12·21·79

THE
RADIO FORMAT
CONUNDRUM

Radio programming is one of the most volatile and challenging functions of broadcasting. The formats that radio stations use vary greatly and are subject to constant re-appraisal and change.

The Radio Format Conundrum cuts through the maze of criteria used in choosing a radio format to provide both professionals and students a well-organized, detailed look at every aspect and strategy of this extremely important decision-making process.

The book explores the many basic commercial radio formats in use in the United States today, along with some of the known variations. Discussed at length are such formats as contemporary music, country and western, Black ethnic, lush or highly-orchestrated music (good, beautiful, adult), all-news, all-talk, religious, total-service, classical, educational and adult block. The descriptions of the formats include not only the basic characteristics and the advantages and disadvantages of each but also cover the mechanics of constructing such formats. Case studies, sample scripts and charts supplement the text by clarifying the points made.

While successful radio formating ultimately depends on an instinct for public needs and desires, *The Radio Format Conundrum* offers the background necessary to make intelligent and creative format decisions.

The Radio Format Conundrum

EDD ROUTT
Broadcast Consultant

Dr. JAMES B. McGRATH
Chairman, Broadcast-Film Arts Department
Southern Methodist University

FREDRIC A. WEISS
Assistant Professor, Broadcast-Film Arts Department
Southern Methodist University

COMMUNICATION ARTS BOOKS

HASTINGS HOUSE, PUBLISHERS
New York 10016

Library of Congress Cataloging in Publication Data

Routt, Edd.   The radio format conundrum.

    (Communication arts book)
    Bibliography: p.
    Includes index.
    1. Radio broadcasting—United States.
I. McGrath, James B., joint author.   II. Weiss,
Fredric A., 1943–   joint author.   III. Title.
PN1991.3.U6R63   384.54′0973   78-9068
ISBN 0-8038-6355-1
ISBN 0-8038-6357-8 pbk.

Published simultaneously in Canada by
Copp Clark Ltd., Toronto

Printed in the United States of America

CONTENTS

2071983

ACKNOWLEDGEMENTS

One is never so learned in a given discipline that he can go it alone on a work such as *The Radio Format Conundrum*. Literally dozens of broadcasters, musicians, and theorists were consulted during the sometimes painful process of compilation. Gordon McLendon's *Cielo,* near Lake Dallas, Texas, was the scene of work for the first chapters. The author spent week-ends on that sprawling, ranch-like estate for more than a year putting the pieces together. Don Tolle, musician, writer, and singer, described the moods of today's musicians and helped identify some of their music. Marsha Hayslett and Kitty Norwood, two old friends with backgrounds in broadcasting and creative writing, helped in editing and organizing. Ira Lipson, program director, KZEW, Dallas, gave advice. Ken Dowe, long-time morning man at KLIF and former national program director for the McLendon Stations, advised on several of the formats, as did Don Keyes, owner of WNYN, Canton, Ohio, and former national program director for McLendon Stations. Bonneville Broadcast Consultants kindly allowed us to describe the Bonneville good music systems. The people within the Schulke organization did likewise.

We gleaned unashamedly from such excellent broadcast publications as *Television/Radio Age, Broadcasting,* and *Broadcast Programming and Production*. The Schafer automation people, along with those at Harris-Intertype, provided pictures and explanations of automation equipment.

Jim Davis and Charlie Van Dyke of KLIF gave advice and counsel throughout the work, and contributed most helpfully in the areas of contemporary music formats and music research.

As usual, my wife Norma typed and re-typed the manuscript. My secretary at WRR, Fay Hartline, typed part of the first draft and was helpful in editing. My colleagues in the broadcast industry aided unknowingly in hundreds of ways, as the authors studied, purloined, and critiqued their formats. Stations studied most closely were KNUS, KVIL, WBAP, KZEW, KBOX, WRR, WRR-FM, KRLD, KKDA, KNOK, KFJZ, KOAX, KMEZ, KMGC, KSKY, KPBC, KCHU, KERA, KVTT, and KWJS.

The co-authors, Dr. James B. McGrath, Chairman, Broadcast-Film Arts Department, Southern Methodist University, and Dr. Fredric A. Weiss, Assistant Professor in the department, came along late in the work and saved the author's good name and reputation. The work load while I was managing KLIF was such that without Drs. McGrath and Weiss, the book would never have been finished.

The book is not everything it should be. No book on radio station formats can be. The scene changes too fast, too dramatically, too often. We can only hope it mirrors the format conundrum at a time of significance.

Drs. McGrath and Weiss collected their own sources during the course of this work, so I will leave to them the task of identification.

EDD ROUTT
January, 1978   Mobile, Alabama

I wish to thank the following broadcasters for the assistance in providing information: Tom Allen, Operations Manager, KBOX, Dallas, Texas; Andy Bell, General Manager, KSKY, Dallas; Harold Gibson, General Manager, KPBC, Dallas; Chester Maxwell, KBOX, Dallas; Richard Sutcliffe, Southern Methodist University, Dallas; Don Thompson, Operations Manager, WBAP, Fort Worth, Texas; Al Veck, WSM, Nashville, Tennessee; J. C. Webster, General Manager, KMGC-FM, Dallas; Bob Wilson, Program Director, KVTT-FM, Dallas.

JAMES B. MCGRATH, JR.
Dallas, Texas

The broadcasters who spoke with us indicated a need for this book and were willing to express their ideas in exchange for learning from others: Chuck Smith of KKDA; Nat Jackson of KNOK; Eddie Hill of WRR-FM; Bruce

McKenzie of KERA-FM, and Lorenzo Milam of KCHU. All of the broadcasters whose thoughts we share understand that radio programming is a neverending process. If we have captured that process long enough to examine, it was worth their time and effort.

FREDRIC A. WEISS
Dallas, Texas

FOREWORD

You have in your hands a tool box. Use it well and prosper. When Don Barrett was National Program Director of the McLendon Stations, before entering a very successful career in the motion picture industry, he first explained the "tool box" concept to me. Basically, it says that the person who desires a career in radio needs every edge possible to get started and an undying dedication to growth in order to succeed. To start, put everything you can into your "career tool box." Then, when called upon, you can do anything. It's strange that even at the biggest radio stations in the nation, the professional broadcaster may still be called upon, on occasion, to perform tasks that require skills placed in the "tool box" early in the career. It could be that a First Class FCC license is a good addition to the "tool box." A college degree, knowledge of electronics, basic accounting skills, a knowledge of marketing, audio production training, typing, retail selling (even if it's in a jeans shop in the summer), or many other items could all fit well into a radio "tool box" you will use for the balance of a career in the most exciting profession available for pursuit. In fact, it was Gordon McLendon who said at the *Radio And Records* convention in Dallas in 1977 that "radio . . . just the word alone still creates within my body the greatest thrill I have ever known. Radio is beautiful."

The Radio Format Conundrum is actually a tool box of radio information. What is presented within the following pages is a clear and accurate accounting of radio's past (and a knowledge of the past is necessary to project for the future), its current "state of the art" at the time of this publication, and some exciting predictions. It is up to the new, youthful, determined broadcaster and dreamer to prove these predictions correct or off target. That is one of the reasons that I hope the work finds its way into the hands of many hungry radio adventurers.

The world is full of "experts." It is even more full of people who spend their careers trying to act like experts. There are, in fact, a few who have actually done something to move radio in new directions. You will find the thoughts of many of these true innovators in the pages of this "tool box." One of the authors, Edd Routt, is a fully-rounded professional. His career includes success in on-air performing, news operations and management, corporate level operations nationally, local and national sales, and general management. Additionally, Edd has enjoyed the personal and professional friendship of Gordon McLendon for years. Edd spent a number of years working closely with Gordon when construction was underway at one of the most exciting radio group operations in broadcast history.

This book also includes many surprises. In my experience, I have not seen in one volume so many concepts, rarely shared, placed together in a meaningful order.

I feel certain that the authors' intent is multi-fold. But certainly, their purpose in this work included a chronology of much of radio's brilliant history, a clear delineation of its present status, and motivation enough to insure that at least one person who reads this book will be moved sufficiently to do something with the industry that will deserve the creation of a new chapter.

It is important to understand that radio's growth has been so fast and so exciting that current top level broadcast executives hold seminars just to try to keep in touch with new engineering, programming, and management breakthroughs.

In the beginning, radio was much like the television we know today. There was drama, variety, concerts, news reports, and the like. Saturday afternoon to many, meant Milton Cross with live opera broadcasts. Occasionally, there were records played (or as my grandfather put it, "that darned canned music"). As the years moved on, Monitor on NBC and Don McNeal's Breakfast Club on ABC were the last hold-outs from the original programming concepts. But even as Top 40 was rocketing radio into a new phase and American radio got "McLendonized," there were still clear choices in radio sounds. You could choose red, for example, or blue, or yellow. Today, your selections include blue-green, morning yellow, autumn rust, or any possible shade of slight difference you can find in a rainbow. There are now that many format choices on radio . . . and another band to get it on too. AM and its traditional ways did not satisfy the radio listeners. FM stations, generally held by the licensee until they could figure out what to do with them, became test labs. And many of the tests worked. Now it's full blown competition on two radio bands with FM listening well above the 50% mark in many markets in the nation. Where is it all going? That will be determined by what the listeners want and how well the radio craftsperson constructs a station in accord with needs and desires of the listeners. Listening to them can tell you what they want. When you know that, you still must master how to deliver it. Radio has entered another phase of super-growth in all areas of station operation. A "good idea" used to be enough to make it air worthy. Now, those ideas can all be pre-tested off the air to reduce the margin of error.

Yes, competition is critical.

The Radio Format Conundrum is also a challenge. Edd Routt and his colleagues bring you to the present and a bit beyond with this compilation of free thinking from many of the industry's best. Use it well; for as I said at the beginning, this book is also a "tool box." Build something beautiful.

CHARLIE VAN DYKE
Richardson, Texas
January, 1978

CHARLIE VAN DYKE is one of the nation's most respected broadcasters. He is morning personality and Program Director of KLIF, Dallas, his hometown. Mr. Van Dyke was previously Program Director and morning personality at RKO's KHJ, Los Angeles. In his earlier years, he was "McLendonized", in his words, as afternoon personality at KLIF, and learned the Drake-Chenault techniques at CKLW, Windsor, Ont. Other experiences include WLS, Chicago, and KFRC, San Francisco. Mr. Van Dyke is known as a "workaholic" in the business, spending from 12–15 hours daily on the job. His beautiful voice is legend, and his performance as an air personality is virtually without peer. He is one of the industry's top-paid personalities.

1

Introduction

SYNTHESIS OF RADIO PROGRAMMING

Radio station formats are infinite in variety and subject to constant reappraisal and change. A *formula* that stresses progressive rock music today may, by a quick decision of the programmer, feature rhythm and blues music tomorrow. A different announcer or staff of announcers can change the personality of a station almost overnight. A changed configuration of news programs on a given station may suddenly change that station's total impact on an audience. Format changes are frequently made on the basis of educated hunches, abstract guesses, competitive station activities, and mere whims.

Usually, a station's *initial* format is developed to fill a specific programming void in a specific market. However, once the decision has been made to program contemporary music, country music, ethnic music, all-news, all-talk, or adult music, the format may, and likely will, be subjected to a dozen subtle or obvious shifts and adjustments. Why? Because execution of conceptualities is the essence of any format. Two stations may begin programming the same formula on the same day with the same capital; and, within 90 days, one will have left the other behind in ratings. The subtleties of execution, the abilities of the programmer to detect weaknesses or irritants, and his ability to com-municate those deficits to his air personalities make the difference.

No single element of a format can account for a station's success or failure in the ratings. A top-flight news department can be dragged down by "wrong" music, consistent mechanical difficulties may annoy a listener who will never return to the frequency of the offending station. Disc jockeys who neglect to provide the time and temperature may disgust the listener who depends upon the station for such information. The announcer who babbles on and on about the performers and labels of his records may be tuned-out by the listener who demands topicality of his air personalities. As one veteran licensee observed, "It isn't the big, obvious, and correctable things that ruin a format; it's the little, subtle discrepancies that slip by, day after day, uncorrected, that ulti-mately land you at the bottom of the ratings."

Another relevant truism is, "It isn't the music you play, it's what you put between the music." These criteria would apply to any format, regardless of whether it is music or talk, AM or FM. A *certain* consistency and flow must be found or the station will not attract the listeners. There is no magic formula. It is much like the talented cook who puts a "pinch" of this and a "dab" of that into the stew, but is unable to explain to anyone else just how everything fell together. Make no mistake, experience and knowledge are required in great abundance by the individual who is programming *any* major facility in a major market. These qualities can be properly delineated. But the feel for "pinches" and "dabs" will quite often decide who wins ratings and makes money, and who will have to change formats and rates. These are the same qualities that make some surgeons great and send others into general practice. It is rarely the obvious that puts one formula station behind and another ahead.

Station formats must be geared *to the times and to the service area*. The approach that worked well in Chicago won't necessarily work in Los Angeles; the plan that "killed 'em" in Des Moines may fall flat in Canton. And the Top 40 jock who stormed the market in New York may become a serious liability to a licensee in Birmingham. The jock whose "blue" material was laughed at and repeated in Los Angeles could be thrown off the air and chastised in Kansas City. Social mores, while generally becoming more liberal throughout the na-tion, are, nevertheless, different from market to market.

Only when a station has a monopoly is it always possible for a station to be "all things to all people." Any time a market has more than one station, each attempts to appeal to listeners of different economic and cultural status. It would be folly for a market's *second* station to emulate the sound of the first, unless, perhaps, the first station is doing an abominable job in executing its for-mat. If the first station is programming to the "youth audience," the logical approach for the second facility would be a format appealing to an "adult audi-ence." If a market already has a well-operated country and western station, the other facility might employ contemporary music. When a market has a dozen stations, it often is impossible to find a total "void"; in which case, the newcomer must select the weakest station and vie for a share of its audience. In major markets, the competition is nothing short of audio war. The two black stations may be after each other tooth and nail. Three lush music FM operations reach urgently for the audience of the old-line network block station. An all-news format is established to appeal to those same adults. Two AM "rockers," with most of the 18–34 adults, are imperceptibly losing audience to a progressive rock station that attracts males 18–24. The competition is vigorous, expensive, unnerving, and exhilarating. It is a kind of war that takes, not human lives, but economic fortunes, and sends them down the proverbial drain.

The ease with which listeners can switch stations denies radio the freedom to abuse. The listener, once hooked on a TV drama, has to suffer through five to ten units of advertising if he is to sate his interest in the plot. Not so with radio. There is no plot to follow: there is only entertainment and information. When the broadcaster becomes offensive in language, manner, or commercial load, he is easily turned off in favor of a less offensive dial setting. Radio programmers, therefore, simply must walk on egg shells throughout the broadcast day. There is never a time to ease up and say, "forget the listener."

Radio remains a personal medium, while TV becomes more and more impersonal. Fans listen and watch "programs" on TV; they identify with local news programs and establish a one-way personal relationship with the local anchorperson. In radio, people listen to "stations," although they do, occasionally, identify with a local personality. "I heard it on KXXX," is a commonality when a station message or piece of music is cited. "Did you hear what Archie said last night?" is a commonality in TV, without regard to the network or the call letters of the station. Talk-show moderators on radio, of course, are hailed by name and in some cases the station call letters become secondary. The same applies to long-tenured DJs and announcers, such as a Howard Miller in Chicago or a John B. Gambling in New York. But, by and large, radio is personal and TV is impersonal in terms of listener identification with the facility and/or performers. The TV station often can be a disinterested public servant and be adored by the populace if it carries listeners' favorite programs. Radio, primarily a service medium, must provide extensive local services and be consistent as a local, personal friend. Otherwise, it will suffer the consequences in terms of lost ratings and revenues. The rise of adversarial citizens' groups in the mid-'60s and early '70s created a new awareness on the part of the licensees to public needs, tastes and desires. While music remained standard fare for radio, greater efforts were being made to splice in public affairs and other types of non-entertainment programs, to satisfy demands of small public groups and the government.

The principal objective of *any* radio station format is to satisfy a specific public desire or need, adhere to government regulations, and make a profit for the investors. The *format* is the magical difference between winning and losing. But sure-fire formulae seem to be in a decline. McLendon, Storz, and Bartell set a basic recovery pattern for radio in the early 50s. Great segments of the industry were traumatized by their stunts, while a joyful, youthful public urged them to become zanier and zanier. There were no major innovations in music programming until about 10 years later when Bill Drake and Dave Chenault presented their "much more music" format. A significant part of the problem is the inability of even the most seasoned broadcaster to objectively evaluate a station's programming. It is almost impossible to get two non-associates in radio broadcasting to totally agree on what, for example, a Top 40 radio station is and what makes it altogether different from, perhaps, a station featuring or emphasizing a "much more music" sound. An individual is simply unable to view, without some bias, any format formula not of his own creation. A team of programmers, working together for weeks and months to create a new format, eventually may meld their thinking, at least toward the common goal of the moment, until they give reasonably parallel descriptions of the plan. But if asked to describe another format in the same market, odds are that each member of the team will articulate a *different* interpretation. John Wheeler Barger, young attorney-turned-broadcaster, once told a class at Southern Methodist University that he believed it impossible to objectively evaluate the effectiveness of a station sound, pointing out that programmers subconsciously permit subjective interpretations that retard most efforts at total objectivity. Thus, if he is correct, neo-radio formats are the products of men and women who sense public needs and desires, share those needs and desires, but must simply sit by and hope their programming will succeed in fulfilling those needs and desires.

The principal objective of this text is to examine several basic commercial radio formats in use in the United States today, along with some of the known variations. These will include formulae identified as contemporary, country and western, Black ethnic, lush or highly-orchestrated music (good, beautiful, adult), all-news, all-talk, religious, total-service, classical, educational, and adult block. The examination will deal with broad categories of music and the *mechanics* of constructing such formats. Although efforts will be made to explain how such formats are executed, the student may expect inadequacies as this text must lack the benefits of actual sound. Examination of the synergistics of "pinches" and "dabs" of human ingenuity that create the format conundrum will, hopefully, enable creative students to understand the problems and search for new answers.

EVOLUTION OF TECHNIQUES

Benjamin Franklin, in 1798, wrote that "in this world nothing is certain but death and taxes." If Franklin were alive today, he might add, "and change in radio station formats." Dan Rustin, writing in a 1972 edition of *Television/Radio Age,* said: "Trying to track a trend in radio news is like trying to hit a knuckleball. Every pitch is different and there's no telling whether it will break up, down, or sideways." The same may be said for *radio,* the news notwithstanding. Before television, radio was so entrenched in American life that people thought it would last forever. The "soaps" captured huge female audiences from coast to coast. Sports fans thrilled to vivid play-by-play descriptions of major league baseball games. Families everywhere spent thrilling hours every evening listening to radio drama, musical variety shows, and stand-up microphone comedy. Politicians were using the medium to reach the electorate. The *electronic medium,* indeed, was here to stay, but radio was not to continue as its principal representative. Television traumatically displaced radio as the country's main source of entertainment. The tube simply had another dimension to offer. Radio performers quickly made the transition from microphone to microphone *and* camera, or they got out of the business.

For years, many radio station owners buried their heads in the sand and refused to believe things had changed. This was particularly true of the "old-line" network affiliates, such as KRLD in Dallas. These stations continued to produce "blocks" of programs, even though most broadcasters believed the listenership was pitifully small. The whole world had gone television crazy and that's where people sat, glued to their sets. TV receivers were expensive and not easily available. Many television stations established "viewing rooms" where non-set citizens could come to the station and watch monitors.

Popular music stations had existed and profited long before TV became the primary entertainment medium, and they continued to prosper. Independent stations everywhere sought to pull audiences from the radio network affiliates. The technique in pre-TV days was considerably different from today's approach, but the primary commodity of "indies" was still the music of the day. A typical "good-music" format would include uninterrupted sweeps of music, followed by brief news and weathercasts and by clustered commercials and public service announcements. Other independent stations attempted to emulate the network stations by programming syndicated mystery and soap-opera-type shows, the "Tommy Dorsey" hour, "Hit Parade" shows and musical variety blocks. These stations, the ancestors of TV, are found today in non-affiliated UHF and VHF properties, and what McLendon, Storz, and Bartell did was simply embellish the old Hit Parade idea with youth-oriented music and information and, most important, zany stunts that made radio "fun" to listen to. Just as history doesn't make it clear who put the first commercial radio station on the air, no one is sure whether McLendon or Storz developed the first Top 40 format. The truth lies somewhere between these two innovators; each was adept at taking a seemingly stale or antiquated idea and presenting it as a fresh and stimulating program. The Top 40 idea became a commercial success partially because audience rating services such as Hooper and Trendex began to publish results of surveys. Soon, the idea that "we're NUMBER ONE" attracted time buyers at advertising agencies, and the race was on.

The Top 40 formula was copied from coast to coast. Some operations set up Top 50 or Top 100 formulae; others dropped to the Top 20. Announcers turned into disc jockeys, and broadcast stalwarts cried and bemoaned the shouting and screeching that went into the microphones between the records. Government officials were appalled. Newton Minow, in his famous "vast wasteland" speech, alluded to radio as a "cacophony of bells, screams, and whistles." And while the "responsible" old-line network stations continued to program long, 15-minute newscasts, Arthur Godfrey, variety shows, commentaries and other traditional fare, the Top 40 operators were sweeping the nation's youth audiences (12–34) and capturing the bulk of the advertising dollar. Time salesmen for the old-line stations were aghast at high rates being charged by the "noise making" stations. But the stage had been set, and most of the traditional type stations fell into line. There were notable exceptions, such as WSB in Atlanta and WCCO in Minneapolis, but by-and-large the programming of contemporary music became standard fare.

All of this was happening in the late '40s and the early '50s. Radio was becoming less and less important in the daily lives of Americans, and many radio station licensees were bailing out. Independent radio stations kept on playing "hit parade" music and broadcasting some sports events, but they were offering nothing new.[1] Music was music, whether heard on the radio or from a record player. Radio revenues declined as advertisers added more television to their marketing plans. Techniques were crude, and the cost of TV spots was relatively high; but advertisers quickly sensed the value of audio messages *with* pictures!

Radio Begins Re-awakening

In Dallas, Omaha, and a few other markets in mid-America and other areas, some new ideas were emerging in *radio*. In Dallas, young Gordon McLendon was almost oblivious to television. He was building a radio network called the Liberty Broadcasting System. He had tried to sell the idea to the Mutual Broadcasting System, but was rejected. So, with verve that was to become his trademark in the industry, McLendon moved in with one of his "firsts" in radio. He offered the country major league baseball on a *daily* basis. Not only was McLendon to provide fans with a massive dose of the national pastime, he was to provide them with their first wire-re-creation of the nation's top sports events. McLendon didn't see the games; he hired Western Union to provide him with an encoded, cryptic description of each inning. He added the sound effects: crowd noises, the crack of the bat on the ol' apple, cries of beer and hotdog salesmen, and his own voice and energy as he brought fans to the edge of their chairs with vivid, sometimes inventive descriptions of the action on the field.

---

[1] In the early days, an "independent" station was one without a network affiliation. To be without a network was a handicap, as the most entertaining and professional programming came through network lines. Today, the radio networks usually just complement local programming. TV "independents" do compete today, but do not enjoy the ratings and revenues of the affiliated stations.

This was innovative, and it was something TV could not do. McLendon, known as the "Old Scotchman," even at age 25, expanded into football, basketball, tennis and other sports. Later, he added a few country music programs. Altogether, there were over 400 radio stations from coast to coast tied into the Liberty Network. But, it was not to last. Baseball and football magnates discovered what a good thing the young Texan had going and decided to deny him the right to broadcast their games. And so it ended.

Rockers and Rollers

Next, radio people came up with the idea of making radio the joy medium. One Southwest promoter claims *he* originated the idea of playing music that would appeal to 14–15 year-old emotions. "I told McLendon this was the only way to go in radio," the individual averred. Whoever came up with the idea first, it worked! In Dallas, McLendon started programming "Hits of the day" in three-hour segments followed by three-hour segments. Announcers became "disc jockeys" and provided "chatter" between the records. News was broadcast in five-minute segments on the hour and half hour. "Your news and music" station slogans were being heard all over the country. "Listen to us and win an album." "Listen to us and win a vacation." "Get the news first on KLIF." "All music, all the time, every day, seven days a week, 24 hours a day." "Woweeee!!!" And young America was "turned on." Adults thought the music terrible. Advertisers wouldn't buy that "kid stuff" radio. Undaunted, broadcasters kept plugging. Programmers put announcers on top of flag poles to get attention. Broadcast marathons from store windows became a craze. If a station in Cleveland gave away $1,000 in cash to a lucky listener, a station in Los Angeles would give away twice that amount. Radio was going wild. One station put two announcers in an airplane to see how long they could stay aloft. Refueling was done in-air. DJs broadcast from underground studios and offered prizes to listeners who could find them. C. E. Hooper started his famous "Hooperratings," and it was then that stations started yelling, "We're number one!!!" Music! Contests! News! Hot News! Mobile News Units:

OPENING:	(Siren up and under) First News First!
VOICE:	(Excited, heavy) First News First!
	KXXX now takes you to the scene of a major news story!
REPORTER:	This is your KXXX on-the-scene reporter, and we have just witnessed a four-car pile-up at the intersection of Main and Commerce. Police say there is at least one fatality, with five other persons injured. Let's see if we can get an investigating officer to the KXXX microphone. Officer . . . officer . . . can you tell us what happened? Etc.
CLOSING:	(Big, excited) You have just heard a major news story reported from the scene by KXXX mobile news unit number 25. Stay tuned to KXXX for First News First!

The jock in the control room would then play a commercial and/or return immediately to the music. Those were the days, also, when announcers were admonished to "shut up and play the music. Give the time, the temperature, identify the record, then shut up and play the music."

The Top 40 format was so effective that even a novice broadcaster could "take" a market in 30 days. Daytime-only stations were knocking off big 50,000-watt network operations that had held the market captive for years. Fulltime operators stormed into markets and knocked off the daytimers. Better financed operators would then knock off the fulltimers. Programwise, it was chaotic, exciting, rewarding. Advertisers sensed the excitement and began buying time on the rockers. Audience research proved people *were* listening and responding. Studies showed that young people had money and would spend it. These same studies showed that young people would switch brands, respond to new marketing ideas, and that people over 50 were set in their ways and couldn't be changed.

Top 40 radio was working and continued to dominate until the mid-'60s. These successes were AM stations (*Amplitude Modulated* stations, with a frequency response of up to 7,500 cycles per second). A few FM (*Frequency Modulated*) stations began timidly going on the air. Few homes and practically no cars had receivers for FM signals. "FM Music" was being played, but it was syrupy and dull. "FM" music was for "Old Folks." Most FM's were owned by AM licensees, as "insurance" against the time when FM might become a viable part of the electronic medium. And then it happened. The AM spectrum was crowded, and the FCC imposed a "freeze." One might be able to buy an AM station, but building one was out of the question because you simply couldn't find an available frequency in important markets. And even if you could find a frequency, most of the known formats were being properly executed. Most large markets had at least two Top 40 operations, a network block operation or two, a country and western, and perhaps an ethnic format. Could FM be made to work profitably, with few FM receivers and practically no voids in the programming spectrum? Of course it could! Radio had again become profitable business, and it was inevitable that someone would have an idea that would sell FM to the American public. It was touted as the "high fidelity" electronic medium, then the "stereo" medium. Music could be more faithfully reproduced on FM than on a hi-fi record player at home because of FM's frequency response (range) of up to 15,000 CPS. FM became known as *the* medium for good music, for "FM music." Then, some "unconscionable" broadcaster dared to put a rock and roll record on FM. Sinful! FM had been reserved as the private domain of "good music." Another operator then decided if FM was good for rock music, why not country music? And soul music? *Any* kind of music??

In 1966, FM set saturation was about 48% of the homes in the country. By 1975, set saturation had reached 93% in homes, about 30% in automobiles, and FM listenership represented 36.4% of all radio listening. Detroit, with 41.1%

led the major markets in FM listening. Washington, D.C., was second with 40.7%, and Philadelphia was third with 39.7%. Overall, FM listening increased 81% between 1970 and 1975. Largest FM listening gains in the five-year period were in Chicago, whose share was up 137.6% and in Boston, up 104.2%. Fifty highly successful FM stations were booming by the mid-'70s. With in-home set saturation approximating that of the AM sets, FM was playing the same music as the old AM Top 40s, but with an important added dimension, *stereo*. Stereo retailers were doing an enormous business. Consumers of all ages were flocking to stores to buy stereo sets. The in-thing was to buy stereo "components"—big speakers, precision turntables, 8-track stereo cartridge players, reel-to-reel playbacks, and exotic receivers and amplifiers wired to pick up sensitive stereo signals from FM stations. And, to many, if a station didn't broadcast virtually pure stereo it was "nowhere." FM station operators began promotions to sell FM receivers. Rate concessions were made to retailers who would promote FM receiver sales in newspapers and on television. Some FM operators banded together to promote weekend sales of FM car receivers. They banded together in the National Association of Broadcasters (NAB) and became NAFMB (National Association of FM Broadcasters.) They sponsored all-channel legislation, hoping to force set manufacturers to build sets with AM and FM circuits.[2]

AM operators, who became as confident of their superior position in the market as the big network affiliates had 20 years earlier, were becoming concerned. Audiences were diminishing (55.1% in 1975). Out of nowhere, FM stations were showing healthy shares of audience, particularly in the young demographics where AM had been undisputed king. Even the adult-oriented FM's were growing, as more and more homes and automobiles boasted FM receivers. And so the stage was being set in the early 1970s for AM radio to enter another big programming era. The changes were to be based on experiments conducted earlier by Westinghouse, Metromedia, McLendon, and the old-line radio networks. In the late '50s and early '60s, McLendon had produced all-news formats on XETRA (a Mexican station serving Southern California) and WNUS in Chicago. WINS in New York went all-news in 1965, and the CBS owned-and-operated (O&O) WCBS joined the race three years later.

McLendon had scored heavily in Dallas, Houston, Shreveport, El Paso, Milwaukee, and other markets with his Top 40 format. Broadcasters would quake in their boots when they heard "McLendon is coming." He had the experience, the know-how, *and* the money to topple just about any Top 40 operation anywhere. Interestingly, he never did go head-to-head with his co-innovators, Todd Storz and G. Bartel.

[2] In October, 1975, the NAFMB changed its name to National Radio Broadcasters Association (NRBA). FM had grown up, literally, and was inviting AM stations to join them and work toward building a better *radio* industry.

2

Format Considerations

MUSIC

The principal commodity of the vast majority of radio stations throughout the world is music, but only in the United States is the field so splintered as to almost defy definition. Tom Ratner, writing in *Television/Radio Age,* noted that "music programming on radio is swinging into an era of fickle formats and shifting audiences." The awesome variety of music available to Americans is due, doubtless, to the competitiveness of the music production industry, stimulated somewhat by the demands of radio stations for "something different" with which to compete in the highly diversified marketplace.

Before any meaningful discussion can occur on the subject of broadcast music, it is necessary to establish the terms used to describe different forms of music available to broadcasters. Only in the area of classical music is there virtually universal agreement, and even then the music may be divided into heavy and light, and then further defined by devotees of opera, symphony, ballet, chamber, concert or cathedral.

Many of the terms used to describe modern music would make no sense to a language Puritan. Really "funky soul" is a term used by Frank P. Barrow to

10

describe some music played in a Black-oriented format. Jim Clemens spoke of "real" country music and "pop" country music. Another programmer described a danceable piece of music as "disco," and some radio stations program entire formats of "disco-stereo." Words are coined, distorted and mutilated, sometimes as the programmer looks for ways to label or tag a format, a piece of music, a frame of mind. And words that may be understood by everyone in a given geographic area may not be understood in another. So "you pays your quarter and takes your chances" when you begin discussions about mass-appeal, popular music. **Some commonly-understood terms and their definitions are:**

C & W — The letters mean "Country & Western," but the term may be falling into disrepute. Rarely is any "western" music played anymore. And "country" music is generally preceded by "pop," "blue grass," "progressive," "Nashville" or, maybe, "Texas," "Austin," or "modern."

Pop/Adult — "Chicken" rock or hit singles. Does not include hard rock or Black/soul. No abrasive sounds. Vocalist often emphasized as "personality."

Progressive — Any piece of music that reflects new interpretation. Progressive Jazz was performed in the '40s and '50s by Stan Kenton, because it was a *new* form, different from the accepted Jazz of the day.

Top 40 — Another term that is losing popular favor in the industry. Originally, when McLendon and Storz coined it, the expression meant simply that only the most popular 40 pieces of rock 'n roll or contemporary music were being programmed. Innovators developed such original exprssions as "Top 30" and "Top 100" to be a little different.

R & B — These letters mean "Rhythm & Blues," and the music originally was played by Black-oriented stations. It is still used, of course, but principally by non-Blacks.

Soul — This term has largely replaced R & B in the vernacular of the industry. Soul music is supposed by many to belong exclusively to Blacks, but it may be heard on many different types of contemporary music stations. The term Black/soul is often used to identify music that is aired only by Black-ethnic formats.

MOR — These letters mean "Middle of-the-Road," a term used to indicate no extremes. Programmers use it to indicate they do not program Hard Rock or Soft Rock, but rather something in between.

Ethnic — Ethnic music is simply music that appeals to a group of people with definitive ethnic backgrounds. There is Black Ethnic, German Ethnic, Spanish or Mexican Ethnic music.

Prog/Rock — Progressive Rock music. Again, the term "progressive" is employed to indicate a new form or interpretation of music. Emphasis is generally placed on instrumentation, production, and/or lyrics rather than melody.

AOR — Album-Oriented Rock.

Rock — Derived from Blues and/or Jazz. The original form had a distinctive and prominent, monotonous beat. The term is used generically to describe today's "in" music.

Contemporary Rock — Simply differentiates between rock music being played this year from that played in years past.

Gold/Oldies — A piece of music that was a big hit of the past.

Good Music — Generally means lush, highly-orchestrated, melodic music. The term is used primarily to differentiate a piece of music from rock or some other form of music.

Gospel — Used to describe some religious music. But gospel on a Black ethnic station is considerably different from gospel on a C & W station, and may often be called "spiritual" or "Black Spiritual."

Jazz — A loose term, usually meaning it is not really commercial. Musically intellectual, it is essentially free extemporization. Jazz to Louis Armstrong meant one thing; to Stan Kenton it meant another. Jazz music is not necessarily written, but it is always "interpreted." A jazz musician may perform a piece of gospel music and, in so doing, produce a piece of "jazz." New Orleans jazz has a distinctively different flavor from modern, or today's jazz. Jazz, then, may be in the mind of the conceiver.

Blues — Composer Don Tolle said, "Blues music communicates pain." In this context, Blues could spring from every type of music. A "bluesy" piece might be a slow tempo in a soul format, a hard rock format, or a country format. The earlier history of the Blues belongs almost entirely to the Negro. Oral tradition traces it back to the 1860s. The conventional harmonic foundation is, for the most part, a European contribution. Some students believe blues came from several areas, including America, Spain, India, Arabia, the Caribbean, and New Orleans. As with other forms of Jazz, there are various developments for mass consumption. These include R & B, Rock and Roll, etc.

Album — At one time meant mainly lush, very MOR. Now it may be any music. Recently, manufacturers began producing albums of hits and misses. Radio stations simply tape (cart) the cuts they wish to use. In earlier times, albums included a few proven hits and were filled out with pieces of lesser stature.

Nashville Sound — Modern country music, produced in Nashville, Tennessee, with a distinctive "sameness" year after year. The "Austin Sound" reflects a type of progressive country music produced first in Austin, Texas.

Underground Music — As undescriptive of a type of music as the old "FM Music" tag. In the early '60s, FM programmers invented the "underground" sound. Basically, this was music written and performed by unknown artists. Underground popularity stemmed from the fact that here was music *never* played by regular rock stations, AM or FM. Many of the so-called unknown artists became quite popular.

Western — Music performed with guitars and violins and other stringed instruments as background for ballad-type lyrics. Often the music is entirely subordinate to the lyrics and may be mistaken for country music. Western "swing" is a brighter form of the original. There are few, if any, stations programming pure western music.

Country — Music performed with a variety of instruments, including electrically amplified guitars, bass fiddles, and violins. Country music is almost always subordinated to the lyrics.

Bluegrass — Country music, basically performed without amplification and possessing many of the original tones and expressions. It is a "bluesy" kind of music that expresses pain, sorrow, worry, longing.

Progressive/Country — A blend of country and rock music. Willie Nelson and Waylon Jennings brought this form to light in the early '70s.

These are some of the terms programmers use to identify music and/or station formats. But it is not easy to get general agreement that a format supports one description or another. The Pulse, Inc., did a recent survey on listener habits. The questions the survey sought to answer were what formats attracted males, females, and teenagers. In the study, various terms were used to describe radio station formats. Pop Standard, Standard Pop, and Standard were classified as basic MOR or Personality. Contemporary, Contemporary Pop, and Pop Contemporary were considered Top 40, Rock, Stereo, or Oldies. Album, Show, Movie, were defined generally as Beautiful, or "Good" Music.

Much of the tag tangle comes from broadcasters who really don't know what they're playing or, at least, are unable to make their plan fit a specific and known format.

A station that pretends to be a real Top 40 operation but plays no really hard rock music is often called a "Chicken Rock" station. And there are managers and salesmen who will describe the format one way to one customer and a different way to another customer. "We're a very conservative Contemporary MOR station," a salesman might tell the ad manager for a bank. "We're really swinging and eatin' up those teens," the same salesman might tell a jeans shop owner.

Scott Shannon, in discussing the format of WQXI in Atlanta, Georgia, calls the station's format "Top 40." "We're contemporary," he told an interviewer from *Broadcast Programming & Production* magazine. "But then, we don't think of the station as any one kind of format . . . it's just 'Quixie,' " he explained. Yet a programmer from another city might monitor WQXI and declare the station to be distinctly Top 40. Jim Clemens at WPLO said he hates to put a tag on any kind of format, but he used Modern Country "for lack of a better term."

"We play Olivia Newton-John, John Denver, The Amazing Rhythm Aces, Michael Murphy and, at the same time, we play Merle Haggard, Mo Bandy, and George Jones. I think it's hard to put a label on music today. Freddy Fender certainly is country, yet every rocker in the world played him . . . what we do here is blend it all together."

Terms, tags, and labels change from generation to generation, each adopting nomenclature to suit the times and the moods. In the '20s, King Oliver's Creole Jazz Band regarded such artists as Paul Whiteman "symphonic jazzmen." It was a time when Louis Armstrong and his cornet produced what was known as that "great blue New Orleans Sound." Oliver's jazz was, as Armstrong said, "beautifully creative . . . always some little idea . . . and he exercised it beautifully." Bessie Smith, in 1925, was called "Empress of the Blues." Her records sold in the millions, but only in the South and the ghettos of the North. Her sound, according to the poet, Langston Hughes, "was too basic for the general public," and few white people in the '20s even knew her name. During this period, the great Fats Waller, in responding to a white visitor to Harlem, said, "What's Jazz, lady? If you don't know, I can't tell you." And a modern day wag said white people can't explain "soul." "They think it's acid indigestion," he said.

The '20s abounded with the work of Whiteman, George Gershwin, Duke Ellington, Mamie Smith and her Jazz Hounds, the Club Wigwam Orchestra, Ruth Etting, Trixie Smith and the Jazz Masters, and Ethel Waters. Gershwin's rendition of *Rhapsody in Blue* was called genuine jazz. At that time, about 60,000 families in the country owned radios. This figure had jumped to about 14,000,000 by 1930. People did listen to music performed mostly live "over the radio," but they also danced to it in such places as The Cotton Club, Connie's Inn, The Savoy Ballroom, The Saratoga Club, or The Alhambra Ballroom. *Variety,* in July of 1923, noted: "Colored singing and playing artists are riding to fame and fortune with the currently popular demand for 'Blues' disc recordings and, because of the recognized fact that only a Negro can do justice to the native indigo ditties, such artists are in great demand." And these artists were performing such tunes as "Alabamy Bound," "Jazzbo Ball," "Shaking the Blues Away," "Give Me That Old Slow Drag," and "Oh, Daddy."

Gershwin had a reputation as a Jazzman. His way of performing such pieces as "I've Got a Crush on You," "Lady Be Good," "The Man I Love," and "Someone to Watch Over Me," was called jazz, although all of these selections were performed as straight ballads by orchestras and singers not regarded as jazz purveyors. Jazzmen loved to play and improvise around the written music, and it rarely sounded the same way twice. It was also during this period that "ragtime" came on the scene. Tags were, perhaps, more applicable in those days when things were simpler.

While "ragtime" was a new term in music, swingers of the era were using such words as flapper, booze, mobsters, and hooch. The great economic crash was en route, but peace-loving Americans, following World War I, were living it up as though there were no tomorrows. It was Jazz, Barbershop Ballads, Blues, Ragtime, Polkas, sports cars, booze, and good times.

The 1930s saw the arrival of the Big Band era, the Era of Swing.

> It makes no diff'rence if it's sweet or hot
> Just give that rhythm ev'rything you got
> Okay, it don't mean a thing
> If it ain't got that swing.
> *"It Don't Mean A Thing"* —Duke Ellington
> Irving Mills

While Adolph Hitler was preparing to ignite World War II in 1938, before dawn one wintery day in New York City hundreds of teens started lining up in front of the Paramount Theater. They literally spilled out onto the sidewalk, stopping traffic. A special police squad was called to contain the "riot." But the trouble outside was nothing compared to what soon broke loose inside. When the early morning movie was over, a band on an elevated platform rose from the orchestra pit. Some 3,000 kids screamed, yelled, and the music began. There was dancing in the aisles. Woodstock? With Rock, pot, and pills? No, it was Benny Goodman's band and the music was "swing."

In the early '30s, radio was described as a "pervading and somewhat Godlike presence" which has come into our lives and homes. The depression had knocked much of the joy out of living in America, and Jazz was said to be dead. Sweet bands, playing the schmaltzy sounds popularized by Guy Lombardo, were up front. Goodman was trying to revive Jazz under the name Swing. Both were characterized by a driving rhythm and improvised solos. Goodman filled the halls and airwaves with the strong beat of drums, fantastic resonance of brass, dramatic precision of saxophones, and the improvisation of hot soloists. Other musicians of the period were Artie Shaw, Tommy Dorsey, Bob Crosby, Glenn Miller, Count Basie, Harry James, Jimmie Lunsford, and Duke Ellington. It was an era of jive talk. "Alligator" meant a devotee of "swing." "Cats" were musicians in the "swing" orchestras. "Long Hair" was an unaware person and, musically, one who preferred symphonic music. "Kicking Out" was being very free, improvising. "Jiving" meant hep, and "trucking" was a finger-wagging, hip-tossing walk. Radio's Hit Parade was on the air from coast to coast, and youngsters were dancing the jitterbug. Psychologists of the day felt the swing and jitterbug crazes were getting out of hand. The music was said to be "dangerously hypnotic, cunningly devised to a faster tempo than 72 bars to the minute. Faster than the human pulse!" It should be encouraging to contemporary generations to know their parents went through the same kind of establishmentarian revolution.

Female singers in the '30s were called "canaries" and included Ella Fitzgerald, Marion Hutton, Mildred Bailey, Billie Holiday, Helen O'Connell, and Martha Tilton. While there were 14 million radios in use by 1930, there were still relatively few broadcast stations, and most of these were tied into the networks. A few independent stations, such as KSKY in Dallas, programmed "Hit Parade" music. And teens in Greenville, Texas, and Hoboken, New Jersey, listened to the independents while their parents turned in the network stations for Amos 'n' Andy and Fibber McGee and Molly. Mass music was big, but public attention to it was tiny compared to today.

President Roosevelt was pushing liberal legislation and trying to get the country back on a solid economic footing. Churchill and his colleagues in Great Britain were unsuccessfully trying to discover how to stop the maniac Hitler. And in New York, citizens spent $150 million to present the New York World Fair.

Programming music in those years (1930–40) was still simple. There were few available surveys, and programmers experimented with new artists and songs. If a band made it at a supper club, chances were its music would be okay for the airwaves. It was popular music, and it wasn't splintered. Country music was normally performed in beer joints and rural night clubs. Progressive music rarely made the airwaves, and when a band became too "kicked out" the mass audiences went away. There was nothing resembling automation or reverb units then, and DJs were called announcers. Microphones were crude by today's standards, and fidelity of music reproduction was poor, but few realized it.

The recording industry got off the ground in the mid-'30s and probably would have advanced much more rapidly had World War II not come along. Radio stations were using some of the product, but jukebox operators were the industry's biggest customers. Music was recorded on "78s"—that is, on seven-inch discs at a speed of 78 RPMs (Revolutions Per Minute.) The major radio networks of the time refused to broadcast recorded music because technicians feared the fidelity was too poor, and because the networks were promoting "live" radio. Much of the attitude continued into World War II. CBS had a policy against "recording and playing back" the broadcasts of such famous war correspondents as Ed Murrow and William Shirer. But the recording industry, an off-shoot of the music industry, must be given much credit for the development of modern radio, for without recorded music the small independent stations that were slowly coming to the fore would have had to employ "live" orchestras to perform. The economics of using live performers, of course, would have inhibited the growth of "independent" radio. ASCAP (American Society of Composers, Artists, and Publishers) had a monopolistic hold on the music business and did not include Country and Western and Negro or "race" music in its catalogue. It wasn't until broadcasters themselves got together in 1940 and formed BMI (Broadcast Music Inc.) that mass-appeal music began to appear on the air. ASCAP simply didn't think jazz and blues music had mass appeal and clung instead to the licensing of Broadway and Hollywood productions of the classier type. Song "pluggers" became record promoters and BMI urged programmers to air BMI-licensed music and "keep the profits in the family." Television, the baby boom following World War II, and an affluent post-war society contributed significantly to growth of the music and record industry. Retail sale of records was under $50 million in 1940,. moved to around $200 million by 1946, and to an astounding $400 million by 1957. Record companies became the not-so-strange bedfellows of disc jockeys and programmers. A few "plugs" of a song on the air would set the cash registers to jingling.

The war years of the '40s brought dramatic change. Zoot-suiters on the West Coast went to war with soldiers, sailors, and marines. Girls knitted argyles for their fellows overseas, and the fellows looked at pin-up pictures of Betty Grable, Lana Turner and June Allyson. Drive-in restaurants with pretty girl hops were the rage, and everyone danced to such songs as "Juke Box Saturday Night," "Slow Boat to China," and "Elmer's Tune." Rum and Coca Cola wasn't just a drink, it was a song popularized by the Andrews Sisters. Young folk of the day idolized Roy Rogers, Franklin Roosevelt, Abe Lincoln, Joe DiMaggio, Louisa May Alcott, Vera-Ellen and Douglas MacArthur. When Americans went to war, the airwaves were filled with "Praise the Lord and Pass the Ammunition," "GI Jive," "White Cliffs of Dover," "They're Either Too Young or Too Old," "When the Lights Go On Again (all over the world)," "This is the Army, Mr. Jones," "He Wears a Pair of Silver Wings," "I Left My Heart at the Stage Door Canteen," "He's A-1 in the Army and A-1 In My Heart," and "Don't Sit Under The Apple Tree" (with anyone else but me.) Everyone was chortling or crying over George Baker's Sad Sack and Bill Mauldin's Willie and Joe cartoons.

In 1945 playwright Tennessee Williams had a hit with *Glass Menagerie,* and his *Streetcar Named Desire* was a 1947 smash. During the same decade, Arthur Miller's *Death of a Salesman* swept the country, and "Nature Boy" was a 1949 hit. Unemployed ex-GI's joined the 52-20 Club to draw unemployment pay of $20 a week for 52 weeks.

But it was 1944 when the bomb hit America in the skinny form and shape of one Frank Sinatra. He was known as the King of Swoon, and teenage girls literally fainted at his performances. In October, 1944, there was a riot at the Paramount Theater in New York (remember the riot Goodman caused a decade earlier at the same theater with his new music called "Swing?") Seven hundred police were called in to restore order. Sinatra had a much wilder reception than had been given Goodman, Bing Crosby, or Rudy Vallee. *Newsweek Magazine* confessed that Sinatra was baffling "as a visible object of adulation." Harry James, who discovered Sinatra working in a New Jersey roadhouse, said he looked like a wet rag. And there was resentment, too.

While Sinatra was thrilling the teenagers, American soldiers were being killed in Bataan, Corregidor, Bastogne, France, and Germany. Some officials threatened to charge him with encouraging truancy because thousands of girls skipped school to hear him sing. They wore dangling shirttails and bobby socks and danced the Lindy, slow or fast. Sinatra held his popularity during the war years with such songs as "White Christmas," "Fools Rush In," and "Night and Day." His smooth, velvety, tender and silky voice, his hungry gaze, drove teenage girls wild until around 1949 when the fans turned to Frankie Laine, Perry Como, and Billy Eckstine.

The war started and ended in that decade and, as hundreds of thousands of young men returned to campuses, a new electronic miracle was emerging—television. Its impact on radio and on the habits of millions of people was not, at the time, imagined. The British experimented with television as early as 1928 and had a regular TV service originating from Alexandra Palace in 1936. World War II stopped all further development, and it wasn't until the mid-to-late '40s that the "boob tube" started attracting mass interest in this country and elsewhere.

Television was to change the habits of virtually every citizen and help bury music the young warriors grew up with and fought by. Rock and Roll was just around the corner in those dim, wispy days of the early 1950s, and it was to be recorded on the new 45 RPM "singles." Milton Berle, host of the Texaco Star Theater, was one of the country's leading comedians and was soon to become "Mr. Television." Traditional radio was still strong, with Duffy's Tavern one of the notable "family hour" shows.

Music went from Pop to Rock in the '50s. Collegians were popping off with such expressions as real george, crazy, hep, bread, flip, green, geets, chic, bear (ugly girl), heavy cream (fat girl), cool, hang loose, yo yo (square), drag (anyone or anything considered dreary), wheels, passion pit, grounded, hardeeharhar (sarcastic response to someone's bad joke), and drag (auto race from standing start).

It was a time of beat folk music, performed first in dimly lit coffee houses. The beats favored songs of protest, Negro blues, and depression ballads. Visitors to New York in the mid-'50s swarmed to Washington Square, headquarters of the new cult. Those American-bred Bohemians, products of the Korean War, called themselves the "beat generation." Totally disillusioned with the American dream of prosperity and conformity, "beat," to them, meant beaten down. Later, they tagged themselves "beatniks" and spoke a peculiar argot of such words as chick, dig, bug, spade (Negro) break and "like," an all-purpose pause-word and qualifier. They smoked marijuana (pot, Mary Jane), slept in "pads," and dug rarified jazz by such artists as Miles Davis and Thelonius Monk.

Rock and Roll radio emerged in the early '50s. McLendon transformed KLIF in Dallas from a stuffy variety format to Top 40, and Todd Storz did the same with KOIL in Omaha.

The first political convention was televised in 1952 as 70 million people watched World War II hero General Dwight Eisenhower nominated by the Republicans and Adlai E. Stevenson by the Democrats. Old line radio held on but its grasp on the country became more tenuous with each new TV set purchased.

Rock and Roll of the '50s was a thundering, ear-shattering mixture of C & W and R & B. The rhythm of rock was overpowering, monotonous, and youngsters played it at a deafening volume. Movements of singers, including the gyrations of Elvis Presley, were scandalous.

> "Make me feel real loose, like a long-necked goose.
> Oh, baby, that's a what I like."

Alan Freed, one of the country's first "disc jockeys," probably coined the expression "Rock and Roll." It was inspired by an old Blues lyric, "My baby rocks me with a steady roll." But rock stations of the period also played Eddie Fisher, Harry Belafonte, Perry Como, Lena Horne, Julie London, and Rosemary Clooney. Such songs as "O, My Pa Pa," "Jamaica Farewell," and "Come On-A-My House," were blended with Bobby Darin's "Mack The Knife," Frankie Avalon's "Venus," Little Anthony's "Tears On My Pillow," and Ricky Nelson's "Poor Little Fool." Patti Page, Jo Stafford and Kay Starr sang the schmaltzy products of the early '50s before Presley turned Rock and Roll into a national teenage religion. The four-sided music of the first half of the decade began to fade as Presley's "Heartbreak Hotel," "Don't Be Cruel," and "Love Me Tender" took over. Bill Haley's all-white Comets came up with "Rock Around the Clock" and a Black group called The Chords produced "Sh-Boom." Dances included the Hip Jive, Bop, Stroll, Circle, Calypso (modified cha cha) and the Slop. As far as youth were concerned, few of the old-time artists of the early '50s survived the transition from Pop to Rock. Pat Boone was one, along with Connie Francis, and Debbie Reynolds.

The music world of the 1960s more or less just "let it all hang out." Great Britain awarded the Beatles The Most Excellent Order of the British Empire after they had become a roaring success in the United States. In 1963, the ageing jazzman, Benny Goodman was invited to tour the Soviet Union, a nation which previously had regarded jazz as a prime example of American decadence. The same year, the first international Jazz Festival was held in Washington.

Joan Baez, a 21-year-old Californian with waist-length hair, sang folk songs in Carnegie Hall, and all tickets were sold two months in advance. By 1963, she had sold more records than any female singer in history. This *was* the period of folk music, and teens and young adults alike were warm to it. But all music didn't fall into the gentle area of good times and bad. The generation of the '60s had turned to the dissonant and unmelodic strains of avant garde, electronic music. A five-piece band would have enough electronic gear on stage to open a small retail business. Speakers and speaker-cells were huge. Guitars, drums—everything was amplified. Radio stations installed reverb equipment to further enhance the sound. Jocks worked standing up or sitting on stage stools and wore amplifier headphones in efforts to "get with it." A Dallas jock, Mike Selden, programmed an "acid rock" sound on KNUS and experimented with "phasing," a technique of playing two copies of a recording simultaneously.

Amid this cacophony of sound were the youth trips, love-ins, beautiful freaks. Marijuana was everywhere and becoming legal in some states. The decade saw the arrival of flower children, love children, gentle people, free people. Burt Bacharach and Hal David produced ''What The World Needs Now is Love, Sweet Love.'' Some young men preferred leaving the country or going to jail rather than fight for the U.S. in Vietnam.

Twiggy became known internationally as a model and Timothy Leary as a proponent of drugs. Jefferson Airplane, The Doors, The Beach Boys, Arlo Guthrie, Bob Dylan, and Judy Collins were popular in such places as New York's East Village and Thompkins Square Park, in Drop City, USA (Colo.), Brook Farm, and Hog Farm. In the summer of '69, 400,000 young people gathered on a 600-acre farm and made Woodstock, N.Y., a part of history. It was a decade of assassinations. The President died from a rifle shot—allegedly fired by Lee Harvey Oswald. Martin Luther King and Bobby Kennedy, the President's brother, were killed. And the Blacks of America began showing their muscles. They rioted in Watts, Newark, Detroit, under the urgings of Malcolm X (killed in 1965), Stokeley Carmichael, and Eldridge Cleaver. LeRoi Jones, the Black playwright, produced ''Toilet,'' ''Slave and Dutch-man,'' and James Baldwin wrote ''Go Tell It On The Mountain.'' It was the heyday of Raquel Welch, James Meredith, Diahann Carroll, and the incredible freak, Tiny Tim. Betty Friedan wrote *The Feminine Mystique,* and Jacqueline Susann the oversexed *Valley of the Dolls.* Pop art, spurred by Andy Warhol, was big. The ''funky look'' was in, and the term, ''fitted misfits,'' seemed, for older people anyway, appropriate for the times. Boris Pasternak wrote *Doctor Zhivago*—and the *Saturday Evening Post* was no more. Beatlemania swept young generations throughout the world, and records by the Black singer, gui-tarist Jimi Hendrix, graced turntables of radio stations from coast to coast.

Rock and Roll music, with its distinctive, uptempo beat, was as perma-nently established in the world as Strauss waltzes and Jazz. As their parents had with the older forms, young people communicated via rock and roll; they could relate to a vocalist singing about ''dirty old blue jeans.'' Such songs as ''Boll Weevil'' (looking for a home) were performed by country, rock—even sym-phonic musical groups. Stevie Wonder, writer and performer, did ''You Are The Sunshine of My Life.'' ''Behind Closed Doors'' started as a country piece, went to rock, then soft rock (contemporary adult.)

In the '60s the FCC became concerned over songs that extolled the virtues of drugs, and McLendon began banning music with dirty lyrics from his sta-tions. But drugs, particularly marijuana, were in. And the composer, writer, and performer, Don Tolle, said it was natural that musicians would write and perform under the influence of drugs, just as earlier generations had under the influence of alcohol.

Early in the decade of the '70s, musicologist and programmer Alden Diehl, noted that ''the pop music scene is characterized by a spectacular up-surge of 1950s-style music and a demand for nostalgia.'' And he observed that programmers were more frequently aiming at both young teens and adults as their target audiences. Diehl explained that, in the 1960s, music had been highly polarized and congealed, "with distinct music forms appealing to specific age groups," and he credited the Beatles with having brought about the change.

The decade also saw the departure of the unstructured acid rock and/or underground stations, and the emergence of the formatted Prog/rock stations (now AOR). Announcers for these stations were "laid back," never raising their voices. Loud commercials and ones that lacked believability were banned. If an advertiser wanted to promote a going-out-of-business sale featuring fantastic discounts, the "laid back" jocks would refuse to read it, preferring to note only that a certain store was having a sale and that the prices were right. Music was played in "sets," and there was considerable freedom on the part of jocks to play their own choices. One set, bright and uptempo, might be called the "Sunshine Set." Another might be a "War Set" of heavy, foreboding sounds. News was keyed directly to the anticipated audience. Ignoring the U.N. and foreign affairs, they reported on congressional discussions on legalizing marijuana, or on what coal miners were doing to the landscape in Pennsylvania or what oil producers were doing to the coastal waters of California.

It is true that, in the early '70s, there was demand for nostalgia, but it looked as faddish as the hoola hoop and the twist of the '60s. Competition among rock stations was grinding. Audiences were getting harder to identify, capture, and retain. And the music was almost *everything*.

In earlier days, program directors and music directors had a fairly easy task of deciding what music would be aired. The options were relatively few. In the mid '50s, with the advent of rock and roll, directors began doing music research—crude though it was. Research, then, meant calling record stores to learn which songs were selling well. As competition grew, research was intensified. Information on what was selling in the record stores was still needed, but many stations sent researchers into the field to *talk* to people about their musical tastes. Results of these studies determined, not only what was desired in the way of music, but where during the broadcast day it would be played and how often. Records that received quick response from the public and then quickly fell to the bottom of the charts could be determined ahead of time through research. "The Purple People Eater," a novelty tune of the late '50s, is an example of a record that quickly caught fire and just as quickly burned out.

PERSONALITIES

Every disc jockey on every rock 'n roll station in the world is a "personality" or thinks he or she wants to be one. Some become genuine big-time stars, others score locally and stay there, but most just fade into oblivion. Larry Lujack wrote one of those "with so and so" biographies about "superjocks" and declared, "I'm just plain fantastic—the best damn rock-'n-roll DJ of our time or any other time." Lujack *is* a personality! He made it! And the station that hires him must be prepared to pay big money and cope with a lot of temperament. Stardom or star-status invariably sensitizes an individual's picture of himself, and it is management that has to pay the tab.

The question, of course, in considering a format, is, "Does the licensee really want to assemble a personality formula?" There are hard rock formats that deemphasize personality by compressing program elements so tightly that the DJs never have an opportunity to express their personalities. The original Drake-Chenault format disallowed personality development. "Play the music and shut up" was the prevailing guideline. KVIL in Dallas put together a "Personality MOR" format that attracted 25-plus listeners. Jocks were paid $25,000 a year and more, depending upon demand by other stations for their services. KLIF, during the same period, had at least two DJs earning nearly $40,000 a year.

Some licensees argue that "you're digging your own grave when you build personalities." The more popular DJs become, the more effort is made by other stations to hire them. This invariably drives salaries to unprecedented heights. And salaries, of course, must be related to the dollars the "talent" is bringing the station through high ratings.

The Drake-Chenault team of programmers were credited with the *sterilization* of Top 40 radio when they installed their "much more music" concept at client stations throughout the country. It was a high pressure, noisy kind of approach that literally left no room on the clock for the DJ to expose personality. To the extent possible, there was never a time when music wasn't being heard by the listener. Time, temperature, and station IDs were given over the opening bars of the record. If there was talk, it was in news and commercials. The jock was expected to keep the pressure on, keep the music flowing, never letting 'em up for air. Chenault was "dialing up" his clients from a Los Angeles bungalow and giving hour-by-hour directions to programmers. Chenault's concept hit big; *Time* published a story on the team and ran a picture showing Chenault directing his empire from a fancy swimming pool float.

But "personalities" have *made* contemporary music radio since those wild, innovative days of the early '50s. The original Drake-Chenault concept faded, as did the later "Q" format which also emphasized more music, less talk, sound effects and pressure, pressure, pressure. Intelligent, relevant talk is necessary in a long-tenured format. KLIF in Dallas has been a personality Top 40 from the beginning and successfully withstood assault after assault on its dominant position. Only in the mid-70s was the big 50,000 watt original McLendon flagship station seriously threatened—and then it was by KNUS, a McLendon-owned FM in Dallas, and KVIL AM/FM, a Fairbanks station.

Some of the top-paid jocks in the nation in the 1970s included Charlie Van Dyke, KLIF, Dallas; John Gambling, WOR, New York; J. Akuhead Pupule,

KGMB, Honolulu; Dan Ingram, WABC, New York; Larry Lujack, WLS, Chicago; Dr. Don Rose, KFRC, San Francisco, and Charlie Tuna, KHJ, Los Angeles.

Of course, the high-priced DJs usually draw significant ratings and are, therefore, entitled to greater remuneration. Many jocks live from book to book, that is, rating period to rating period. In life and death struggles for numbers, the jocks who are overtaken by a competing station often find themselves on the street, looking for another job. It is much the same with anchorpersons on local and national television newscasts. As long as the personalities can maintain a saleable rating position, they are safe. When the ratings bomb, it is assumed that the personalities bombed and they are, therefore, replaced by other personalities.

One licensee, years ago, decided to copyright certain "air" names for exclusive use by his rock stations. Thus, when Jim Smith came to work he was known as "Charlie Chattersby"—a name owned by the station. If Jim Smith didn't perform satisfactorily as Charlie Chattersby, management simply hired Tom Brown to come in and perform under the Chattersby title. Good air names, however, are copied unconscionably by DJs the country over. A Jay Jay Jackson may be playing the hits in Seattle, Dallas, Kansas City, Oklahoma City, Los Angeles and Miami—all different jocks but all claiming the air name Jay Jay Jackson.

Many MOR stations and most good music stations make no effort to develop personalities. The names of announcers are not promoted, and only rarely are announcers permitted to identify themselves on the air. There is no need for those stations to build personalities. The *music* is the product, by and large, and personality development only gets in the way and distorts the aim of the programmer. Some automated stations have gone so far as to pre-record intros and outros and have dropped all pretenses of even having personalities on the air.

NEWS

There is considerable argument *against* the implied requirement that *every* commercial radio carry some non-entertainment programming. News is part of every station's non-entertainment category of programming, and, often, in the case of good music stations, for example, it is regarded as a "throwaway." The industry seems stuck with tradition; all radio stations have always carried *some* news, so it follows that all radio stations must *continue* to carry some news. But many hundreds of U.S. stations should not broadcast news because they are ill-equipped to do so and because their listeners do not tune in such stations for news.

It is a truism that any program element that flies into the face of the *reason* a person tunes in a given station tends to defeat the format. Thus, a listener tuning for good music and finding a newscast will be disappointed and will probably continue the search for music. This is an age of format specialization, and the broadcast spectrum is filled with a department store variety of music, news, talk, religion, and public service and public affairs programming. There is no justification for news being the *only* thing stations have in common. The good music or progressive rock station cannot compete in the news field with all-news and/or network stations. It is in incredibly bad taste for a highly-trained music specialist on a classical or good music station to deliver one or more minutes of wire copy that he neither understands nor can interpret. News, in this case, becomes an unpleasant interruption in an otherwise pleasant flow of music.

The FCC rules do not require that each station program news, but the *general feeling* among communications lawyers, FCC staff members, and broadcasters themselves is that if a station doesn't schedule some news, it will be regarded as *not operating in the public interest*.

Many broadcasters are criticized by their colleagues for airing poor-quality news reports. Low budget stations simply can't afford the talent required to produce quality newscasts. Many rockers, in order to make the news more palatable for their absolutely disinterested teeny-bopper listeners, have resorted to either sensationalizing or "keying" stories to the audience with which they identify. The "keying" technique is infinitely more desirable, but the station continues to do a poor job of "covering the news." Such stations may ignore important political activity in India or a White House announcement that touches half the lives in the country, while concentrating on an ecology problem in Northern California. A counter argument here, of course, is that there are many specialized newspapers and magazines and that, if print can successfully specialize in limited news areas, broadcasting can, too. But the ambient radio listeners who are searching for news won't be satisfied and, indeed, may be misled, if their dialing leads them to one of the "earthnews" programs or to a sensationalized newscast that implies a Cleveland rape story is the biggest news of the day. There are no qualified arguments for sensationalism, just as there were none for the newspapers' era of yellow journalism. There may be some support for a station specializing in earth or financial news, but even this limited effort should perhaps be listed as information rather than news *per se*.

News should be *considered* when planning *any* format. But it should be considered in the light of available capital, market competition, and format suitability. The licensee must serve the public interests, needs, tastes and desires. Poorly-executed newscasts provide a *disservice!* The Schulke good music format, for example, is designed to provide listeners with beautiful, highly-orchestrated music. If news must be aired in such formats, every effort should be made to persuade the FCC to permit a very low percentage in the total broadcast week. Two minutes per hour, 12 hours a day, would produce 168 minutes per week or 1.6% of the total week for a 24-hour station. Broadcasters simply should not be required to program news when they have neither the resources nor interest in doing the job properly. Audiences *do* sweep the dial for programming that interests them at a given moment. "I don't want news and markets on the classical station. Yes! I'm interested in news and markets but when I want them I'll tune the station that specializes in news and markets. I tuned the classical station for classical music! Don't louse it up with inept, poorly organized, badly delivered news that has either been ripped unedited from a wire machine or simply read from a newspaper." That's one argument. It has been correctly said that all-news formats cut across all other formats in a market. Adult listeners tune C & W stations for country music, rock music stations for the latest pop hits, and good music stations for relaxing, easy-to-digest beautiful music. But when they want news, many tune an all-news station.

No licensee would program rock music without resources to employ rock music specialists and buy the latest reproduction equipment.

No licensee should induce any element of programming into a format if that element can't be executed competently.

So it is with news programming.

Most of the discussion on news matter is contained in the chapter on Information Formats. News *departments* at radio stations range in size from zero news persons to staffs of 20 to 30 with specialists in business, politics, agriculture, culture, etc. Time allocated to news by music stations ranges from 2 minutes an hour on good music stations to 50 hours a week by adult block formats. The minimum effort is for the announcer on duty to read headlines ripped from the wire or plagiarized from the local newspaper. It is possible, however, for a station to provide quality news service economically. There are several possibilities:

ONE NEWSPERSON — Prepares and delivers two 5-minute newscasts hourly in the 6a-9a period, spends the balance of day gathering and writing local news for delivery by jocks, and leaves "voicers" for use by jocks who do news in later periods.

TWO NEWSPERSONS — News Director handles morning-drive writing and voicing chores, spending the balance of the day gathering and rewriting. The number two newsperson spends the early part of day gathering and writing, and delivers two 5-minute newscasts hourly in the afternoon drive period.

THREE PERSONS — The third addition to the staff would handle all inside duties, and deliver the newscasts in the 9:30-3:30 period.

As each new staff member is added, professionalism is added to the station's news product. Disc jockeys *read* news as they might read commercials, but a trained newsperson with basic journalism skills is necessary to write and voice a believable newscast. The successful, news-oriented station will continue to build on the staff indicated above until the newsroom is staffed around the clock, seven days a week.

KLIF's first news department was built in such manner. At first, there was a desk, typewriter, telephone, microphone, and one news person. Later, a "mobile reporter" was added, along with a mobile news unit. This unit consisted of a station wagon equipped with a two-way radio and police/fire radio receivers. The mobile reporter gave "on-the-scene" reports through the base station located in the studios. These reports would sometimes be taped and replayed on regular newscasts by the "inside man." Later, at KLIF, a small console and an old Magnacorder were added to the newsroom, giving the newscaster much more control over the product. Some of the first taped actualities in the country were broadcast over KLIF by this arrangement. A second mobile unit, then a third and fourth were added, along with reporters to staff them. When more space was required, walls were torn out and new desks moved in. The staff grew to 15 persons before management decided to approach news in a different manner and eliminate all of the mobile news operation. The news continued to be hard and fast, but more use was made of the telephone and the small, compact cassette recorders that had become available.

A good news department subscribes to one or more of the wire services. Some two-way radio equipment is employed, not on a regular basis, but as needed in case of special stories such as fires, floods, people jumping from tall buildings, or traffic reports. Much of the material in the chapter on Information Formats will be helpful in setting up a news department and planning a news policy.

COMMERCIAL LIMITATIONS

To reduce the "commercial load" of a format seems inimical to the interests of the investors in a commercial radio station. After all, that's how stations make money—through the sale of as many commercial minutes as possible in each hour of the broadcast day. In the early days of Top 40 programmers hated heavy commercial loads, but as they didn't seem to affect audience shares, nothing was done about it. Many stations ran as much as 30 minutes of commercial matter during prime periods. Some station sales managers explained, tongue in cheek, that "our policy is to never run commercials back-to-back, but sometimes we have to." And back-to-back they did run them—sometimes as many as seven minutes of solid advertising, broken only by quips on time and temperature checks by the jock. Surprisingly, DJs developed considerable skill in being able to politely force commercial after commercial into the ears of listeners.

In the mid-to-late '60s, the trend toward more music and fewer commercials began. FM stations, unable to sell time because of sparse audiences, began to promote the fact. "Hey, look!" they proclaimed, no commercials, just wall-to-wall music. The early FM rockers, faced with the same problem, quickly learned that the absence of commercials was gathering audiences for them. It soon became generally apparent, through research, that the over-commercialized format could be defeated by a station that refused to run an unlimited number of spots. Further, the FCC was beginning to respond to complaints about the heavy loads, and the National Association of Broadcasters moved in to establish guidelines that limited to 18 minutes the amount of commercial matter subscribing stations could run. Not everyone, of course, adhered to the guidelines, but those who did were said to be "safe from FCC interference" in that respect. Many stations were promising the FCC they would adhere to the self-imposed limit of 18 minutes per hour except during political campaigns when the demand for time often skyrockets.

Competition, however, was the principal element in reducing commercial loads. The cost of commercial time went up. Stations that were averaging $20 per minute for 18 minutes an hour simply cut the load in half and charged twice as much for the remaining 9 minutes. In other instances, owners took a financial beating until their ratings increased sufficiently to merit the higher spot rates.

After television, many advertising agencies began de-emphasizing the importance of good quality radio commercial production. Coca Cola, for example, sometimes produced one theme for use on five different formats. The spot may have been excellent for the Top 40 stations but totally inappropriate for good music, C & W, R & B and all-news formats. It was uncommon in those days for a well-heeled licensee or programmer to refuse to air a commercial considered too noisy or too schmaltzy for the station's "sound." As radio reasserted itself, and as programmers became more demanding, agencies and clients slowly turned around and again began putting more time and effort into radio commercial production. It is now common to hear the same product or service advertised on five different stations with special treatment given five *different* styled commercials. The music *theme* or melody can be detected in each of the commercials, but the treatment varies according to the format. Modern Coca Cola commercials for a Black-ethnic station's audience might feature a heavy, bluesy vocal, while the commercial for a Top 40 operation hammers away with the basic rock and roll background. Commercials are "keyed" to the standard formats and enhance rather than detract from the station sound. It represented a step forward by an industry that had been selling time to anyone for virtually any price offered. Broadcasters have always been charged with a degree of responsibility for the *content* of commercials, but few have bothered to police the veracity of commercial messages. Most notable in this area were the underground or prog/rock stations who purport to "tell it like it is." If a commercial isn't believable to the prog/rock station's young and "with it" audience, the station will not air it.

Too many station programmers still consider commercials a throwaway. This is a mistake. It is known that bad commercial writing and production will "tune out" the audience, while a good, well-produced commercial will hold and even attract audiences. Every commercial should complement the format, rather than detract from it.

OUTSIDE PROMOTIONS

The "outside" promotion differs principally from the on-air promotion in that it involves the station or station personnel in visually public situations. A prime example of an outside promotion is a rock concert. The station books the talent, hires the hall, and advertises the event. Extremely popular stations need no outside help in promoting such shows. Numerous announcements on the station will usually do the job. Weaker or less popular stations must resort to using outside media, such as newspapers.

These promotions are designed to build *image,* rather than attract listeners to the frequency. Such events do both, but the main effect is to "make 'em love us!" Too, such concerts often result in a considerable profit for the station.

After the successful promotion of a rock concert, stations often will bill themselves as "KXXX, the station that brought you The Beatles!" Or, during and after the promotion, the entertainers themselves will cut station breaks. "Hi, this is so-and-so of Jefferson Airplane, and I just want to say you're listening to the swingingest station in the city, KXXX!"

The public concert, of course, is only one such promotion. Others include Family Picnics, A Day at The Beach, Easter Egg Hunts, Sock Hops, Ski Trips. One is limited only by the imagination.

At Christmastime, some stations ask listeners to bring toys to the station for re-distribution to the poor. One station threw a party for the first 100 listeners to call in their names and addresses. The party was hosted by the jocks, and winning listeners had a chance to "rub elbows" with their "favorite deejays."

Such promotions, obviously, attract primarily the young. They tend to bore or disgust the 25-plus audiences. Author Peter Marin made the point: "It is not that what is done among the young is different or extreme; it is simply that what is done feels differently in quality, in resonance. It is a sense of warmth, of slowness, and delight that seems to enter the flesh and abide there."

Some stations, particularly those in the rock and country fields, use mobile studios and broadcast from such places as shopping centers, county fairs, and athletic events. Technology is such that a complete broadcast studio can be assembled in a mobile home and transported to any location for use. Most stations tie the studio to the station's main control center with telephone lines; others use microwave equipment. In any event, the best assembly provides a quality broadcast, and listeners normally are unable to tell from the sound that the broadcast isn't coming directly from the main studio.

Here are some outside promotion ideas which may be executed in a variety of innovative ways:

1. Book a popular entertainment group into a local high school auditorium, municipal auditorium, or sports arena.
2. Stage a snake race at a high school football field.
3. Stage a county fair. Rent a building, sell advertisers on renting space

and buying advertising on a "50%-off" sale. This may also be called a "sales promotion," as the station should earn money from it.

4. Install a "flag-pole" sitter in a tower on a main thoroughfare.
5. Stage disco-hops, renting a dance floor and use jocks to play danceable music along with that which the station regularly programs.

These are "outside" promotions—where the principal thrust is to attempt to gain visual recognition. They often relate directly to "on air" and sales promotions. For example, Girl on The Billboard is an old promotion that fits into all three areas.

These are the steps:

1. Find a sponsor, such as the local Coca Cola bottler.
2. Rent a large billboard on a main thoroughfare. Build a platform on the billboard, and top it with sand to simulate a beach.
3. Hire a good-looking boy or girl to reside on the "beach" during the period of the promotion.
4. Paint the billboard brightly with copy that explains vaguely why the person is on the beach and asks the viewer to tune KXXX to learn what is going on. The sign might also include the sponsor logo.
5. Prepare announcements explaining the promotion. *Any* person *seeing* the board is invited to call the station and relate the "mystery" number on the board. Each caller receives a six-pack of sponsor product. Meanwhile, each caller is invited to guess the telephone number of the "beach-comber" who lounges all day in the sun on the billboard beach. Clues are given hourly to stimulate excitement. The prize is limited only by the planner's budget and imagination. The person who guesses the mystery telephone number may win a trip around the world with the beach comber or, if that isn't practical, (and it usually isn't, for obvious reasons), an amount of cash equal to the trip. Too, tons of sponsor product may be thrown in, along with the sand (for the yard) and a variety of smaller prizes, such as clothing, appliances, and radios.

To make such an effort profitable for the station, the sponsor may be required to buy a long-term schedule in exchange for the "free" plugs received during the promotion.

Outside promotions can often cause the station embarrassment and bring down the wrath of the establishment on the heads of the owners and managers. Listeners have been killed or seriously hurt while searching for "treasures." Fights have broken out at rock concerts, and teens have been arrested for alcohol and drug abuse at sock hops. Insurance to protect the licensee against damage suits is usually available and should be purchased.

ON-AIR PROMOTIONS

Anyone considering a youth-oriented format must also consider promotions that will stimulate listeners and urge them to invite others to tune the station.

> Cash Call!
> The fourth caller wins $185.00!
> Identify the mystery voice and win a trip to Europe!
> Treasure Hunt, worth $25,000!
> Listen to me! I've got money to give away!

Promotional give-aways are routine fare at most rock stations, but are avoided by many adult-oriented and progressive stations. The on-air promotion is designed to do one fundamental thing: attract and hold listeners. Audiences usually benefit materially when two strong rockers begin a "hype" campaign. If station "A" offers $25,000 in prizes, station "B" may offer $50,000. In some cases, the prizes have been only *offered;* the contests were designed to be won when the dollar value was relatively low or designed to not be won at all. The FCC becomes interested in the mechanics of a contest when listeners complain that the rules were changed in mid-stream or that the contest was rigged. Any time a station contest is planned, the licensee should assume the prize will be won and be prepared to hand it over, whether it's a check for $1,000 or a new motorcycle. Every such contest must be conducted completely above-board. Any sign of fraud or misrepresentation may put the station license in jeopardy. Scores of licensees have paid heavy fines for running rigged contests. Such malfeasance includes *not* hiding the object of a treasure hunt, faking famous voices in a "mystery voice" contest, and *not* doing anything the programmers promised the listeners they would do.

Contest ideas are endless.

Examples:

1. Give away a motor home, worth $12,000. Display the motor home at the station or in a heavy traffic area with appropriate signs. Ask listeners to identify the "mystery castle." One person knows the answer, and he is a banker or CPA sworn to secrecy. The "one person" selects a castle, perhaps in Italy, identifies it on a card, and seals the card in a vault. The holder of the secret then writes clues to its identity, and these are given on the air. The first clues may be very remote to the actual castle, but they should become easier as the contest wears on. Listeners are urged to "stay tuned" for clues and mail in their guesses on post cards. The first person to identify the mystery castle wins the motor home. If two persons identify the castle simultaneously, the motor home is sold and the cash proceeds divided equally. Listeners

will flood the station with postal guesses. Others will bring them to the station by the dozens. Professional contest enterers may send as many as a thousand guesses, after spending time in the library looking up all the castles in the world.

2. In the mid-60s stations ran silly "apple peel" contests. These were particularly popular in college towns, where students were already cramming themselves into small cars and telephone booths. In this contest, stations offered a substantial prize for the longest apple peel. In one market, the manager of a supermarket called the station manager to complain that "those darned college students are buying all the big apples in my store." Entrants would very carefully peel the skin from the apple and seal it in a box or envelope and mail or bring it to the station. One winning entry was 12 feet in length.

3. When the public was going wild over the book and movie, "Jaws," a Dallas station jumped into the swim with a "Jaws" contest. The technique was tricky but effective, and certainly timely. Listeners were invited to call the deejay and take a chance on "getting into the water and out again before being eaten by the shark." The jock, after getting the listener on the telephone, would play a tape containing a "splash." That meant the listener was "in the water." In from 12 to 60 seconds, a loud CRUNCH, CRUNCH, CRUNCH would be played, meaning the listener had been eaten. The longer the listener "stayed in the water," the more money could be won. Of course, listeners who were eaten by the shark won nothing.

4. Two deejays went in opposite directions in an "around the world contest." Listeners were invited to call in or write guesses on (1) who would win the race, and (2) the exact date and time the winner would complete the trip.

5. The "rear window" or "bumper" sticker contests drew excitement. Working with a multi-store retailer, the station distributed bumper stickers to listeners who were asked to place them on rear windows or bumpers. Each sticker had a serial number and, if that number was called on the air, the holder had to (1) call the station within, usually 3 minutes, and (2) be able to prove that the bumper sticker was on the car at the time the number was called. There are many variations of this contest. One station called out auto license numbers and, if the winner's car had a station sticker on it at the time, the prize could be claimed.

6. A variety of on-air contests:
   A. Flagpole sitter—guess when he'll come down.
   B. Hi-Low—guess a $ figure between $600–$1500.
   C. Cash Call—Guess the jackpot exactly and win it.
   D. Guess the serial # on a $1,000 bill and win it.
   E. Find the station's "mystery person" from hourly clues.

There are inherent dangers to the station license when programmers execute such promotions. In 1975, the FCC strongly considered the possibility of prohibiting promotions during rating periods. It is common industry practice to hold off on big-dollar promotions until the April–May/Oct.–Nov. period when Arbitron conducts surveys in most major markets. A station may, month after month, give away a few prizes or a few hundred dollars in a steady flow. Then, during the rating period, the idea becomes to up the ante to, perhaps, $100,000! This is called "buying" the listeners and is effecitve primarily with youth-oriented rock stations. Teen audiences are said to be fickle because they move with the contests and excitement; the bigger the prize and the wilder the contests, the more teens and 18–24 audiences the station is likely to attract.

Aside from the possible risk of being cited on a "hype" charge, there is always the danger that someone on the staff might rig a contest. When this has been done, it usually has been to prolong the contest and thus gain more mileage from the promotion. While the licensee may not have participated in the rigging, he will be the one to pay the fine or lose the license when it is discovered. When a contest is rigged, it is almost certain that someone will suffer an attack of conscience and report the matter to the FCC. The cost of discovery can range from a small fine to $10,000 to loss of license. The gain simply isn't worth the risk.

It is a heartbreaker when a listener wins the jackpot on the first day of the promotion, but this possibility is insignificant when compared to the possible loss of license if the owner is convicted of rigging the contest.

The FCC resolved, in part, the "hype" controversy in 1976 when it decided to keep hands off such station activity. Broadcasters had complained that small stations, who could afford to advertise *only* during rating periods, would be hurt by an anti-hype regulations. Others argued that the marketplace would take care of the situation through reports on hypoing from the various rating companies. Time buyers are generally conscious of special promotions as they search a rating book for a station that attracts the demographics desired by the agency's client. The best outside advertising plan, of course, is to promote year-round. But newspaper space, billboards, bus backs and sides, taxi backs, and television time are expensive, and a majority of station owners cannot afford a long-term plan. These owners argued that they should continue to be allowed to promote when it would do them the most good, e.g., during a rating period. While the FCC decided to keep its hands off such station matters, the FTC (Federal Trade Commission) maintained its interest in unfair trade practices, and stations may still face serious litigation if they are caught trying to promote themselves to diary holders or to persons who may be called in a telephone coincidental survey. Example of promotion to be avoided:

"Hey out there, if you're keeping a diary this week, be sure to note that you've been listening to KXXX! We are number one and want you to help make sure we stay number one."

Stations have run big money contests during telephone coincidental surveys. "If your phone rings today, answer it with 'I'm listening to KXXX!' If you do, you may win $1,000. Here's how it works. All day every day this week, KXXX personalities will be calling telephone numbers at random. If they call you, answer 'I'm listening to KXXX' and you win the money." A competitor complaint to the FTC could result in a cease and desist order being given the station owner. That could result in high legal and court costs, plus a problem at renewal time when the FCC considers any litigation the licensee may be involved in. Further, rating services (Arbitron, in particular) became sensitive to "diary-oriented" promotions and threatened legal action and deletion of call letters of offending stations from the reports.

COMPETITION

Only a blind person would conceive a particular format and then simply begin execution without special consideration of what is already being done in the market. Each format should be designed to provide, if not a unique service, at least one that is markedly different from those already in use. The solution is easy if there is no All-News, no Classical, no Contemporary MOR. One simply fills the void. But when a market already has one or more of the known formats, it becomes a highly complex problem. The Dallas market has a variety of good radio stations executing with unusual competence a wide range of commercially successful formats.

There are a number of ways to get a "reading" on a market before deciding precisely the form your format will take. First is the task of preparing a local "radio dial" to give the programmer a quick graphic of where the stations are located on the dial and their relationship to each other. Some markets are "far left" or "far right" markets, while others are mid-dial markets, ones where most of the highly popular stations are situated in one general area on the dial. Dallas has a mid-dial market.

Prior to 1960, planners paid little attention to stations on the FM band. But with each passing year, it became more apparent from Arbitron, The Pulse, Inc., and other rating services, that FMs share of listening was increasing. In the early '70s, well after the myth of "FM music" had been crushed, FM stations in many parts of the country had higher ratings than AMs. KNUS (FM) in Dallas is one prime example of how an FM-only operation can overtake an AM-only (KLIF).

"Ah, that's just an FM—we don't have to worry about those stations!" That kind of remark can bring disaster to the programmer who believes FM stations aren't competitive.

Once the local radio dial has been completed, the programmer might then analyze the latest Arbitron or Pulse to learn who is listening to what station. One of the best means of analyzing a station's audience is through development of "skew" sheets. These, as illustrated, will give the programmer a pretty good idea of a station's audience composition. In the examples, KNUS, the leading FM rocker in Dallas, has the largest share of teens, and *these teens* represent the largest percentage of the station's total audience. Teens are not identified by sex in either Arbitron or Pulse. The young demographics, it will be noted, continue to make up most of KNUS' audience. As one moves on to older audiences, it may be seen that they listen less to KNUS and more to KRLD, KOAX, and WRR. Skew graphs are particularly important when one is planning to enter a highly competitive contemporary music format. In Dallas, should anyone want to put yet another rock format on the air, particular attention would have to be paid to KNUS, KLIF, KVIL (AM & FM), KFJZ (AM & FM) and KKDA (AM & FM). These all program one or the other variety of rock music. KVIL skews to the older demographics (25–49). KNUS, KLIF and KFJZ-FM skew younger (12–34), while KKDA, a Black ethnic station licensed to Grand Prairie (AM) and Dallas (FM), picks up a broader or flatter composition of age groups.

Until 1974, KLIF was the dominant rock station in Dallas. KVIL was somewhat adult contemporary MOR, as was WFAA. It was not a competitive market, insofar as rock stations were concerned. KLIF was tops and that was it. When Fairchild Industries bought KLIF from the McLendon group, the McLendon family was left with KNUS (FM). KNUS had been for sale, but Fairchild declined to purchase it with the AM station. Bart McLendon, son of the founder of McLendon stations, assumed the management of KNUS and, with the help of veteran programmer Ken Dowe, began programming "against" KLIF. At first it appeared there would be no competition. FM still hadn't arrived in Dallas, and no one took the challenge seriously. But with each passing Arbitron sweep, KNUS' audiences grew. Programmers stopped thinking "FM" and simply thought "radio." Finally, in Arbitron's Oct–Nov study of 1975, KNUS actually came out ahead of KLIF in total audience, 12-plus. It was the first time any FM had beaten any AM in Dallas on the same or similar format. Both stations gave away money by the thousands of dollars. Both hired hotshot jocks to lure young listeners. Each station employed the most talented music directors available. KLIF had the advantage of range, and thus did better in the total survey area. But KNUS had the advantage of stereo, and this, apparently, contributed to its victory. One station promoted the world's greatest radio contest. Another station promoted the world's *last* radio contest. KLIF flooded the market with billboards, bus backs, TV commercials, and newspaper ads. KNUS lashed back with lesser volume but equally effective "outside" advertising. KNUS' efforts were geared more to teens (the promotions and the music) with the result that KNUS achieved the highest ratings among that group. KLIF skewed its effort more toward the 18–34 group and, consequently, led the market in those demographics.

Meanwhile, KVIL (AM/FM) was purchased by the Fairbanks group in Indianapolis. Almost immediately, KVIL's new management started an unprecedented promotion campaign. The AM station (a daytimer) fared poorly, even under simulcast conditions, but the FM more than made up for this deficiency. Within three years, KVIL had jumped from nowhere among rock stations in the market to first. KVIL claimed to have an *adult contemporary* format, heavy with personality. Its promotions were geared to the 25-plus audience. Results? An audience made up predominantly of 25–49 listeners.

Just prior to the grinding competitive battle between KLIF and KNUS, the Belo Corporation re-tooled its AM and FM stations. The old WFAA (FM) changed call letters to KZEW and began programming progressive rock. The old format was "good music," and it had been a loser. Progressive jocks were brought in from Detroit, Chicago, Austin and other points. The format was an almost instant success, knocking KAFM, the market's first prog/rock station, out of the picture. WFAA (AM), on the other hand, executed an *adult contemporary,* directly in competition with KVIL, and did not succeed. Some gains were made, initially, but KVIL's personalities and outside promotional campaign made the difference. Late in 1975, the daytimer licensed to Grand Prairie, KKDA, acquired an FM station in Dallas and entered yet another contemporary music format into the scramble. It must be understood that Black-ethnic stations do not attract Black-only audiences. People of all ages and backgrounds in Dallas listen to Black-oriented stations and freely admit it to survey companies when questioned about listening habits. There are few who are only FM listeners, rock listeners, or country listeners. There are just *listeners*—and broadcasters strive constantly to broaden the base of their formats to attract as many of these *listeners* as possible.

When a licensee is unable to fill a total void in a given market, he must then decide which of the existing formats he will challenge. Dial position and power are two principal considerations, along with, of course, financial resources. It takes a great deal of money to employ *better* announcers and *better* programmers, to buy more outside advertising, and to give more money away on the air. But these are the elements required to overtake an existing format.

In Austin, Texas, several years ago, the manager of a full-time AM invited the manager of a daytime AM to lunch. The conversation:

AM Fulltimer: Mr. Bates, you're leading this market with a daytime AM station and we've decided to go after you.

AM Daytimer: Well, Mr. Rathbone, shoot your best shot. We'll make you wish you'd never heard of rock and roll.

AM Fulltimer: Just a minute, Mr. Bates. I'm over here to try to save us both a lot of money and headaches.

AM Daytimer: Oh, how's that?

AM Fulltimer: Just this. In a dozen markets in the last couple of years, a well-done rock format on a fulltime station has overtaken a well-done AM daytimer. Shreveport is the closest example. KJOE was leading the market in Hooper and it was a daytimer. The owners thought they'd never be knocked off. Then, KEEL changed format and went rock, and in

30 days had pulled out in front of KJOE. The difference? The fulltimer developed audience continuity with these young listeners we're after, and the owners of KEEL had virtually unlimited capital to buy talent and promotion.

AM Daytimer: So what's all this got to do with my station?

AM Fulltimer: Just this. We're going into the rock field, and we're prepared to spend the money to beat you.

AM Daytimer (not too skeptically, this time): And just how do you think money will beat us?

AM Fulltimer: Easy. We're putting five mobile news units on the street, and we'll cover everything from fender benders to visiting Congressmen. We've purchased a 100% showing in billboards and bus and taxi backs, and, more important, we're going to offer your program director, your morning and afternoon jocks from $2,000 to $5,000 a year more in money. I know they're loyal to you, but these are young folks trying to get ahead in the world, and I believe they'll accept my offer. Consider this a battlefield, if you will. I have the superior forces, and I'm here to tell you in a gentlemanly fashion that we're going to lick you.

AM Daytimer: (really getting interested, now): Okay. So what do you expect me to do? Just lie down and play dead?

AM Fulltimer: As far as contemporary programming is concerned, yes. But I have an idea for an option that might interest you.

AM Daytimer: And the option is . . . ?

AM Fulltimer: Go country. You'd have no competition and probably won't have for a lot of years. Country is going great everywhere. You'll have the field all to yourself, and I'll have the rock field. What do you say?

AM Daytimer: I'll think about it.

AM Fulltimer: Fine. But just remember. For every $1,000 you give away on the air, I'll give away $5,000. For every mobile news unit you put on the streets, I'll put out five. And everytime you get a decent jock, I'll hire him away from you. Now, please. Let's don't get into a dog fight that'll cost us both a lot of needless worry and certainly more money than either of us could like to put into the Austin market.

AM Daytimer: I'll let you know.

The daytimer manager did think about the conversation and decided that, after all, a country format wouldn't be so bad. The scheme worked, and both stations became highly successful.

The KAFM/KZEW conflict presented a short-lived study of how a station becomes vulnerable when it fails to maintain a purity of format. KAFM, sister station of KRLD (AM), was the only prog/rock format in the market. The demographics were principally 18–34 males, with few females of any age.

Prior to the arrival of KZEW, KAFM began to think of itself as a "rocker"— and began trying to compete with other rockers.

To compete with rockers, KAFM had to broaden its music base and, in so doing, destroyed the reason its listeners tuned in the first place. One cannot mix elements of various formats in the contemporary field and expect to maintain high ratings in any demographics. By the time KZEW went on the air, KAFM, (programmers believe) had already weakened itself to a point where its audience had dialed out and gone back to the second favorite stations. Thus, KZEW had a wide open field when it entered the prog/rock market. KZEW did not make the same mistakes. Music was carefully controlled within well-defined boundaries. DJ "style," too, was controlled, as were commercial content and load. While KZEW was an almost instant success, two years were required (four Arbitrons) for the graph to level out. KZEW's loyalty to its format also produced female listeners after the first year. Women, traditionally, react more slowly to new format variations.

The more the licensee can learn about his *radio* competition, the better able he will be to prepare a plan around a new and different or better executed format. There are, obviously, other media seeking shares of the market's available advertising dollar, but none will affect the new format as dramatically as other radio stations. Modern radio *has* arrived, and most marketing specialists include radio in their advertising plans. In the '50s, with the birth of television, huge radio budgets were cancelled in favor of the new extra-dimensioned electronic medium. After years of struggle and change, professional broadcasters were able to convince marketers that people did listen and that merchandise and services could be sold via the old medium of radio.

Tom Johnson, former publisher of the *Dallas Times Herald,* told a group of Dallas broadcasters that his paper's principal competitive aim was to "compete with ourselves," doing everything possible every day to make the *Herald* a better newspaper. This concept of competition makes sense. Counterprogramming is often frustrating and non-productive. Station A schedules a Sunday morning talk-show. Station B follows with a similar program. One operation hires a two-man rock team for the morning show. The competition follows suit and adds a team in afternoon drive. Competition against one's own standards is often more productive than direct, head-to-head competition with another station. Programming competition arises when two stations seek precisely the same audience. While C & W formats indeed do seek 18–49 audiences, they tend to compete with *each other* rather than with a rock station going after the same age groups. There is competition among every format for the advertising dollar, even when a particular station doesn't reach the advertiser's consumer target. Thus, banks will buy time on teen-oriented rockers and head shops will buy time on good music or all-news stations. These are not common buys, of course, but do illustrate how stations compete for shares of advertising budgets.

NON-ENTERTAINMENT, PSAs

Competitively formulating music, personalities, and news is the beginning of a viable format, whether it is ethnic, rock, C & W, or another. There remain the legalities of complying with the Rules, Regulations, and Guidelines of the FCC. There are commercial limitations, a certain number of public service announcements to run, along with, perhaps, some public affairs and instructional/religion/agriculture/educational programming. While the area may appear vague to the newcomer, veteran practitioners of the broadcast arts have come to understand with great clarity the public interest "requirements" of the FCC and their devastating effects on programming.

Some actions violate a law, a rule, or a regulation. Others violate a Commission policy or guideline. Others violate neither, but may be predicted to cause some consternation among staff members at the Commission because, perhaps, of citizen complaints about certain programming. It was never against "the law" to broadcast sex-talk shows on KLIF in Dallas. It was being done successfully in other parts of the country, so why not Dallas? This talk format started essentially in Los Angeles, then spread to most other regions of the country. It wasn't until the shows reached the heartland audiences that citizens began to complain to Washington. When FCC Commissioners couldn't adequately respond to the complaints, word came down through stations' legal representatives in Washington that it would be smart to drop them. One Commissioner admitted that the programs broke none of the rules, but publicly wondered if such programs were really "in the public interest." That one statement was enough to make most licensees tremble and, at the same time, "get back to playing music."

There is no law or rule that says a station must broadcast news, public affairs, public service announcements, or any of the "other" types of non-entertainment programming we hear on the air.

But when an entity applies for a license to broadcast, it must make certain "promises" to the Commission that it will broadcast in the public interest. For example, the applicant *proposes* to broadcast 100 public service announcements per week, of no special duration. The proposed 100 units, then, become the "law" for that station so far as the Commission is concerned because, when the license comes up for renewal, the Commission expects the licensee to have *performed* as *proposed*. Another station may have proposed to run 150 units of public service time per week and that figure, then, is the "law" for that particular licensee.

The same is true with news and other non-entertainment programming. If the licensee proposes to run 4½ minutes of news per hour with 60% of it local, that becomes the law under which the station operates. Should the licensee fail to run that amount of news with the 60–40 ratio, then he must explain to the FCC's satisfaction why. Should the licensee promise to run four hours per week in public affairs programming or religious programming, he is expected by the Commission to do just that.

Must the licensee promise to run a certain quantity of non-entertainment programming? Yes. Again, the Commission does not specify how much of this material is to be aired, but it makes it clear to the industry that no station can really operate in the public interest, convenience, and necessity without such programming. Applicants usually depend upon Washington attorneys who specialize in communications law and FCC moods to help them determine what will be an acceptable "proposal."

These non-entertainment programming requirements, then, must be dealt with by the programmer, no matter how repugnant they may be to him.

"What do you mean, I've got to program four hours of religion between 8 a.m. and 12 noon every Sunday? Why do we have to schedule 168 public service announcements per week? Do I really have to program a five-minute program from my Congressman, along with doing a two-hour talk show on Sunday night? These are bummers! I'll kill my audience; they'll tune out and listen to another station. I can never make this station number one if I have to put that junk on the air."

Typical bleating from the rock operators, but once the principals have stopped screaming and started thinking, solutions are found. The broadcaster without a conscience simply buries such programming in "washout" hours and lets it go at that. PSAs are run after midnight. Public Affairs programs are scheduled for late Sunday night, while religion is often relegated to the 4 a.m.-8 a.m. period Sunday morning. These are "safe" dayparts for nonentertainment programming and usually do not hurt the overall effect of the format.

Some solutions:

PSAs may be aired anytime—including morning and afternoon drive—without killing the format.

Public Affairs programming may be accomplished entirely by a Sunday evening or Sunday morning telephone talk show. But the shows must be well planned and deal with controversial issues to be effective as audience gainers. Talk shows also have been scheduled in the 10-11 p.m. 12 p.m.-1 a.m. Monday through Friday without devastating the format. Again, these shows must contain controversy if they are to gain (and not lose significantly) audiences.

Religious programming can be appealing to young audiences if proper care is taken in the selection of ministers. It may be "nice" to have the oldest, most establishmentarian church in town on the air, but it would be better programming to have a liberal young minister who relates to your demographics. News can be handled similarly.

Prog/rock stations have been particularly effective at airing "relevant" news to young audiences.

These problems are, of course, not so serious for variety, all-news, and news/talk formats. Former FCC Commissioner Nicholas Johnson, during a visit to Dallas, praised the local news/talk station for its format "because it gives so many people an opportunity to get on the air and express their views." Indeed, such formats do deliver, in many cases, as much non-entertainment programming as all the other stations in town. But one wonders if that "public access" role should not be left to public stations.

There has nearly always been the gnawing, irritating question of the electronic medium's role in U.S. society. The British solved the question rather abruptly by putting all broadcast authority in government hands. Some private broadcasting exists in Great Britain now, but in the beginning the BBC (British Broadcasting Corporation) held full control and was financed through the sale of *licenses* to those who wished to listen to radio or view television. Some argue that, because the license fees were split between the BBC and other departments of the government, radio was actually subsidizing the government of the English people, rather than the other way around. Russia solved the problem by not only taking over all broadcasting, but also by dictating all programming. The BBC, at least, is an independent authority responsible for programming in such a way as to "broaden the interest" of the listeners. Canadian radio combines the British-U.S. system. The government operates the CBC stations, while permitting private citizens to be licensed to operate commercial stations. The CBC sells commercials on its stations, but the sales effort is rather uninspired.

Most U.S. broadcasters do not see themselves in the role of "broadening the interests of the listener." Rather, the aim has been to entertain *and* to inform so long as we can inform in an entertaining way. Radio in America is a *business*—and businesses in America are supposed to earn a dollar profit by selling more than it costs to operate.

For music stations, there apparently is no resolution to the problem. If heavy non-entertainment programming is placed in prime times on a rock station in a competitive market, the station will lose its audience. This is simply an historic truth. Without substantial audiences showing up in research, no station can survive in the marketplace. Therefore, non-entertainment programming is buried in what some refer to as 'throwaway' time, e.g., early Sunday morning and late Sunday night and between midnight and 5 a.m. Some will argue that these times indeed are not throwaway times, but they are the least commercial and the least listened to, and nonentertainment programming placed there will do the least damage to the format.

There is a move afoot to encourage *specialization* in formats, which would resolve the problem to some extent. In this plan, a good music station (KOAX, Dallas) would not be required to broadcast news (other than weather emergencies) or other non-entertainment matter. The station would provide a "good music" service to the market, free of canned PSAs and badly-done, uninspired newscasts and public affairs programming. Listeners would always know they could get virtually uninterrupted music when they tuned to that dial position. If they wanted news, they could tune to WFAA—knowing that WFAA is a news-talk station, geared to handle their needs for information, discussions on public affairs, and other so-called non-entertainment programming. Another station might specialize in sports, another in all-talk, etc. Such specialization might relieve the broadcaster *and* the listener of the frustrations of mixing pure entertainment with a government-dictated schedule of "public interest" programming.

KZEW in Dallas resolved the problem to some extent by scheduling news of special interest to the peculiar culture of its identifiable audience. A Sunday morning talk show dealt with such subjects as the legalization of marijuana and abortion. The essence, of course, is to provide non-entertainment programming that is in itself *entertaining*.

TECHNICAL AND FINANCIAL LIMITATIONS

Radio broadcasting is not a business for timid investors. There are relatively few really financially stable operations, such as WSB in Atlanta, WCCO in Minneapolis and WBAP in Fort Worth. With more than 7,000 radio stations in the nation, hundreds upon hundreds are hand-to-mouth operations. A station, particularly in the rock field, that is highly successful during the first half of a year, could very well be on the rocks in the second half of the year if it fares poorly in the April-May Arbitron, which is published around mid-year. Any rock station's hold on youth audiences is shaky, at best. The leader today can be tomorrow's loser. And any loss of audience is almost immediately emphasized by a loss of revenue.

Any station that wishes to compete for number one total audience position must spend great sums of money on talent, equipment, outside promotion, and on-air giveaways. The alternative? Use a format that is attractive to listeners but does not cost a fortune to operate and promote. Many daytime AMs employ automation equipment and a minimum staff to program C&W or Good Music formats. Many FMs do the same on a full-time basis. "I'm not getting into that *rock* fight" is often the expression that is heard. Some students argue that on-air giveaways are not necessary to gain salable audiences. And they can point to successful stations that do not give away thousands of dollars. But for every rocker that does not give away money, we can point to half a dozen that do. It would not be uncommon, to support the first argument, for a station to spend thousands of dollars during an Arbitron sweep and *actually lose audience*. Such activity "only during a rating period" has been frowned upon by the industry and indeed can create legal problems for the licensee. Year-round, balanced promotion is what the Commission *and* many broadcasters desire.

The FCC, before it will grant or transfer a license, attempts to verify that the applicant has adequate funds to operate the station *at a loss* for a certain period of time. The optimum situation, according to one Washington lawyer, is where the licensee has enough money to operate the station without earning one cent during the first year of broadcasting. This, unfortunately, is often not the case as most licensees are not that well financed. Too often, stations are opened with inadequate funds by operators relying on "letters of credit" from banks and other lending institutions. Equipment may be obtained on a long-term lease-purchase plan, and other essentials are traded out. Money to finance programming plans is often a problem that is ignored with the inevitable result that the owners find themselves in serious financial trouble. And with the Commission's "three-year" rule, adopted shortly after World War II to prevent trafficking in stations, the licensee can be between a rock and a hard place because:

1. Can't sell the station to recover or stop losses.
2. Can't program the station adequately to obtain audiences.
3. Without audiences, can't sell time on the station.

In at least one situation, it was a case of minimizing operating costs because the investors were not willing to provide sufficient operating funds to bring the station's programming up to a competitive parity. Old-time announcers were hired at minimum wage, just to spin the few good music albums left in the station. There was only one salesman, who also did a stint on the air. The station sounded bad—and continued to sound that way for two years until the three-year rule was met, and new owners were allowed to take over.

In planning make-ready and operating budgets, the person responsible should always overestimate costs and underestimate revenues. Ideally, a planner should figure to the penny what will be spent and what will be sold in commercial time. Unfortunately, this is not practicable, as there are so many unknowns and imponderables in the industry. Certain cost factors can be nailed down, but it is difficult to know what the rating books and competition will force a station to do. A serious slump in ratings may result in the licensee having to discharge "luxury" personnel and revert to an austerity program. A sudden influx of competition can force a nominally successful operation to spend thousands of unbudgeted dollars on promotion and outside advertising. In any budget, there should be funds available for contingencies, such as increased competition, serious technical problems, and resultant operating losses.

"We're going to 'poor boy' is an expression commonly heard among small market or small station operators. They do, and in many cases with astounding success. KVIL was for many years a "poor boy" operation that made a profit for its investors. KSKY, with a religious format, is reputed to have made a profit every year for the past 25 years. The station does no noticeable outside advertising and in no way competes with other Dallas stations for mass audiences. The desire to "keep out of the rat race" has prompted many broadcasters to set up a basic music service and just grind along, keeping expenses down and maximizing profits to every extent possible. Others jump into the rate (rat) race because they think they can win it.

It is important that a radio station gain and keep financial solvency because of the business's position or image in the community. Broadcasters literally live in a fish bowl, and the image reflected is worth at least as much as the transmitter and towers. Payroll checks that bounce and bill collectors pounding on the door are conditions that soon will spread to advertisers, who will lose confidence in the station and its management. Financial planning is the answer.

POWER CONSIDERATIONS

In the early days of commercial radio, the power of the station's transmitter was critical. The 50,000-watt clear channel facility was easily the best buy in a market, regardless of format. Radio in those days was much like television today. Dallas, for example, in 1945 had about four major stations, each affiliated with one of the national networks. Aside from those network affiliates there were two or three "independent" stations. KLIF, a leader in the market today, was a daytime independent that had to fight for every dollar. The big net affiliates were KRLD, WRR, WFAA, and WBAP. The formats were essentially the same, and broadcasters didn't have a clue as to what types of people listened. The fact is, everybody listened at one time or another—just as everybody listens to and watches television today. And power simply became a matter of arithmetic: the more power, the more listeners. The other Dallas "indies" were KGKO, KIXL, and KSKY.

As television developed and stole radio's thunder, the network affiliates were slower to react, and the independent stations began taking over. Stations developed local flavors that appealed to local audiences; so much of the net affiliated programming was national or regional in scope that local programming was de-emphasized. Many old-time radio "announcers" spent their lives just giving "station breaks."

In the mid '50s, big power stations, generally, were experiencing fierce competition from the independents. It was common for a 5,000 or even a 1,000-watt station to have greater audiences and earn more money than the big, overstaffed, anachronistic 50,000-watt network affiliates. If a station could reach the local market, that was enough, because listener surveys were taken "locally"—not 50 miles away where *other* local stations were hammering away at their local audience. Radio, therefore, became a *local* medium. Huge national ad budgets were going to television networks. National "rep" firms were beginning to sell "ratings" and "shares."

Product advertising, of course, gave some consideration to power but generally, if an advertiser wanted the San Francisco market he would buy a station that effectively covered *that* market rather than a big power station that had

ineffective coverage of San Francisco, and also of 50 other municipalities. Retailers, of course, didn't kid themselves at all; they bought the local station that
reached the local market.

The advent of sophisticated rating services, such as Arbitron and Pulse,
brought back some consideration for power. These two companies surveyed
listener preferences, in not only a SMSA, but also in what Arbitron called the
"Total Survey Area" and in what Pulse called the RSA, Radio Survey Area.
To be more specific, the Dallas "metro" area consisted of Dallas and five
surrounding counties. The "Total Survey Area" included Dallas and 65 or so
surrounding counties. Competent buyers would often specify listenership in the
TSA, and many of the low power stations couldn't compete in this particular
buy. So, after a lapse of many years, the power stations started coming back.
The low-power station might lead the field in the metro survey with an average
audience of, perhaps 20,000 persons. The power station might only have
15,000 average quarter-hour audience in this local metro universe. But in the
total survey area, the local rocker might pick up another 5,000 audience, bringing its TSA figure to 25,000, while the power station could easily double its
audience to 30,000. Again, it is important to remember that in *any* total survey
area, 75–90% of the buying power may be concentrated in the much smaller
"metro" area. A product such as Coca Cola might be interested only in the
local audience. In many, many instances, rather than try to reach consumers in
a market 100 miles from the recognized trade area, the buyer will simply go to
that distant market and buy the most effective local station there.

In mid-1975 Arbitron developed a report on market ADIs (Area of Dominant Influence.) This was done so that radio stations could effectively compare
their ADI listenership with that of television. Previously, it was a case of com-
paring apples and oranges. Radio pitched "metro" figures for, perhaps 6 counties, or TSA figures for 65 counties. Television pitched figures for 28 counties,
which might be the in-between size of an ADI. The Dallas-Fort Worth SMSA
is made up of 11 counties; the TSA held at 65 counties, and the ADI is 28
counties. Under Arbitron's new ADI publication for radio, it now is possible
for a media planner to compare apples with apples: radio vs television in the
ADI. It is quite possible that a combination of radio stations can more economically reach a target audience than one or a combination of television stations.
This was radio's argument, and Arbitron's response was publication of ADI
figures for radio. It is apparent, therefore, that power has again become a big
consideration when buying radio. If a station's signal doesn't reach throughout
the ADI, it can't possibly have listeners in the null areas. Low-power stations,
therefore, cannot always compete *because* of their low-power.

Power, in FM radio, is not as critical as antenna height. Two stations with
equal power and equal antenna height can effectively compete in terms of geography. But if one of the stations has an antenna height of 1,500 feet, and the
other has only 700 feet, the station with the lowest antenna is at a disadvantage.
On the other hand, a station with 50,000 watts of effective radiated power

(ERP) and an antenna height of 2,000 feet, covers a good deal more geography than the 100,000-watt station with a 500-foot tower. Antenna height means "height of the antenna above average terrain."

Because of a relatively new trend to "weight" certain audiences, power takes on another important role in the radio buy. Not only do buyers "weigh" certain age groups, they also weigh certain geographic groups. A station's audience in San Francisco might be given 100% weight, while those listeners in Sacramento, nearly 80 miles away, might be weighted only 50%. But this 50% weighting of a distant audience could be the difference between a big order and no order at all.

Power stations have another advantage over low-power stations in certain areas where man-made interference is a factor. A Dallas station may be heard in Abilene, for example, but would have a poor signal in downtown Fort Worth. Abilene is 180 air miles from Dallas, while Fort Worth is only 30 miles. A low-power station's signal has difficulty in getting through the steel and concrete of downtown Forth Worth, while the big 50,000-watt facility does not.

Power isn't the only technical consideration when putting together a competitive format. Modern, high quality studio equipment is necessary, including microphones, tape recording equipment, cartridge recording and playback units, consoles, audio compressors and limiters, microphone compressors and, in some instances, automation and stereo equipment. It is possible to put a station on the air with low cost and/or used equipment. When this approach is used, highly skilled technical personnel are required to keep it operating. This is an example of a shoe-string operation that could not compete in a major market. Many stereo FM operations employ "audio specialists" whose technical skills include the ability to get the most out of available equipment. Oscilloscopes are often used to technically determine good stereo separation and to make certain the station is modulating to the legal and technical maximum. FM has gained musical audiences because of its superior ability to reproduce recorded sounds. It would be foolish for an operator not to make maximum use of the equipment.

MARKET EVALUATION

Each city in the world exudes a distinctive flavor or mode of living. Chicago has been described as brawny and broad-shouldered. San Francisco's delightful climate and colorful history, combined with her cable cars and rolling hills, make her excitingly different from Detroit's auto industry and New York's population amalgamation. New Orleans is said to be the birthplace of Jazz. Fort Worth is known as "cowtown" because the flavor of the west is still evident. Milwaukee, Los Angeles, Miami, Cleveland, St. Louis, Dallas—each is different. New Orleans is known as the city that "care" forgot.

How does a city make its living? What sort of people live there? What is the ethnic mix? How many persons in the 18–24 age group? How many are between 50–64? What has been the growth pattern? New York is a city that includes virtually every known race, color, creed. There is a huge Black population, a growing Hispanic group that includes Puerto Ricans, Mexicans, Spanish. Every language is spoken somewhere in the Big Apple. It is a mercantile city, an international seaport. It is crowded, busy, industrious. It is a cultural center of the world. It is a "white collar" market. Detroit is a "blue collar" or "lunch pail" market. Heavy industry is in Detroit, Akron, and Cleveland. Miami is a retirement town. Cities surrounding Dallas and Philadelphia are often called "bedroom" cities because their residents live there and work in the big city.

It is not enough to understand the competition. The broadcaster must be acquainted with the "soul" of the market if he is to effectively identify with it and program to its citizens. Marshall Pearce of WSMB in New Orleans described his market:

"New Orleans is a tough market. It's basically composed of so many different types of people because it's a port city. It's generally a loose society. I think it is one of the few cities in the world where you can put one-and-a-half million people on the street during Mardi Gras . . . of all races, colors and creeds . . . and not have a major incident. There are mixed neighborhoods all over the city . . . but we've never had the real black ghettos like some other cities . . . and I think it's left us with a little better temperament than most of the cities of the country."

Bob Mitchell, program director at WTIX, tries to make his station "sound like New Orleans," pointing out that WLS "sounds like Chicago" and WABC "sounds like New York." "Most of our announcers were born and raised here. New Orleans is a very different and unique city. When you talk about crawfish, and red beans and rice, people from outside of New Orleans don't even know what you're talking about. Announcers from other cities can't pronounce the French street names here. We try to *be* New Orleans on the air. We try to relate to the people here."

Ty Bell, program director of WYLD, sees New Orleans as a "mesh of cultures." He envisions New Orleans as an "invisible point where people are into rock music and out of soul, or out of soul and into classical. Music is a prime interest in this city, and people are exposed to it from elementary school on up."

"The people are really proud of and into the city itself. If you really want to die your early radio death in New Orleans, make fun of the city the first time you hit the microphone . . . and you'll never live again."

Doug China of WWL put it this way: "I don't really know why this market is different from any other market . . . but it is. I think it has to do with the ethnic complexion of the market. It's pretty unique in that New Orleans itself is over 60% black, so there is a great influence there in so far as rock music is concerned. I guess more black hits have come out of here than anywhere besides Detroit. More black records have broken here on white stations. The people here are unique in that they subscribe to the theory that New Orleans is the city that 'care' forgot. The natives particularly. I don't know of another city that goes off on a ten-day drunk once a year! . . . that is at Mardi Gras time.''

3

Contemporary Music Formats

The *contemporary music* format eludes clear definition. It changes from week to week, year to year. What *appears* to be a Top 40 format in Dallas may be called something else in Cleveland. From time to time, industry publication writers note that one trend or another is developing and that "contemporary formats appear to be in a high state of change." This is true, but not news. This format changes almost weekly. One period may see some actual polarization of music types and forms. The very next period may witness a traumatic synergizing (homogenization) of types and forms, only to have the following period embrace re-polarization.

Perhaps all of this is natural. Rock music *is the now music* for 12-49 audiences and each succeeding generation finds something new and exciting in the music spectrum. And while the youth audience is fickle, so are the young men and women who try to second-guess the public's taste in music and program to that youth audience. E. Alvin Davis, program director for WNOE in New Orleans, told an interviewer, "It's hard to tell what I'm liable to do. I don't even know that. When I believe it's something that will enhance our success, I'm all for doing it." Davis was responding to the question, "Are you likely to initiate a jingle package in the future?" His response was typical of the often sensitive PD who guides his format as much by instinct and feel as by knowledge and experience.

It is apparent that tastes in music can quickly become jaded. Programmers try to detect *ahead of time* the various cycles that history has shown are sure to occur over and over again.

HISTORY

Musicologist and programmer Alden Diehl believes "the whole history of this business has run in cycles. In the 1960s the music was highly polarized and congealed. You had distinct music forms appealing to specific age groups. You have to credit the Beatles with having the most profound influence in this development." Diehl, in 1973, said, "now the pop scene is characterized by a spectacular upsurge in 1950s-style music and a demand for nostalgia. Young teens and adults are more easily lumped together in target audiences."

The late 1970s saw programmers aiming at smaller demographics and specific psychographics. KVIL in Dallas claimed its principal audience was 25–34, earned good money, wore fine clothes, frequented the best restaurants, and drove sports cars. KZEW, a progressive rock station, claimed to program to the same *age* group, but its main audience was men, 18–24. KFWD, an album-oriented rock (AOR) station, aimed at the 18–34 audience, while KFJZ FM (Z-97) went for teens through the 24 levels. KLIF, during the same competitive period, strove for 18–49 audiences.

TYPES OF STATIONS

For discussion purposes, contemporary music stations will be identified as follows:

1. Top 40, with variations
2. Progressive Rock
3. Album-oriented Rock (AOR)
4. Black (Soul/Rhythm & Blues)
5. Disco-Stereo
6. MOR (Middle of Road, Chicken Rock)
7. Progressive Country

Every known type and tempo of new pop music will eventually have at least a small exposure in one or more of these formats. The "skew" graphs in this chapter will indicate the different demographics attracted by each formula, and the word-for-word transcript of one representative hour of two different stations will indicate the amount of talk permitted, the style in which the news is

SKEW-GRAPH

KLIF (CONTEMPORARY/PERSONALITY)

		10	20	30	40	50	60	70	80	90	
TEENS	93,800			27.7%							
18-24	90,900			27.0%							m= 47% w= 53%
25-34	70,800			20.9%							m= 43% w= 57%
35-44	42,900		12.7%								m= 38% w= 62%
45-54	15,100	4.5%									m= 33% w= 67%
55-over	25,500	7.5%									
TOTAL	338,900										

KVIL-AM/FM (CONTEMPORARY MOR)

		10	20	30	40	50	60	70	80	90	
TEENS	72,800		19.7%								
18-24	85,600			23.2%							m= 40% w= 59%
25-34	106,900			29.%							m= 40% w= 59%
35-44	58,300		15.8%								m= 41% w= 58%
45-54	23,200	6.3%									m= 39% w= 60%
55-over	21,100	5.7%									m= 45% w= 53%
TOTAL	367,900										

KNUS (TOP 40)

		10	20	30	40	50	60	70	80	90	
TEENS	82,800			33.7%							
18-24	76,700			31.2%							m= 49% w= 51%
25-34	55,300		22.4%								m= 39% w= 61%
35-44	24,900	10%									m= 29% w= 71%
45-54	3,600	1.5%									m= 22% w= 78%
55-over	2,700	1.1%									m= 33% w= 67%
TOTAL	246,000										

(Cumes, 6AM-12M, Monday-Sunday Dallas/Ft. Worth Metro)

SKEW—GRAPH

KFWD (AOR)

		10	20	30	40	50	60	70	80	90	
TEENS	35,700			23.5%							
18-24	66,900					44.0%					m= 50% w= 49%
25-34	36,300			24.0%							m= 78% w= 21%
35-44	6,100	4.0%									m= 18% w= 81%
45-54	5,900	3.8%									m= 59% w= 40%
55-over	900	.5%									m= 0 w=100%
TOTAL	151,800										

KZEW (PROG-ROCK)

		10	20	30	40	50	60	70	80	90	
TEENS	56,400			27.4%							
18-24	94,500					46.%					m= 64% w= 36%
25-34	35,700		17.4%								m= 73% w= 26%
35-44	12,700	6.1%									m= 22% w= 77%
45-54	4,600	1.8%									m= 58% w= 41%
55-over	1,300	.6%									m= 46% w= 53%
TOTAL	205,200										

(TEEN-ORIENTED ROCK) KFJZ-FM

		10	20	30	40	50	60	70	80	90	
TEENS	102,800					46.3%					
18-24	67,200			30.%							m= 49% w= 50%
25-34	24,200		10.%								m= 49% w= 50%
35-44	17,700	8.%									m= 20% w= 79%
45-54	7,700	3.4%									m= 44% w= 55%
55-over	2,200	.9%									m= 59% w= 40%
TOTAL	221,800										

(Cumes, 6AM—12M, Monday—Sunday Dallas/Ft. Worth Metro)

KRLD (ADULT-BLOCK)

Scale: 10 20 30 40 50 60 70 80 90

Age	Cume	%	m=	w=
TEENS	8,900	2.6%		
18-24	22,700	6.7%	56%	43%
25-34	65,100	19.3%	55%	44%
35-44	66,300	19.7%	60%	39%
45-54	65,100	19.3%	52%	47%
55-over	108,300	32.1%	54%	45%
TOTAL	336,400			

KBOX MODERN (C&W)

Scale: 10 20 30 40 50 60 70 80 90

Age	Cume	%	m=	w=
TEENS	17,100	9.%		
18-24	36,500	20.%	20%	41%
25-34	37,900	21.4%	42%	57%
35-44	34,400	19.4%	63%	36%
45-54	28,000	15.8%	49%	50%
55-over	23,000	13.%	88%	9%
TOTAL	176,900			

WBAP TRADITIONAL (C&W)

Scale: 10 20 30 40 50 60 70 80 90

Age	Cume	%	m=	w=
TEENS	31,700	.6%		
18-24	48,700	.9%	59%	40%
25-34	86,700	15.4%	60%	39%
35-44	110,600	21.%	56%	43%
45-54	90,100	17.1%	55%	44%
55-over	158,100	30.%	53%	47%
TOTAL	525,900			

(Cumes, 6AM-12M, Monday-Sunday Dallas/Ft. Worth Metro)

KKDA-FM *(BLACK-ETHNIC)*		10	20	30	40	50	60	70	80	90	
TEENS	33,300		25.6%								
18-24	40,700			31.3%					m= 46% w= 53%		
25-34	32,300		24.8%						m= 39% w= 60%		
35-44	13,500	10.3%							m= 45% w= 54%		
45-54	6,800	2.9%							m= 52% w= 47%		
55-over	3,300	2.5%							m= 42% w= 57%		
TOTAL	129,900										

		10	20	30	40	50	60	70	80	90
TEENS										
18-24										
25-34										
35-44										
45-54										
55-over										
TOTAL										

		10	20	30	40	50	60	70	80	90
TEENS										
18-24										
25-34										
35-44										
45-54										
55-over										
TOTAL										

(Cumes, 6AM-12M, Monday-Sunday Dallas/Ft. Worth Metro)

TOP 40 CLOCK
TYPICAL MORNING DRIVE HOUR
15-Min CM

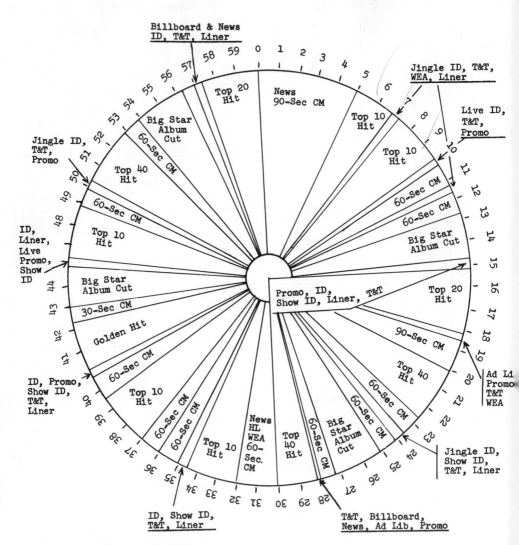

T&T – TIME & TEMPERATURE
WEA – WEATHER
HL – HEADLINES
CM – COMMERCIAL MATTER

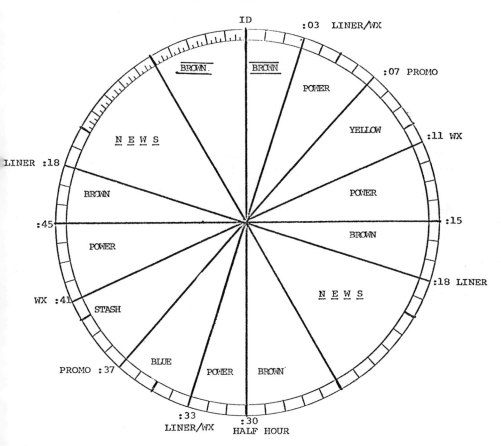

MONDAY–FRIDAY
6AM – 9AM

ID

:03 LINER/WX

:07 PROMO

:11 WX

:15

:18 LINER

:30 HALF HOUR

:33 LINER/WX

PROMO :37

WX :41

:45

LINER :18

BROWN

BROWN

POWER

YELLOW

POWER

BROWN

N E W S

N E W S

BROWN

POWER

STASH

BLUE

POWER

BROWN

ONE SUPER STASH REPLACES ONE BLUE OR YELLOW PER HOUR.

ONE SUPER GOLD REPLACES ONE BROWN PER HOUR.

MUSIC CODE: "0"   OR   "1"

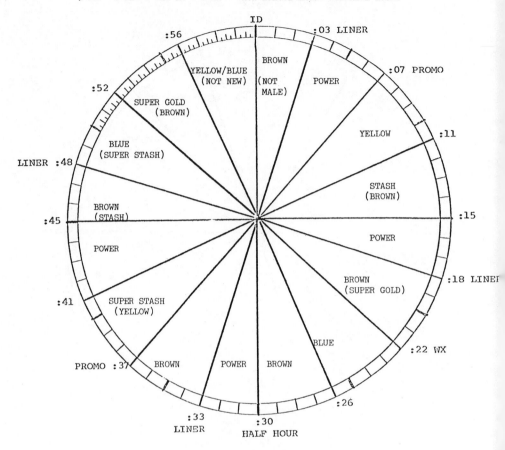

* Image replaces one Brown in scheduled hours.

  OPTION: Even hours: play bracket catagories.

        Odd hours: play non-bracket catagories.

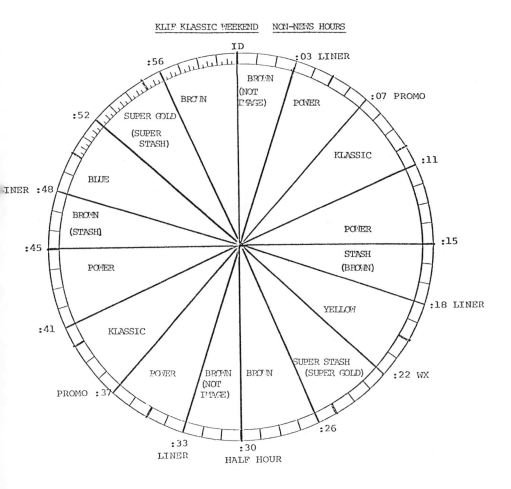

Image replaces one brown as per schedule.

OPTIONS: EVEN Hours: play bracketed categories only.
          ODD Hours: play non-bracketed categories only.

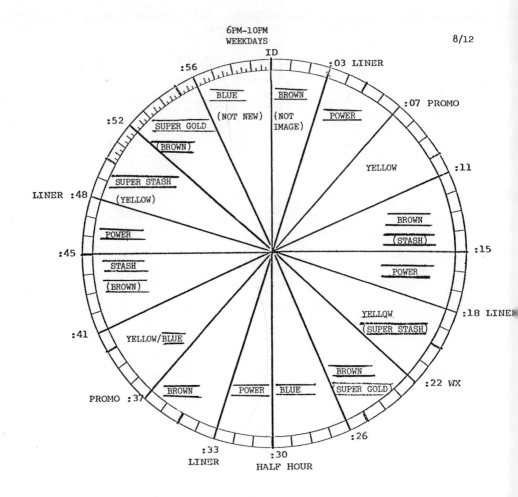

6PM-10PM
WEEKDAYS
8/12

* Image replaces one Brown in scheduled hours.

OPTIONS: EVEN hours - play bracket options.
          ODD hours - play non-bracket options.

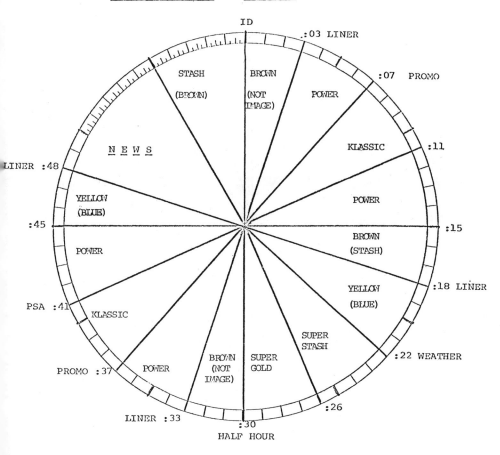

Same data here as non-news hours.

59

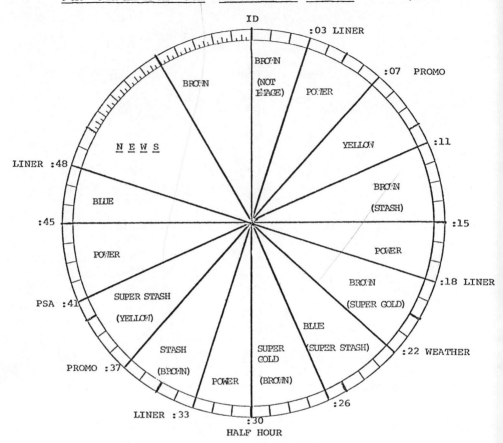

* Image replaces one brown in scheduled hours.

OPTIONS: EVEN HOURS, play bracket categories.
          ODD HOURS, play non-bracket categories.

handled, and the music that is employed. The old idea that "if you heard one rock station, you've heard 'em all" is no longer applicable. The jock, the news, the contests, the program inserts (such as a brief on-air telephone conversation with a listener) all combine in differing recipes to produce a unique radio product. Escoffier's ingredients for a souffle in the hands of a fry cook would likely produce something other than a recognizable edible. By the same reasoning, the ingredients for a successful rock station in the hands of an incompetent program director are not likely to produce more than something that sort of sounds like a rock station.

BASIC TOP 40

The genesis for most modern contemporary music formats *in the world* was the "Top 40" plan devised by McLendon, Storz, and Bartel in the early 1950s. It consisted principally of music, light chatter, and news. Promotions in which money, merchandise and services were awarded listeners were a vital part of the over-all plan. Disc jockeys were selected for their sexiness, their voice, their ability to communicate excitement. Basic service consisted of time and temperature checks. Any idea of doing anything more than entertain the listener was out of the question. Why not? Radio had always entertained; why must it now do otherwise? One of the most difficult things for a Top 40 format to accomplish is the *non-entertainment* programming that the FCC insists upon.

Dallas is one of the most competitive and innovative markets in the country. Of 32 stations licensed to operate in the cities and towns of the Dallas-Fort Worth SMSA, 10 are devoted to programming contemporary music. Another four are C&W stations, while three push religious formats. There are two "good music" formats, four ethnic Black, three all-news and one Adult Block variety. KLIF was the original Top 40 station in Dallas, while KFJZ pioneered the effort in Fort Worth. Within a 20-year span, almost all of the other stations have attempted, in one way or the other, to emulate the "rock" sounds of KLIF and KFJZ. And it wasn't until the mid-1970s that a Top 40 station beat KLIF in the ratings: KNUS, an FM owned by the McLendon family and operated by Bart McLendon, son of Gordon McLendon.

The essence of a Top 40 format is *people*. And with the proliferation of rock formats in virtually every market, the object is to put together a team of highly articulate, "hip" jocks who are simply better entertainers than those on competing stations. With every station having access to about the same music, the differences that exist between formats must be in the manner in which a particular group of people execute the concept of Top 40.

The elements of a Top 40 plan:

1. Personalities
2. Music—Music Research

3. On-Air Promotions
4. News
5. Community Involvement
6. Sales Promotions

Every station programming popular music employs these elements, and the manner in which they are employed makes the difference. Remember, it is rare when one station has music that is not available to competitors. A station may get a couple of days head start on a record, but no more. If it is a hot new single by a currently hot artist, listeners themselves may notify their favorite station that someone else is playing it. In any event, no station can for long have exclusive play of a new piece of music.

The basic Top 40 format has a broad demographic appeal. It aims at teens, 12 through 17, and at adults 18 through 49. It is this broad mass appeal that has made the format vulnerable to other rock formats that aim at a more narrow demographic base. But the Top 40 station that counter-programs, say, a progressive rock station, tends to lose its identity and consequently its audiences. The idea that a station "can't be all things to all people" must have originated with a Top 40 programmer who finally saw the light and stayed on course, allowing competitors to do the same.

Talent Search

Considering the above elements of a Top 40 plan, let's deal first with the personalities. In this hypothetical situation, we'll select a group of air personnel with deep backgrounds in major market contemporary operations.

First, scour the market and find out who is good and who can be moved at a not-too-unreasonable cost. Jocks love for licensees to fight over them because no matter who wins the jock ends up making more money and gaining wider recognition.

Bert Daily moves to K-Triple X radio!
Wolf Man Bill signs $100,000 contract with competitor!
K-Triple X goes after K-Triple K!

And the hiring dialogue goes something like this:

Program Director:	Hey, man, let's rap. We're putting together this heavy bunch of studs and we're gonna stomp the competition.
Disc Jockey:	Lay it on me, man; if the bread's right then *it's* right.
Program Director:	What's that dog you work for now laying on you, man?
Disc Jockey:	Two bills a week, plus fringe.
Program Director:	Cheap, cheap, cheap. Always thought so. We got the afternoon drive marked down for you and we're gonna put your name in lights.

Disc Jockey:	Yeah, man. But the bread, man. How much is the pay?
Program Director:	We've got a 100% showing on billboards and your name and picture will be on one-quarter of them.
Disc Jockey:	Nice, man, nice. But does your station pay any money?
Program Director:	Yeah, man. We're gonna pay you two-fifty a week. That's a whole two thousand six hundred a year more than you're doing now, and we got the fringes.
Disc Jockey:	Okay. The money's right. If I like your plan, maybe I'll get on your boat. I got to have freedom, man; freedom to express myself; freedom to have a good time on the air; freedom to do my thing and say my thing. I want to entertain, man; and if you're gonna lash me up in one of those tight, clinical operations that stifles the real me, then that ain't for me.
Program Director:	Cool it, man. This is real Top 40 radio we're talking about. You can play radio; you can play the personality. We want your personality to shine like a baby's behind.
Disc Jockey:	So, let's see it on paper. If I like it, I'll be over in two weeks—assuming they don't fire me when I quit in which case I'll be over after I take a few days vacation.

The language in this dialogue, of course, is admittedly a bit silly and was used to illustrate the idioms of the programmers and performers. The same conversation, under different circumstances and with different people, might have been as straight and formal as that between a banker and his principal depositor.

Ideally, of course, the station would be staffed by leading personalities from the home market. Barring this unlikelihood, the programmer must seek help from other markets. This may be done through contacts in other markets and by advertising in trade journals. A typical method of pirating help is to call a friend in another market and ask if the competition there has "anyone who is hurting you?" If so, one gets the name and station and makes that personality an offer. This may be preceded by a trip to the market to "monitor" that personality to determine if he can fit into the new plan. In the advertisement in trade journals, the format idea is vaguely described and tapes and biographies are solicited.

Top operator in major market seeks afternoon drive jock. Top dollar, top billing. Send tape and resume to Box 123, Broadcasting.

If you're a highly successful morning man in one of the top 20 markets, answer this ad. Big power station in major market seeks morning man to knock off the competition.

Programmers, as a group, are consistent in describing what they really want in "personalities." One New Orleans program director wanted "my jocks to be real people . . . more than just a voice in between records.'' Yet this same programmer argues that only *minimum* information be given in drive periods. His station pushed music sweeps of 10 to 15 minutes duration, breaking the music only for important information and commercial matter. His policy involved ''clustering'' commercials to ''get them out of the way.'' Jocks talk *only* over musical bridges or piece intros. Admittedly, this hard policy held mainly for morning and afternoon drive, but if personalities are to be developed these key periods should be used to develop them. No personality can emerge under these conditions. This programmer doesn't really want *personalities*—because they interfere with his concept of ''much more music.''

Another programmer may truly emphasize personality and virtually destroy the basic idea of a Top 40 operation. A two-man (or, two person) team in morning drive may play one record per half-hour of programming. This is *not* Top 40. It *is* personality radio. The personalities are well-prepared and they talk about everything from football to art shows. They pull off situation comedy, excel in one-liners, invent characters. They pay little attention to the music. KVIL's (Dallas) Ron Chapman achieves good balance; his show includes considerable adult contemporary music, but Chapman injects a lot of himself and his helpers (news persons, traffic reporters, sports reporters, characters) into the programming. The skew graphs indicate that Chapman's principal audience is 25–35 with 59% of these being women. While Chapman does not program hard-rock music during his show, he does balance his personality with a good flow of adult contemporary MOR. During this same period, KNUS employed Kevin McCarthy and Dick Hitt (a famous Dallas newspaper columnist with a dry wit) as a two-man information team. They put heavy emphasis on sports, politics, listener involvement. KLIF faced these stations with Charlie Brown, who involved a fictitious ''Clydee,'' a newspaper boy, as well as the news people and an airborne traffic reporter, Charlie Deaton. In spite of this, KLIF played considerably more music during morning drive than either KNUS or KVIL.

Scheduling

The Top 40 ''clock'' indicates one technique programmers use in communicating format structure to disc jockeys. Normally, the clock would not be so detailed. The disc jokeys would be permitted to interpolate the general idea in order to let their personality come through. This particular clock (A) indicates a commercial load of about 15 minutes, a bit heavy for a major market rocker in an extremely competitive situation. Some stations reduce the load to eight or ten minutes under the correct assumption that too many commercials cause listners to tune-out.

Not shown in the wheel, of course, are news bulletins and possible mobile unit reports from the scene of news events. These would be inserted when appropriate with the disc jockey adjusting his schedule to compensate for them.

This basic Top 40 pattern can be significantly adjusted without destroying the Top 40 concept. For example, the 5-minute newscast on the hour may be programmed at five minutes *before* the hour. The half-hour news break may be eliminated altogether and made up in other, less-critical time periods. One object of programming news at five minutes before the hour is to enable the programmer to play music starting *at the hour* when the competition will likely begin airing news. With youth-oriented stations, news is considered a tune-out. Many stations would carry no news if the FCC didn't insist upon a certain amount of non-entertainment material.

Another variation that does no damage to the basic concept is the programming of news 20 past and 20 before the hour. This "20–20" idea has been employed for basically the same reason the "five-before" is used. It is assumed that listeners tune a rock station for music and *anything* that interferes with music is a tune-out. Therefore, programmers struggle constantly to make non-music programming as bright and interesting to the listener as possible.

Clocks "B" through "G" represent one programmer's efforts to develop a music and interruptions (stop sets) formula. Music is well-researched, coded, and played in a specific order. This plan provides the jock little or no freedom to decide the "type" of music to be played at a specific time. Each type of music may have dozens of selections, with the jock being given little latitude even in title selections.

The "B-thru G" clocks were designed by Jim Davis when he was program director of KLIF. These clocks specifically direct the jock to play certain pieces of music in a certain sequence.

Power is the highest rotation category. Consider the rotation as circles. The power rotation is the smallest circle, closest to the hub. Normally, there are nine or ten pieces in this group, the hottest of the current hits. These songs are played every two and one-quarter to two and one-half hours.

Yellow is a current rotation of up-tempo songs either breaking into the survey or just coming back down out of power rotation. Normally, there are eight or nine of these, and about two are played each hour.

Blue is the same as yellow, except they are down tempo.

Super Stash is a re-current group of songs, not on the current survey, that achieved great listener acceptance recently. Listeners still request they be played. These songs display a much longer life than regular hits. There are seven of these songs and they are changed weekly. One is played each hour, a procedure that may be altered when the programmer is dayparting.

Stash is a group of 17 "near recent" hits, generally within the last nine months. These are still familiar favorites, and may be heard frequently on juke boxes. Davis believes they are favorites of middle demographics (18–24). One is played per hour.

Super Gold is a collection of 53 "monster" goldens, top 10 super hits of the past three to five years that have stood the test of time for listenability. These are usually by the "core" trend groups of the time. One is played per hour.

Brown is the balance of the gold library, filed by years and given daypart codes. These are assigned to the jock for airplay according to the time of day, season, and age of the song. Within brown, there are normally three rotations of repetition, based on vintage.

Image is an album cut, from albums that are in the top 10 in local sales. Nine select cuts from these albums are played with irregular frequency throughout the day, but in particular at night to give the station a contemporary album flavor, without giving up the base of familiarity.

Klassics are vintage records, "roots of rock" records that go back as far as the early '60s. These are played on weekends to attract the attention of the people who grew up with KLIF and to bring back the emotional experiences they may have felt at that time. Certain songs from the Klassic category are day-part coded, indicating when play is permitted in any shift and on any day. This information is provided the jock by a series of code numbers displayed by each title.

Promotion

The "promos" indicated in Clock A may cover a variety of station promotions. These are a critical portion of the program package, and must be produced with high quality and excitement. The promotions themselves must be topical and relate to the audience the station believes it is reaching. Of all the things stations have offered listeners, nothing has been as effective as cash.

> Win a house!!
> A trip around the world! Dinner out!
> Win $10,000!!!!

The appeal is obvious.

Top 40 format promotions must be carefully planned and scrupulous care must be taken in their execution. Sloppy execution may not only cause listener indifference, but may also involve the station in legal difficulties. When prizes are offered, they must be available for winning. Audiences must not be deceived because they as well as the FCC are unforgiving when a station makes more of a contest or promotion than really exists. For example, if a station runs a "Million Dollar Sweepstakes" there must be some basis for using the term "Million Dollar." What is a million dollar sweepstake? Can a listener win a million dollars? Or, would there have to be 1,000 winners before a million dollars were paid out? Furthermore, when a prize is offered there must be a reasonable expectation that someone will win it. The contest cannot be so difficult as to defy *any* winners. On the other hand, a contest that is too simple will be quickly won and the station will have lost its prize without any significant gain in listener attention.

An example of an impossible-to-win contest would be "Find A Zirch" contest. Find a Zirch and KXXX will pay you $100! If there is no Zirch anywhere in the world, and there isn't, then no one will win.

A too-simple contest might be "find the lucky house number." In this contest, programmers designate a section of town, a street within that section, and a house number on that street. Again, it is best that only a very few persons know the exact number and street. Air personnel who are exposed to the secret information should sign a statement confirming they will keep this and all contest secrets to themselves. After these details are handled, the station then begins broadcasting clues to the exact location of the "mystery street number." Obviously, this will work with any "hidden" item, whether it is a $50,000 check in a bottle or a castle in Germany.

Probably the best on-air promotions are those that give away cash on an escalation plan. One successful promotion involved four mystery voices giving the station's call letters. Each mystery voice was asked to articulate one letter of the station's name. Mystery person #1 spoke the "K," #2 did the "R," while numbers 3 and 4 did the "U" and the "F." These were collated onto a tape and made a part of the promotional announcement. On the first day of the contest, listeners were offered $1,000 if anyone could call the station within a certain period of time and identify all four of the voices. Interest was heightened when a caller would get one name but miss the other three. The disc jockey would respond, "You have one name correct, but the other names you mentioned are incorrect. Try again." Now, listeners know that of the four names, *one* of them will fit. The next caller guesses at one of the four names, and adds three new ones. And so on. Each day the prize may build by $1,000 or any other amount. In one case, the prize reached $15,000 before the four names were finally accurately identified. It is *absolutely* necessary that only a minimum number of persons know the winning combination in such contests. Any effort to cheat or rig the contest could cost the station its license.

The idea of any on-air contest is to create listener excitement. The contest should be fresh, unique in the market, expertly produced and handled. In one such contest, the disc jockey "missed" the first winning entry and awarded the prize to the second winning entry. Result? The station, in response to a scary threat from the first winner, had to come up with another identical prize. In this case, it was a $14,000 error because the prize was a fully-equipped motor home!

A typical "running" promotion is "Cash Call" where the station maintains a continuous budget (however small) to keep the interest of those listeners who enjoy contests. Properly handled, the gimmick is sufficiently soft-pedaled to preclude annoying those who aren't interested in small-scale contests. In Cash Call, the jackpot may be increased several times a day as listeners *fail* to guess the precise amount of the jackpot. The amount added to the pot varies with each addition to prevent listeners from detecting a pattern and "sandbagging" the station. The morning jock may add $2.85 to the pot, while the mid-morning jock may add $3.21.

Promotional announcements are often used as follow up to stimulate long-term or regular listening. Rock stations normally have a high turnover in au-

dience—and this is one method employed to reduce turnover. For example, reaction of winners is often recorded and played back later in the week. The
promo might go like this:

> IT PAYS TO LISTEN TO KXXX! MARY SMITHSON OF 2344 ELM
> IN OURTOWN LISTENS . . . AND THIS WEEK SHE WON $500!
> (Actuality) Who is this! Yes, I listen to KXXX! You're putting me on!
> (Squeal) FIVE HUNDRED DOLLARS . . . WHEEEEEEE!!!! YES.
> . . . IF YOU DON'T BELIEVE IT PAYS TO LISTEN TO KXXX . . .
> JUST ASK MARY SMITHSON OF 2344 ELM IN OURTOWN.

TALENT PERFORMANCE

While listeners to Top 40 plans are amused or titillated by the promotions
and the quality of station production of them, the burden of really hanging on
to that listener still is on the disc jockey. He is the one who ties it all together.
When the microphone switch is open, the jock has behind him the licensee's
capital, the program director's ingenuity, the sales department's commercial effort. Every effort will have been in vain if the jock doesn't perform. What is
expected of the jock?

He must be *interesting.*

How?

By relevancy. Humor. By being someone listeners can identify with. The
jock must understand his audience, what they are doing at a particular time of
day, how they are being affected by the current weather.

> This is Johnny B at big 99 radio . . . yyuuukkkk have you looked outside
> yet this morning . . . it isn't cloudy. It isn't foggy. IT'S POURING
> DOWN RAIN!! 48 degrees . . . and 20 minutes before EIGHT
> O'CLOCK. And it's the Rams against the Cowboys this Sunday at Texas
> stadium.

Here the jock may segue to music or an announcement, maintaining a
bright, fast-paced morning show tempo. This audience is young, busy. Teens
are gulping breakfast, getting ready for school. The adults are getting ready for
work. Time and temperature *is* important to everyone who is up against a
schedule. Weather reports tell mothers how to dress the children. Fathers who
have to be at work at a specific time schedule departures around radio reports
on traffic and street conditions. The Rams-Cowboys game *reminds* the whole
family, perhaps, of weekend plans to either see the game live or visit friends
houses to watch it on television.

Programmers spend endless hours trying to find a balance between the old
basic Top 40 and the relatively new much-more music concept which virtually

eliminates the development of personality. The following transcript exemplifies how elements of both old and new are combined to produce a "new" and different format. Read the transcript of the show, then compare your thoughts to those of the authors at the end of the show. The transcript is of a real show, but the names and call letters have been changed so that the student may develop a more objective view.

A ONE HOUR RADIO SHOW

SOUND: Music, faded for: (Theme of S.W.A.T.)

Jock: Lots of fun on K-N-O-P, Dallas. Billy Boy here. Welcome Back.

No, no, no, not high school, YOU know where you are...in the valley

of the shadow of the time clock...there's nothing wrong with con-

sistency though.

SOUND: Music, up: RIGHT BACK TO WHERE WE STARTED FROM

SOUND: Music, under.

JOCK: K-N-O-P...and your basic wizard of the airwaves, Billy Boy. What

ever you do, don't hit that snooze alarm until I tell you the latest

about Linda Lovelace..

SOUND: Music up slightly, then a high-pitched bleep

JOCK: Oooopps...sorry. Too late, the hand is quicker than the ear...ha ha ha

SOUND: Music up: STORY OF THE TIN MAN

JOCK (Music out) K-NOP. And the story of the tin man. Oz never did give

nothing to the tin man that he didn't already have (whisper laugh)...

and a shot of penicillin will clear that right up. Six o six now...

with Billy Boy...the terror of the office...ah, yes...the office girls

around here really...how do you say ADORE me. 'Smatter of fact,

I got one trying to beat my door down right now... LOCKED HER IN

MY ROOM!!

CM: Commercial - Pepsi (Cued tight to "my room")

Segue to

SOUND: Station Promo ($25,000 Giveaway)

SOUND: Music - SQUEEZEBOX

JOCK: (Over music) K-N-O-P. The Who: SQUEEZEBOX. 6:11 now with Billy

Boy. If you, er, have something you'd like to cry on some-body body's shoulder about, here it is (pat, pat, pat) right here. The proverbial crying shoulder (sings, now) Oh, it's crying time again, you're gonna wake up. Ha, ha, ha. If you've got something you'd like to bemoan this morning, give me a call at 742-5542 or 263-KNOP. The understanding ear of Billy Boy at 6:11.

Segue to

CM: Commercial - Dallas Power & Light

Segue to

DM: Commercial - Titche's Department Store

JOCK: (Over music) The tears of a Clown on KNOP, or, they won't have Scoop Jackson to kick around any more. Huh, ha ha ha ha. Would those of you out there who voted for Henry in the Texas primary, please go back to sleep.

SOUND: Music - TEARS OF A CLOWN

JOCK   (Over music) K-N-O-P, Billy Boy. The thought for today, 'bout memory (mumble) wood mouth forgot it.

SOUND: Music - SILLY LOVE SONGS.

(Note: Jock made his remark <u>over</u> the opening bars of SILLY LOVE SONGS, in effect talking over a segue)

JOCK: K-N-O-P and THE SILLY LOVE SONG, Paul McCartney and Wings. That one got a standing ovation at the concert the other night. It's up to 6:19 and we hear the rip and read sounds of Joey Brown (News Director)

NEWS: Ahhh (disdainfully)

JOCK: That's not true. You're not a rip and reader, are you?

NEWS: Are you kidding me?

JOCK: Ah, ha ha ha ha!

NEWS: Who besides me would write this libelous, slanderous material?

JOCK: Hey listen, I didn't mean to get personal

NEWS: Welllll...

JOCK: Just because I likened you to Paul Harvey...

NEWS: No no no no!

JOCK: We shouldn't take shots at other people, should we?

NEWS: Where are you going with this, Billy Boy?

JOCK: I wasn't going anywhere!!!

NEWS: Ha ha ha ha!

JOCK: Matter of fact, I was planning on staying right here.

NEWS: Yeah...

JOCK: But that's what I get.

NEWS: Uh, this week of sports coverage is just starting to get me now...
if I sound a little bit off in the fog.

JOCK: It's because you have a tennis ball stuck between your teeth!!

NEWS: Something like that.

JOCK: Ha ha ha ha!

NEWS: It gets a little strange when you're the last person to leave Moody
Coliseum...and you know...there's a little sign "Will Joey Brown
please turn out the lights."

JOCK: Ha ha ha ha ha!

NEWS: Ha ha ha ha ha!

JOCK: You're beginning to realize this tennis game is a racket, isn't it?

NEWS: Yeah, uh...

JOCK: Uh, ha ha ha!

NEWS: Oh...

JOCK: Oh...ouch!

NEWS: Well, we're getting serious...anyway we've got the Byron Nelson going
on. Ted Allison's got that all day. We've got two quarter final
matches at Moody Coliseum tonight at WCT...so we're in serious business.

JOCK: AND...I have tickets to give away to the Byron Nelson golf classic
again today...

NEWS: All right.

JOCK: So, I'll be doing _that_ while you're doing _that_.

NEWS: Okay, good. We have about 61 degrees outside right now (details

         local weather) then, This is Joey Brown with the "new day" report

         of KNOP Information.

      1.   Convenience food story

      2.   Eating out on Mothers Day

      3.   FBI tries to discredit Martin Luther King

      4.   Voicer -- reporter on City Council story

      Brown billboards story: "The gov goes for smilin' Jimmy,
                          Truday Smith reports next on KNOP
                          Information.

CM: Pizza Hut 60-sec

      5.   Voicer - governor - Carter, includes actuality from governor.

      Brown billboards sports: Borg over Dibbs

CM: Perfume 60-sec

      6.   Borg beats Dibbs (story included stroke-by-stroke of last
          two or three points recorded by Brown at game)

      7.   Ranger Baseball

      8.   Dallas Public Library getting into progressive/country music

      9.   Area Weather

NEWS: ...and a high of about 75

JOCK: Huh?

NEWS: 'Bout 78. That's a definitive. Thank you, Billy Boy.

JOCK: I'm gonna be holding your cue cards higher next time around, ha ha ha.

NEWS: Ha, ha. Right now it's 61 downtown. This is Joey Brown, now on

         KNOP...more music with Billy Boy.

SOUND: (Tightly cued) Music...WHO LOVES YOU

JOCK: (OVER music) KNOP FM in your car. Little past 6:30 now...your

         morning wake up call, Billy Boy...with the Dial Tone Blues.

SOUND: Music - FOOLED AROUND AND FELL IN LOVE

JOCK: (Over music) KNOP will give 4 folks a chance to scramble for

         $25,000 cash...in front of thousands of people at The Cotton Bowl

         Saturday night...for the big soccer game...keep listening and find

         out how you can win.

SOUND: Music up - MY EYES ADORED YOU

JOCK: (Over music briefly, then music out) KNOP and Frankie Valli - MY
          EYES ADORED YOU. This is Billy Boy at 6:39...(now on telephone)
          here's one maddern' a wet hornet.

WOMAN: (On phone) I am mad. I don't care whose toes I step on this
          morning. I really don't.

JOCK: Uh, okayyy.

WOMAN: I have been...I take my kids to school.

JOCK: Right.

WOMAN: And those fools driving down Illinois in that school zone...like they
          can't read...they might not have no kids going to this particular
          elementary school, but I have two nieces go there...and I would really
          appreciate it if they would go to a class to learn how to read...
          you know, so

JOCK: Breaks up with laughter.

WOMAN: They won't go through there speeding. Really, I know that a lot
          of listeners are listening and drive down Illinois in the morning...
          by the sub police station.

JOCK: Uh huh.

WOMAN: I got news for them. If they don't stop, I'm gonna take me a tablet
          and pencil and get their drivers license...and take it down to
          police station...because it doesn't make sense for people to know
          that is a school zone...and they drive like a bat coming out of you
          know where.

JOCK: Ha ha ha ha. But if they drive like a bat out of you know what,
          you'd know where they'd wind up...

WOMAN: Right, but yet and still, why should some elephants hit a 6 or 7
          year old child. Get hit...or get messed up for life.

JOCK: That' right.

WOMAN: From dumb people that can't read.

JOCK: That's right. You people going through school zones...slow down this
          morning or you'll be forced to eat my wife's cooking tonight.

CM: Exxon 60-sec

           Segue to

SOUND: Produced ID, using synthesized KNOP tone.

           Segue to

SOUND: Music - BREAKING UP IS HARD TO DO

JOCK: (On phone again, with music still in BG at beginning) KNOP.

WOMAN: Billy?

JOCK: I think so.

WOMAN: Stop talking about your wife the way you do.

JOCK: Oh, well.

WOMAN: I'll bet she's the sweetest person.

JOCK: Ha ha ha ha.

WOMAN: You know what's gonna happen?

JOCK: What?

WOMAN: One of these days you're gonna find yourself like a football coach
           that had a disastrous season.

JOCK: Laughs.

WOMAN: Everybody was mad at him. And he only had one friend and that was
           his dog.

JOCK: Laughs.

WOMAN: Even his wife was mad at him. So he told her every man should have
           at least two friends. She agreed and went out and bought him
           another dog.

JOCK: Breaks into wild laughter, tight cue to

CM: Skillerns Drugs

JOCK: (Over music) LOVIN SPOONFULS on KNOP. And do you believe in magic?
           You don't? Then how do you explain I'm never late for work.

SOUND: (Music up) LOVIN SPOONFULS

JOCK: (On phone and over music briefly) Morning, KNOP.

MAN   Billy Boy?
CALLER:

JOCK: Yes, indeed!

MAN: Will you please give me two tickets to the Byron Nelson?

JOCK: Well, we're not quite ready to give 'em away yet. We'll be doing
         that a little after 7 o'clock...keep listening.

MAN: Is there a contest or something?

JOCK: Well, it'll be one of those call-in-and-win-type of things.

SOUND: Music - COME ON OVER.

JOCK: (Music out) K-N-O-P and Olivia Newton John - COME ON OVER.
         Billy Boy at 6:52. I'm sitting here doing that old thing about
         watching my hand...ha ha ha...and I didn't even have any papers
         this morning...it's real strange.

NEWS: Ha ha ha.

JOCK: Ahghhhh you know that bit?

NEWS: Oh, yeah.

JOCK: Uhh, look at my hand (oh, groan) WHAT AM I DOING??

NEWS: How'd you like a little fashion show this morning?

JOCK: Uh, wait a minute.

NEWS: Coming down the ramp

JOCK: Wait wait wait wait

NEWS: No, this is serious. Coming down the ramp, the fat kid behind the
         microphone has; up, has on a dazzling knit yellow Munsingwear
         shirt. What this is all about is that the good folks at Sanger
         Harris didn't want us to look too shabby while we're representing them
         at the WCT and the Byron Nelson this week. So they dropped by
         yesterday and dropped off some sports shirts from the sporting goods
         department at Sanger Harris.

JOCK: We don't want to say that Joey is one of those journalists that goes
         for the jugular, but instead of a little penguin on his shirt they
         gave him a buzzard.
         (both laugh)

JOCK: You noticed that!

NEWS: Yeah, right off.

JOCK: Ha ha ha.

NEWS: Right on!

JOCK: Well, here we are. Another cloudy day. And the clouds are
          supposed to go away.

NEWS: Yes, I think I have the weather situation under control now.

JOCK: Well, tell us about it.

NEWS: Showers this morning and then clearing this afternoon. Looks like
          they'll be able to get the opening round of the Byron Nelson in.
          High about 72-73 today...so it's a little on the cooler side.
          This is Joey Brown, KNOP Information.

                    1. FBI story, rewritten.

                    2. FTC charges Chrysler with deceptive advertising

                    3. Gov endorses Carter

                        Brown billboards Borg story

CM: Pepsi

                    4. Borg-Dibbs (with actuality)

                        Brown billboard Byron Nelson golf story

CM: Sanger Harris

                    5. Byron Nelson story

SOUND: Music, tightly cued to last word of Nelson story.

          7 o'clock hour begins

Let's examine the performance of the jock in this early morning period at
KNOP. The performer was bright, uptempo. His use of clichés was minimal.
His banter with the newsman was amusing. As the transcript indicates, there
were sections of the hour when it appeared Billy Boy was executing a much-
more-music format. Bridge music held throughout these sections, comment was
minimal, and program elements were tightly segued, e.g., commercial cartridges started about two beats (one second) before the jock's last word; opening bars of the next piece of music segued tightly into the commercial with
remarks of the jock spoken over those opening bars.

The idea of this Top 40 format is to plan the unexpected for the listener.
The woman, whose southern accent couldn't be properly duplicated here, com-
plaining about careless drivers in the school zone. The other woman chiding
Billy Boy about his remarks about his wife's cooking, and told her tale about

the losing coach. These were bright program inserts that added humor to the overall performance.

There were several places where Billy Boy might have added time and temperature checks but didn't. Had the program director been listening, he surely would have admonished the jock. Many people are beginning their day at 6:00 a.m. and need the basic services of local radio (time, temperature, traffic.)

Throughout, the personality of Billy Boy came through. His dialogue with the news director was fairly typical of the informal way some programmers have of getting into and out of the news.

The news prepared and delivered by Brown appealed basically to the young adult listener. The banter about the weather, the Byron Nelson and the WCT was entirely appropriate as these are two of the biggest sporting events in the area and manage to capture about everyone's attention. Had the news content been of a more ominous nature much of the chatter would have been inappropriate. This is where professionalism and "gut instinct" play a vital part in the jock and newsperson's performances.

The 6–7 a.m. period carried nine commercial units, about a normal load for this format. There were *eleven* pieces of music aired. In no case did Billy Boy formally identify songs, artists, labels. He played around with them, as when he said "The tears of a clown on KNOP."

The next transcript is an example of a more personality-oriented format. The jock injects more of himself into the program, makes good use of the newsperson, and minimizes the importance of music. It takes a *strong,* well-known personality to sustain this plan. The jock appeals to an older, more sophisticated audience.

MODIFIED TOP 40

DJ: Hey, it's 7 o'clock in the morning on KSIL, and this is the

             kind of morning that you should play music like this...on a

             morning that it's kinda misty blue outside with rain in Oak

             Cliff and Arlington. Right now...and chances of it continuing

             are still around a little.

SOUND: Music up – MISTY BLUE

CM (segue): CM – VOGUE

CM (segue): EXXON

PROMO: Teaser on Rematch of Cowboys and Steelers Promotion

             (Segue) Music, GET UP AND BOOGIE

DJ: KSIL (each letter pronounced distinctly) 8 minutes after,
             almost 9 minutes after 7 o'clock in the morning. Raining in
             various parts of the Dallas-Fort Worth area. The showers are
             supposed to go away. It's raining outside our window right
             now, as I notice. I'll just see if we can hear it on the roof.
             You can hear it pitter-patter up there - listen! (Sound
             effect, rain.) Sure, boy. Pitter pat on my windowpane this
             morning. And just in time for Winn Dell to come in and talk
             about the Byron Nelson golf classic and other things that take
             place under roofs that don't get involved in the rain (ha ha.)

SPORTS: Yes, I've read of those, too. They wished they could have
             roofed Preston Trails I'm sure yesterday.

DJ: Boy, I bet they did.

SPORTS: (Goes into sports, detailing golf, TV ratings from sports
             coverage, WCT, story on Arthur Ashe motivating junior tennis.)

DJ: Yeah, then if you can come back and eventually win the, uh,
             you know, World Championship of Tennis and win that gold tennis
             ball they have made up you get to meet the designer.

CM: COLT 45

DJ: Of course, when Winn Dell speaks of sports in the morning on
             KSIL, he does so for the Dallas and Fort Worth Dodge boys and
             continues to here at 13 minutes after 7.

SPORTS: (More sports news, Texas Rangers, Dodgers scores)

DJ: Okay, thank you, Winn Dell. I happen to know there are some
             ladies and some gentlemen I'm sure who are leaving the area
             and heading toward Austin for a speech tournament today and I
             have a song for them next.

CM: GABBERTS FURNITURE

SOUND: Produced ID.

DJ: Yes, Melanie World and Karen Katen and Belinda Doyle all from
             Wylie are heading to Austin to do a little talking today so
             here's for you.

MUSIC: EVERYBODY'S TALKING.

NEWS: 18 minutes after 7 o'clock on KSIL and we're keeping an eye on

                that radar scope and right now it shows an area of heavy thunder-

                storms right now between Granbury and Fort Worth to about 50

                miles east of Dallas. These storms are just south of the

                metropolitan area which could account for the rain reports

                out of Oak Cliff and Arlington and Highland Park and University

                Park. There is another storm east of us around Paris (Texas)

                now and all of the storms are still moving to the northeast

                at 35 miles an hour.

                (News items...)

                     1. Texas Medical Association

                     2. Southwest Airlines Strike story

                     3. Shooting

                     4. Chrysler and FTC

                     5. California Governor Brown

                     6. Byron Nelson update with Toby Roddy

CM;   AUTO DEALER

NEWS: Roddy continues with Byron Nelson classic

                Weather Forecast, current conditions
                For Don Smith, Toby Roddy, Tom Kent and Ted Arrendale Ford,

                I'm Clyde Black.

SOUND: Produced ID

DJ: (Over music) and would you believe that while you were listening

                to that I had an early morning conversation with Tommy Lee,

                Details shortly.

MUSIC: NIGHT THEY DROVE OLD DIXIE DOWN.

DJ: KSIL, 7:27 in the morning.

CM: MARGIE'S

                Segue

CM: SKAGGS ALBERTSON'S

DJ: That's 28 after 7; 7:28 if we wear a digital and Hal Kemp is

	up in the air and we better check with him cause I don't know how long he's gonna be able to stay here. Good morning, Hal.
INSERT:	Traffic and weather report from airborne announcer.
CM:	FUNTASTIC
DJ:	Ah, yes, Betty Abrams, not Barbara. Betty, good morning. 7:30 in the morning. Yes, I did have a conversation with Tommy Lee, just a couple of minutes ago and I will share it with you in about 5 minutes here on KSIL.
MUSIC:	HEART OF GOLD.
DJ:	KSIL 7:33 in the morning. Before I do anything with Tommy Lee, here here's uh uh, supposed to be, a quick report that's live from another good friend of ours at KSIL. I mentioned your name on the air yesterday, Rick Novac in Presbyterian Hospital and you were the one that led the fight for law and order to get KSIL on their house monitor system.
CALLER:	Right on.
DJ:	Yeah, what were they playing up there before that?
CALLER:	Uh, you want me to name the stations?
DJ:	Well, I don't real...yeah, it's all right 'cause they got their choices.
CALLER:	Well, they were playing KAAA, KBBB, and KCCC.
DJ:	Yeah, say all that background stuff, right?
CALLER:	Yeah, stuff that makes you go to sleep. That's even after they give you a pill.
DJ:	Yeah, you you had a great line the other day. You said that if you're getting well you need KSIL, right, ha ha?
CALLER:	Right. If you if ya need to get well get KSIL.
DJ:	There ya go. We could make a billboard out of that. Well listen, are you getting better?
CALLER:	I'm gettin better since I got KSIL.
DJ:	On the speaker?
CALLER:	Right.

DJ: Now tell me what's happened since then. That's the story.

CALLER: Well, since then I've had several people from the administration

           staff and the co-workers around here come through and they say

           thank you for getting KSIL on the radio because they all like

           to listen to it.

DJ: That's wild. So they were...they, they, you you (stuttering,

           looking for words) were fighting a fight and thought you were

           all alone. It turned out you had friends and they weren't going

           to the upper, huh?

CALLER: Right on. We're all one big happy family, now ha ha.

DJ: Ya know...don't get too close...we want you to get out of there

           okay?

CALLER: Right on.

DJ: That's a great staff out there but don't get 'm emotionally

           involved, alright, Rick?

CALLER: Oh, ya know, I wouldn't do that. They get too excited ha ha.

DJ: Okay, thank you, Rick.

CALLER: Okay.

DJ: Bye, bye.

CALLER: Bye.

DJ: 26 minutes before 8 o'clock in the morning on KSIL.

CM: NATIONAL BANK OF COMMERCE

CM: WEIR'S COUNTRY STORE

DJ: Speaking of good ole boys, as you, oh, by the way speaking of

           good ole boys, if you goin' to Weir's Country Store today

           or Weir's Furniture you just uh say Happy Birthday to Dan

           Weir. He's the he's the honcho in charge of the place there

           uh you tell 'im that Ina Rose told me that it was his birthday.

           She's sneaked (she snitched on him is what it is) and we all

           know he's getting older but I didn't know it was today. O kay.

           23 minutes before 8'oclock now. Tommy Lee is a put on. We're

           pretty confident of that. Uh, but the fact is that he's such

a good put on that I always enjoy hearing from him. He is
alleged to be a farmer from Zion Hill, Texas, callin' me from
the pickup truck phone. A telephone in his pickup truck right?
And I know I'm being put on, but its always fun because he's
always fun when he calls and if, if it sounds at the very
outset of this conversation like I really wasn't interested
in hearing something funny this morning, we had a late party
here at KSIL, a lot of us last night, if, if it sounds like
I wasn't interested in hearing something funny this morning,
that's correct, I wasn't ha ha but here's the way it started.

DJ: Good morning, Stu Dew.

CALLER: (Using hick, ignoramous dialect) Mr. Dew, how are you this
           mornin'?

DJ: Wait a minute, it's too early for you! You don't normally get
           into town until much later in the morning.

CALLER: Well, yeah. Tried to get an early start 'cause its raining
           and everything thought I'd better get out early and try to get
           on up here to Dallas.

DJ: Well, it's good to have you in town. What brings ya to town
           during all the rainstorms?

CALLER: Well, I kinda have a little kind of emergency. I had to come
           up here uh my Uncle Oily Bob is in the hospital up here and
           I had to come up here and see about him.

DJ: This is almost a familiar pattern with him and medical treatment.
           As I recall you've told me about him and uh various forms of
           uh uh hurt before.

CALLER: Yeah, well see, he hadda little accident well actually it all
           started a couple of years ago uh there's a feller bought a farm
           uh next to him.

DJ: Uh huh.

CALLER: And uh

DJ: Is that in Zion Hill?

CALLER: Yeah, right there in Zion Hill and I got him uh he wanted to trade Uncle Oily Bob. Oily Bob had a milk cow that he wanted. He traded him a set of golf clubs for it.

DJ: (Hysterical laughter) wait a minute. A set of golf clubs for a milk cow?

CALLER: (After DJ laughter subsides) well anyway, after that, Uncle Oily Bob he just became a fool about that golf.

DJ: (Great laughter) a lot of people do.

CALLER: Yeah, he went crazy over it and he had a high point in his life yesterday.

DJ: Oh, really.

CALLER: Yeah, uh he got invited to come up here to play in this big golf tournament in that, in that am pro pro am tour.

DJ: That pro am thing, the Byron Nelson. He played in that?

CALLER: Well yeah he come up here, but he didn't get to play cause uh it rained and everything. But that kinda, you know, we talked about it before you know he loves to you know hit the juice a little bit?

DJ: Well we know he sauces just a tad, yes.

CALLER: Oh a little bit and he was out there on the golf course and yesterday he commenced bragging 'bout how far he could hit a golf ball.

DJ: Oh, ha ha ha.

CALLER: And he just kept a bragging 'bout it and he ug ug ug he did it twice further than anyone out there.

DJ: He said that?

CALLER: Yeah he did and you know there's some boys out there who can pocket it, too.

DJ: Well...ha ha ha...yes.

CALLER: But anyway.

DJ: They do have a little clout, yes.

CALLER: Uh right. But anyway, uh they commenced a bettin on who could hit the furtherest and they were gonna have a contest there.

DJ: Uh huh.

CALLER: To see who could hit it the furtherist.

DJ: Uh huh.

CALLER: And it got all rained out and they couldn't have their contest.

DJ: Oh, really.

CALLER: They went on into the locker room there and they kept a drinkin'
          a little bit and they kept a talkin' 'bout it.

DJ: Sure.

CALLER: And Oily Bob kept a talkin' 'bout how far he could hit it.

DJ: Yeah.

CALLER: But they decided to settle it right there in the locker room.

DJ: Okay. How'd they do that (laughter)?

CALLER: Oily Bob had a terrible accident. He came out with 47 abrasions.
          He had 32 cuts he had about 17 bruises and a light concussion.

DJ: Laughter.

CALLER: What happened though is they didn't do no fighting or nothing.
          But what happened is he took a full swing on that golf ball
          in the tile shower.

DJ: (Hysterical laughter)

CM: (Segued to laughter) THE CAP

DJ: (Laughter continues) I'll bet that thing is still bouncing.
          19 minutes till eight now.

CM: SMITH VILLAGE CADILLAC

INSERT: Produced ID.

DJ: (Over music) well it's KSIL coming up to 17 minutes before 8
          in the morning. Get this for a people's choice total. Know
          this amount if I call you $5,400 dollars...54 hundred bucks
          even. And this is by the Andrea True Connection.

MUSIC: MORE MORE MORE.

DJ: The Andrea True Connection. I like it fine, thank you very much on KSIL. Winn Dell takes a look at high school and college things in just a moment.

CM: SAFEWAY

DJ: 14 minutes till 8.

CM: TOYOTA TOWN

DJ: Okay, 13 minutes till 8, Winn Dell watches high school and college action and reports.

SPORTS: Sports News

            Richland College Karate Playoffs

            Junior High Track Meet

            Baseball scores

            Basketball coach report

            Tennis

            Golf

DJ: Thank you Winn Dell for keeping on top of all that. And keeping on top of other things, we thought he was going to set down but he's still up there apparently; the weather hasn't forced you down yet, that's Hal Kemp, right?

KEMP: Traffic report (followed by conversation on giving away WCT tickets)

CM: TURTLE CREEK VILLAGE

DJ: KSIL, 10 til 8

MUSIC: LOVE WILL KEEP US TOGETHER.

NEWS: 7 minutes before 8 o'clock on KSIL and its been another one of those wild weather nights around Texas (details weather)

            Arlington School releases scholastic achievement tests

            Dallas Schools

            Food & Drug Administration warning

            Price of potatoes in Idaho

            Network sports billboard

CM: ALKA SELTZER

```
CM:        SEARS

NET SPORTS:  To 8 o'clock.
```

This is personality MOR in its purest form, with the DJ working more as an emcee than as a spinner of records. For the listener who wants music, there was very little. The jock really threw himself into humor, information, situation comedy. In this one-hour period, there were *six* pieces of music and *fifteen* units of commercial matter. In this case, the programmers determined what the market was thinking about (the Byron Nelson, bad weather, traffic conditions) and addressed themselves to those topics. Music was secondary. In heavily-talk shows, the commercial load becomes less important because listeners are already "tuned-in" to talk; comercials become *part* of the programming rather than an interruption.

AOR (PROG-ROCK) VARIATIONS

The AOR sound is, among other things, attitudinal. A definite life style is implied. A Navy recruiter complained that his superiors wanted him to buy stations that reach 18–24 men, but he didn't want the prog-rock stations "because those guys listening are anti-establishment, smoke pot, and wear long hair." And the recruiter didn't want "guys like that in the Navy."

The term "prog-rock" began fading in the late '70s, making way for the term, "Album Oriented Rock" (AOR). The style of the plan didn't change basically, but the demographic base was broadened due mainly to "mass audience" stations picking up on the popularizing some of the artists and groups previously aired only by the prog-rock stations. Peter Frampton, for example, was featured for more than a year on prog-rockers before the mass audience stations noticed him.

Jocks on AOR stations are "laid back." That is, they never pressurize their delivery. It's a "cool" attitude. AOR Jock language might go something like this:

```
MUSIC:  Buckingham.

JOCK:   Buckingham there.  And that group will be in concert this

        Saturday at City Auditorium.  8 o'clock, I believe.  Most

        local agencies have tickets; check it out if the group

        turns you on.  The time?  Who cares.  Roll a fresh one

        now, as we put on a little "Yes."
```

The jock delivers in a laid-back mode, working the microphone very closely. A lot of breath can be heard, occasionally. The idea is intimacy, close identification, togetherness. The language is very cultish, very "in." Notice the jock didn't tout the performing group. He *assumes* his audience knows the group, appreciates the group because the group is "in," and may or may not care to hear it live.

The reference to "roll a fresh one" obviously refers to marijuana, pot, the weed, "M", "MJ." The language of the pot smokers changes so often, it is hard for the "square" person to keep up. Jocks, therefore, can openly and freely discuss the use of pot, even though many states still have stringent laws against possession and use.

Much of the music played on AOR stations is not played on any other format, although Ira Lipson, program director for KZEW, Dallas, laments the fact that "the number of artists who belong to AOR exclusively grows smaller each year." Some of the artists and groups who belong *almost* exclusively to AOR stations include Dan Fogelberg, Yes, Jesse Colin Young, Traffic, Dave Mason, and Steely Dan. Some artists who were closeted for long periods of time on AOR and later graduated to mass audience stations include Frampton, Boz Scaggs, Fleetwood Mac, and Steve Miller.

The original concept of handling commercial matter on prog-rock and AOR formats has changed as higher ratings increased demand for commercial time. But, still, commercial matter *is* handled differently, as is over-all production. There are no jingles, for example, such as those used by the up front Top 40-type operations. An AOR jock, for example, would never deliver a hard-sell commercial.

```
Hankins Department Store is having a fire sale!

Everything reduced from 25 to 75 percent! Come

one, come all, come early while selection is good.

You may never experience another such sale in

your entire life. Hankins! Hankins! Hankins!

The fire sale of your life. Located 2121 Main

Street. That's 2121 Main Street, Hankins....

biggest fire sale ever.
```

This commercial would force the AOR jock to regurgitate. Many would resign their jobs before delivering such a commercial. Allowed to rewrite the work, the jock would probably say:

```
Uhhh...Hankins store over on Main Street...got a

sale on. Pretty good cuts on jeans and tank tops.

They say you can save some bread...and they're calling
```

```
it a fire sale, or something like that.  Might check

'em out.  Couple of examples:  jeans that were priced

at 14 bucks last week...you're supposed to be able to

get 'em now for 8 dollars.  Uhh...that's Hankins on

Main...2121, I believe.
```

Control rooms of AOR stations may be very dark, just enough light for the jock to see the controls and cartridge labels. Pop-art posters adorn walls. This atmosphere is conveyed to the listener by the jock's laidback, "into it" attitude.

The news is delivered in much the same manner. It also is laid back. Congressional activities, violence, stock markets, military actions, and other establishment-type news, isn't covered. An arrest concerning pot usage will be mentioned, and probably editorially commented on. Violence in a London "punk rock" demonstration may be discussed. For the most part, programmers have tried to perceive what their distinctive listeners want and give it to them.

OTHER VARIATIONS

One unique aspect of the AOR format is the tremendous diversity of its music. While some programmers claim the AOR plan is more structured than the old prog-rock or underground format, the idea is to *sound* unstructured. The sequence of music may be planned very carefully, for example, but it is supposed to sound as though the jock is simply expressing his current mood with the music played. AOR stations, and there are hundreds of them, mainly on FM, say they're attempting to offer an "alternative" to the main-stream rockers.

The splintering impact of diversified musical artistry is apparently never-ending. Programmers, charged with the responsibility of building *some kind* of audience for their stations, continually search for groups of listeners who aren't being served.

Black-oriented stations are different from other black-oriented stations, according to how the programmer perceives his audience. One station may program more disco (danceable) music. The other may avoid so-called "white music." More emphasis may be placed by jocks on black jargon, while another may have jocks "play it straight."

The prog-rock programmer may skew to more mass audience performers while another may continue to play unknowns who fit into a general pattern pre-established by the programmer.

Stations have tried programming "stereo disco" music, which, allegedly, is a total format of danceable music. These operations have not been wildly successful, as the "solid oldie" operations were not. A mix and blend of currently popular music obviously is required if the station is to achieve commercially viable numbers.

The future of contemporary music formats is limited only by the imagination of programmers.

Go for teens! Skew young folks! Be sophisticated. Return to the original Top 40. Young people are more sophisticated now. Use the laid back approach. It worked in Philly! It worked in Chicago. Crack the barrier. Play solid music for three months, no commercials. Research that piece of music! Research the market. What are the 18–49 audiences buying, listening to, dancing to? Listen to the folks! Play what they want! Cut the commercial load, that'll get listeners. Listeners hate commercials. Hate contests, except they'd all like to win a color TV or a trip to Hawaii. Eighty percent tune any station for music. When the music stops, they'll punch you out. To hell with teens, they're too fickle. Let's program to 25 plus audiences. Slow building, but once you get them, they'll remain loyal. More sports! Hide the news, it's a tune out. Make the jocks shut up and play the music. Jocks are popular with only 20% of the audiences, according to surveys. We're AOR! We're prog-rock! We're Top 40, no, we're personality oriented; we play contemporary music, but nothing for teens, nothing for Blacks. We skew young, you skew old. Entertain, inform!

Radio, a science? A craft? A trade? No, a lifetime of wildly, exhilarating conjecture.

RESEARCH

Without competent research, programming a music station may be compared to flying in fog or playing tennis in pitch dark. Far too many radio stations rely on gut instinct, or by the primitive research method of gauging a record's popularity by local and national sales. Studies have indicated that people who patronize record shops aren't necessarily radio listeners, and vice versa. There are industry standards for measuring radio and television audiences, but none has emerged for measuring the kind of music people want to hear and at what periods they'd like to hear it. Indeed, there are enormous efforts underway to correct the lack of music research, but it is still scattered. The RKO Radio group has had a major effort underway for several years, and many stations have a primitive plan in one form or the other. Some of these methods will be discussed in this chapter.

For sales purposes, the industry has a number of research services available, including Arbitron, Pulse, Mediatrend, C.E. Hooper, The Source, International Demographics, and several regional services. These firms, using various methodology, contact people at home, at work, at play, and ask them to identify their favorite radio station. This oversimplification suffices only to broadly explain the general aim of the services.

Arbitron uses the "diary" method principally to survey listening habits, as does The Source. Pulse uses a one-on-one interview method, while Hooper, Mediatrend and International Demographics use the telephone. International Demographics is useful mainly in determining the "quality" of the audiences, as to income, education, and product and service preferences. Only The Source, among the better known of the other services, attempts to provide qualitative data.

The diary method requires a listener to keep track of listening for a seven-day period. The listener records which stations were tuned in, duration of listening, time period of listening, and where the listening occurred. From the resulting data, Arbitron determines the relative popularity of the stations in the survey area.

Rating services are not universally loved or hated. Those stations coming out on top of a survey usually tend to praise the service, while the losers claim foul and incompetence. But it remains that these services are a vital part of the broadcast industry, and will continue to determine who makes money and who loses until something more efficient comes along.

Unfortunately, there is no national company that provides intelligence on the *local* popularity of music. A record that is selling widely on the national scene, may be totally unloved in Dallas or Kansas City. A Top 40 list *nationally* may vary as much as 10 records when compared to a Top 40 list *locally*. So, national sales may be considered, but cannot be the last word when the local programmer is attempting to determine what music to air.

A Basic Step

The oldest method of attempting to determine the popularity of various pieces of music is to call record stores in the station's service area. It is important to select stores in *many* parts of your service area, because the outlet in a poor neighborhood will sell a different kind of music product than the one in the city's fanciest shopping center. A store near a high school will cater to the needs of high school youngsters, while the shop next door to a book store will appeal to yet another demographic.

Get to know the store! Establish one contact, then stick with that person each time you call. Set a day and time to call each week, so you'll have a chance to really *discuss* sales. Visit the store from time to time, get to know your contact and, more important, stand aside and casually observe the people as they purchase records. Are these the listeners to your radio station? What seems to be their lifestyle? Observe, listen, tune in on people—because that's what radio programming is all about. Is the store a big, full-service operation, or is it a funky little hole in the wall that sells posters, papers, and pipes as well as records? What is the volume of the store? Does it sell 20 or 200 records a day? All of these elements must be considered if the programmer is to gather valid data for use in selecting music. Be aware that record promoters know of the record store survey technique and are capable of influencing the answers you receive from you contacts.

```
PROMOTER:  Hey, good buddy!  When the PD at KXXX calls today,

           tell him my record is selling like crazy!  I'll lay

           a dozen freebies on you if you'll do that!
```

To avoid this kind of hype, change stores from time to time or if you feel you're receiving doctored information.

Telephone contact with you record store may go something like this:

```
MUSIC DIRECTOR:  Good morning, Mary.  It's Joe and I hope you

                 can talk to me about sales this week.

MARY:            I'm ready, let's begin.

MUSIC DIRECTOR:  Okay, what about the new Eagles album?

MARY:            Going fine.  We sold out our inventory last

                 night.  Believe we actually moved around 50 yes-

                 terday.

MUSIC DIRECTOR:  Mary, you're located near Central High, aren't you?

MARY:            Yeah.  Can't believe those kids have that kind of

                 money.  Oh, they bought out our 8-track tape supply

                 too on that album.
```

The dialogue continues until the music director has gotten the picture of dozens of current songs. It has been pretty well established that singles (45 RPM) are purchased mainly by children and the poor. The development of sophisticated stereo equipment during the 1970s led to heavy sales in albums and tapes. Record manufacturers and A&R (artist & repertory) people are directing most new product be placed on album. When an artist develops a new song, it may now be issued on album along with 10 or 12 other selections by the same artist. The new cut, to be sure, is touted as though it were a new single, but the profit in an album is far more significant than in a single. Some of the major record producers in 1977 were talking about discontinuing singles altogether. Under this plan, stations would get their "samplers" or promotional copies on tape, rather than on the traditional single.

The survey of local sales can be a valuable tool for the programmer in determining the correct music for *the* station and *the* market. To some extent, results do reflect local preferences, but sales pictures alone will not suffice.

A Second Step

To refine the process somewhat, the programmer compares local sales figures to national charts from such publications as *Billboard, Record World, Cash Box, The Gavin Report* and *Radio & Records* (R&R). Each piece of music is charted weekly, giving the programmer an idea of how a song is trending. *Billboard* and *Cash Box* base their ratings on sales *and* air-play. R&R uses air-play only as the basis for evaluation, while Record World uses sales-only as its principal base. Air-play statistics are gathered by those publications using that technique from key stations around the nation. If KXXX in Philadelphia is playing a record, the record may be given six points. If a station in Sacramento, California is playing the same record, it may receive only four points. Some of the brightest and most experienced music personnel are working in the major markets, and their decisions would naturally carry more weight than, say, a relatively unknown and inexperienced programmer in Shreveport, Louisiana. Hence, sales and air-play are important when trying to determine the relative popularity of a given piece of music.

Here's an example of how information gathered from national publications may be charted:

Last Week's Chart

Weeks On	Last Week	This Week	Title	Billboard		Rec World		Cash Box		Gavin		R & R	
				LW	TW	LW	TW	LW	TW	LW	TW	LW	TW
7	14	10	Southern Nights	23	17	20	18	15	12	18	11	40	28
6	18	9	Rich Girl	17	6	12	4	19	10	17	4	30	15

The above product of this second-stage research serves to help the programmer determine which pieces of music to keep on the playlist, which ones to add or delete, and how to rank them. The programmer still has the task of *how often* to play each song and *in which* daypart. Further research will help answer these important questions.

Every Top 40-type station in every major market is kept aware of *new* music on a weekly, sometimes *daily* basis. The record companies, through promotion representatives, thrust dozens of new products on program directors or music directors every week. Only station program executives should decide which piece of new music goes on the air. Some stations play only established hits; others will chance a new record if it is doing well in other parts of the nation. A San Antonio station manager "sticks to the hits." He refuses even to see record company reps. Other stations court the reps in efforts to ascertain priority treatment when major groups produce new music.

A Third Step

Request lines are open at most youth-oriented rock stations and a wealth of information can be gleaned from these telephone calls. Who is asking for which song? What is the age and sex of the caller? When does the caller normally listen to the radio station? With the answer to these questions, the programmer is equipped to begin dayparting his music with some precision. Instinctive dayparting is not difficult when a piece of music clearly appeals to a teen or ethnic audience. During school months, teens are available to listen in afternoon drive and in the 7p-12m slot. Music with distinctive teen appeal is slotted in those periods, and on weekends. If a station's nighttime signal reaches into a predominantly ethnic area, special consideration may be given to music that has a recognized ethnic appeal. But it is simple to make these determinations. The difficult part is determining precisely what is teen and what is ethnic and what is not, and when must the records in other categories be aired. These questions, to some extent, can be answered if the station takes telephone requests. Normally, the jock is too busy to maintain consistent records of calls, so many stations employ students part-time to handle the chore. Here is an example of such recordkeeping:

KXXX REQUEST SHEET		SUN MON TUE WED THU	FRI SAT	SUN Day/Night Date_____	
Song	Total	6-11 child/12-17 males/	18-24 males/18-24 females/etc.		
Do Run Run	26	ᴜᴴ ᴜᴴ ııı	ᴜᴴ	ıı	ᴜᴴ ı
Fly Like	21		ı	ᴜᴴ	ᴜᴴ ᴜᴴ ᴜᴴ
Rich Girl	25			ᴜᴴ ᴜᴴ ᴜᴴ ıı	ᴜᴴ ııı

The demographic spread will vary according to the target audience. A teen-oriented rocker may not measure persons over 24. A MOR rocker might exclude all teens and break-out adult males and females. Research of any kind is to determine if the music is hitting the target audience.

The programmer now has the results of telephone surveys of sales at local record shops, a break-out of how national publications rate the major songs, and a survey accomplished through listeners calling on the request line. But there is more.

A Fourth Step

The development of call-out research is one of the latest methods of measuring music, particularly new music. The listener list is compiled from the names of persons who are known to be in the station's audience. Contest winners, for example. Those who write to the station, praising or complaining; any person who is a potential listener to the station or a *similar* station.

Once a list of 500 to 1,000 persons has been established, a letter is sent to each describing the plan. A single one-page letter is adequate, along with a self-addressed card on which the respondent indicates willingness to go along, telephone number, and best time to call. Each week, starting on Monday, the calls are made. Operators should use a preference system, from one to seven:

(1) My favorite
(2) Like it a lot
(3) Like it, but getting tired of it
(4) It's okay
(5) Don't like it
(6) Really hate it
(7) Never really heard it

The current list of songs, plus any potential adds, and less any long-lived hits due to go to stash, is recorded onto casette. Not the entire song, of course, but a key line, phrase, or a hook. The average length should be 5- to 10-seconds, with new songs being given perhaps 15-seconds. About 4-seconds of dead air between pieces should give the telephoned-listener adequate time to make a judgment.

Programmers who have worked this formula estimate 25–30 bits of music are about all the listener can tolerate. As the music is played down the telephone line, the respondent is able to give the answer and speak to the operator, even over the music.

In this example, teen through 49 demographics are used. At the beginning of the call, the operator determines the age and sex of the respondent, then moves to that demographic block, and works that block through each sheet. Note that only one artist and song are covered by each survey sheet. A dot or check-mark is made as the respondent responds to each piece of music.

To tabulate, reverse the value given by respondents, so that the most popular pieces of music will receive the highest number of points. In other words, ones are worth seven, twos are worth six, etc. For example, the Eagles' "Hotel California" received a total of 46 points from men 18–24. There were 10 respondents so men 18–24 gave the record a 4.6 rating (46 divided by $10 = 4.6$.)

Using this procedure, the programmer can easily determine not only how well a record is doing generally, but may also determine specifically which record appeals to which demographic group. It is often surprising, for example, to learn that a particular record is rated higher by women 25–49 than it is by teens, when instinct and experience would indicate a predominately teen appeal.

There are two schools of thought on this procedure. Nationally-known programmer and researcher Todd Wallace argues *against* playing bits of music on the telephone. A record might get unfavorable response, for example, if the

Here is the tabulation form:

Music Survey Work Sheet

Week of _____

ARTIST *EAGLES* | SONG TITLE *HOTEL CALIFORNIA*

7	6	5	4	3	2	1		7	6	5	4	3	2	1		7	6	5	4	3	2	1

MEN 18-24   MEN 25-34   MEN 35-49

44 ÷ 10 = 4.6   (4.6)   (4.0)   (5.4)

WOMEN 18-24   WOMEN 25-34   WOMEN 35-49

(5.5)   (4.4)   (5.8)

MALE TEENS 12-17   FEMALE TEENS 12-17   TOTALS   TOTAL

3	4	9	11	21	16	16	= 395

395 ÷ 80 = 4.94

(5.5)   (4.3)   140

programmer has selected the wrong "bit" to play down the phone line. The respondent might be turned on by the song's open, refrain, or close; while the programmer thought another part of the song would be the most popular and recognizable. Not hearing the "familiar" part of the song, the respondent might give a rating of seven (never heard of it).

Wallace's technique was simply to identify the song and the artist to the respondent and elicit an answer on the scale indicated. If the respondent hadn't heard the record, there would be an indication that it simply hadn't caught on yet, Charlie Van Dyke, morning jock and program director for KLIF, Dallas, believes it takes a minimum of two or three weeks for any record to develop mass appeal, in spite of the possibility that half the radio stations in the country could begin playing it within a week of release.

Van Dyke is recognized as one of the leading music researchers in American radio. The "KLIF Call-Out Totals" chart is an example of how he compiled one week of call-outs in Dallas. He endorsed the Wallace concept of call outs, and does not play bits of music for the respondents.

A Catch-all Step

Once the programmer has checked all the routine sources and gone through the basic steps, there are certain involvements that would be helpful. Juke Boxes? Maybe. One problem is that juke boxes in neighborhood bars and taverns may reflect only the tastes of that particular neighborhood. Too, new records often do not reach juke box operators for several weeks after they have hit the airwaves. Van Dyke believes juke box plays may be important for determining the "burn out" factor for a record. Often, station personnel become sick of a record before it has really caught on with the listening public. Hence, a song may be pulled from the charts before it is really burned out with the people who count . . . the listeners.

Restaurants with live shows and discos sometimes reflect the popularity of a piece of music. Programmers cannot live by charts and graphs alone; they must go into the real world and find out what people are singing and dancing to.

The Test

Now, unless the programmer is prepared to exercise judgment, instinct, and experience—all research is for naught. If the programmer is a *leader,* all aspects of judgment and research are synergized and a decision is made. If the programmer is a follower, then the decision has been made by a leader at *another* station.

Van Dyke believes valid judgments can be made only after thorough research, involving one or more of the steps described. But he also believes the data gathered are nothing more than a scramble of arithmetic if the programmer isn't then prepared to make decisions. True, heavy decisions aren't required on *every* piece of music *every* week. But 10 *wrong* records on a hit list of 40 can make 20% of the music *wrong* and can consequently drive away listeners in droves. As an example, Van Dyke cited a Helen Reddy record, "You are My World," that appeared to be bombing nationally, but had hit the top five in Houston and Chicago. One key element in the decision *not* to play the record was the lack of air-play from *other* Dallas stations. Van Dyke didn't believe KLIF's demographics for that particular record were strong enough to make it a hit in Dallas. If KVIL, KNUS and KFJZ had been playing it, maybe. But,

TITLE	M→ 18-34	25-34	35-49	F→ 18-24	25-34	51-49	TEENS 65	
1. Handyman	4.1	5.0	4.0	4.3	5.5	3.0	4.5	✓
2. Star Wars	5.0	7.0	1.0	4.0	2.7	5.0	4.0	✓
3. I Just (Want to be your everything)	4.3	1.0	4.0	5.16	5.0	4.3	4.91	
4. Old Schoolyard	4.83	1.0	1.0	2.6	4.16	3.0	4.58	✓
5. Signed, Sealed, Delivered	5.0	1.0	6.0	5.16	6.3	6.3	5.08	✓
6. Don't Stop	4.91	5.0	6.0	4.41	5.6	4.0	5.0	✓
7. Whatcha Gonna Do	4.6	1.0	4.0	3.6	3.83	1.3	4.25	✓
8. On & On	3.16	1.0	1.0	4.6	4.16	2.6	3.08	✓
9. Higher & Higher	5.3	5.0	7.0	4.45	6.0	4.0	5.41	✓
10. Give a Little	4.3	1.0	7.0	3.83	3.6	1.3	3.5	✓
11. Best of my Love	4.83	7.0	4.0	4.3	5.3	4.3	4.08	✓
12. Just a song before I go	4.6	3.0	1.0	5.0	4.0	4.3	4.08	
13. Barracuda	6.0	6.0	3.0	4.5	3.83	3.3	5.25	
14. Strawberry Letter #23	4.5	1.0	4.0	3.3	3.0	1.3	2.4	
15. Black Betty	3.6	7.0	5.0	4.83	2.6	3.3	4.0	
16. Christine 16	2.0	0	1.0	3.0	2.0	1.0	3.4	✓
17. Smoke from a distant Fire	2.4	N	1.0	4.3	1.0	2.0	2.4	✓
18. You & Me	3.6	O	6.0	4.7	6.0	5.0	5.5	✓
19. Float On	3.2	ø	1.0	3.0	1.0	3.5	1.8	✓
20. Do you want to make love	3.8	8	6.0	3.0	7.0	4.0	5.3	
21. Easy	4.6	8	3.0	4.7	4.0	3.5	4.0	
22. Telephone Line	4.2	A/0	4.0	3.3	5.0	2.5	4.3	✓
23. Da Doo Ron Ron	3.4	m/0	2.0	4.0	4.3	6.0	5.5	✓
24. I'm in you	5.8	P	6.0	5.0	6.3	5.5	5.3	✓
25. Your Smiling Face	5.2	w	4.0	2.0	4.7	2.0	2.4	✓
26. almost like a love song	1.8	E	7.0	4.8	4.0	6.5	3.3	✓
27. Jungle Love	2.5	D	4.0	2.3	4.7	2.5	3.4	✓
28. Fantasia	2.0	D	7.0	1.8	2.5	2.5	3.5	✓
29. Jet Airliner	5.0	V	3.0	3.5	2.3	3.5	5.2	✓
30. Knowing me, Knowing you	4.5	0	6.0	5.0	6.7	5.0	6.4	✓

98

alone, they believed, the record would not get off the ground. Experience! Instinct! And, courage to make the decision.

One of the toughest decisions to make is when to add songs. Some of the national publications refer to "breakers"—that is, music that in the professional judgment of other programmers will reach the top 10 nationally. These "breakers" may go well in a Southern California market, and die in Miami. This is a case where the programmer's knowledge of and feel for the market is critically important. A "breaker" in Detroit may have high appeal for an industrial market that is composed of a high percentage of Black listeners and other blue-collar workers. It could go to number one in Detroit in a week. The same record would not fly in Dallas, because the social and ethnological composition in the market is entirely different.

One reason so many broadcasters distrust record companies is that promotional people will "sell" a local programmer on airing a certain record, "because it's doing well in Chicago" or because "so and so in Los Angeles is playing it," or, at the worst because the record promoter bought the programmer a new stereo set last month (an illegal act called "payola" which subjects both giver and receiver to fines and/or imprisonment.)

Ultimately, it doesn't matter who in which market is doing what with anything! What matters is that the record is right for your station and your market.

4

Country Music Formats

Where's that gal with the red dress on,
    Some folks calls her Dina,
Stole my heart away from me.
    Way down in Louisiana.
Take me back to Tulsa,
    I'm too young to marry.

Bob Wills and Tommy Duncan

HISTORY

Beginning in the 1920s with cowboy bands live on many local stations, and the development of the "National Barn Dance" on WLS Chicago in 1924, and a year later the "WSM Barn Dance" from Nashville (later to be called the "Grand Ole Opry"), country music began its infectious hold on many segments of the American public. At that time, broadcast historians report, "the impact of the country western programs was tremendous," and it's still the same today.[1]

According to some sources, WSB, Atlanta was one of the first big radio stations to put country music on the air in the early '20s, and WBAP, Fort Worth, broadcast a "barn dance" over two-thirds of the country with its clear channel reach.[2] But it was Saturday night broadcasts of the "Grand Ole Opry," from WSM, Nashville, that established country music as a popular

[1] Lawrence W. Lichty and Malachi C. Topping, *American Broadcasting: A Source Book on the History of Radio and Television* (New York: Hastings House, 1975), p. 298.
[2] *Broadcasting*, September 18, 1972, p. 34.

staple of radio programming that has lasted over 50 years. An entire industry grew up around this program in Nashville, and to this day people drive 500 miles to see the "Opry" broadcast live.

During the 1930s, in spite of the economic depression, both the recording industry and radio began to build a powerful economic base. The innovation of playing records on the air to increase both the listening audience for the radio station and the retail sales for the recording companies proved to be an unbeatable economic and entertainment combination. Great recording stars like Bing Crosby helped to popularize country music by crooning pseudo cowboy songs such as "Empty Saddles," "Navajo Trail," and "Sierra Sue." Ken Maynard introduced Western songs in his motion pictures in 1930. Five years later Gene Autry and Roy Rogers became immensely popular singing cowboy songs in Western movies, and they enjoyed a replay as radio stations spread the sales of their records by constantly spinning the discs on the air.

As in the 1920s, when radio stars like Uncle Dave Macon, "The King of the Hillbillies," Uncle Ezra, and the Hoosier Hotshots toured the fairs and dancehalls of the midwest, the combination of radio and live stage performances became a potent force. During the 1930s in Texas, the "Lightcrust Doughboys" were a sensational radio hit in Fort Worth, and they always ended their program telling where they'd be playing at small town dance halls the next week.

In the 1940s during World War II many able-bodied males were in the Southland where three-quarters of the military bases were located. Everytime these chaps from Milwaukee or Brooklyn turned on their radios, they were introduced to country music and many of them came to like it.

The '40s brought dramatized western songs like "Mule Train" and "Ghost Riders in the Sky," recorded by ballad singer Frankie Laine. These records were tremendously popular on both the juke box and the radio stations, and as in the case of the personal appearance-radio combination and the motion picture-radio combination, the juke box-radio combination proved to be an economic bonanza for country radio stations, honky tonks, and recording artists and companies. Quasi-country songs like "Pistol Packing Mama," "Sioux City Sue," and "Slipping Around," made strong invasions into what had always been called "popular music."

In the 1950s a great blow was dealt to the country stations by the advent of rock 'n roll. The unkindest cut of all was that country stars like Elvis Presley, Conway Twitty, and Jerry Lee Lewis made rock music that blew country music off the air and off the charts. The combination of country singing with the heavy beat of rhythm and blues produced rockabilly and rock 'n roll that made a heavy impact on country fans, especially in the case of the younger listeners. But in the end the influence of rock on country was good, because it brought a change in country that gave it a broader base of popularity than it had ever had before.

By the 1960s rock had gotten so extreme that many listeners, especially in the age twenty-five up, were looking for some optional music to listen to. A new kind of country music called modern or progressive was beginning to develop. Artists like Roger Miller were producing songs like "King of the Road," that were very popular. Country began to have a different sound. Double fiddles, mandolins, banjos, and pedal-steeled guitars were dropped. Singing styles became more up-beat. Arranging became more complicated and sometimes 26-piece orchestras were used for recording.

Recording techniques were advanced by new technological developments. Stereo radio, playbacks, and recorders made listeners more sound-quality conscious, and the great multi-track recording innovations began influencing and changing the sound coming from the studios.

Stations began to tighten their formats to match the new music. The loose, chatty rhythm of the small town country station was streamlined by superimposing format radio onto the country structure. Segued music-under-everything techniques with attractive jingle IDs, well-produced PSAs and commercial spots, news and weather on the hour made for a full, continuous sound. Country radio changed to a full service radio station that played a wide range of country music.

The music form broadened so that a lot of new ears were attracted to country stations. The influence of Elvis Presley brought country a quicker rhythm from rock. Glen Campbell, Lynn Anderson, and Charley Pride brought a more up-beat ballad style which meant that Nashville had departed from the hard country approach to a more diversified sound. As this kind of music caught on, more stations began to go modern country. DJs and program managers from top-40, MOR, and rock backgrounds were attracted to the modern country station. These people were not rooted in traditional country music so that more of the modern country began to be played. The jocks added some Lynn Andersons and Charley Prides to the Wanda Jacksons and the Ernest Tubbs.

In the 1970s the appeal of country stations grew. By the middle 70s there were 1,100 stations playing country music.[3]

The listenership grew and became even more broad-based; bankers, truck drivers, insurance executives, laywers, and blue collar workers listened to country stations. The modern country stations have broken the time buyer's prejudice of the "chip-kicker" image that stuck for so many years. Agencies never thought of trying an airlines account or a Cadillac account on a country station. "We never had a man walk up to our counter wearing a steel helmet and safety shoes," would be a typical comment from an airlines time buyer.[4] But this prejudice is over. Station managers say that they don't have to restrict their commercials to ranch beans, country meat markets, horse sales, and western wear. Country stations in large markets get every kind of account from

[3] *Broadcasting,* September 27, 1976, p. 66.
[4] *Broadcasting,* September 18, 1972, p. 38.

Fords to Rolls Royces. Station managers will tell you that there is no stereo-
typed country account. The snuff dipping, tobacco chewing image is a thing of
the past. Large market stations for the most part are not concerned about the
"country" image, although there are still a few "closet" country fans who
won't admit they like the music and this causes some stations to soften the
country image. But for the most part country stations in large markets are
openly and proudly country. As one station manager said, "We want people to
know that we know what we are doing. We know the music and we're a
country station and we don't apologize for it." KJIM, Fort Worth, Texas, carries the title "Red Neck Radio" in its ID.

Some country stations settle for a happy medium. They may have a cowbell on their ID, but their commercials are strictly out of the modern jingle
production houses. Others may have an updated women's trio ID, but play
country music under most PSAs and commercials. Some use a kind of Drake
format. They simply rely on the music for the country sound, and their commercials, PSAs and DJ chatter are very straight. The jock tells the names of the
artists and the records with no comments of a country flavor and no attempts at
humor. After the record, the jock identifies the artist and the selection, punches
up a commercial on the cart, gives time and weather, and then goes on with the
next record without comment.

COUNTRY JOCKS

The jock is one of the key elements in protraying the image of the station.
Country station managers stress "believability" as the outstanding trait of the
good DJ. Sincerity is emphasized and also the ability to deliver what is promised to the listeners. Managers choose down-to-earth people with good air
voices who can relate to the audiences. The managers don't require "country,"
"southern," or "western" accents. The ability to relate to the audience on a
one-to-one basis is the main requisite.

The jocks are required to be well informed and "topical" in their chatter
base. The managers expect them to be well aware of what is going on, and they
are encouraged to read extensively to keep abreast of current developments in
human interest items and general news. Transcripts reveal that the jocks work
in humorous comments based upon news events. During a country-wide mass
innoculation program, one jock remarked after playing "There Ain't No Cure
for the Summertime Blues," that perhaps queueing up for a free shot might
help.

Managers search for jocks who can adjust rapidly to the particular geographic coverage area. They look for people who can quickly assimilate the
slang, argot, and updated idiomatic expressions that will make the jock sound
indigenous to the area and enable the jock to communicate intimately with the

listeners. The managers tend to think of radio as a very intimate medium that communicates with one or two people in a car, on the beach, or in the kitchen.

Jocks are encouraged to use humor in achieving a friendly relationship with the listners, but are cautioned not to use it if it seems strained. Recordings of country jocks reveal that humor is used to achieve a free and easy, conversational relationship with the listener. After a commercial on washers and dryers, a jock said that his daughter always had a problem with using dryers. "I believe that she could shrink a human body if she could get it in that dryer." When a young listener called in to ask how to prepare for a career as a DJ, the jock said to practice by going hungry four days before pay day.

The country jocks will use the recording artists as a basis for their humor. One jock remarked that the female country star of the record he had just played, "really does some excellent album covers." After spinning a dolorous lost-lover type song, the jock said after the singer had his blood pressure checked, the doctor said, "Yep, he's alive." When a listener requested an Elvis Presley number the jock remarked, "Old Elvis shakes, rattles, and rolls so much he can't get 40,000 miles out of a pair of pants to save his life." A light banter is kept up much of the time by the jock who sings along with the ending of the record and makes remarks about the song lyrics. After playing a "woman stealer" type of record, the jock said, "I am no thief, but if I were to take it up as a profession, that would be a product I would go for."

The jocks occasionally try to get some laughs out of the commercials. After an "uncola" commercial, the jock called his program the "un-radio show." After a comic dramatized commercial on a hamburger fast food chain featuring onion rings, the jock said, "Yes, you fool, she loves the onion rings more than she does you. She's going out and have an onion ring with me tonight." Sometimes the jock will make fun of himself. For example, after a flub the jock said, "I've got lockjaw of the tongue."

Some of the country jocks' chatter is in praise of the recording artists. As the record ends complimentary remarks are heard such as: "Oh, what a great country song that is;" "She does fantastic singing;" "She's lovely, lovely, lovely;" "He ain't had a bad song yet;" "Great performer." In addition to praise, some station managers like a little gossip about the artists mentioned occasionally, and the jocks scan the usual trade journals for choice incidents in the artists' lives.

The lyrics of the story ballads or "saga songs" as they are sometimes called, are very sad and nostalgic. The jocks take these lugubrious lyrics pretty lightly. One jock after hearing a sad, philosophic lyric about the soul crying out in the stillness of the night said:

> You ever been sittin' around the house late at night and its nice and quiet and you were just dog tired and all of a sudden through the stillness your soul cries out for rest, that's ridiculous, I don't believe that, that's silly.

The jocks also promote country music. Two stations in a large market played promos for "Country Music Month" and mentioned that one of their jocks was attending the country music DJ convention. One jock added to the station ID, "Where all the great country music is," and "We brought country music to the metroplex ten years ago and we are glad we did." Phrases such as "Soft country stereo," "Your stereo country station," "Good country music" flavor many of the station breaks.

Some country station managers want the listeners to make a strong identification with the station, to feel that the station is theirs, and to enjoy some access to the station. For this reason the country jocks are asked to use the telephone extensively. Telephone calls from the listeners are featured and calls that are particularly humorous are recorded while the records are spinning and then played back after the records are finished. The jock is very friendly and intimate with the listeners and even calls some of the women "darlin' ". Request lines are used freely and jocks try to play any request that comes in. A warm, easy-going dialogue is maintained as revealed in this transcript:

Woman on telephone:	Hello, Jack.
Jock:	Hello there.
Woman:	How are you tonight?
Jock:	Well, I was checked out just before I came aboard. O.K. go on.
Woman:	I would like to hear "Paradise" by Len Anderson.
Jock:	"Paradise"?
Woman:	Uh, huh.
Jock:	Well, I will put it on for you.
Woman:	O.K., sure thank you.
Jock:	Thank you for listening, bye, bye.

- -

Woman:	Hello there, Jack.
Jock:	Hi.
Woman:	How you doin' tonight?
Jock:	Well, I seem to be O.K., how are you?
Woman:	Oh, I'm fine. I tried to get in touch with my favorite DJ.
Jock:	Did you?

Woman:	Yeah.
Jock:	Did Ken answer the phone?
Woman:	No, I'm talkin' about you.
Jock:	Oh, Oh, I see. O.K., now talk to me.
Woman:	O.K., I just wanted to get you to play me a song before I go to bed.
Jock:	Yeah, I'll be glad to.
Woman:	I picked out a real pretty one, for me and Howard.
Jock:	Well, I'll do it one more time.
Woman:	One more time, eh. I don't think you'll ever refuse me.
MUSIC:	UP
Jock:	I wouldn't dare.
Woman:	Just pick out a pretty love song.
Jock:	Thank you, dear. Bye, Bye.[5]

A one-to-one relationship with the listener is promoted by encouraging the jocks to make personal appearances. Some of the jocks have country bands and some write country songs. They appear at dancehalls and rodeos around the country making themselves more visible to the listeners. At WBAP, Fort Worth, the traveling country jocks are called the "Country Gold Gang," and they use some of their chatter time on the air to promote these trips:

Friday, Hal King will be at the Lewisville Danceland in Lewisville, Texas, and the next Tuesday, he will be appearing with Box Car Willie at the Silver Saddle in Grand Prairie, Texas.[6]

All in all the country jocks are a friendly group, knowledgeable about the music and the artists, certainly doing their part to promote country music by their chatter, the busy request line, and interviews with traveling country recording stars who are on junkets pushing their latest pressings. They have become a friendly voice in the night to many lonely people, and someone with whom to share the love, enthusiasm, and knowledge about country music. With their personal appearances at various rodeos, square dances, and concerts they have become a very visible part of the electronic community.

[5] KBOX, October 13, 1976.
[6] WBAP, Fort Worth, October 13, 1976.

APPEAL OF COUNTRY MUSIC

The growth in the number of country stations is due to the strong appeal of country music. It has the double appeal of telling a story to cast a nostalgic mood and doing so with great artistry in singing and playing. The dramatic quality of the singer's interpretation of the lyrics backed by skillful instrumentation and excellent recording techniques casts a strong spell. But! The lyrics are the heart of the song. According to one country operations manager, the country songs are like mini-soap operas, but are more effective because they are more true to life and less like caricatures than the soaps. The lyrics reflect what is happening in life and deal with deep emotional issues. Country music talks about common problems that appeal to a broad cross section of people— hard times, love, hate, war, and alcoholism. The problems are current. A song about a lonely rodeo cowboy, who is always traveling and working, appeals to the busy executive, sales representative, and policeman, because these people are too busy to really communicate with their families. The early cowboy songs were sad because of the lonely life of the cowboy. The current country songs are sad because of the lonely lives of the truck drivers, traveling salespeople, and manufacturers representatives.

As in the case of the soap opera, the country song lyrics are concerned with love and infidelity. The lyrics sing dolefully of lost lovers, cheating lovers, and lonely lovers. One station manager said that the songs deal with "sin and redemption." There seems to be a strong moral overtone, and those participating in infidelity seldom seem to be happy about it. There are frequent references to God, repentance, and helplessness in regard to a feeling of "sin" or doing someone wrong. The lyrics ask for forgiveness and a desire for "one more chance." Many songs reveal the despair of those who have strayed away from parents, wife, lover, and how the wanderer longs to return home to love and affection. These common problems and heartaches of life written in a language that people understand and communicated by excellent writers, musicians, arrangers, and recording technicians account for the strong popularity of country music. As one program manager said, "Country music is influenced by whatever is going in the media scene (television, motion pictures, radio, and theatre), and what is going on in the lives of people. As long as it reflects and responds to these current experiences, it will be popular."

Another reason for the popularity of country music is that it is well done. The singers have come up through a tough school, playing countless bars, high school gymnasiums, and small dance halls as they start out, learning to play several instruments and learning to play and sing all kinds of music. By the time they make it to Nashville, they have been thoroughly seasoned in their art. Once they become just a little bit known, they begin to play many local radio and television shows, and they drive hundreds of miles appearing in many exhausting one-night stands. This constant exposure helps to professionalize their art and give them a first-hand knowledge of their fans, and with this comes the awareness of how to please these fans.

Country music has been helped by the establishment of the country music business in Nashville. Nashville has attracted talented side-men, efficient recording engineers, and bustling publishing houses which serve as an active support system to nourish the country music stars. The "Grand Old Opry," as an active country memorial institution, keeps country music on the airways and before hundreds and thousands of people who drive there each year to see and hear it all first-hand. Both the new country artists and the old timers perform on the "Opry." Whether it is a tourist attraction for those who are only vaguely interested, or a shrine for those who are ardent fans, Nashville has certainly contributed to the popularity of country music. The continuous broadcasts of the "Opry" on WSM since 1925, and the swarm of country DJs that filter in and out of Nashville feed the professional interest and knowledge of country radio for local stations throughout the country.

SCHEDULING

Since country stations appeal roughly to ages 25 to 64, they seldom daypart, except for tempo. They play the same music for the 24-hour period. During drive-time they will program more news, and there may be more bright chatter in the morning drive-time and perhaps more topical conversation than in the evening. Because of the increase in the woman work force, some urban country stations use news and conversation program items designed for working and professional women during drive-time. The music, however, is much the same for the 24-hour period.

A station manager said that consistency in country music programming was very important, and that listeners have the right to expect the same kind of music whatever time they tune in, morning or midnight. The reason for this is that country stations are adult oriented and do not have to change their programming (as rock stations do) to meet the habits and school schedules of young children and teenagers.

FULL-SERVICE COUNTRY

The managers of country radio intend for their stations to be full service radio stations and not just music stations. Music will be a strong entertainment factor and will carry the country image, but news, weather, and public service programs which involve the listener are important contributions to the format. One manager said he didn't believe that people listened to his station just for the music. He believes, for example, that weather forecasts are considered to be a very important staple of programming, a high interest item, and a basic service. As one station manager put it, "Weather has an appeal that nothing else has." He added that the rating service he subscribed to backed his opinion about weather. Another station manager said that he wanted his weathercasters to be highly identifiable people with strong air personalities. WBAP, Fort Worth, has had the same weather man, Harold Taft, for many years, and he is very popular with the listeners. WBAP does two full weathercasts each hour in the evenings with weatherman Harold Taft on cart followed by a live tag from the DJ with the temperature. KBOX gives four full weathercasts each hour in the evenings.

NEWS

News is stressed as an important part of the country station's programming fare, and the station managers have no wish for the country station to become a lost music land as was the case with some FM programmers, where news was virtually ignored. Don Thompson, Operations Manager, WBAP, emphasizes the value of the long-time affiliation with NBC News as an important plus for the station's service image and a big draw for listeners. As one WBAP jock said preceding a newscast, "There is so much going on in the news, don't go away."

KBOX has six news staffers and they try to stay on top of vital news events, endeavoring to anticipate when something is getting ready to break and staying with the events to keep the listener up to date. KBOX features five-minute newscasts on the hour and then in the morning and afternoon drive-time, the station programs news on the half-hour. Headlines are broadcast on the half-hour on Saturdays. From 9:00 p.m. to 10:00 p.m., KBOX has four newscasts; a sportscast, a newscast (national and state news), and a newscast with local, international, national news, sports, and weather.

PUBLIC SERVICE

KBOX stresses public service as an essential part of the concept of the country station being a full service radio station. The public service involvement has a three-part plan: (1) campaigns, (2) special projects, and (3) continuing programs. The campaigns are developed from the station's Community Relations Council which is made up of representatives from city, county, police, church, federal, private, and non-profit organizations. An example of a campaign is the "Stay in School Campaign" which was directed at potential school drop-outs and spots were aired urging students to stay in school.

Special projects generally take the form of benefits organized by the station to help out a particular group or individual. KBOX sponsored a trout fish-ing tank at a boat show to benefit the Muscular Dystrophy Association, and co-sponsored a donkey baseball game to benefit a family whose home had been destroyed by a tornado.

Continuing programs are those ongoing programs which last a year or more. Examples of these programs are the assistance given to the National Organization of Women (NOW) to create the Rape Crisis Center, and production of continuing weekly program series such as "Behind the Wall" (an analysis of the problems of rehabilitating prison inmates), "Consumer Alert" (an educational program for consumers), "Youth and Their Community" (a radio forum for highschool students), "Black History" (a history of blacks in America), "Amigo Forum" (presentation of self-help programs for the minority community), and the "Feminist View" (an exploration of the obstacles confronting women in today's society).

WSM, Nashville, uses on-the-air spots to raise money to buy presents for foster children during the Christmas season. The management saves part of the Christmas money for a picnic for foster children in July, when most people have forgotten about this needy group. WSM promotes events like "Holiday on Ice" and gives one-half of the proceeds to charity.

WBAP's public service philosophy is to program PSAs that are locally produced. They try to determine the needs of the community and then produce spots that communicate these needs. They believe an awareness of the community problems and the use of skilled communicators to express the needs is the best approach. A frequently programmed PSA is the "WBAP Date Book" which tells of events in the community such as a high school reunion. Other public service programming features remotes dealing with problems in the Indian community, a campaign to build a Four-H Club Center, and PSAs concerning the YMCA basketball program for children.

PROMOTIONS

KBOX uses a free country music show at the Cotton Bowl to keep the station's image before the fans. The show runs for seven hours and features country stars. KBOX management says the event serves as a gesture of appreciation to the listeners. Preserving the country image, KBOX joins with the City of Mesquite, Texas, to present the All-American Youth Rodeo. The KBOX jocks are on hand to make awards to the winners. An annual event is the KBOX Country Fair, an attempt to revive the old time country fair where artists and craftsmen gather to sell their wares, and people congregate from miles around to visit with old friends, purchase merchandise, and be entertained by the musicians. KBOX management presents some country recording stars and invites merchants to put up booths and exhibit their products. On one day, in spite of cold rainy weather, a crowd of 30,000 attended and 30 merchants had exhibitions.

WBAP gets promotional help from their disc jockeys. Three of the jocks have country bands and play and sing. They travel about the region and keep the call letters before the eyes and ears of the fans. Two of the jocks are writers of country music which brings some prestige and the true country stamp to the station. Both KBOX and WBAP employ the usual media—television, billboards, newspapers, radio, mail-outs, and contests for promotional purposes. The billboards are generally huge portraits of on-the-air talent. An example of a promotional contest is the "Guadalajara Weekend," used by KBOX. The prize is a free weekend in Guadalajara and the hurdle is to identify the Guadalajara song of the hour.

STATION ORGANIZATION

There are five departments in the country station: operations, sales, office, news, and engineering. The chief administrative officer is the general manager. The operations manager, sales manager, and office manager report directly to the general manager. The operations manager (a term which seems to be replacing the title of program manager) is in charge of everything that goes on the air, so that the news director, chief engineer and the DJs are under the operations manager's jurisdiction. The operations manager also oversees music. The office manager is in charge of the secretarial and clerical personnel. The sales department may be divided into local and national operations, and in this case there will be a national sales manager and a local sales manager. The general manager and the sales manager do promotion concerned with marketing projects related to products and sponsors. The operations manager handles promotion when it pertains to music, the scheduling of promotional spots, and the nature of the spots produced and those voiced live by the DJs. Corporations which own both AM and FM outlets will have an FM manager and/or an FM operations manager, and these officers will be on line with their counterparts in AM, under the general manager.

THE FUTURE OF COUNTRY MUSIC

The future of country radio looks bright. The National Association of Broadcasting's "Future of Radio Study" states that the largest population growth in 1985 will be in the South Atlantic region.[7] This is fertile country radio territory. Because of this growth in population, the region will have the greatest increase in radio revenues. The U.S. Census Bureau reports a shift in population to the rural areas.[8] When the city folks move to the country they

[7]*Broadcasting,* April 4, 1977, p. 45.
[8]*The Dallas Morning News,* April 14, 1977, p. 4D.

will be innoculated with the country music bug, since that's what they will be hearing on the rural radio stations. This happened in World War II, when the recruits from the north were sent to the training camps in the south and they became fans of the country music they heard there.

> The Opry was on every radio in every barracks, and there wasn't any way these kids from New York and New Jersey could get away from it. It had to rub off on 'em.[9]

Technological advances will contribute to the popularity of radio in 1985. FM quadraphonics and AM stereo will stimulate the public's desire for the audio medium, especially music programming. There will be pressure to increase the number of radio stations and an expansion of the AM band and additions to the FM channels are predicted. The number of clear channel stations may be augmented. Among these new stations there will be many country stations to serve the ever growing rural audience with that good old country sound. It may be streamlined, perhaps, influenced by the varying currents of contemporary melodies, but still speaking to folks' problems in an appealing way that large segments of the population will relate to.

Transcripts

The following transcripts illustrate the mix and flow technique of KBOX and WBAP. Try to imagine a country jock who is trying to entertain and inform his listeners.

```
KBOX - C&W

DJ - JACK WESTON (JW)

NEWS - KEN DAVIDSON (KD)

KD:     Station Promo. Fanfare with old fashioned big voiced announcer.

        "Today's country is on K-Box." Women's trio jingle "KBOX."

        Announcer: "And Jack Weston does it all for you." Trio: "Dallas

        and the great southwest." Segue into "I Love You."

MUSIC:  "I Love You." Bill Anderson.

JW:     (Cuts record out) This space is for rent right here. (Record back

        up and under) I don't like to see anything wasted. Oh, I love you.

        Bill Anderson on the Jack Weston Show. KBOX in Big D. 1480 Radio.
```

[9] Paul Hemphill, *The Nashville Sound: Bright Lights and Country Music* (New York: Simon and Schuster, 1970, p. 151.)

Country Music 24 hours a day. 9:03 on a Wednesday night, we thank
you for joining us. Here's Bobby Lewis.

MUSIC: "I Would Do Anything." Bobby Lewis. Under for:

JW: For your love I would do most anything. Except sell my soul.

MUSIC: Out.

JW: Now for my love I'd sell your soul. (Chuckles) But that's a dif-
         ferent story. Bobby Lewis in a new version of an old song at 9:06,
         on the Jack Weston Show from KBOX. Hello.

MUSIC: "Hello."

SOUND: (FILTER MIKE) (WOMAN'S VOICE) Jack Weston does it all for you.
         Segue into Woman trio: "KBOX" ID.

JW: Eight minutes after nine o'clock, on the box in Big D. If you got
         a chance to hear Ken Knox on his show, I hope you did, he had his
         special feature on Elvis Presley. The thing he didn't tell about
         old Elvis though is that old Elvis shakes, rattles and rolls too
         much. He can't get 40,000 miles out of a pair of pants to save his
         life. MUSIC UP ON LAST THREE WORDS.

MUSIC: "Nights Are Getting Colder."

JW: (MUSIC UNDER) You ever been sittin' around the house late at night
         and its nice and quiet and you were just dog tired and all of a
         sudden through the stillness your soul cries out for rest, that's
         ridiculous, I don't believe that, that's silly.

MUSIC: UP AND UNDER FOR:

SOUND: Woman's voice on telephone or filter mike. Hello, Jack. JW: Hello
         there. Woman: How are you tonight? JW: Well, I was checked out
         just before I came aboard, OK, go on. Woman: I would like to hear
         "Paradise" by Lynn Anderson. JW: "Paradise." Woman: Uh, Huh.
         JW: Well, I will put it on for ya. Woman: OK, sure thank you.
         JW: Thank you for listening, bye, bye.

MUSIC: "Paradise."

JW: "Paradise," Lynn Anderson. She's Lovely, Lovely, Lovely, nine fourteen, on the Jack Weston Show, KBOX in Dallas, where all the great country music is, we're around until twelve midnight tonight. I hope you get the opportunity to stay with us. It's another lovely day in Dallas for a Wednesday, you could not ask for better, and for the next couple of days, well here's what they say. Partly cloudy t-h-r-o-u-g-h the night time some cloudiness and coolness tomorrow with a twenty percent chance of rain tomorrow night. Chance of rain is slipping closer for the weekend. Either a weekend coming up quickly or me washing my car. Those are two sure ways to get rain in a forecast. Low tonight and tomorrow night near 58 degrees, tomorrow's high 78, on Friday it goes up to 75, we'll have light and variable winds turning southerly at 10 to 15 miles per hour, too-morrow night. Excuse me. I got lockjaw of the tongue. Clear and 72 out at DFW Airport, at our studios near White Rock it's 68. A volunteer who knows photography and film development is needed at the West Dallas Center. There are many needs for many people in our area. Call the Dallas Voluntary Action Center and find out where exactly you may fit in to their all-so-important program. The **New York Yankees and Kansas City Royals** are all locked up in the American Baseball League playoff, and they'll uh make that final decision come tomorrow night. And uh Cincinnatti Reds for second year in a row, have captured the National League pennant. So the series this year will either be Cincinnatti and the Yankees or Cincinnatti and Kansas City. We shall soon know!

SOUND: Drum beat and music roar under Announcer: Imagine spending Thanksgiving weekend in Guadalajara. SFX: cymbal crash and drum beat. Announcer: Six lucky KBOX couples will win. Prize includes airfare for two via Mexicana Airlines, two days and three nights furnished by the beautiful El Tapadeo, a princess hotel resort and $200.00 spending money, plus there'll be cash prizes every day during the contest. Here's what to do. Fill out and mail a newspaper coupon or send a postcard with your name, address and phone number to Guadalajara Weekend, KBOX, Dallas 75238. Then be listening for the Guadalajara song of the hour. Once an hour from eight a.m. to eight p.m. starting Monday, October 25th we'll draw an entry and place a call. If we call you, and you know the title of the Guadalajara song of the hour, you'll win the cash jackpot for that hour, and become eligible for the grand prize drawing for the six Guadalajara weekends. Hourly cash jackpots are for $14.80 and increases by $14.80 each hour until there's a winner. All entries must be in our hands by 12 midnight, November 12th. Contest ends November 14th. Grand prize drawing will be November 17th. We'll see you in Guadalajara.

JW: (Singing) Guadalajara, Ole! Da! Da! (Laughs) Don't forget to see tonight's Dallas Times Herald because the KBOX coupon is in it. People call us every once in a while or see us out at the State Fair in a Dart Toss booth and they say, Weston, how do you guys do it? Anytime anybody asks you for something on the telephone you always, always seem to have an answer. Well, my **friends**, that's not always true. Sometimes things (Laughs) work out like this:

SOUND: RECORDING TELEPHONE: WOMAN'S VOICE: Hi, Jack, could you play my song? JW: By what, by who? Laughs. Woman: You heard me. JW: What's a trog? (PAUSE) Woman: J-a-c-k. JW: That sounds like, that sounds like a frog (laughing) that's got problems. A trog. What is a trog? Woman: Well, its a group. JW: Oh, well I don....that must not be country music. Like I've heard it before. Woman: Oh, really. JW: I don't know, I've never heard of a trog. But it doesn't sound that way. How bout some **thin' else.**Woman: Oh, well, I'll have to think about it. JW: OK. Woman: OK. JW: Well, call me again. Woman: Allright. JW: Bye, bye. MUSIC: UP. JW: See, you can't win 'em all.

SOUND: KBOX JINGLE ID.

JW: (OVER MUSIC OF ID) I don't think I even tied that one.

SOUND: ID OUT AND SEGUE INTO:

MUSIC: "Good Woman Blues."

JW: (Coming in over music) The Weston show at K-Box, hello.

WOMAN: (PHONE) Yes, could you play "Kentucky Rain."

JW: "Kentucky Rain" by Elvis.

WOMAN: "Uh, huh."

JW: You didn't get enough of Elvis on the Ken Knox show, huh?

WOMAN: No, I never get enough of Elvis.

JW: Laughs. Well, I tell you what, we'll send him right over. How'll that be?

MUSIC: UP.

WOMAN: Oh, Good, Thank you.

JW: LAUGHS.   Ok.

WOMAN: Uh, huh.

JW: Well, bye, bye, now.

MUSIC: UP

JW: You can get service on this program. You can get service on this program.

MUSIC: UP. "Kentucky Rain" Presley.

SOUND: (OVER "KENTUCKY RAIN") (SLIGHT ECHO EFFECT) Howdy Folks, howdy. This is Big Tex. The biggest voice in the world with the biggest welcome, from Big D, Dallas, Texas, home of the biggest and best fair in the world, the State Fair of Texas.

SOUND: Jingle ID.

SOUND: MUSIC UNDER ANNOUNCER WHO GIVES PITCH FOR KBOX DART TOSS BOOTH WITH PROCEEDS GOING FOR MS. ALSO PITCH FOR STATE FAIR. (CART). COUNTRY MUSIC THROUGHOUT.

SOUND: Jingle ID.

SOUND: Sounder intro's Ken Davidson with KBOX News.

    1. President Ford story and Jimmy Carter story.

    2. Texas Legislature and Narcotics Act. Controlled Substances Act.

    3. Michael Wayne Moore Sentence.

    4. Spying on University of Texas Football Team Practice.

    5. Temperature.

SOUND: Sounder introduces ABC Entertainment Radio. "News In Brief."

    1. President Ford and Swine Flu Story.

    2. Watergate - Ford Story.

    3. Loan Rates on Feed and Grain Rates increased.

SOUND: Jingle promo for Country Music Month.

MUSIC: "Her Name is Boing."

JW: The Weston Show at the Box in Big D, Good evening.

WOMAN: (call in) Hello, Jack.

JW: Hello.

WOMAN: How are you tonight?

JW: Well, they say OK.

WOMAN: Well, that's good

JW: I was checked out thoroughly.

WOMAN: Well, that's good.

JW: Chuckles.

WOMAN: Would you play "Strangers" for me by Johnny Duncan?

JW: (friendly voice) I don't see why not.

WOMAN: You're awful sweet.

JW: (CHUCKLES) Okay, thanks for callin'. Bye, Bye.

SOUND: MUSIC: UNDER: KBOX constantly strives to render the very finest in
    programming and public service. Your suggestions will be given
    consideration by writing to General Manager, KBOX, Dallas, 75238.

MUSIC: "Stranger" Johnny Duncan.

JW: (CUTTING IN OVER RECORD) I like to see a girl who's energy conscious,
    don't you? Johnny Duncan and "Stranger." That's a gal by the name
    of Janey Frick that sings with him on that song. (MUSIC OUT) It's
    nine thirty four with country music month rolling on through Dallas
    the month of October and this of course is KBOX (MUSIC UP) the station

that brought country music to the metroplex nearly 10 years ago.
We're glad we did.

MUSIC: "Drop Kick Me Jesus Through the Goal Posts of Life."

JW: The Weston Show at K-Box, hello there.

WOMAN: (ON PHONE) Hello there, Jack.

JW: Hi.

WOMAN: How you doin' tonight?

JW: Well, I seem to be OK. How are you?

WOMAN: Oh, I'm fine. I tried to get in touch with my favorite DJ.

JW: Did you?

WOMAN: Yeah.

JW: Did Ken answer the phone?

WOMAN: No, I'm talkin' about you.

JW: Oh, Oh, I see. OK, now talk to me.

WOMAN: OK., I just wanted to get you to play me a song before I go to bed.

JW: Yeah, I'll be glad to.

WOMAN: I picked out a real pretty one, for me and Howard.

JW: Well, I'll do it one more time.

WOMAN: One more time, eh., I don't think you'll ever refuse me.

MUSIC: UP.

JW: I wouldn't dare.

WOMAN: Just pick me out a pretty love song.

JW: Thank you, dear, bye, bye.

MUSIC: "Help Me Make it Through the Night." Sammy Smith.

JW: (CUTTING IN OVER RECORD) Sammy Smith in a song called....

MUSIC: (SAMMY SINGS THESE WORDS GIVING THE TITLE) "Help me make it through the night."

JW: (OVER MUSIC RECITES WORDS) I took the ribbon from her hair, I let it fall, and it was Rene Richards, my gosh.

MUSIC: UP.

JW: (OVER MUSIC) What kind of deal is this!

MUSIC: "Woman Stealer" Johnny Carver.

JW: (OVER MUSIC) "Woman Stealer." Tell you what, I am no thief but if
I were to take it up as a profession that would be a product I would
go for. Johnny Carver from his album "Afternoon Delight," "Woman
Stealer" on the Weston Show. Eighteen minutes away from ten at K-box
right now. Linda Ronstadt has a song that goes like this.

MUSIC: UP. "That'll Be the Day."

JW: (OVER MUSIC) Linda Ronstadt on K-Box, she does fantastic singing, and
also (LAUGHS) does some really excellent album covers, as witness
to her last one if you have seen it. 16 minutes away from ten on the
Box in Big D, Jack Weston Show, on your radio, good to have you along,
late on Wednesday night. We're wrapping up the 12th thing, no 13th,
no wonder I'm behind, I lost a full day in there rapping up the
13th day of, of October and heading toward the Ken Knox show, he'll
be in at 12 tonight.
(JW SEGUES RIGHT INTO READING A PSA) Generals and politicians take
their lumps alike in a Theatre Three Satire "The Road to Rome," and
the front production makes for a great evening out. Call 748-5191
for reservations and show times. (JW SEGUES INTO READING WEATHER FORE-
CAST) Well, the weather for Dallas partly through the night, increasing clouds and we'll have cooler temperature and a 20% chance there'll
be some rain tomorrow night, low in the morning 58 degrees. High
about 78 and then on Friday its going to get up to about 75, for the
high, light variable wind in the forecast changing to southerly at
10 to 15 miles per hour, tomorrow night. In Dallas the sky is clear,
at the airport 72 degrees, at our studios near White Rock it's 67.
Takes me a while to find it. Every night when I come in they put
the thermometer around here in a brand new place I have to scan around
the room. It's kind of handy though, that's one way to find some
things we've lost. You have to look for the thermometer, you run
across two or three things that you haven't seen around here for

awhile cause they've been shuffled around and they're put underneath or behind something and they get kind of lost you know when they get kinda shoved out of the way, so when you are searching out the thermometer every night, you know, you uncover a lot of those things that have been missing. Jist about fifteen minutes ago, I found two old secretaries.

COMMERCIAL: Kraft Caramel Apples voiced by woman with country music under.

COMMERCIAL: Seven Up.

MUSIC: Jingle ID.

MUSIC: Under.

JW: Thirteen away from 10 now, this is Jack Weston with the Un-radio program (he is making a gag from the preceding Seven Up Uncola commercial) late at night, here's Don Williams, his brand new one called "She Never Even Knew Me," it's a good one too, listen.

MUSIC: "She Never Even Knew Me," Don Williams.

JW: (OVER MUSIC) Ten minutes away from ten on K-Box. Don Williams, his brand new one, "She Never Even Knew Me". If you've ever seen Don perform before you know what a great entertainer he is, and he really is. I don't mean anything about Don, Don scarcely gets a whole lot excited, he's kinda cool, calm, and really together fella, really with his feet on the ground. He is, he is calm. When they check old Don's blood pressure, they come back and give him a reading and say, "Yep, he's alive."

MUSIC: "Summertime Blues"

JW: (OVER MUSIC SINGING ALONG WITH THE RECORD) Ain't no cure. They start giving swine flu shots again, there's a possibility. "Summer Time Blues" Joan Libby and **Olivia Newton-John** on the Weston Show, it's eight away from ten in Big D on a Wednesday night. Lovely young girl called me just a while ago, who is about to graduate from Sky Line High School, this year, and she is quite seriously thinking about getting into the radio disc jockey business, and going to East Texas State

University in Commerce, and majoring in that. She called me a while
ago and wanted to know what is the most important thing to do to train
yourself for being a disc jockey, and of course, I was able to tell
her that right off the bat. What you really need to do to get in
practice for this profession is...is going hungry about four days
preceding pay day.

MUSIC: UP.

JW: That'll get you right in shape for this business. Here are the Statler
         Brothers in their newest.

MUSIC: UP. "I Thank God I've Got You."

SOUND: JINGLE ID.

SOUND: Sounder intros KBOX News at 9:55 p.m.

         1. Weather

         2. Armed Bandits Story

         3. YMCA Debates on Prostitution Story

         4. National Legal Secretaries Week

         5. Plane crash in Bolivia

         6. Boston trial of anti-war activist, Susan Sachs
             (Voicer)

         7. One liner sports: Royals and Yankees. Score. Playoffs.

COMMERCIAL: Salvage Carpets.

         8. Weather Forecast

SOUND: Jingle ID

MUSIC: "Suspicion."

WBAP - C&W

DJ - HAL KING (HK)

SOUND: Jingle ID.

MUSIC: "Fire at First Sight" Linda Hargrove.

HK: There's a gold nugget here from Linda Hargrove and there's "Fire
         at First Sight." Eight minutes after eight o'clock as we resume
         business here on the Hal King Show. Wanta' say good evening to

"Sweet Thing" who's listenin' this evening, by the way congratula-
tions on your forthcoming wedding.

MUSIC: UP. "She's Living It Up Now" Freddy Fender.

HK: Freddy Fender, "She's Living It Up Now" and I'm living it down,
twenty minutes after eight o'clock, seventy four degrees in the metroplex.

SOUND: COWBELL.

HK: You got the Hal King show here from WBAP 820 celebrating Country Music
Month which is October. By the way Bill Mack's gonna head up to
Nashville Friday and spend a couple of days at the country music
DJ Convention and once in a while Bill's going to be callin' in and
givin' us a report on what he's seeing and what he has been doing.
(CHUCKLES)...all right, and Oh, that's uh there at the country music
capitol, you be sure to be listenin', all right. Oh well, just a
little humor injected there. Well if you're hungry, Roger & Leslie
for Jack in the Box restaurant.

COMMERCIAL: DRAMATIZED. COMIC. ENGLISH ACCENT. CART.

HK: Yes you fool, she loves the onion rings (IMITATING ENGLISH ACCENT)
more than she does you. She's going out and have an onion ring with
me tonight. (LAUGHS)

COMMERCIAL: JINGLE ARMOUR HOT DOGS. KIDDY CHORUS.

HK: Well, a young man here from Athens, Texas.

MUSIC: UP.

HK: Here's Tony Douglas to sing about that rodeo cowboy from Sweetwater,
Texas.

MUSIC: "He's a Rodeo Cowboy from Sweetwater Texas."

HK: Thank you, Tony, Tony Douglas, sixteen minutes after eight o'clock,
here on the Hal King Show, WBAP, 820.

COMMERCIAL: (INTERRUPS ABRUPTLY) Horse Sale. Announced by sponsor. Texas
accent.

COMMERCIAL: JINGLE G.E. WASHERS AT BRUMBAUGH.

HK: Well I think one of those dryers would be just the thing we need
           around our house. My daughter Toby does the laundry...and washin'
           she has no problem with, but she's got this thing about dryers. I
           believe that she could shrink a human body if she could get it in
           that dryer.

SOUND: JINGLE ID. SAYS "GOLD NUGGET" AT END.

MUSIC: UP.

HK: Good old you know who is back in town.

MUSIC: "Good Old You Know Who." TO FINISH.

HK: Lester Flatt and the Nashville Grass at twenty minutes after eight
           o'clock, and there's "Good Old You Know Who." Let's check the weather
           here with good old you know who.

WEATHER MAN: Weather forecast. CART SAYS AT TAG: "Hal will you read the
           current temperature, please."

HK: (AT A LOSS) Well, wait a minute, (CLEARS THROAT) Twenty minutes
           after eight o'clock, here Harold, and the wind, and the winds are
           out of the Southeast. Just about, maybe one mile an hour. The
           temperature now is 71-72 degrees, and that's all the weather now
           from Harold Taft at the WBAP weather center.

COMMERCIAL: JINGLE. EDISON'S CATALOGUE. AND STRAIGHT PITCH.

MUSIC: UP.

HK: Well, here's Vernon Oxford, "Clear Off Your Own Tables, Boys, Go
           Fetch Your Own Beer."

MUSIC: "Clean Your Own Tables, Boys" Vernon Oxford

HK: (OVER ENDING BARS) There's Vernon Oxford, clean your own tables
           boys, I tell you what, I don't think that Vernon's had a bad song
           yet. I think that's about the fourth song that he's had so far this
           year that's really done great things and uh, Old Vernon, he ain't
           had a bad song yet. 8:25 and 71 degrees. And the Hal King Show
           from WBAP 820, all Texas radio.

COMMERCIAL: Longhorn Ranch Wear.

COMMERCIAL: PSA YMCA.

HK: (ANSWERING PSA) Well he's big enough there sonny.

MUSIC: UP.

HK: Here's Red Stegall.

MUSIC: UP. "Rosie Do You Want to Talk It Over."

HK: (OVER LAST BARS) That's the number eight song from the WBAP Gold Rush Gazette. "Rosie Don't you Wanta Talk it Over." There's Red Stegall and the Coleman County Cowboys. You're listening to the Hal King Show from WBAP 820 where we've got about twenty-nine, thirty minutes after eight o'clock, in fact it is 8:30. Wanta' remind you that C. W. McCall will be with us tonight at 10:30 talkin' about C. B.

MUSIC: UP.

HK: Here's Ann Murray now, she's going to sing about some things here. Don't be scared there dear, just step right up to the microphone, that's it.

MUSIC: "Things."

HK: (OVER LAST BARS) Oh, yes. That's Ann Murray at thirty-three minutes after eight o'clock on the Hal King Show from WBAP and it's Gold Nugget time right now, Teddy and Doyle of the Wilburn Brothers, "Oh Look What She Did to the Little Roadside Tavern."

MUSIC: "She Burned the Little Roadside Tavern Down."

HK: Gold nugget there from Teddy and Doyle of the Wilburn brothers, "She Burned the Little Roadside Tavern Down," WBAP time now is twenty-five minutes before nine o'clock.

COMMERCIAL: Ranch Style Chili. Announcer with country western music under. Live tag about coupon in newspaper.

SOUND: CHEERS AND APPLAUSE.

 Thank you and we are really glad to be with all of you, and thanks for that applause and we're going to get things underway here with Brother Joe Anders this time singing a little song. We're gonna probably surprise you. We're gonna sing a brand new one called

"Ida Red," Yes-suh.

MUSIC: "Ida Red." (this has a real old fiddler sound) Bob Wills and his

Texas Playboys.

HK: There's the late Bob Wills and "Ida Red"...Twenty-one minutes now

before nine o'clock, and here's Charley Pride with a whole lot of

things to sing about...be happy.

MUSIC: "I Gotta Whole Lotta Things to Sing About."

HK: Yes-suh. Charley Pride, everybody, nineteen before nine, now.

COMMERCIAL: Transeason Oil.

HK: Well, we've got a gang of requests for this song here...just gonna

play it right now for you. It's the number six song from the WBAP

Gold Rush Gazette, here's Loretta Lynn "Somebody Somewhere Don't Know

What He's Missin' Tonight."

MUSIC: "Somebody Somewhere Don't Know What He's Missin' Tonight."

HK: (OVER LAST BARS) Oh, what a great country song that is, "Somebody

Somewhere Don't Know What He's Missin' Tonight." There's Loretta

Lynn. It's exactly fifteen minutes before nine o'clock.

COMMERCIAL: Mr. Transmission. Announcer with CW music under.

Plus jingle at end.

MUSIC: UP.

HK: A gold nugget now from the late **Lefty Frizell,** "I Never Go Around

Mirrors Because I Can't Stand to See A Grown Man Cry."

MUSIC: "Grown Man Cry."

HK: (OVER LAST BARS) I never go around mirrors because I can't stand to

see a grown man cry. Gold nugget here from the late **Lefty Frizell.**

Twelve minutes now before nine o'clock on the Hal King Show from

WBAP 820 all Texas radio.

COMMERCIAL: "Marathon Man." Recorded with Live Tag.

MUSIC: UP.

HK: Connie Smith, "I Just Don't Want to Talk It Over Any More."

MUSIC: "I Just Don't Want to Talk It Over Any More" Connie Smith.

HK: (OVER LAST BARS) Connie Smith, and "I Just Don't Want to Talk It Over Any More." Well to find out what is going to happen weather-wise here's Harold Taft.

SOUND: Harold Taft Weathercast. Ends by saying: And what is it (the tempera-ture) right now? You can see the thermometer.

HK: Yes I can, at this time of night, I'm still able to see that far, Harold (chuckles) 71 degrees in the metroplex and winds comin' out of the southeast at about zero miles an hour.

COMMERCIAL: Six Flags.

HK: Here's Johnny Russell.

MUSIC: "She's In Love With a Rodeo Man."

HK: (OVER LAST BARS) Johnny Russell, she won't go home with you cowboy because she's in love with a rodeo man.

SOUND: WBAP Date Book: Item: High School Reunion.

SOUND: Promos about appearances of WBAP Jocks. Announcer with country western music under. Called "WBAP Country Gold Gang."

HK: (OVER MUSIC) Thank you Tom Casey. Also add a footnote on that on Friday Hal King will be at the Lewisville Danceland in Lewisville, Texas, and the next Tuesday he will be appearing with Box Car Willie at the Silver Saddle in Grand Prairie, Texas.

MUSIC: UP.

HK: Here's John R. Cash and the Tennessee Three.

MUSIC: "It's All Over."

HK: (OVER LAST BARS) Johnny Cash and "It's All Over" and that's the latest from Johnny Cash and the Tennessee Three. We've got about a minute and a half here before news time at nine o'clock. At nine 0 five, of course, the Hal King Show resumes musically but there's so much goin' on in the news don't go anywhere. Just be sure and stick around there and get yourself some education.

MUSIC: UP. FIDDLE MUSIC.

5

Black Ethnic Formats

(*Soul, Rhythm and Blues, Disco*)

Daddy-O, Mommy-O, this is Jocko, engineer aboard the big Rocket Ship Show, the fastest moving show on the radio, saying greetings, salutations, oo-poo-pa-doo and how do you do . . .

> "Jocko" (Douglas Henderson) on WADO, New York. (10:00 p.m.) and WDAS, Philadelphia (5:00 p.m.), 1960.

If you want to hear a fast-talking DJ personality like "Jocko" just listen—at a discotheque—not on today's soul radio station. On most Black stations "personality" has been replaced by formats which leave little time for improvisation. The DJ takes a back seat to a total station sound. Play lists are tight, music is "controlled," and even commercials are "programmed."

The more than 250 stations that have a "Black" format program any combination of Top 40 rhythm and blues, soul, gospel and jazz music, news of interest to the Black community, talk, and consumer information. They have in common the desire to reach the largest share of the 20 million Black listeners and non-Blacks who are attracted to their sound. It is not difficult to recognize a Black station while scanning the radio dial. One hears Blacks speaking to Blacks. One hears infrequently the "jive talk," clichés, hard-sell commercials for major appliances "on easy credit terms," and the incessant appeal to buy a particular record or product which were almost universally characteristic of Black radio stations until the '70s.

126

DISCO

Nat Jackson, program director of KNOK, Fort Worth, believes the pendulum has swung about as far as it can go. "We de-emphasize personality. We have made our sound more listenable. We have found that our listeners get turned off by a lot of talk, so we have cut back on our commercial loads." KNOK serves Fort Worth, Dallas and the "Metroplex" with daytime—only AM and 24-hour FM stereo stations. They simulcast a "DISC-OK" format with the exception of a gospel program heard at the noon hour when the AM splits from FM. "We aim for the sophisticated-type listener. We are not super-Black. We will play something that will appeal to everybody, Black, White, Mexican-American," says Jackson. "KNOK plays mostly music by Black artists with some cross-over records by artists like Leo Sayre and Rod Stewart. I don't discriminate with our music per se. You've got to go at it with an open mind. You have hecklers out there that call and say 'get that White music off!' They don't understand broadcasting from the side that the professional does."

Twenty percent of KNOK's programming is jazz, about 5% is news, talk, and public affairs and the remainder is disco-type music. According to the program director, KNOK is 95% on top of all the R & B hits. "Timing is very important with many different records. Sometimes you can jump on a record too fast and just when you are tired of playing it yourself it is just beginning to break in the market." Jackson believes that "an individual programmer or music director who is really hip and on top of the music, is a true music lover, and has a good music ear, can listen to a record and decide if it is 'in the groove.' If it's a hit, it's there. We stay away from records that are really hyped." Jackson listens to his request line very attentively, follows up to see why a record was requested, listens to it, and sees if it fits the format. About half of the music on KNOK is from albums. "You really have to look at your day parts and what type of audience you're trying to hold at that particular time," says Jackson. "One must consider all of the potential listening groups, teens, 18–34, and the older set. One must consider when each group might be listening." He prefers more disco sound and a lot of up-tempo. Most of the actual selections are made by a music director. Once the basic play list is set announcers do not stray from it. They can pick from three different categories as long as they keep a particular flow going at all times.

There are six announcers (two women) who generally work five-hour shifts, six days a week. They follow a format clock which varies, along with the announcer's style, with the time of day. KNOK plays three records and then "back announces." It attempts to keep its commercials down to about 12 minutes per hour, usually in stop sets of three minutes.

Nat Jackson feels a need to educate the listener and to use the best English on the radio. He feels that the education of children today will be reflected in their character and listening habits five years from now. "You can't just shoot 'em a bunch of jive and pop your fingers."

KNOK has three 10-minute news blocks in the morning, consisting mostly of local stories and current features because it is felt that most people get their national news from television. In the morning and afternoon a male-female approach is used with both announcers live. Listeners have written that they enjoy KNOK's newscasts. Jackson remarks, "the big introduction into the news is really the form of yesterday. Today just sneak right into the news. This keeps the listener tuned longer." KNOK subscribes to the National Black Network which provides news and public service material, most of it aired on Sunday. Reaction to an Ossie Davis-Ruby Dee story hour has been so favorable that the station plans to run similar programs.

KNOK runs pre-recorded public service announcements which are aired at night. Live PSAs are read over records during the day, to give the announcer something topical to talk about. The station regularly airs recorded announcements of community events phoned in by listeners. Agencies supply Black stations with "soul-versions" of commercials with Black announcers and jingle singers and with a sound designed to reach the Black market while providing work for the artists.

KNOK faces the difficult problem of having an FM sound coming across the AM band. Jackson notes: "If you know you are listening to FM you are listening to stereo, you know what it is supposed to sound like, and you have an FM receiver. AM listeners are not ready for it yet." KNOK's disco-type format is suited to the "sophisticated cat who gets off his job and stops by the lounge and has a few drinks and wants to boogie a little and let his hair down." It considers itself reaching everybody in the Dallas-Fort Worth Metroplex. "All Blacks in town don't make up a viable market," Jackson notes, "so you have to do the whole market to survive. We don't segregate ourselves. I don't think most stations can afford to do that. The station that does fails."

SOUL

KNOK can best be compared to a contemporary Top 40 station. KKDA, another North Texas Black-oriented station, licensed to Grand Prairie, is more like a progressive rock station. KKDA is actually two stations as its daytime AM is programmed independently from the 24 hour FM-stereo, which is licensed to Dallas. "K-104" is the name given to the FM sound developed by program director Chuck Smith. He believes that talking *at* people, as opposed to talking *to* people, has run its course. The format is built around a one-to-one approach between listener, personality on the air, and the radio itself. "The only thing you can do is try to present the information, music, and personality in such a way so as to encourage people to hang on for long periods of time." This, Smith believes, is accomplished by playing a carefully selected combination of contemporary, Black, soul, and jazz music in sets of three cuts or more interrupted only for brief stop-sets of commercials, announcements, news, information, and the introduction of the forthcoming music sweep. Each element is carefully controlled. Even commercials are programmed. Smith's approach is based on his belief that "people don't want to hear a guy yell and scream and go high energy. On a typical station much of what is said really means nothing." He says "We always want our people to be delivering some good, constructive information in a very communicative way and we don't throw away any breaks at all."

KKDA dislikes spots like concert promotions which say "this will be the greatest disco show in Dallas" because people are disappointed when it is not. He says the station must fight "the traditional feeling that Black people on radio can't read." There was resistance when the station wanted to have spots read live, without distracting music underneath.

KKDA-FM has five full-time and two part-time announcers. The AM side has three full-time and one part-timer. Most work four hours, with the exception of the midday to 5:00 p.m. and 7:00 p.m. to midnight shifts. The announcers don't pick the music at all. It is selected by the program director who provides guidelines which the announcer must follow. They are given album and singles "work sheets" and a "control sheet" which they must follow. The guidelines provide for the playing of a set number of albums and singles within an hour. Some titles would be circled as "must play" while others are selected by the announcer from a given category, such as "groups." A typical week's play list and control sheet are shown below.

KKDA ALBUM SHEET

1.	Message in the Music	O'Jays	P.I.
2.	Have a Good Time	Al Green	HI
3.	Rated Extraordinaire	Johnnie Taylor	Columbia
4.	Unpredictable	Natalie Cole	Capitol
5.	Maze	Maze	Capitol
6.	The Best of the Staples	Staple Singers	Stax
7.	Deep in My Soul	Smokey Robinson	Tamla
8.	The Jacksons	Jacksons	Epic
9.	Hutson 2	Leroy Hutson	Curtom
10.	Bristol's Creme	Johnny Bristol	Atlantic
11.	Songs in the Key of Life	Stevie Wonder	Tamla
12.	Ahh the Name is Bootsy Baby	Bootsy's Rubber Band	Warner Bros.
13.	Part Three	K.C. & the Sunshine Band	T.K.
14.	Little Funk Machine	Street Corner Symphony	ABC
15.	Unfinished Business	Black Byrds	Fantasy
16.	Home is Where the Heart Is	Bobby Womack	Columbia
17.	Hardcore Jollies	Funkadelic	Ju-Par
18.	Ask Rufus	Rufus/Chaka Khan	ABC
19.	Tempts do the Tempts	Temptations	Gordy
20.	Billy Preston	Billy Preston	A&M
21.	Love and Touch	Tyrone Davis	Columbia
22.	Coming Back for More	William Bell	Mercury
23.	Something Special	Sylvers	Capitol
24.	Motown's Preferred Stock (1)	Various Artists	Motown
25.	Loleatta	Loleatta Holloway	Gold Mind

26.	Moods and Grooves	Ju-Par Universal Orchestra	Ju-Par
27.	Color Her Sunshine	Willie Hutch	Motown
28.	Motown's Preferred Stock (3)	Various Artists	Motown
29.	Second Breath	Denise La Salle	ABC
30.	A Soulful Experience	Rance Allen Group	Truth
31.	Greatest Hits	Al Green	HI
32.	Where Will You Go	Archie Bell/Drells	TSOP
33.	It Feels So Good	Manhattans	Columbia
34.	Too Hot Too Stop	Barkays	Mercury
35.	Ted Taylor	Ted Taylor	Alarm
36.	Stand by Me	Johnny Adams	Chelsea
37.	Motown's Preferred Stock (2)	Various Artists	Motown
38.	A Man and a Woman	Isaac/Dionne	ABC
39.	Truth is the Power	Mighty Clouds of Joy	ABC
40.	Passport to Ecstasy	Banks & Hampton	Warner Bros.
41.	Ten Years of Gold	Aretha Franklin	Atlantic
42.	Family Reunion	O'Jays	P.I.
43.	Method to the Madness	Undisputed Truth	Whitfield
44.	Best of the Dramatics	Dramatics	Stax
45.	Spirit	Earth, Wind & Fire	Columbia
46.	Solid	Michael Henderson	Buddah
47.	A Whole Nother Thang	Fuzzy Haskins	Westbound
48.	K.C. & the Sunshine Band	K.C. & The Sunshine Band	T.K.
49.	Intimate	Leon Haywood	Columbia
50.	Gold	Ohio Players	Mercury
51.	Collector's Item	Harold Melvin/Bluenotes	P.I.
52.	Especially for You	Al Hudson/Soul Partners	ABC
53.	In Flight	George Benson	Warner Bros.
54.	Happy Being Lonely	Chilites	Mercury
55.	Etta is Betta than Evvah	Etta James	Chess
56.	Sing About Life	Ebonys	Buddah
57.	Never Say You Can't Survive	Curtis Mayfield	Curtom
58.	Purify Bros.	James & Bobby Purify	Mercury
59.	So So Satisfied	Ashford & Simpson	Warner Bros.
60.	Let 'Em In	Billy Paul	P.I.

KKDA Singles

1.	Don't Leave Me This Way	Thelma Houston	Tamla
2.	I've Got Love on My Mind	Natalie Cole	Capitol
3.	Tryin' to Love Two	William Bell	Mercury
4.	Good Thing Man	Frank Lucas	ICA
5.	Feel Free	Four Tops	ABC
6.	Look Into Your Heart	Aretha Franklin	Atlantic
7.	Ain't Gonna Bump No More	Joe Tex	Epic
8.	People Users	Philadelphia Story	H&L
9.	I Tried to Tell Myself	Al Green	HI
10.	Too Hot to Stop	Barkays	Mercury
11.	Just Another Day	Peabo Bryson	Bullet
12.	Love is Better in the A.M.	Johnnie Taylor	Columbia
13.	Somethin' 'Boutcha	Latimore	Glades
14.	Gloria	Enchantment	UA
15.	I Can't Say Goodbye	Millie Jackson	Spring
16.	At Midnight	Rufus/Chaka Khan	ABC
17.	Sometimes	Facts of Life	Kayvette
18.	Ha Cha Cha	Brass Construction	UA
19.	There'll Come a Day	Smokey Robinson	Tamla
20.	Don't Touch Me	Shelbra Deane	Casino
21.	There's Love in the World	Mighty Clouds of Joy	ABC
22.	I Wish	Stevie Wonder	Tamla
23.	I'm Your Boogie Man	K.C. & the Sunshine Band	T.K.

1. 40	B	12	2	38	
2. ALBUM	9	1	5	4	
3. EXTRA					
4. 40	8	4	6	9	
5. ALBUM	4	6	19	21	
6. NEW	1	6	2	5	
7. 40	14	13	26	23	
8. ALBUM	24	2	18	26	
9. EXTRA					
10.					
11. 40	10	7	10	11	
12. ALBUM	8	9	15	17	
13. EXTRA					
14. ALBUM	12	20	22	14	
15. 40	13	21	16	19	
16.					
17.					
18.					
19.					
20.					

(Note: Numbers refer to album sheets and singles play list.)

131

24.	Sweeter Than the Sweet	Staple Singers	Warner Bros.
25.	I Wanna Get Next to You	Rose Royce	MCA
26.	Darlin' Darlin' Baby	O'Jays	P.I.
27.	If a Peanut Farmer Can do It	Ed Townsend	EGA
28.	Where is Your Woman Tonight	Soul Children	Epic
29.	The Pride	Isley Bros.	T-Neck
30.	Fancy Dancer	Commodores	Motown
31.	Reaching for the World	Harold Melvin/Blue Notes	ABC
32.	Phoenix/Say a Little Prayer	Isaac & Dionne	ABC
33.	Fallin' in Love with You	Jimmy Ruffin	Epic
34.	Dreamin'	Loleatta Holloway	Gold Mind
35.	What Do You Do	Donnie Elbert	All Platinum
36.	We Don't Cry Out Loud	Moments	Stang
37.	Just One Step	Little Milton	Glades
38.	Blessed is the Woman	Shirley Brown	Arista
39.	Time is Movin'	Black Byrds	Fantasy
40.	Comin' Round the Mountain	Funkadelic	Warner Bros.
41.	Feel the Beat (Everybody Disco)	Ohio Players	Mercury
42.	Dream	Justice of the Peace	Metroplex
43.	Gonna Lay a Little Soul	Creators	Coconut
44.	Super Band	Kool & the Gang	Delite
45.	Laying Besie You	Eugene Record	Warner Bros.
46.	Let's Steal Away	Luther Ingram	Koko
47.	We Should Really be in Love	Dorothy Moore/Eddie Floyd	Malaco
48.	You Turned me on to Love	Johnny Bristol	Atlantic
49.	You're Throwing a Good Love Away	Spinners	Atlantic
50.	Easy to Love	Joe Simon	Spring
51.	Love to the World	L.T.D.	A&M
52.	Have Yourself a Good Time	Major Lance	Columbia
53.	Only Love Can Mend	General Johnson	Arista
54.	Be My Girl	Michael Henderson	Buddah
55.	Freedom to Express Yourself	Denise La Salle	ABC
56.	Let's go Down to the Disco	Undisputed Truth	Whitfield
57.	I Wanna Be Where You Are	Reality	Buddah
58.	Fill This World with Love	Ann Peebles	HI
59.	Hummin'	Nat Adderly	Little David
60.	We've Only Just Begun	Bobby Womack	Columbia

New at KKDA

1.	On Ya Face	Earth, Wind & Fire	Columbia
2.	A Dreamer of a Dream	Candi Staton	Warner Bros.
3.	It Feels So Good	Manhattans	Columbia
4.	I'm Qualified to Satisfy You	Barry White	20th Century
5.	While I'm Alone	Maze	Capitol
6.	Standing in the Safety Zone	Bobby Womack	Columbia

Smith notes that program director control is necessary to make sure that all the music is played and to eliminate announcer bias. He says, "There are some realities in life that have pretty much taken the freedom out of the hands of the announcer, like you have the freedom to drive down the road but you don't have the freedom to drive down the left side of the road."

He selects the music by carefully researching his target audience. This is accomplished by phone requests, checks on record stores, and by watching the reaction of people at concerts. KKDA will even play "cut-outs" from the $1.99 bins in record stores. Smith believes music is "strictly emotional and purely subjective and local. If you like it, it doesn't matter whether it's number twenty-nine in Cash Box or what's the number one in New York.'' He even tries to strike a balance between the tastes of "progressive" Dallas and the "more conservative" neighboring city of Fort Worth. The problem is to avoid the tendency to get too far ahead. Unlike KNOK, KKDA plays very little cross-over music (pop). "It's where the audience takes us. We don't try to force them," says Smith. "People are very sensitive and we think there is enough of our kind of music to keep us busy and we can't even play all of that." According to Smith repetition is one of the things that tend to make people not want to listen. He eliminated as much repetition as possible. "There is no way you can tune in to K-104 and know you are going to hear a particular song." This is in sharp contrast to a Top-40 format. "This could be a liability or it could be a plus," he says.

KKDA-FM is tailored to younger demographics 18–34 while its AM is tailored for 25–49 year olds. Chuck Smith says he doesn't mind that 12-year old kids or 50-year old men are listening, but he wouldn't go to extremes to attract them. AM programming is about 15% gospel, 5% jazz, 5% blues and 10% talk. A unique feature of KKDA's format is its presentation of news. It "jabs" the listener by opening with a live announcement and follows with several male and female voices delivering individual stories from carts with music fronts.

Commercials are programmed by dividing an hour into a set number of "stops" or interruptions, each containing a limited number of commercial units which do not exceed a maximum number of minutes. For example, 60 minutes of programming might contain six stops with two units each of 30- or 10-second commercials, for a maximum of 12 units, totalling 9 minutes. If only three minutes were used for commercials, the other 6 minutes would not be used. The station must convince sponsors to tailor their commercials to fit KKDA's approach. It will rewrite a spot to fit its format, taking away the "hype, pounding, yelling and screaming," and showing the sponsor how it could be done. It will not accept commercials for x-rated movies. Public Service Announcements are read live, thus allowing the station to respond to the people who listen to it. "Good PSAs sound like a good piece of information," says Smith. "They communicate and people get some good out of them."

Smith looks for announcers who are able to sell, and are willing to work within the station's rules and guidelines. "Some people confuse ego with personality," he says.

KKDA-FM has tried for a mass appeal with a sophisticated presentation. It seeks to expand its audience while losing neither its broad popularity nor its style. "I want to be successful with a low key, common sense approach," comments Smith. "Play lots of music, treat people like they're human beings—its how people want to be treated."

REALITIES

KKDA and KNOK compete with half a dozen contemporary stations in the Dallas-Fort Worth market and with each other. KNOK's Nat Jackson says, "All radio stations in the same market are after the same thing you're after— listening ears." Chuck Smith recognizes the limited appeal of KKDA's format. "After a guy has given up on all of the others, if he's not satisfied—if he likes us—fine." The program directors of both Black-oriented stations note that other stations in the area will play as many as three Black records in a row to pick up a percentage of the Black audience. Jackson says: "This is intended to attract the average listener who just happened to tune in. The other stations really play only the top Black records that have crossed-over to the pop charts." Smith adds: "These stations don't cross very real boundaries." KKDA's research indicates that its listeners also tune to KNUS and KLIF (pop) KRLD (news/adult) and KNOK. Jackson remarks that KNUS, KLIF and other pop stations in the area are the last to go on R & B music.

Neither program director feels bound to his particular current format. KNOK's Jackson watches larger markets for new ideas in programming techniques and has seen good results with the disco-type format. "Disco right now looks like it will be around for a while. It's just a new version of soul. If it dies out you ease over into another area." KKDA's Smith sees changes in the audience. "Either you've got to change with your audience or you've got to attract a new audience."

KKDA and KNOK publish their play lists which are distributed by record stores. Samples follow:

HISTORY

In the early '70s a consultant to Black radio stations remarked that his main job was to raise the stations to the level where they "are not an embarrassment to my White friends."

It was only a few years ago that "soul" stations were severly criticized by government officials, academicians and pressure groups. In 1968 FCC Commissioner Nicholas Johnson told members of the National Association of Television and Radio Announcers that the responsibility for a station's contribution to the Black community falls on their shoulders. He warned that "soul music is not enough" and protests might arise if program changes were not made. He called for imaginative programming to advance the cause of Blacks. His suggestions: Negro history via radio drama; Black culture other than pop music; information in short or long pieces; investigative reporting; editorializing; local programming with members of the Black community, and minority training programs.

The Office of Communications of United Church of Christ claimed that

KKDA Rock'n Soul
TO DALLAS - FT. WORTH

KKDA PLAYLIST

#	Title	Artist	Label
1.	GOT TO GIVE IT UP	MARVIN GAYE	TAMLA
2.	WHODUNIT	TAVARES	CAPITOL
3.	WHILE I'M ALONE	MAZE	CAPITOL
4.	THE PRIDE	ISLEY BROTHERS	T-NECK
5.	SHOW YOU THE WAY TO GO	JACKSONS	EPIC
6.	SO CALL ED FRIENDS	LEE MITCHELL	FSA
7.	AIN'T NOTHING YOU CAN DO	ALBERT KING	UTOPIA
8.	I CAN'T GET OVER YOU	DRAMATICS	ABC
9.	HUSH HUSH	QUINCY JONES	A&M
10.	KEEP THAT SAME OLD FEELING	SIDE EFFECT	FANTASY
11.	UPTOWN FESTIVAL	SHALAMAR	SOUL TRAIN
12.	IT FEELS SO GOOD	MANHATTANS	COLUMBIA
13.	HE NEVER LEFT ME ALONE	SHAW SINGERS	MESSENGER
14.	I'M GOING DOWN	ROSE ROYCE	MCA
15.	NOW DO U WANTA DANCE	GRAHAM CENTRAL STATION	WARNER BROS.
16.	PEOPLE GONNA TALK	TIP WATKINS	H&L
17.	THIS I SWEAR	TYRONE DAVIS	COLUMBIA
18.	I DON'T LOVE YOU ANYMORE	TEDDY PENDERGRASS	P.I.
19.	I'M YOUR BOOGIE MAN	K.C. & THE SUNSHINE BAND	T.K.
20.	HOLLYWOOD	RUFUS/CHAKA KHAN	ABC
21.	BREAK IT TO ME GENTLY	ARETHA FRANKLIN	ATLANTIC
22.	SIR DUKE	STEVIE WONDER	TAMLA
23.	EASE ME YOURS	COMMODORES	MOTOWN
24.	EASE ME YOURS	JACKIE MOORE	KAYVETTE
25.	YOU DIDN'T HAVE TO PLAY	JOE SIMON	SPRING
26.	BODY VIBES	OHIO PLAYERS	MERCURY
27.	SUNSHINE	ENCHANTMENT	UA
28.	YOUR LOVE IS RATED X	JOHNNIE TAYLOR	COLUMBIA
29.	BEST OF MY LOVE	EMOTIONS	COLUMBIA
30.	SHOW ME LOVE	CURTIS MAYFIELD	CURTOM
31.	KISS IN 77	JAMES BROWN	POLYDOR
32.	GIRL	BILLY PRESTON	A&M
33.	LEANIN' TREE	ARTIE WHITE	ALTEE
34.	SLIDE	SLAVE	COTILLION
35.	ALL BECAUSE OF YOUR LOVE	OTIS CLAY	KAYVETTE
36.	I WRAPPED UP	FRANKLIN SINGERS	CHILAND
37.	I LIKE THE FEELING	LUTHER INGRAM	KOKO
38.	SPELLBOUND	BARKAYS	MERCURY
39.	ME AND MY MUSIC	SPINNERS	ATLANTIC
40.	MORNING TRAIN	5 BLIND BOYS OF ALABAMA	JEWEL

NEW AT 73 **NEW AT 73**

#	Title	Artist	Label
1.	YOU'RE GONNA WALK OUT ON ME	EDDIE FLOYD	MALACO
2.	BABY DON'T CHANGE YOUR MIND	GLADYS KNIGHT & THE PIPS	BUDDAH
3.	DON'T GIVE UP	WORLD WONDERS	CHERUB
4.	PARTY LAND	BLACK BYRDS	FANTASY
5.	THE SOUL OF A MAN	BOBBY BLAND	ABC

ALBUMS **ALBUMS**

#	Title	Artist	Label
1.	A REAL MOTHER FOR YA	JOHNNY GUITAR WATSON	DJM
2.	COMMODORES	COMMODORES	MOTOWN
3.	GO FOR YOUR GUNS	ISLEY BROTHERS	T-NECK
4.	TRAVELIN' AT THE SPEED OF THOUGHT	BROTHERS JOHNSON	A&M
5.	O'JAYS		P.I.
6.	AHH THE NAME IS BOOTSY BABY	BOOTSY'S RUBBER BAND	WARNER BROS.
7.	NEVER SAY YOU CAN'T SURVIVE	CURTIS MAYFIELD	CURTOM
8.	MORNING, NOON & NITE	REV. ISAAC DOUGLAS	UA
9.	UNTIL YOU COME AGAIN	OHIO PLAYERS	SAVOY
10.	ANGEL	ANGELS	MERCURY
11.	SWEET PASSION	ARETHA FRANKLIN	ATLANTIC
12.	ME FOR YOU, YOU FOR ME	LITTLE MILTON	GLADES

JUNE 1, 1977

KKDA AND SMITH MEMORIAL CHAPEL ARE PRESENTING A FREE GOSPEL CONCERT FRIDAY, JUNE 10th, AT 8 P.M.

AT TERRELL MIDDLE SCHOOL IN DENISON, TEXAS.

FEATURED WILL BE:

REV. GENE WEST AND THE RELATIVES

TRUTH AND SOUL

THE INSPIRATIONAL OUTREACH CHORALE FROM DALLAS AND THE SIMPSONETTES, THE ANTIOCH CHOIR, THE THE ARRAY OLIVE AND ST. PAUL CHURCH CHOIRS FROM DENISON.

SPECIAL GUEST MC'S WILL BE KKDA'S STEVE LADD AND WILLIS JOHNSON.

GET THERE EARLY. MAKE SURE YOU GET A GOOD SEAT. IF YOU'RE ONE OF THE FIRST FIFTY TO MAKE IT IN, YOU GET YOURSELF A FREE GOSPEL ALBUM.

A GOSPEL CONCERT IN DENISON, TEXAS

PRESENTED BY

KKDA AND SMITH MEMORIAL CHAPEL . . . .

AND IT'S FREE FROM SOUL 73

Disco Notes

DISC-OK 107

KNOK JOINS KOOL FOR JAZZ FESTIVAL

KNOK and the Disc-OK 107 Gang will be very much involved with the first annual Dallas-Fort Worth KOOL Jazz Festival which has been scheduled for Texas Stadium, Sunday, May 29.

Produced by festival impresario George Wein, this major event will mark the beginning of an important series of great music for the Dallas-Fort Worth area. The lineup of artists is outstanding:

Natalie Cole

The Spinners

Al Green

Ronnie Dyson

The Mighty Clouds of Joy

For the past 10 years Wein has been presenting highly successful festivals in major stadia across the country. Last year's KOOL Jazz Festivals, which played in Cincinnati; Houston, Kansas City, San Diego, Oakland, Hampton, Atlanta, Milwaukee, Washington, D.C. and Pontiac, attracted over one-half million patrons.

Texas Stadium will provide a perfect setting for the KOOL Jazz Festival and more than half of the stadium seats will be used for the concert with the stage being located on the 50 yard line. There will be limited seating on the field.

Tickets for the First Annual Dallas-Fort Worth KOOL Jazz Festival are priced at $9.50, $8.50, $7.50, with a limited number of field seats at $12.50. Tickets are now on sale by mail order with over the counter sale starting April 15.

Check KNOK for more details and how to Disc-OK jocks will be involved in this big Festival.

DISC-OK CAGERS PLAY FOR CHARITY

Last week the KNOK Disco-OK Cagers were looking to even their record at 6-6 for the season.

But, with the demand growing heavier each week for their basketball services, the OK Cagers may find that 500 record hard to maintain.

Coach Nat Jackson explained that the basketball team has received a large number of requests for action. They were booked to meet the North Side High Faculty in Fort Worth and were dickering with the Park South YMCA in Dallas for a match.

"We are very particular about these games," Jackson pointed out. "We play only for charity and we want to be sure that we know where the money is going and how it is being used."

Clubs and organizations seeking to raise funds for a worthy cause should contact Nat Jackson at KNOK to schedule the OK Cagers for a charity basketball game.

Besides Jackson, the team includes Bill Wright, Larry Hemphill and Nathan Jenkins from KNOK. Jackson admitted that he rounds up a few ringers from outside the station staff to complete the lineup.

"It all depends upon the time and day when we play," Jackson said. "But generally we use all of the station people we can get to play."

The OK Cagers will continue their basketball act on as long as there are teams trying to build a reputation on beating a bunch of broken down ex-athletes who have turned Disco-Jocks.

(Continued on page 4)

136

the "soul package formula" failed in its responsibility to communicate. It cited the exclusion of drama and Black music other than soul, "rip 'n read" news, and "shouts from personalities bordering on hysteria." This "Black style" consisted of "hip" Black English talk used to sell overpriced and inferior products while avoiding responsible reporting of important local issues.[1]

A Stanford University study of Black-oriented stations found that the station had tremendous "audience power" and "profit power" while failing to serve the public interest. The R & B format was descried for its hit list which excluded other forms of Black-oriented entertainment, the quality and quantity of commercials, and its news. Changes in programming based on changes in profits and ownership were proposed.[2]

Added to this criticism was the simple fact that audiences had become more sophisticated and diverse. With this came the ever-increasing awareness of buying power within the Black community and the development of appropriate marketing strategies. Broadcasters, increasingly sensitive to the realities of the socio-economic changes, revised their programming accordingly. Input from professional Black broadcasters in management and decision-making positions, coupled with new trends in specialized radio programming, raised the overall quality of the stations.

In 1973 a reviewer for *The Washington Post* described Black radio: "It's flamboyant, up-tempo, filled with jive talk and hyperbole, and thunders forth like a continuous Saturday night party." That same year Frankie Crocker, program director of New York's WBLS (FM), topped popular WABC with a "Black progressive" format. Crocker used a highly produced and polished approach borrowed from AM. He combined jazz, R & B, Latin and Gospel music, programming every cut to produce a "total Black experience in sound."[3] He believed one could educate while providing entertainment.

During the '60s much of the music which could previously be heard only on Black stations was regularly played on top 40 stations. Songs by British artists led by the Beatles and Rolling Stones, competed for chart position with artists recording for the Motown group. Stevie Wonder, The Temptations, Supremes, Four Tops, Marvin Gaye, and The Miracles had hit after hit on the Tamla, Motown, Gordy and other Detroit labels owned by Berry Gordy, Jr., a Black man. The "Motown Sound" paved the way for soul music with its driving, danceable beat. It differed from the rhythm and blues of the '50s in its appeal to both Whites and Blacks and its formula approach. Meanwhile, rock and roll records produced by and for Whites were accepted on pop stations with

[1] Douglas O'Connor and Gayla Cook, "Black Radio: The 'Soul' Sellout." *The Progressive,* vol. 37, #8 August, 1973. Reprinted: Ted C. Smythe and George A. Mastroianni, *Issues in Broadcasting.* Palo Alto, California, Mayfield Publishing Co., 1975.

[2] Anthony J. Meyer, S.J., *Black Voices and Format Regulations.* Stanford, California, Eric Clearinghouse on Media and Technology, May, 1971.

[3] "Black FM Finds Right Chemistry For Success In New York". *Broadcasting,* March 5, 1973, pp. 52, 54.

their harmless lyrics failing to mask the unmistakable back beat borrowed from Black music.

In 1960 "Jocko" could be heard on two New York area radio stations. Personalities like "Hot Rod," "Dr. Jive," and "Wildman Steve" could be heard blasting from radios in every city. They were often as important as the music they played.[4] They would appear as MCs of concerts featuring a number of rhythm and blues artists. They had substantial freedom to play the records they wanted and could make hits. Jocko, for example, would declare, "that's so nice, let's do it up twice," and proceed to play the record again. The artists featured on their programs recorded for independent labels like Atlantic, Chess, King, and Modern.

Rhythm and blues evolved from the blues which had previously been called "race" music. Groups like the Dominoes, Cadillacs, and Clovers sang of drinking, sex, money and love. White stations avoided these records, preferring to air the pop tunes recorded for major labels by artists like Perry Como, Frank Sinatra, and Doris Day. Black teenagers listened only to the R & B sounds on Black stations and many Whites, turned off by the pop music of their parents, followed suit.

Alan Freed, an Ohio DJ, attracted a large teen following when he played R & B records on White stations. Other pop stations played "sanitized" versions of R & B tunes recorded by White groups for major labels. By the mid '50s Ray Charles, Chuck Berry, Little Richard and other R & B artists crossed over to the pop charts. When Elvis Presley became a hit with his blend of blues, gospel, and country music, the White stations found a winning combination to attract both teens and adults.

The sounds of The Mills Brothers, Ink Spots, Marian Anderson, Ledbelly, Charlie Parker and Billie Holiday were heard in the '40s. In 1947 the first Black-operated station, WVON (Voice of the Negro), Chicago, was established. At the same time a daytime serial with an all Negro cast was started.

That 1947 soap opera was the first for the sponsor and the advertising agency. Thirty years later the Bernard Howard Company would represent Black-oriented stations. Arbitron now takes special ratings of Black communities. Black-oriented news services are offered by the Mutual Black Network and the National Black Network. Advertisers and agencies appeal to Negro-market sub-groups.

Black-oriented stations are predominantly white owned. Only about 33 radio stations are black owned.[5] In 1972 columnist Jack Anderson disclosed "evidence of a new payola scandal in the billion dollar record industry." DJs and program directors, he revealed, were paid with free vacations, prostitutes, cash, and cars in exchange for plugging records. Anderson claimed R & B disc

---

[4] See Arnold Passman. *The Deejays,* New York: The Macmillan Company, 1971.

[5] Jacob Wortham. *"In With The Big Boys,"* Black Enterprise, September 1974. Reprinted in Charles Clift III and Archie Greer, *Broadcast Programming,* Washington, D.C. University Press of America, 1976.

jockeys were furnished wholesale lots of free records and he accused the underpaid R & B jockeys of accepting bribes and promoting their own dances or shows featuring talent provided by the record companies.[6] Subsequent hearings disclosed improper activities on the part of the stations, promoters, and producers of soul records.

THE FUTURE OF BLACK FORMATS

Nat Jackson of KNOK and Chuck Smith of KKDA believe very strongly in a "pendulum effect" in radio programming. The de-emphasis on personality has meant that listeners can't identify the DJ. Jackson says that listeners know the music but they can't tell you who they are listening to. "This really gives broadcasters something to think about down the road." Smith adds: "A person's awareness of radio stations is much more limited than we think."

Industry predictions reveal the movement of young listeners to FM, leaving the AM band to minority and older listeners. The Dallas-Fort Worth stations mentioned here are examining this trend and adapting to it. Smith offers this observation: "There is no doubt that radio is like fashion. We must be sensitive and aware of where the changes are and ride along with them."

KKDA FM: (TRANSCRIPT 11:15 p.m.–12:15 a.m. October 26, 1976) (Erik

            Williams, DJ).

            (11:15 p.m.)

Music: "Rubberband Man," The Spinners

DJ: K-104, The Spinners "Rubberband Man," You heard the Bar-Kays'

            "Cozy," Gloria Gaynor did "Be Mine" and the album "I've Got

            You" and Tyrone Davis started things off for us, "Give It

            Up, Turn It Loose"...Coming your way next Roy Ayers' "Ubiquity"

            The Goldenrod, and the album "Everybody Loves the Sunshine"

            new from Webster Lewis, "Do It With Style," also Bootsy's

            Rubber Bank "I'd Rather Be With You," and you're gonna hear

            Johnny Bristol, "She Came Into My Life."

Commercial: Times-Herald Classified

Commercial: Thomas and Hart Records and Tapes

Jingle: K-104

[6] Jack Anderson. "New Disc Jockey Payola Uncovered," and "Disc Jockey Payola Still Thriving," *The Washington Post,* March 31, and November 29, 1972.

Music: (As above)

DJ: K-104, Johnny Bristol's "She Came Into My Life," in the album

                Bristol's Creed, Bootsy's Rubber Band did "I'd Rather Be With

                You," the new song you heard was from Webster Lewis, "Do It

                With Style," coming your way next, Brass Construction's "Changin,"

                along with Bunny Sigler, "Just Let Me Love You Tonight."

PSA: (live) The Sojourn Truth Players are presenting an Urban

                Communications Workshop Saturday, November 6, at 9:00 a.m.

                and 3:00 p.m. - for more information you either call 335-7403

                in Fort Worth

DJ: It's about 11:40 and I'm Erik Williams at K-104.

Newscaster: Good evening, I'm Shirley Clark.

                (Story of Representative Wayne Hayes and Elizabeth Ray).

Sound: Music Bridge

Cant: (news story re "All the President's Men")....

                I'm Ruth Allen...

Clark: (release of White House tapes)

                (Ford and Carter traveling during campaign)

Sound: Music: bridge Up and under

Cart: Swine flu strikes in Dallas, I'm Sherry Jones. (reads story)

Sound: Music: bridge

Cart: (story about a rock concert and interview with Sly Stone)...

                I'm Noah Nelson.

Sound: Music: bridge

Cart: (college football sports)...

                I'm Duane Carroll

Clarke: (HEW-Medicaid/Abortion; Temperature; weather). For K-104

                I'm Shirley Clarke.

Jingle: K-104

Music: (as listed above and below)

DJ: K-104, that's Bunny Sigler, "Just Let Me Love You Tonight."

	You heard Brass Construction's "Changin," comin' your way next
	Barry White and Steve Ladd (dj), "Don't Make Me Wait Too Long."
Commercial:	Commodores, L.T.D., K.C. and the Sunshine Bank concert promo..
Jingle:	K-104
Music:	Barry White - "Don't Make Me Wait Too Long."
DJ:	K-104, that's Barry White, "Don't Make Me Wait Too Long," its 12:00 at K-104 - KKDA-FM in Dallas and I'm Steve Ladd.
Music:	"I Don't Wanna Lose Your Love," "Shakin' Your Love," "Love's A State Of Mind," "Girl I'm Yours for the Takin"

KNOK (AM and FM) 1:55 p.m.- 3:00 p.m.   Transcript October 28, 1976

(DJ: Bob Stewart)

1:55 p.m.

Music:	"Catfish", Four Tops
DJ:	The Four Tops and "Catfish" on K-NOK...it's 1:54, good afternoon to ya, have a happy day and all that jazz, its 48 degrees in the metroplex...I'll take the third caller from, uh, Big-D Town, uh, from Dallas it's your turn to burn right now..."Car Wash" time, 429-1075, caller number three from Dallas.
Commercial:	(on cart) Body and Soul Fashions, (over disco-music)
Commercial:	Paliament-Funkadelic concert promo.
DJ:	It's 1:56 on K-NOK, I'm Bob Stewart and we want to congratu- late my man in Big-D town, Ronny Ray, O.K., yeah...this is Walter Jackson.
Music:	"Feelings" Walter Jackson
ID:	(On cart, strong with big echo sound) K.N.O.K., AM-FM Fort Worth, Super Disco for Dallas-Fort Worth.
Music:	"Just Keep It Up" (instrumental)
Promo:	(strong echo) Disc O.K., playin' the better music (Disc-O.K.)

Music: "You're Everything To Me" Billy Preston

DJ: Very good, "You're Everything To Me," That's Billy Preston
                on K-NOK...I'm Bob Stewart.

Commercial: Riverside Village, a planned apartment community.

Commercial: Eddie's Fashion Nook.

Commercial: Len Smith's Auto Sales.

Commercial: (Political Spot) Vote Democratic

Promo: Go to the movies in a chauffeur-driven limousine to see "Car
                Wash"..."make the big score..."

Music: "I Can't Say Goodbye" Millie Jackson

Newsman: Good afternoon, I'm Jim Ponds, it's 48 degrees in the metro-
                plex...
                (women's voice with interview) Story about a local high school
                band contest winner.

Ponds: Story-threat on life of Congressman Gonzales.
                Story on increased state inspection of nursing homes (with
                interview, including information on where to complain about
                nursing home practices).
                Story about a dairy cow running for homecoming queen at a
                state university.

Commercial: Campbell's Soup, "Give Me The Campbell's Life" (upbeat, soul-
                version of the jingle).

Jingle: metroplex weather

Ponds: It's going to be (gives weather report)...for K-NOK, I'm
                Jim Ponds.

ID: (cart with echo) Super-Disco, K-NOK

Music: "On and On"

DJ: (over music) You turn it on me baby, yeah, turn it on like a
                faucet baby, on and on and on and on, ha, ha, whatever, that's
                alright, Bob Stewart on KNOK, at 2:22 in the afternoon.

Commercial: Commodores, L.T.D., K.C. and the Sunshine Bank Concert promo.

Music:	"The Pride," Isley Brothers.
Promo:	(cart with echo) Bob Stewart on KNOK
DJ:	Let's sing happy birthday to Anthony Thomas in D-town, John Sivley.
Music:	"So Very High To Go," Tower of Power.
DJ:	"So Very High To Go, yes it is...it's 2:33 in the afternoon, good afternoon to you and yours, how ya' doing?
Commercial:	Parliament-Funkadelic Earth Tour Concert promo
Commercial:	Monig's (department store) Christmas payment plan.
Commercial:	Scorchy (r-rated movie)
Commercial:	Piggly-Wiggly (supermarket halloween specials)
Promo:	(cart with echo) Disc - OK
Music:	"What Are You Doin' The Rest of Your Life" (segue to)...
Music:	"You Brought Joy Inside My Tears"
Newscaster:	Good afternoon, I'm Jim Ponds, its 48 degrees in the metroplex... Story-absentee voting Story of House Subcommittee on Assassinations reported coverup Story of a local Halloween fashion show charity affair Story about attorney Donald Yarbrough's controversial candidacy for a state judgeship
Commercial:	Win free groceries at Trailways' terminal.
Jingle:	Metroplex weather
Newscaster:	For K-NOK, I'm Jim Ponds.
Jingle:	Super Disc OK
Music:	"You'll Never Find Another Love Like Mine" Lou Rawls
Commercial:	Parliament-Funkadelic Earth Tour concert promo.
Commercial:	Body and Soul Clothes.
Commercial:	Sound Warehouse Records and Tapes.
DJ:	2:54 at K.N.O.K...Happy Birthdays go out again to Anthony Thomas of Dallas and John Sivley or John Sibley, O.K. John

Sivley, alright, and also Alvin Burns in Fort Worth, Happy

Birthday everybody may you have many more,...it's been a

pleasure, Don Kendricks (d.j.) is next, this is David Newman

to take me out, a thing called "Brandy"

Music: "Brandy" David Newman (jazz instrumental).

6

Good Music Formats

There is universal disagreement on what is and is not "good music." To the lover of classical music, a waltz by Johann Strauss is "good music." To the country music fan, "Catch A Tiger By The Tail" by Buck Owens may be the most artistic piece ever. Led Zeppelin or Sly and The Family Stone produce "good music" for many whose ears and audio senses are so attuned. Broadcasters, however, have come to understand that in industry terms "good music" means music that is *relatively* gentle, lushly orchestrated, and highly palatable to certain adult (25+) audiences. The "good music" format is one of the oldest being used. In radio's golden era, good music was a mainstay of independent stations. KIXL in Dallas and WPAT in Paterson, New Jersey, were broadcasting easy-listening music with related programming when the big network affiliates were producing soap operas, comedy shows, and other dramatic programs.

HISTORY

KIXL, founded and programmed meticulously for years by Lee Segall, used segue bridges especially created for the station so the opening bars of a piece of music would be in the same key as the closing bars of the previous one. There was no stereo in those early days and no automation. The programming was "live," and announcers had to have deep, resonant voices. Segall had a special program feature called "Think It Over," which offered sage advice to listeners, and KIXL announcers became masters of the pause in delivering them.

The "thinks" were laced into the sound at the rate of, perhaps, two per hour.

```
SOUND:        CHIME, SOFTLY

ANNCR:        Speaking of competition, Benjamin Franklin

              once said, it takes a strong wind to keep a

              good kite in the air. (Pause)

ANNCR:        Think it over.

SOUND:        Segue bridge.
```

Segall solicited contributions of such material from listeners and eventually compiled the "thinks" into hard-cover volumes which he then sold to listeners for $1 each.

Segall was a creative programmer who sensed and met the needs of many listeners in the Dallas market. Surveys were few and unreliable, so Segall simply "flew by the seat of his britches." His genius was in his "feel" for good music. This, of course, is true in all categories of music. Rock stations cannot be programmed by record surveys alone. Music and Program Directors must have a sense of what will or will not be popular with listeners.

It was Segall and others of his ilk who laid the foundation for today's good music stations. And some of the principles established then still hold true. Both the music and the commercials must be non-irritating. Announcers must not shout; instead, they must soothe and charm and, in the words of an irreverent, "chuck gently the ladies under their chins and shake firmly the hands of the gentlemen." It is important to determine the moods of listeners during different hours. Early morning programming may be at a faster tempo to match the mood of listeners hustling to get to work. Mid-day music contemplates a large "housewife" audience and, thus is softer. Tempo increases during the afternoon and, at night, romantic tunes and tempos are employed.

Most good music stations today are automated, or partially automated, and most subscribe to a service that provides taped music. But many licensees still produce "live" programming, even when the music is on tape. In those cases, the announcer is on and off the air, providing the basic services and articulating the titles of the music and the artists. The announcer simply "punches up" the music and other recorded program matter at the scheduled times. This level of live programming gives the station absolute control over the music, and what is spoken between blocks of music. In completely live programming, disc recordings are used. Many stations, including rock stations, "cart" the music to preserve the life of the albums. Stations that broadcast live in stereo often install an oscilloscope in the control room so the announcer can keep the two-channel audio output in proper balance. Live programming of good music has declined simply because the format deemphasizes personality and promotes long, uninterrupted sweeps of music. The announcer has little to do other than break in three or four times an hour to deliver weather, time checks, and station ads. A machine can do this work just as effectively and will never become bored! A few good music stations may interrupt the programming after each piece of music, but these are rare. Other adult-oriented facilities may play music written in the swing era but recently produced by modern artists using modern recording techniques. These are often called adult MOR formats, and the announcers weave in and out between the music just as DJs do on rock formats. Few such stations are successful, and their number diminishes each year.

Good Music radio has come a long way with the development of stereo FM and an endless array of sophisticated automation equipment. Music services provide stations with *everything* required to execute a good music format, up to and including voice tracks to intro and/or outro every piece of music played. Jim Schulke's Stereo Radio Productions (SRP), even provides advice and counsel on engineering, sales, promotion, and commercial production. Schulke, in 1977, had been in the business of producing good music tapes for about seven years and was a recognized leader in the field. His 60 or so client stations were among the best rated in the country. The April/May 1975 ARB showed 15 of his stations overall number one in their markets, 19 were second, 10 were third, 10 were fourth, and 4 ranked fifth among all AM or FM stations in each market. His KOB-FM in Albuquerque was number one in adults 18 plus. Other number one stations included WJIB in Boston, WLYF in Miami, and WWSH in Philadelphia. The term "number one" is often misleading, as most broadcasters can always find a set of demographics and day-parts in which they rank quite high. Schulke's conclusions, however, were correct when considering 18 plus adults, 6:00 a.m.-midnight, Monday through Sunday, Total Survey Area (TSA), average quarter-hour share and/or metro share. While it was not practical to check Arbitrons in each market, it can be safely assumed that Schulke stations were not number one in all day-parts and were not number one in cumulative audiences. Good music stations traditionally do not develop high cumes. Because of this low turnover factor, good music stations can develop high frequency of reach rather economically. In contrast, all-news stations develop high turnover resulting in a lower frequency of reach. People simply listen longer to good music stations than to all-news or Top 40 stations. The longer listening produces the low turnover factor.

Schulke, of course, is not alone in the good music program service field. Bonneville Broadcast Consultants of New Jersey have enjoyed successes in Los Angeles (KBIG), New York (WRFM), Chicago (WCIR), Cleveland (WQAL), and Jacksonville, Florida (WKTZ-FM), to mention a few. Bonneville provides essentially the same services as Schulke to its various clients, but there are major differences in how Bonneville and Schulke *perceive* and *execute* good music formats. It's the old story: give two equally-qualified broadcasters equal facilities, equal capital, and with matching formats one will outdistance the other in ratings and earnings within a year.

Because Schulke's formatting techniques have produced more high-rated stations than any other known good music service, they are described here as the example of how good music stations may be successfully programmed. In mid-1975, Schulke concluded an arrangement with the British Broadcasting Corporation (BBC) to bring all of the beautiful (good) music orchestras of the BBC to the United States for the first time, exclusively on his subscribing stations.

Schulke's basic music design was created for syndication and the complete and immediate control of music mix and flow. *Mix* and *flow* are the key words.[1] In contrast, music syndicated as a result of the success of an originating station often does not have the flexibility of change in flow and mix by market, by season, and in tune with fairly rapid changes in public taste. Schulke believes that dominance of the 18–49 female demographic is essential to success in a *beautiful music* format. Younger male listeners are products of dominance by younger women, in his opinion. For this reason, he believes, it requires more time to generate strong morning and afternoon drive audiences of men 18–49. In direct contrast, progressive rock formats attract men 18–24 first, with female audiences in the same demographics following as the format matures. The time factor varies by market size. It is more difficult in large, highly-competitive markets to make a rapid showing in the ratings. In small markets, (or in major markets where there is a format void), it is easier to promote the new format and quickly attract significant shares of adult listeners. While 18–49 audiences are the demographics most sought by all stations, good music formats and other adult-oriented plans tend to skew to older demographics. For example, Schulke's station in Dallas was fourth overall in the market and in a 1975 ARB, 38.9% of its audience was over 50, while 57.2% fell into the 18–49 demographics. The balance of 3.5% was represented by teens. Of the 18 plus adults, 57.8% were female and 42.2% were male.

Fundamentally, what Schulke or any other music service offers is, first, the taped stereo music and, second, advice based on experience on how to put it all together. The ebb and flow of moods and tempos by hour, by season, and by current listener tastes, require the tenure and expertise of highly sensitive programmers who, according to Schulke, spend as much as two days preparing a single hour of taped music. The technical quality of the recording and the station's ability to faithfully reproduce and broadcast the sound are equally important.

---

[1] Schulke refuses to discuss his formula for "mix and flow" and "matched flow." This is typical of programmers to protect their magic methods. Bonneville was willing to provide even less information.

THE SCHULKE MUSIC LIBRARY

Tapes are ¼ inch, 1½ mil 3M 176 mylar, 7½ IPS, on 10½ inch NAB metal reels in two-track stereo with four segments of 12:00 to 14:30 minutes each. (See glossary for definition of terms.) The average reel of tape has approximately 53 minutes of music. The minimum library available to subscriber stations consists of 120 of these tapes. The actual library in play "floats" between 130 and 220 tapes, depending in part on the season of the year and whether single vocals are recommended because of format competition in the specified market. Once the basic library has been established, subscribers receive no fewer than 80 tapes per year. New tapes are not delivered on a monthly basis but on a judgment of the needs of the library in use and in relation to changes in public taste.

Two tapes are alternated by segments (quarter hour) for complete control of tempo and instrumentation for male or female appeal by hour of the day. In other words, two tapes are in play on two alternating playbacks, and they program a two-hour period. There are divergent male-female and tempo curves for 6–8 a.m., 8–10 a.m., 10 a.m.–noon, noon–2 p.m., 2–4 p.m., 4–6 p.m., 6–10 p.m., and 10 p.m.–6 a.m. The Spring-Summer sound is happier, up-tempo, and more contemporary than the Fall-Winter period, which is more romantic.

Because the tempo and instrumentation curve is changed in two-hour periods throughout the day, and two tapes are in alternate play during each period, the 53-minute average for each tape provides the necessary flexibility. Fill music for use on a third playback deck is also supplied to accommodate hours with low commercial content.

It is important to note here that good or beautiful music stations maintain relatively low commercial loads and are acutely sensitive to the content and production quality of commercials. Commercials often cause tune-out, so while a rocking Top 40 might actually run 18 minutes of commercials per hour, a good music station or a progressive rock station might hold the limit at 8 to 10 minutes per hour.

Schulke furnishes a recommended schedule of tapes for 24 hours of every day in the year. During a typical hour, such as 12 noon–1 p.m., the schedule requires that tape numbers 1088 AC, 1095 AC, 1088 AC, and 1095 AC be played *in that order*. Total play time of these numbers is 55:07, leaving four minutes 53 seconds for commercial matter, public service announcements and news. This is a perfect example of "wall to wall" music that is touted by so many beautiful music stations. Many will promote that "during the next hour, you will hear 55 minutes of beautiful music." Interruptions are kept to a minimum, usually no more than four per hour. For example, tape number 1088 AC is 14:22 in length, leaving 48 seconds in the first quarter-hour for a station break and a 30-second commercial. The second tape is 13:52 long, leaving 1:08 for, perhaps, a station ID, 30-seconds of news headlines, and a 30-second commercial. Tape number three is 13:50 long, leaving 1:10 for local matter. The fourth tape is 13:03, leaving 1:57 for local matter. In the one day schedule reviewed, the fullest Schulke hour called for 55:20 of music, and the briefest was 51:51. It is quite apparent that subscribers must minimize talk and other program material in order to accommodate the music. But the good music format has always tried to satisfy the complaint that disc jockeys and/or announcers "talk too much."

```
Wall to wall music!

55 minutes of beautiful music per hour!

KTLC -- Tender Loving Care (for your ears)!

Good music.  Beautiful music.  24 hours a day.  In stereo.

No promotions.  No contests.  No screaming announcers.  Just good music.
```

Automation equipment has made it possible for good music stations to operate economically, often using as few as three or four persons to handle station business and programming. In the typical hour cited above, the automation package might consist of a brain, four music decks, one announcement carousel or instacart, and perhaps a wild deck for fill music and another carousel for news and/or additional announcements. (See automation section.) Modern automation equipment includes computer components that produce program and operating logs and thus require only a small amount of hourly employee effort.

Those, of course, are the *mechanics* of the format. The automation will do only what it is told to do. It can be pre-set to play tape 1057 AC at a certain time or programmed to react to a 25-cycle tone, inaudible to the human ear. The tone is at the end of each segment of programming (commercial, PSA, news, etc.) When the sensor hears the tone, the electronic brain automatically actuates the next segment or event. Most automation brains can be rigged to operate the programming for up to 24 hours, although this much "walk away" time is not standard. Four to six hours of hands-off time is probably much closer to reality. The more hands-off time desired by management, the greater the investment in tape decks and related equipment. So technology has solved most of the good music programmers's mechanical problems. If a studio engineer can keep the equipment operating, keep playback heads aligned and clean, the equipment will operate smoothly and efficiently for many years.

The *human factor* in good music programming is decidedly more difficult to comprehend for it is here that one person is attempting to detect the ever-changing musical desires of mass audiences. Schulke's plan insures against repeating standard selections over a four-hour period, even by different artists. The system maintains a 90-minute no-repeat structure for modern day standards and the more contemporary songs. The tapes are not designed to rotate evenly. Tempos are moved up or down, and programmers are able to change to a greater or lesser romantic flavor simply with scheduling priorities for each individual tape.

Schulke has devised ways of measuring audience reaction quickly through

such survey companies as C. E. Hooper and through private telephone coincidental studies. When these surveys signal a widespread change in audience
preference and/or acceptance for a specific season, the correction can be made
by scheduling techniques and does not have to wait for the production of new
tapes. All markets, of course, are not programmed exactly to the same
sequence curve. Because of differences in market competition, Schulke may
have as many as four schedule variations.

He argues that his "beautiful" music does attract very young audiences.
This is true to a limited extent, and Schulke believes the beautiful music plan
will continue indefinitely to appeal to younger women. "Essentially, there is a
change in life style when people get married and especially with the first child.
It is at this point that our music becomes an especially welcome addition to
daily living." Standards and modern day standards become more important if
properly mixed with current hits.

Schulke believes that recently there has been a further shift to conservative
tastes in music, emphasizing the basic strength beautiful music has enjoyed for
years. He contrasts the success of his client stations with the "decline of progressive rock and the continuing shift to 'rock' standards by other contemporary stations."

"The most accepted mix and flow is changing more rapidly now than in
the past. It takes more thought and creativity to maintain a strong recognition
factor with people 35–49 and still have a contemporary 'in touch' sound which
is continuously pleasing to long-hour listeners," he maintains. The fact of the
matter is that the beautiful music play list and repeat structure are just as important as they are for Top 40 radio, but because the beautiful music play list is
larger, the relationship is less obvious. *All* play lists must change to meet the
changes in listener desires. Control can be exercised only with a limited library.
Additional control results from schedule priorities. *Matched flow* creation is the
remaining key to an "in touch" sound which is continuously pleasing to long-
hour listeners.

Schulke doesn't describe the subtle factors that go into his matched flow.
Each programmer will have a little different idea about the sequence of play or
"flow" of the different pieces of music. One may open with a bright, big-band
instrumental, followed by a male vocal, then a small combo instrumental and a
mood-breaking Latin beat instrumental. Music is often described as "young"
or "olds." A Benny Goodman piece recorded 25 years ago obviously would be
old. But a Mantovanni version of a tune popularized by Goodman 25 years ago
might be called "new." An original Beatles tune, of course, would not be suitable for the beautiful music format, but a rendition of the same tune by Percy
Faith would be perfect.

There is a constant shifting of play lists in the programmers' efforts to attract as wide a range of age groups as possible. The problem is that if the music
becomes too old, it will not attract the young audiences. The trick, then, is to
find the perfect balance!

Schulke's "creative director" literally creates the tapes for library inclu-

indicated, it takes approximately two days to create an hour of pro-
ng because of the *matched flow* and stringent specifications for each
ation. Mastering and duplicating are accomplished with the problem of
uppermost in mind. Schulke estimates that 70% of a successful FM sta-
hare of audience is on mono receivers. Out-of-home (car, office) listening accounts for most of this mono audience. If a piece of music is recorded out
of phase, with too much emphasis on either the right or left channel, the mono
receiver will not provide high fidelity reproduction.

A one-minute 700 Hz zero level tone is at the head of each tape, preceded
by a 15-second 10d 5 kc tone which is for quality control purposes. The 700
Hz tone is followed by 15 seconds of dead air, and the first segment is preceded
by a 25 Hz tone at 5 db on the left channel for cueing purposes. 25 Hz tones
follow each segment by ½ to 1 second; this tone is used to signal the automation brain that the segment is concluded and that the next machine function
should begin.

During the mastering process, levels are carefully controlled on each selection to preserve dynamic range and at the same time provide sufficient
average and peak modulation for broadcast. This means that the original record
levels have been adjusted for broadcast use when the tape is delivered. This ex-
acting control of levels also means that stringent specifications are required for
duplicating.

TECHNICAL REQUIREMENTS:

The Schulke format may be executed live or automated. Currently, 35%
are live and 65% automated. The automated stations use either Schafer, SMC,
Gates or IGM equipment. Three playbacks are the minimum required. Two
tapes always alternate by quarter-hour segment. A third playback provides fill
music when required. Walk-away time is determined by the number of playbacks and the capability of the programmer in multiples of two hours. Two
playbacks, plus a fill deck provide two hours of hands-off time; four playbacks,
plus a fill deck, provide four hours, and so on. To completely automate, a
motor-driven clock fader is required, as well as a 25 Hz sensor on each playback unit. This is not required for nonsegmented tape music services but is for
those services whose music is programmed in quarter-hour segments.

Schulke recommends mono carts and carousels for best control of phase
and levels. Most of his client stations that started with stereo carts have converted to mono by using the left track to feed both channels. Anyone considering the future importance of stereo commercials need only visit about five
households selected at random and find four of the five receivers out of balance. The system also recommends three single-source cart machines and two
random access carousels to minimize "cockpit" (control room) troubles.

CONSULTATION AND ADVICE:

Any music service provides advice and counsel to client stations purely as a matter of self-interest. The more successful the station, the more likely the station will remain a customer of the service. Drake/Chennault, TM Associates, Bonneville—all provide subscribing stations with virtually unlimited advice and counsel, whether the service provides rock, country & western, or beautiful music.

Schulke and Bonneville even provide a manual, delivered upon signing of the contract, containing the station guidance on station IDs, commercial load acceptance, production, placement, and pace. The approach to news and scheduling are more related to individual market competition, but a general philosophy is advanced as a basis for more specific recommendations. Generally, most services aim to help a station in the use of its talent and other assets to achieve the best overall sound for that facility in that specific market. Through experience with the format under widely varying conditions, music service consultants can advise on equipment purchases ranging from the best antenna to playback tape decks and on such minor details as limitor adjustments and tape guide stability.

Schulke explains his service:

An expert, disciplined outside perspective. It's easy for a station to accept something that it has become used to. We do not have that problem and do have a perspective relating to a great many executions of beautiful music formats with our company and on competing stations.

In working with over 40 professionally operated facilities, we have the opportunity to pass along the best creative ideas, based on results, and suggestions for solving technical problems based on their solutions elsewhere.

MONITORING TECHNIQUES:

Monitoring or listening to a station may be accomplished effectively in a variety of ways. Many program managers often just "take the day off," hole up in a hotel room, and make notes all day on what appears right and wrong about a format. This is the *only* way management can ever really know what is happening on the station. The sporadic listening normally accomplished by a manager tells him little about the overall quality of station programming.

An all-day monitor, for example, might reveal that time checks, weather reports, and station IDs are being given too infrequently. It might indicate an imbalance in music, such as too many Top 10 tunes and too few album cuts.

Schulke's primary tool for creative recommendations are numerous cassette air checks which are critiqued by phone. Probably one of the first program experts to *monitor by phone* was Bill Drake of the Drake/Chennault consulting team. This is about as simple as it sounds. The station has only to install a special telephone number that can be dialed at any time by the consultant. Once the number is dialed, the programmer can sit and monitor for hours. Schulke has a Watts line and thus can easily monitor any client station that has the special telephone number. The results can be the same without the expense and trouble of air travel, baggage, and hotels.

Other programmers simply have engineers make recordings of major segments of the day and listen to the tapes at more convenient times. In some cases, the music is clipped in the middle, allowing the programmer to concentrate on how the announcer or DJ is handling the commercials, intros and outros, and other program matter.

One program expert earns a living by listening professionally to big city stations. By contract, he visits the market unannounced and listens intently for a week. His minute-by-minute notes are transcribed into a typed critique of everything from DJ personality to the quality of commercial production. It is this outside "disciplined" perspective that often is most useful to management in straightening out format problems. Local managers and program directors get too close, become emotionally attached to personnel and methods, and therefore cannot be objective in their evaluations. The outsider has no emotional attachments and can at least *advise* management of potential weaknesses.

ATTENTION TO DETAIL

It has often been said that it isn't the big chinks that kill a format, it is the cumulative effect of little, very subtle chinks that decide who wins and loses in a competitive market. Failure to repeat the weather, failure to provide frequent time checks during morning- and afternoon-drive periods, failure to screen obnoxious commercials, failure to produce high quality PSAs—small errors, perhaps, as they stand alone, but collectively such flaws can eventually pull a station right to the bottom.

In Schulke's good music plan, music is matched flow, both as to fit and mood. In other words, romantic, happy, contemporary and older standards are matched and fitted into a pattern that the programmer belives will be best received by the listener. Intros are often deleted from a piece of music if the intro doesn't seem to fit the pattern. Spacing, termed critical by experts, varies from a seque to 3-½ seconds. As the creative process and flow are so important and often involve cut-out material, Schulke makes every effort to secure album copies in depth. Often the third or fourth copy will produce an acceptable technical sound, where the first three tries did not (about 20% of all albums lack reasonable fidelity to start with, because they are late pressings from the master). Pops and clicks that are editable are removed from master tapes. Sometimes, of course, this is not possible and, when the pop or click is too offensive, the entire master is scrapped.

The programmer at Schulke *plans* the tape and issues detailed instructions to the engineer for mastering. Below is a finished information sheet for a one-hour tape.

PRODUCTION NO: 3088   SERIES CA

	SELECTION	ARTIST	LICENSE	TIME
	25 Hz AUTOMATIC TRIGGERING PULSE			
	I SAY A LITTLE PRAYER	PERRY BOTKIN JR.	ASCAP	2:25
	I'M GONNA CHANGE EVERYTHING	LIVING STRINGS	BMI	4:09
GV	STORMY	PERCY FAITH	BMI	2:36
	IS THAT ALL THERE IS	FERRANTE & TEICHER	ASCAP	3:28
				12:45
	25 Hz AUTOMATIC TRIGGERING PULSE			
	MANNY BLUE	BILLY VAUGHN	ASCAP	2:35
	TO WAIT FOR LOVE	FRANK CHACKSFIELD	ASCAP	3:03
GV	LOVE CAN MAKE YOU HAPPY	PERCY FAITH	BMI	2:35
	CRYING IN THE CHAPEL	ROGER WILLIAMS	BMI	2:16
	GOODBYE	FRANCK POURCEL	BMI	2:21
				13:04
	25 Hz AUTOMATIC TRIGGERING PULSE	CUMULATIVE TOTAL		25:49
	TRUE GRIT	ARTHUR GREENSLADE	ASCAP	2:15
	MY FAVORITE THINGS	ED BLAND	ASCAP	2:13
GV	I'D DO ANYTHING	STRAWBERRY STREET SINGERS	BMI	2:44
	SINCE I FELL FOR YOU	PERCY FAITH	BMI	3:25
	WHEN DAY IS DONE	CHET ATKINS	ASCAP	2:16
				13:05
	25 Hz AUTOMATIC TRIGGERING PULSE	CUMULATIVE TOTAL:		38:54
	THEME FROM IS PARIS BURNING	FRANCK POURCEL	ASCAP	2:37
	BLUE TANGO	LIVING STRINGS	ASCAP	2:58
	IF HE WALKED INTO MY LIFE	PETER DUCHIN	ASCAP	2:42
	SECRET LOVE	FRANK CHACKSFIELD	ASCAP	3:20
	A GROOVY KIND OF LOVE	ARTHUR GREENSLADE	BMI	2:09
				14:00
	25 Hz AUTOMATIC TRIGGERING PULSE	CUMULATIVE TOTAL:		52:54

Here are typical instructions from the programmer to the production engineer:

```
Seg. III

1 - On Manny Blue...fade out beginning at approx. 2:25.  Be out completely

    by 2:35.  Use your judgment on this fade.  Do not make it too slow, but

    rather normal sounding fade-out.

4 - Cut intro (Crying In The Chapel) approx. 12 sec.

Seg. IV

1 - True Grit -- space this approx. 1/2 second.  Not quite a segue.

Seg. I

3 - Support 1st 33 sec. slightly.  Support last 11 sec.

4 - Pop :22, pop 5 sec. from end may not be editable.

5 - Pop 12 sec. from end.

Seg. II

2 - Pop 1:21.  Slight support 1:08 - 1:45.

3 - Boost 9 sec intro and continue slight support through 35 sec.

    Then 0 to 57.  Then slight support to 1:30.  Then 0 to 2:15.

    Then suppress slightly to end.

4 - Will surface noise allow more boost of 1st 20 sec?  Support last

    50 seconds, particularly last 20 sec.  Pop 2:07, 2:51, 2:57.

Seg. III

1 - Suppress slightly sax peaks at 40 sec. and again from L45-2:15.

    Audition and hold up last part of artificial fade slightly.  Would

    this sound better butted?  Or with just a 1/2 sec?  Lever is down

    to almost an inaudible level for 5 to 6 sec.  Use your own judgment.

    The fade on 1 is well done.  Now that it is on 1/4 inch, we're just

    looking for any additional improvement.
```

And so on, until the production is finished. The jargon that crops up in these inside memos is incredible. Consult the glossary for any terms not understood.

Here is a Bonneville hour, with total quarter-hour time indicating time available for other program matter.

U-2070 RI 50822

SELECTION ARTIST	SOURCE	TIME
A1. SUNDOWN - GEORGE GREELEY ORCH.	EDIT 50716-3	1:55
A2. LOVIN' YOU - RAY CONNIFF SINGERS	COL 33564	2:30
A3. NEVER MY LOVE - 101 STRINGS	ALS S5078	2:35
A4. YOUNGER THAN SPRINGTIME - PETE JOLLY	A&M SP3033	2:15
A5. STAR DUST - MANUEL	EMI TWO219	3:15
	TOTAL TIME	12:30

U-2094 R2   50730

A1. IT'S TOO LATE - RIDGEWOOD STRINGS	EDIT 50716-4	1:50
A2. ERES TU (TOUCH THE WIND) - SONNY JAMES	COL KC 33477	2:40
A3. WANDERIN' STAR - FRANCK POURCEL	PARA PAS5022	2:55
A4. YOU AND ME AGAINST THE WORLD - HELEN REDDY	CAP SO11284	3:10
A5. MONDAY, MONDAY - NORWOOD BRASS	EDIT 50716-3	2:20
	TOTAL TIME	12:55

M-1004 R4 51004

A1. MY LIFE - NELSON RIDDLE	BASF MB20887	2:10
A2. UP, UP AND AWAY - DON COSTA	VER V68702	2:30
A3. LEARN TO LOVE - WERNER MULLER	LON SP 44193	2:50
-----PAUSE/TONE-----		
A4. SUNNY - PERCY FAITH CHORUS	COL CS9610	3:15
A5. MYSTERY MOVIE THEME - RAY DAVIES	PYE NSPL41021	1:55
	TOTAL TIME	12:40

M-1019 R3   51004

A1. FAYE'S FOLLY - 101 STRINGS	ALS S5306	2:20
A2. PLAY A SIMPLE MELODY - HORST JANKOWSKI	MERC SR61054	2:35
-----PAUSE/TONE-----		
A3. LULLABY OF BROADWAY - ANDRE KOSTELANETZ	COL CS8939	2:45
A4. DOWNTOWN - PETULA CLARK	WB WS1765	2:55
A5. COQUETTE - TONY MOTTOLA	COMM RS807SD	2:05
	TOTAL TIME	12:40

In contrasting those two good music services, it becomes apparent that there isn't much difference in the selections provided. The differences occur in the editing and in the match and flow. Both services feature some Percy Faith; Bonneville may include a Floyd Cramer selection, while Schulke may use a Chet Atkins. Country and folk and rock artists may be sprinkled throughout the lists, but the *arrangement* of the particular selection is compatible with the programmer's overall intent.

The program "wheel" will indicate to the student the concept of arranging specific hours for specific purposes. Mechanically, every hour will be about the same. More news may be included in some segments, depending upon the licensee's commitment to the FCC. Other hours may contain a full 59:55 minutes of music, leaving room only for a station identification. The wheel is used only to provide graphics for the planner to help him see how the hour will come together.

AUTOMATION

A Dallas Top-40 station in the mid-1950s ran a newspaper ad promoting one of its personalities, Sam Seeburg. Sam really wasn't an exciting personality, but he was always in the studio on time and rarely made a statement on the air that didn't have management's complete and specific approval. Sam would goof, from time to time—play the same record twice or play two or three records back to back without giving station call letters—but these errors were overlooked because of Sam's many virtues. Sam never asked for a raise, hated vacations, didn't engage in office gossip, and never had to leave the control room to go to the bathroom. He also didn't run up long-distance telephone calls.

Sam Seeburg was an automaton and he was on the air from midnight to five a.m.

The station was KLIF, one of the first in the nation to experiment with automation equipment. Sam was composed of two Seeburg automatic record selectors (right out of a jukebox) and one reel-to-reel tape machine that contained commercials and Sam's "chatter." By today's standards, Sam was awful. He was more of an idea that anything else, without form or even an equipment cabinet of his own. There was the hated "dead air" between records. If program events got out of kilter at 1:00 a.m., they stayed out of kilter all night. There was no "brain" as such to put the equipment back on the timetable. But it was a beginning.

The Schafer Electronics Corporation put together Sam's automation system. Paul Schafer was the brain behind the concept, and his company today claims that one of every seven radio stations in the country uses automation equipment in one form or another to handle programming. There are many pro-

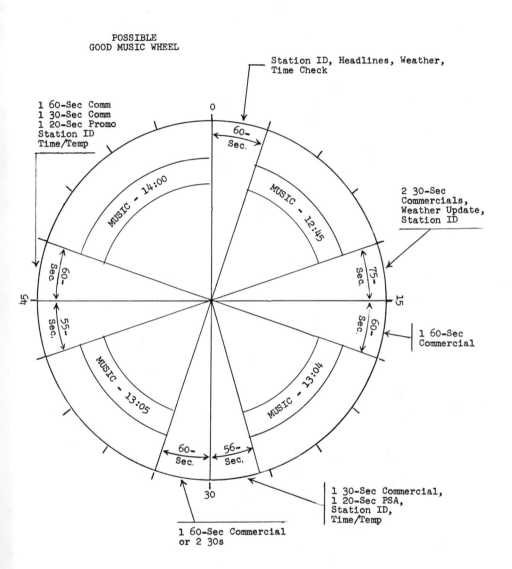

POSSIBLE
GOOD MUSIC WHEEL

Station ID, Headlines, Weather,
Time Check

1 60-Sec Comm
1 30-Sec Comm
1 20-Sec Promo
Station ID
Time/Temp

60-
Sec.

MUSIC – 14:00

MUSIC – 12:45

2 30-Sec
Commercials,
Weather Update,
Station ID

60-
Sec

55-
Sec.

75-
Sec.

60-
Sec.

1 60-Sec
Commercial

MUSIC – 13:05

MUSIC – 13:04

60-
Sec.

56-
Sec.

1 30-Sec Commercial,
1 20-Sec PSA,
Station ID,
Time/Temp

30

1 60-Sec Commercial
or 2 30s

159

ducers of highly sophisticated automation gear, but only two will be dealt with in this text: Schafer and the Harris Corporation.

Automation equipment wasn't desirable or necessary when modern radio was first conceived in the early- to mid-1950s. Those "golden" days involved mostly live shows, live announcers, live commercials. Recording devices were primitive, and solid-state transistors didn't exist. But World War II had produced sophisticated timing devices, both mechanical and electronic, and these were to play a vital part in the development of radio's automation equipment.

"Why should I pay a man $500 a month to sit in my control room from midnight to five a.m., play records, and sound stupid?" may have been the question that started Schafer and other electronic tinkerers to thinking about a machine that would do the same thing, sound brighter and cost less money to operate. The concept of automation didn't click immediately with the rock and roll stations. Rather, it was the good music stations that first took full advantage of the new technology. The rock programmers felt they had to have that "live" sound—and early automation did *sound automated*. Listeners were aware of the unscheduled pauses and breakdowns, the pops and clicks, record changers, and crude sequence devices which crept from one program event to another. Top-40 formats required "personality"—and Sam Seeburg's early descendants simply didn't have it. But the good music stations could get by without personalities, programmers assuming that what people really wanted to hear when they tuned in was music-music-music—wall to wall. The first effort at providing equipment that would simply play music and commercials was *relatively* simple. Ford's first car was *relatively* simple when compared to the highly complex machines on the road today. The original automation equipment contained a simple rotation system that would (1) play a piece of music, (2) play a commercial or PSA, (3) then play another piece of music. This sequence would continue until the tape ran out or the record supply was exhausted and had to be changed. The "brain," at best, was simple-minded.

Sam Seeburg would be proud to watch the Harris Corporation's Systems 90 or Schafer's 903E perform today, executing a Tom Merriman (TM) good music format or a Drake/Chennault XT-40 (Top 40) plan. These systems, while manufactured by different companies, have many similarities but, also, many differences. As automobiles are made to convey people from one point to another, automation equipment, in this case, is made to *program radio stations* with minimum human involvement in the hour-to-hour operation. Each manufacturer has legitimate claims of superiority or efficiency. But, the ultimate result is about the same.

Pictured on the following pages is some of the equipment in use by all types of radio stations. Photographs range from a simple idea (KGRO) to one of the most sophisticated systems available, the Schafer 903E.

The heart of any automation system is the "brain" or control center. It handles the sequencing, timing, sensing, execution. Everything else is enslaved to the control center. Early units of all manufacture contained only this kind of mechanical brain. The development of computers led to the addition of memory banks which, for example, enable bookkeepers to extract exact times-run for commercial accounts for an entire month.

Starting with the control center, then, additional equipment may be added until the automation package will perform every conceivable function. The relatively simple KGRO package contains the brain, instacart unit, and three carousels. As the picture cutline indicates, there is a reel-to-reel machine also tied in to provide for intros and closes for records. Each carousel contains 24 slots for music cartridges. The instacart machine contains 48 slots for commercials, PSAs, and station promos. Harris' System 90 control unit electronically signals each of these units when a certain function is programmed. Example of the sequence:

0:00 – (Reel-to-reel): DJ voice opens show, introduces first record.

0:30 – (Carousel #1): Plays first record.

3:00 – (Instacart): Plays Coca Cola commercial.

4:00 – (Reel-to-reel): DJ voice gives time, billboards upcoming event,

intros next record.

4:20 – (Carousel #2): Plays next record.

The process continues until the reel-to-reel tape runs out, until a new series of commercials must be placed in the instacart machine, or until a different variety of music must be placed in the carousels. Carousel #1 may contain the top 24 hits, Carousel #2 "golden oldies," while the third machine contains album cuts. The machine can normally be counted on to do its part—that is, execute commands of the brain in proper sequence. But it requires a skilled programmer to establish the sequences and prepare voice tapes that give the station a "live" sound. As contemporary music formats require the repetition of much of the music programmed, a good deal more walkaway time can be accomplished with minimum effort. The good music formats could require more equipment, as the music is not repeated as often. Therefore, the equipment packages are sometimes more complex.

Once the basic procedure is established, the equipment can be expanded to handle additional tasks.

Features and functions of the Harris System 90 automation package:

1. All programming, operator control, and display of system operating status is centralized in a single, small portable console (see p. 165 ff.)
2. Micro-computer uses firmware logic—a safeguard claimed by the manufacturer against obsolescence. When advanced operating techniques are developed, firmware instructions may be conveniently changed by changing plug-in ICs. (A hardware logic system would require rewiring—if it could be changed at all.)

3. Expandable as needs expand. Many options and peripherals available. These include memory expansion, source expansion, automatic memory load and dump capability, additional control consoles, and automatic logging.
4. Flexibility in programming, without compromising established format. Format may be changed, often without additional equipment.
5. Choice in programming memory as "sequential" or "main format/sub format."
6. Random access capability in all memory events, permitting last-minute changes and program variations. Indexing of random access sources is completed considerably ahead of "on-air" time.
7. Network join included. Fade-out and back-timed controls. Join a national network, state network, local studio, or a remote broadcast.
8. Automatic voice tracking for intros and outros. Programmable link and fade control between talk tape and sources to insure their playing on the air at the proper audio mix.
9. Time announce control built in by adding two standard cartridge playbacks.
10. Time compare memory simplifies time instructions. Time entries to perform a system action are entered directly into the compare time memory. Time entries can be entered once and caused to occur each hour (repetitive entries.) Or, specific entries can be made to occur at an exact second of a specific hour (hourly entries).
11. Automatic self-correcting restart following power failure, eliminating the confusion of getting the system back in operation.
12. Remote control standard for full system and memory use with live DJ. DJ has convenient access to all system sources, plus tray/shelf selection. DJ may also program events to play automatically for brief periods. The portable console handles this action.
13. Sum channel mono output standard for conveniences in AM simulcasting.
14. Error sensing prevents system from accepting any data from operator that is not valid. Eliminates danger of invalid data causing system failure.
15. One-time bulletin insertion, without altering memory sequence.
16. Built-in monitoring system with single VU meter accuracy. All levels set to exact the same standard—use for source level adjust, alignment, and phase check. Provides for continuous on-air phase checking of stereo source inputs.
17. Clear text and numeric high speed-verifier logging systems available. With either system, every on-air event is logged, as is every event that was scheduled but did not play. Each non-event prints a special character that tells why it did not play.

18. Emergency panel allows bypassing the micro-computer for source and shelf selection and operation.
19. Individual 25 hz sensing with stop delay is built in on each reel-to-reel source card. No optional add-on detectors required.
20. Systems may be integrated into automatic billing and accounting systems.
21. Stereo configuration standard, with costs equivalent to mono.
22. Solid-state audio, logging, and control switching eliminates pops during starting and stopping of sources.
23. Dual silence sensors for system and transmitter monitoring.
24. Multiple consoles may be employed to provide convenient system control points throughout the station.
25. Time entries entered in any order. The compare time memory automatically sorts and selects the entry that is to occur next according to the digital clock.
26. Up to 3,700 events and 32 source inputs—with 1,200 events and 16 source inputs. Fifteen sources can be random accessed.
27. Digital clock setting by keying correct digits directly into the display.

Schafer Electronics and other automation manufacturing firms boast many of the same features and some, perhaps, that are not included above. The Schafer 903E is a single-keyboard 8,000 event microelectronic memory control system that will store events for the most complex format for three days in advance. This system has a two-file memory that separates repetitive program events from non-repetitive, time-oriented events, such as commercials and PSAs.

The 903E stores 3,800 recyclable format events which may be divided into a number of sub-formats, or programmed in straight-line fashion for random access cartridge music selection. There are virtually no limitations on the number of sub-formats that may be used. Each hour for three days may have a different music rotation, for example. In addition, the system provides three days of time-related avails: 60 per hour for 72 hours, enough to pre-program all commercials, PSAs, newscasts, and other time-oriented events over a weekend, or three days in advance.

The keyboard/display terminal is a relatively new feature of all modern automation systems. This device has simply made it more convenient for personnel to program the system and to modify the programming in progress. A more recent innovation is Schafer's "studio" organization of the equipment, as compared to the standard "rack mount" which all companies provide. Harris' capability of locating the display terminal 150 feet from the system (without wire hookup) is another recent convenience.

Automation stories abound. One wag accused Schafer of selling him a machine that sassed the general manager. And an Albuquerque operator once spread the story that his system:

1. Turned on the transmitter carrier at 5:00 a.m.
2. Started the coffee at 5:30 a.m.
3. Activated programming at 6:00 a.m.
4. Awoke the general manager at 7:00 a.m.
5. Had breakfast ready by 7:30 a.m.

The manager then spent a few hours selling time on the station and one entire hour programming the automation system for the next day. The manager finally got out of the business because his one-man operation was "so lonely."

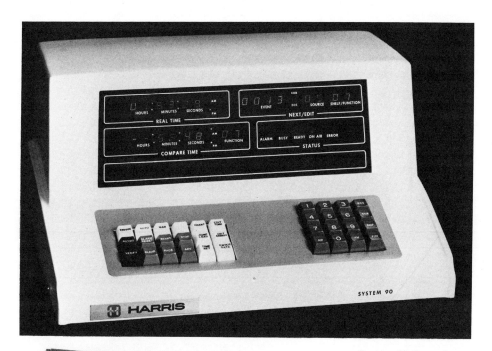

System 90 Console

KGRO-AM, Pampas, Texas.
This system will handle a locally programmed pop music format. Three carousel-type random accessed multiple cartridge playbacks for music; one Instacart multiple cartridge machine for commercials, PSA's, local news, ID's, etc.; and one reel-to-reel (not shown) for a talk tape. System 90 control electronics and control console.

schafer
903 *BROADCAST AUTOMATION SYSTEM*

PRESENTING... THE ALL NEW
schafer 903E

* 8000 EVENT DUAL-FILE MICROELECTRONIC MEMORY

* 3 DAY STORAGE FOR ADVANCE PROGRAMMING

* LOWEST PER-EVENT COST OF ANY MEMORY

* COMPLETE MANUAL REMOTE CONTROL

* ONE-TIME PUSHBUTTON BULLETIN INSERTION

* EXCLUSIVE CLOSED-LOOP CIRCUIT

* NETWORK JOIN CAPABILITY

* PROGRAMMABLE BY TIME AND/OR SEQUENCE

* DUAL ALARM SYSTEMS BUILT-IN

* CRYSTAL CONTROLLED DIGITAL CLOCK

* EXCLUSIVE ONE-BUTTON COMMERCIAL SEARCH

* FOUR-WAY KEYBOARD ACCESS LOCK

* FULL STEREO OUTPUT AND MONITORING

* FIVE YEAR MEMORY WARRANTY

* CHOICE OF STUDIO OR RACK CONFIGURATIONS

In addition to all the advantages listed above, the Schafer 903E has three full days of commercial availabilities and three days of program events, for advance programming and total weekend walkaway! *All that, and the 903E has the lowest cost per-event of any automation system, plus the proven performance of the Schafer 900 series control units.*

Add it up. You'll see that the 903E has three times the capability of any other system on the market, plus the human engineered features that you need in your station every day.

Schafer experts in system planning, financing, programming, taxes, and engineering are as close as your telephone. Call today for details about the new 903E.

schafer
a Subsidiary of Cetec Corporation

Schafer Electronics Corporation
75 Castilian Drive, Santa Barbara Research Park
Goleta, California 93017   (805) 968-0755

Tell me more about the 903E !

name _____ title _____

station/company _____

address _____

City _____ State _____ Zip _____

KBUR-FM, Burlington, Iowa. This system will be used with a Drake/Chenault XT-40 format (Top 40). In addition to the System 90 console and control electronics, it includes four reel-to-reel machines to execute the music; one 3-deck cartridge machine for ID's, weather, etc.; two single playback decks for odd- and even-time announce; and an Instacart multiple cartridge handler for commercials and PSA's. These sources are all called on in the desired program sequence by the versatile System 90 microcomputer, which is controlled by the portable console located up to 150 feet away from the system. This system also includes high-speed Clear-Text logging for complete automatic print-out of the station's program log.

KIKS-AM, Sulphur, Louisana. This system handles TM Programming's good music format. Four reel-to-reels for the music; three carousel-type random accessed multiple cartridge machines for commercial announcements, PSA's, etc. This system employs automatic numeric logging for verification of program execution. Plus System 90 control electronics and control console.

7

The Information Format

As competition grew stiffer in radio markets throughout the country, it became more difficult for operators such as McLendon to simply walk in and achieve overnight success with a Top 40 format. When McLendon entered the San Francisco market via an Oakland facility, he quickly monitored KYA and KFWB and decided not to go up against them. These stations were well-established rockers, and it would have taken years to overtake them. But McLendon had begun thinking more in terms of social responsibility of broadcasters and had conceived the idea of looking for and filling voids in the programming spectrum. He decided on good music, much the same as Lee Segall had been programming for many years on KIXL in Dallas, and similar to the music of WPAT in New Jersey. But McLendon added a twist that made his KABL an almost overnight success. He *romanced* the San Francisco market with poignant bits of nostalgia and eyebrow-raising contests, such as ten cents for the best description of the dark side of the moon.

After San Francisco, McLendon began thinking about an all-news operation. He had had a great deal of experience in airing short newscasts on his other stations, but neither he nor anyone else had tried *all* news. There was plenty of news available, and there were plenty of people available who knew how to find it, write it, and put it on the air. Why not an all-news operation? Well—why not?

The great southern California market was covered by one 50,000 watt signal that generally just didn't impress audiences. It was on a frequency of 690 kcs and originated in Tijuana, Mexico. The station was XETRA. McLendon conceived the idea of obtaining U.S. "sales rights" from the owners of the station, and setting himself up as a "program consultant". With these agreements firmly and legally signed, McLendon, in 1961, started the country's first all-news radio station. The industry perked up. Industry journals hailed McLendon as the most innovative programmer in the business. Los Angeles and San Diego were turned on to the all-news station. Jam-packed freeway drivers had but to "punch up" the station to get a full dose of news; news *anytime,* 24 hours a day, seven days a week. McLendon had always believed that a station must sound approximately the same, every minute of every day, and to the all-new format he applied this thinking. News, nothing but news, around the clock. McLendon's news people would cross the U.S.-Mexico border daily at Tijuana to work their shifts. The station subscribed to all wire services, and it was essentially a rip-and-read operation. Executive and sales offices were in Los Angeles. Commercial tapes were bussed to the border every day, along with logs and other program materials. Logistically, it was difficult, and the operation proved to be very expensive. But it was new, and was well-received by southern California. Business was good, and from this area McLendon moved to Chicago in 1964 to establish WNUS and the country's second all-news operation.

Meanwhile KFWB in Los Angeles and WINS in New York had turned all-news, and the idea had taken hold. All-news had become an accepted format. It was erroneously thought that only a major market, such as Los Angeles, Chicago, New York could support such a specialized format.[1] By 1968, McLendon had abandoned the idea and switched both of his all-news operations to a particularly good brand of lush music in Los Angeles and Chicago, because, with his relatively poor technical facilities, he simply couldn't compete. The XETRA transmitter was almost 150 miles south of Los Angeles and it was an awesome problem getting staff and materials back and forth across the border. In Chicago, WNUS's signal could not be heard in the very area an all-news station should reach—the affluent North Side. Only with a superior signal could McLendon hope to compete with such giants as KNX, KFWB, WBBM and WINS.

It wasn't FM's impact on music alone that brought many AM radio operations to programming all-news. The electronic medium in general had brought

[1] All-News or News/Information formats in 1977 were doing well in Phoenix, Omaha, Houston, and Dallas.

people closer to world events. Events in Europe suddenly concerned the little retailer in Canton, Ohio or Tyler, Texas, because, via electronics, that little retailer had been caught up in international affairs.

TV's ability to bring congressional hearings and other events into the living room of average America further whetted the citizens' interest in news. It would become axiomatic that as turmoil in the world intensified, popularity of all-news operations would rise.

In addition to McLendon's "invention" of the all-news format, interview programs had begun to emerge. Joe Pyne of Los Angeles had scored dramatically in ratings, and his radio show was being syndicated across the U.S. and Canada. Mike Wallace of CBS had scored successes in some very candid interviews, and in Dallas, Jack Wyatt was doing TV interviews with ex-convicts, prostitutes, and other social types that would grab the interest of viewers. Years later, Bill Ballance in Los Angeles launched the first "sex" talk shows. All the elements were there for the modern day information format. It remained only for someone to put them all together into a viable, profitable operation.

The information formats of the '70s characteristically emerge in three forms:

All News
All Talk
News/Talk

A pure information format excludes musical programming of any kind. Many operators have included news blocks and talk shows in a music format, and many have been successful in a variety of areas. Those operators defied a long-held rule that stations must specialize to ever gain sufficient audience to be profitable.

THE ALL-NEWS CONFIGURATION

A one-hour program schedule for an all-news operation may appear as follows:

MORNING
6:00–9:00 - Morning Report
6:00–6:05 - National, World News (Net)
6:05–6:15 - Local News, Weather
6:15–6:20 - Sports (Net)
6:20–6:23 - Local, National Headlines
6:23–6:25 - Stock Markets/Features
6:25–6:30 - Pyramid News (Local, Regional)
6:30–6:35 - National, World News (Net)
6:35–6:45 - Local News, Weather
6:45–6:50 - Sports (Net/Local)

6:50–6:53 - Local Headlines, Weather
6:53–6:55 - Stock Market
6:55–7:00 - Pyramid News (Local, Regional)

Of course, length of news, sports and features vary according to the concept of the programmer, size of the market, and the operating budget. It is almost certain that such a format should include some network news. A typical modern "News wheel" might appear: (See p. 54)

This particular news wheel will accommodate 18 minutes of commercial matter, public service announcements, and promotional announcements. Network news consisting mainly of national and world items is broadcast on the hour and half hour. Each specific information period may be formatted in detail, or the flow may be left to the anchorperson and the engineer (producer). This wheel is intended only to demonstrate the elements of a news hour. The programmer may wish to record the network news on the hour and play it back (delay broadcast) at 15 minutes past the hour, or he may wish to exclude network news altogether. Commercials may be clustered differently and the commercial load decreased, thus allowing more time for news matter. The combinations are *endless*. This wheel encourages a 30-minute flow of mostly different information, with repetition occurring only on top local and national stories. The second 30-minute flow is almost the same as the first, except that all material should be rewritten and/or updated. The networks most certainly will do this, and locally-produced news and features should also be revised. While some listeners tune in and out rather quickly, others tend to listen longer. Objections come primarily from the same story being repeated in the same words quarter-hour after quarter-hour. Rewrites and repetition actually increase understanding of the news and keep listeners tuned for a longer period of time.

Undated feature material may be repeated, but not as often as hard news stories. Even with a widely spaced rotation plan, there should be at least two versions of the feature, with at least the lead sentence or paragraph changed. There are listeners who will hear all four of the broadcasts, and same-word repetition can cause a dial switch.

The typical hour illustration may vary also from day-part to day-part. More sports may be included in morning and afternoon drive when male audiences are more available to listen. Softer feature material may be substituted for sports in the mid-day period. More weather and traffic information might be included in the drive periods as a special service to motorists. Stock market reports may be abbreviated in the early hours, as these will contain information on only the previous days trading. The all-news wheel is the most variable of all formats. Nothing is fixed immovably; conditions change hour by hour, and the all-news teams must be ready to confront these conditions.

In the late '50s and early '60s when McLendon was getting XETRA (called "Extra" News) and WNUS off the ground, the format had been simpler. Most of the material broadcast was "hard news," and the style attracted mostly males of the 25 + demographics. The contemporary belief is that by including features on consumerism, child care, education and related topics, women listeners will be attracted. The idea, simply, is to make the all-news format more entertaining by adding actualities, sound effects, and less formal anchor persons. Anchor assignments have undergone changes, with more women occupying anchor seats. Dual anchors are common, as on television. There is considerable argument over the viability of dual anchor systems. They work for some, not for others, depending, perhaps, on economics and the chemistry of the individuals involved. Sports is getting much more play now than in previous years, due largely to the proliferation of professional teams and divisions. The idea of making news more entertaining does not mean broadcasters treat the news less seriously. There is a time in each news period for by-play between the news people; there are other times when such by-play would be offensive. This impromptu activity is often left entirely to the judgment of the anchorperson or persons.

There are differences of opinion on how much feature or alien material should be included in the all-news format. One argument is that *anything* that decreases the flow of hard news is harmful to the format. "Listeners tune for *news*—not some feature on how to feed a baby or water a plant," the argument goes. Ultimately, these become subjective arguments and do not contribute to the orderly development of a format. The fact is, the plan that works in one market may not work in another. Detroit, with its huge blue collar population, may, indeed, want a stronger dose of hard news. But a slower-paced market, such as Dallas, may react more favorably to feature treatment. So, it may be said that the all-news format creates as many program arguments as a contemporary music station. The music-casters search eternally for the proper rotation and sequence of play for hit records. The news operators argue over where and how much business news to air. When does the format have too much sports? At what point does the format contain too much hard news? How often should a feature be repeated? Should production aids be used?

Every station broadcasting news claims something different, *really* different, about its format. One station in New York claimed it was the first, in 1958, to use tape inserts during news reports and the first to include a commentary as the tag item of a regular newscast. But a Dallas station said it was using tape inserts as early as 1955, even before the now-common endless-loop tape cartridge was in use. The Dallas station simply recorded actualities reel-to-reel, then turned the Magnacord playback on at the moment the actuality was needed. Mike Stein, former news director of WNEW, New York, believed the key to newscast style is writing. "Most stations have newscasters talking in what I call 'newscasterese.' We try to get our staffers to talk on the air the same way they would in conversation," he added. And good writing is the basis for this delivery style.

KNX in Los Angeles has a computerized traffic control reporting system, supposedly the first of its kind in radio news. There are over 700 miles of freeway in the Los Angeles area—a lot of traffic to cover. KNX used Xerox

Data Systems computer equipment to provide 20 regular traffic reports during peak travel hours. Other stations, to handle morning and afternoon drive traffic reports, have hired policemen to interpret otherwise dull and meaningless police reports on traffic pile-ups. Still others have stationed mobile ground units at critical points to give updates. Others have employed fixed-wing aircraft and helicopters.

The methods employed to gather and broadcast news on an all-news format are virtually endless and are limited only by the station's finances. A panoramic graphic might include:

The "panoramic" indicates the breadth and scope of a maximum-effort operation. The drawing does not show editorial offices, administration suites, secretaries, bookkeepers, or other personnel not required to produce the news report. In this elaborate arrangement, editors and re-write personnel receive the raw material of finished news in a variety of forms.

THE STAFF

In putting together a news staff, management's first effort, obviously, is to find and employ the top person, referred to as news director, editor, managing editor, or other appropriate title. These individuals, particularly in the case of an all-news operation should have had considerable experience in this specific format. They must understand and endorse the licensee's *concept* of the operation, and must be in a position to push and enforce station policy. Only with this kind of management-editor rapport can a station expect to succeed. Because the station will be dealing exclusively in information, the editor should have a broad, general educational background, as well as experience, and he should be an administrator capable of directing the activities of many other newspersons. It isn't enough to be the best reporter or editor on the staff. The editor of an all-news operation must also have the intelligence, knack, and patience to guide, stimulate and control the activities of subordinates.

Once the editor has been selected, management should develop the plan of action, from the smallest detail of re-write and story life to the image management would like to present to the public. An operation manual should be written, detailing the "do's and don't's" of the plan. Here is a basic manual that might be used as a starter. It is not intended as the last word in operating manuals, and the ideas may be employed at any news department, whether the station is all-news or not.

KXXX's News Policy

INTRODUCTION

This News Policy and Operations Manual is intended to give news personnel guidance in the day-to-day performance of their duties.

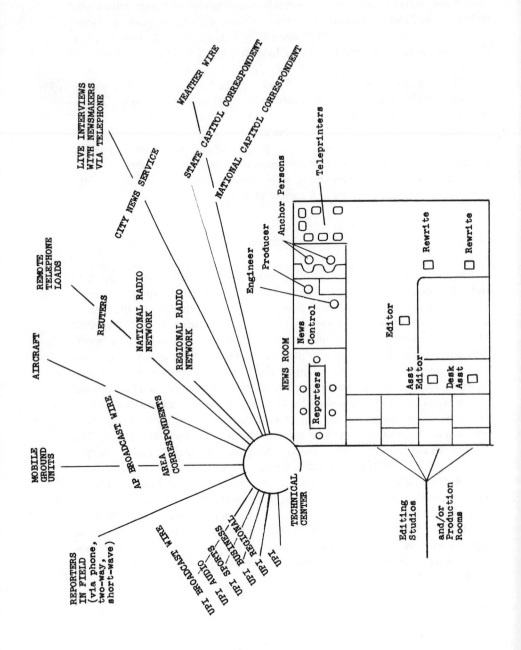

MOBILE GROUND UNITS

AIRCRAFT

REMOTE TELEPHONE LOADS

REUTERS

LIVE INTERVIEWS WITH NEWSMAKERS VIA TELEPHONE

CITY NEWS SERVICE

WEATHER WIRE

STATE CAPITOL CORRESPONDENT

NATIONAL CAPITOL CORRESPONDENT

NATIONAL RADIO NETWORK

REGIONAL RADIO NETWORK

AP BROADCAST WIRE

AREA CORRESPONDENTS

REPORTERS IN FIELD (via phone, two-way, short-wave)

UPI BROADCAST WIRE

UPI AUDIO

UPI SPORTS

UPI BUSINESS

UPI REGIONAL

UPI

TECHNICAL CENTER

NEWS ROOM

Reporters

News Control

Engineer

Producer

Anchor Persons

Teleprinters

Editor

Asst Editor

Desk Asst

Rewrite

Rewrite

Editing Studios

and/or Production Rooms

174

Personnel are expected to work by the spirit, if not the letter, of each guideline. If exceptions must be made, such exceptions should be discussed with the Editor or General Manager.

Please keep this material in your possession; do not Xerox, and do not loan your manual to anyone outside the station. There are no secrets herein, but it is internal paper and we want to keep it that way.

From time to time we will add, delete, or modify portions of the manual. You will be expected to post these changes and otherwise keep your copy up-to-date.

The Management
September, 1977

STATION NEWS POLICY
(Background & Explanation)

It is the responsibility of the licensee to determine policy supporting the methods and procedure the station will use to find, prepare and broadcast news material. It is the specific duty of the General Manager to ascertain on a day-to-day basis that the licensee policy is carried out. The licensee may delegate the responsibility, but it cannot be *absolved* of responsibility. Any policy set by the licensee must include procedures that insure accuracy and fairness in the presentation of news material.

The following 10 points, taken from the Radio-Television News Directors Association's Code of Broadcast News Ethics, represent the broad policy under which the News Department operates.

Broadcast News Ethics

1. The primary purpose of newspersons—to inform the public of events of importance and appropriate interest in a manner that is accurate and comprehensive—shall override all other purposes.

2. Broadcast news presentations shall be designed not only to offer timely and accurate information, but also to present it (news) in the light of relevant circumstances that give it meaning and perspective. This standard means that news reports, when clarity demands it, will be laid against pertinent factual background; that factors such as race, creed, nationality, or prior status will be reported only when they are relevant; that comment or subjective content will be properly iden-

tified; and that errors in fact will be promptly acknowledged and corrected.

3. Newspersons shall seek to select material for newscast solely on their evaluation of its merits as news. This standard means that news will be selected on the criteria of significance, community and regional relevance, appropriate human interest, service to defined audiences. It excludes sensationalism or misleading emphasis in any form; subservience to external or "interested" efforts to influence news selection and presentation, whether from within the broadcasting industry or from without. It requires that such terms as "bulletin" and "flash" be used only when the character of news justifies them; that bombastic or misleading descriptions of newsroom facilities and personnel be rejected, along with undue use of sound and visual effects; and that promotional or publicity material be sharply scrutinized before use and identified by source or otherwise when broadcast.

4. Newspersons shall at all times display humane respect for the dignity, privacy and the well-being of persons with whom the news deals.

5. Newspersons shall govern their personal lives and such nonprofessional associations as may impinge on their professional activities in a manner that will protect them from conflict of interest, real or apparent.

6. Newspersons shall seek actively to present all news the knowledge of which will serve the public interest, no matter what selfish, uninformed or corrupt efforts attempt to color it, withhold it or prevent its presentation. They shall make constant efforts to open doors closed to the reporting of public proceedings with tools appropriate to broadcasting, consistent with public interest. They acknowledge the newsman's ethic of protection of confidential information and sources, and urge unswerving observation of it except in instances in which it would clearly and unmistakably defy the public interest.

7. Newspersons recognize the responsibility borne by broadcasting for informed analysis, comment and editorial opinion on public events and issues. They accept the obligation of broadcasters for the presentation of such matters by individuals whose competence, experience and judgment qualify them for it.

8. In court, newspersons shall conduct themselves with dignity, whether the court is in or out of session. They shall keep broadcast equipment as unobtrusive and silent as possible. Where court facilities are inadequate, pool broadcasts should be arranged.

9. In reporting matters that are or may be litigated, newspersons shall avoid practices which would tend to interfere with the right of an individual to a fair trial.

10. Newspersons shall actively censure and seek to prevent violations of these standards, and shall actively encourage their observance by all newspersons.

The following are guidelines and specific instructions that are used to implement the News Policy:

Department Organization

1. The News Department shall be under the daily guidance of a Managing Editor, who shall be responsible directly to the General Manager of the station.
2. The Managing Editor shall be responsible for recommending reporters, editors and broadcasters to be employed in the News Department. The General Manager shall rely upon the Managing Editor for recommendations in the hiring, disciplining and dismissing of all news department personnel, but responsibility for same shall remain with the General Manager.
3. The Managing Editor shall assign each news department employee specific duties for which the employee is qualified and shall be responsible for the quality of that individual's productivity.
4. The Managing Editor shall be responsible for certain administrative details in the department, including but not limited to:
   a. approving weekly time sheets
   b. requisitioning supplies for department
   c. requesting pay increases for department employees
   d. naming Assistant Managing Editor and other subordinate editors
   e. setting day-to-day operational procedures
5. The Editor on duty is responsible to the Managing Editor for the composition of any news broadcast. In the absence of the Managing Editor, the Editor on Duty shall be responsible to the General Manager.

Special Interest Stories

Special interest stories shall not be included in the news broadcast unless, in the judgment of the Editor on Duty, such stories are deemed to be valid news.

Examples:

(Business)

A retailer who has purchased a schedule of announcements on the station requests that the station cover his "grand opening." The *Editor on Duty* decides. Should the person making the request wish to appeal, he should appeal to the Managing Editor. Further appeal should be to the General Manager. Such story will be run only if the Managing Editor and General Manager *agree* that it should be run. It is *not* big business news when McDonald Hamburgers adds another store in the market. It *may* be legitimate business news when the president of McDonald's addresses a civic group and makes pronouncements on the economy. No advertiser shall be entitled to any news coverage simply because he is an advertiser. Neither shall an advertiser be excluded from news coverage, simply because he is an advertiser. Any editor making a decision *to air* or *not air* shall be responsible *only* to the Managing Editor for his decision.

(Political)

No political figure, elected or appointed, shall be *entitled* to any special coverage. Coverage of elected and appointed officials' activities will be conducted by the news department, but only to the extent that, in the judgment of the Managing Editor and subordinate editors, these activities constitute bonafide news.

The exception to this rule will occur during political campaigns involving legally qualified candidates for public office. It shall be the responsibility of the Managing Editor to ascertain that *every* candidate involved in a particular race is provided with equal coverage, no matter how remote that candidate's chances for election, or to otherwise follow the FCC's most recent guidelines or rules relating to political reporting.

Section 315 and the Fairness Doctrine shall guide editors in their decisions on stories involving political figures, in or out, and on controversial issues. It is a hard policy of the licensee to ascertain that both or several sides of all controversial issues will be covered, no matter how unpopular one side or the other may be.

(Intemperate Language)

Individuals express themselves in different ways. The lawyer or public relations person may be eloquent. Except for patently obscene, profane or indecent language, which will not be broadcast under any circumstances, the Editor on Duty will make the judgment of whether an expression shall or shall not be broadcast. The Editor on Duty has a social responsibility in this instance and should consult with the Managing Editor or General Manager when in doubt.

There will be instances when the voice and words of a newsmaker should not be aired, when the editor should voice the *meaning* of the voice and words of the newsmaker. The objective here is clarity, and the editor must ask, "Does this taped actuality convey the speaker's meaning, or should I write and voice the meaning?"

Example: Khrushchev: "We will bury you." Did the speaker mean, *literally,* that the USSR will destroy the USA? Or was the word "bury" a euphemism for outdistancing economically, industrially or socially?

Militant: "It's time for our people to buy some bullets." Is the speaker issuing a call for violence? Or is "buy some bullets" a euphemism for "get tough" or "fight harder" or "work harder"?

There can be no hard-and-fast rule governing the editor's judgment in such instances. In the militant instance, some stations aired the remark while others deleted it. In the Khrushchev instance, editors and reporters have argued for years over the former premier's meaning. It is a matter of *editorial judgment* which the Editor on Duty must make on the spot. The Editor must be responsible for the decision and able to justify to management the decision. Actualities with obvious calls for violence should not be aired; such calls should be reported, but in the language of the Editor.

Example: Newsmaker: ". . . and I say we have taken all we can take. I say it is time we picked up our guns, clubs, pitchforks, and attacked the White House. It is time to kill, kill, kill!!''

(NOTE: The Secret Service doubtlessly would be interested in this speaker, as his statements indicate a threat on the White House occupants.)

Editor's Report: "In a fiery tirade, the speaker issued a call for violence. He used the words, "kill, kill, kill" and said it was time his people picked up weapons and attacked the White House. Other speakers at the rally quickly voiced opposition to such action and urged the crowd to keep calm and let the problem be handled through due process of law."

The Editor, in this case, conveyed the meaning of the speaker's words, but eliminated the "passion" from the delivery of the message. This was an obvious effort to incite a riot, a vigorous call for violence. No station should be *used* in this manner. The Editor has a responsibility to the public to *edit* such stories to convey the meaning of the speaker but to *eliminate* the danger of actually inciting a riot. No Editor would want to feel responsible for the death of another person. If one person killed another as a result of actually hearing a passionate call for violence, that Editor could be, at least morally, responsible for that death.

(Fairness/Balance)

"News" is no more than a report on what *people* are saying and doing. It should reflect the activities *of* society, and occurrences *in* society. It should always be true, never manufactured, contrived, twisted. It is the job of the reporter and Editor to gather, sift, evaluate, untangle, write and broadcast these sayings, doings, activities, and occurrences. Trained, conscientious personnel are required to make such judgments. Even skilled professionals, with years of experience, differ over what is and what is not news. Some reporters take no responsibility for what they report. If newsmaker "A" says political figure "B" took a $10,000 bribe, some reporters will put this on the air *without* ever bothering to ascertain the truth of such a damaging statement.* Such reporters believe they have done

* Libel and slander laws vary from state to state, but it is possible that a station and the reporter writing and airing such a statement could be held liable.

their jobs; that it is not their responsibility to determine the impact of the story; that their jobs are to report what is done, not weigh its impact on society or on the individual charged. The more responsible reporter, upon getting such a story, will immediately check with the person charged or with other sources who would know if such a charge contains any truth. Obviously, if *police* charge someone with theft, if a grand jury charges someone with accepting a bribe, the story may be reported without the necessity of further immediate checks. But if one citizen charges another citizen with theft or bribery, or any crime, criminal or civil, the story should be checked before it is aired.

Example: Newsmaker: "That company has no minority employees; it discriminates against Blacks and Mexican-Americans. The company has interviewed seven minority applicants in the last month and has not hired any of them. I say the company is guilty of racial discrimination."

It would be *unfair* to let this stand alone as a news story. Such charges should be reported simultaneously with the company response. The following is an example of how the story might be handled.

"AT A MEETING OF THE CHAMBER OF COMMERCE BOARD TODAY, MRS. A. E. SPARKS CHARGED THE AJAX COMPANY WITH RACIAL DISCRIMINATION. THE CHARGES WERE IMMEDIATELY DENIED BY T. C. DAVIS, PRESIDENT OF AJAX. AT THE MEETING, MRS. SPARKS VOICED HER FEELINGS:

(Actuality: The company has interviewed seven minority applicants in the last month and has not hired any of them. I say the company is guilty of racial discrimination.)

THE STATION REACHED MR. DAVIS AT HIS OFFICE, AND TOLD HIM OF MRS. SPARKS' CHARGES. DAVIS DENIED THE CHARGE:

(Actuality: "Twenty-five percent of Ajax employees are either Black, Mexican-American, or American Indian. We conduct interviews with prospective employees every day, and if an individual is qualified we hire him or her without regard to race, color, or sex. We may have rejected seven minorities last month, but it was not because of their races.")

THE COMPANY, WHICH HANDLES A NUMBER OF GOVERNMENT CONTRACTS, SAID IT HAD CERTIFIED TO THE FEDERAL GOVERNMENT THAT 25% OF ITS EMPLOYEES ARE MINORITIES AND THAT IT IS AN EQUAL OPPORTUNITY EMPLOYER.

That's *fair* treatment of the story.

(Accuracy)

Accuracy will never be compromised in the News Department. No story can have any meaning unless it is true and unless it is reported *accurately*. Inaccuracies in one medium (radio) are often repeated and enlarged in another medium (newspaper). The facts of a story, regardless of source, should be checked and re-checked before the story is aired. In radio news, it is permissible to round off large figures, e.g., $106,892.50 may be reported as "one hundred six thousand eight hundred," or, "nearly $107,000," or "just under $107,000." But reporting $5,000,000 as $500,000 is not acceptable.

Accuracy in reporting also means reporting statements and incidents "in context," e.g., the avoidance of pulling a strand from the fabric and reporting the strand as the whole truth. Example:

> Newsmaker: "I am violently opposed to conditions. We must kill to maintain our dignity. We must kill bigotry; we must kill hate; we must kill poverty."

If the reporter quotes the speaker only as saying "We must kill to maintain our dignity," he is taking the statement out of context and therefore giving it a meaning different from that intended by the speaker.

Accuracy must be maintained in the News, even when it means delay in getting an important story on the air.

(Form and Style)

1. Foreign names, words and phrases will usually be given local or area pronunciation. Thus, "Guadalajara" will be pronounced GUAD-UH-LUH-HARA. There will be exceptions, such as Wagner, the composer. His name will be pronounced VAUG-NER.
2. NEVER say "6 a.m. this morning." This kind of redundancy is absurd. "Six a.m. today; two o'clock yesterday afternoon.
3. Beware of unconscious crutches: *"Good morning,* this is Bill Smith and in the news *this morning* the City Council will meet *this morning* to discuss zoning laws. And the weather *this morning* is fair to partly cloudy, etc."
4. Beware of excessive personal identification. The appropriate place to identify yourself is at the end of a story, if you're performing as a *reporter,* and at the beginning and end of a 15-minute local block, if you're an anchor person. In 5-minute blocks, identify yourself only in the opening *or* closing line.
5. Too often, we hear repetition (ad nauseum) of story lines, indicating lack of "feel" for the programming. Following is the kind of situation to avoid:

ANCHOR: COUNTY COMMISSIONERS HAVE AGREED THAT A TAX INCREASE IS THE COUNTY'S ONLY WAY OUT OF THE CURRENT BUDGET CRISIS. HERE'S A REPORT FROM JUDY JOLLY

DAR: This is Judy Jolly. County Commissioners have agreed that a tax increase is the County's only way out of the current budget crisis. We talked with County Judge John Jones this afternoon at 3 p.m. and here is what he said.

(Actuality: We have agreed that a tax increase is the County's only way out of the current budget crisis.) I'm Judy Jolly, KXXX News.

A more correct way to have handled *this* story:

ANCHOR: THE COST OF LIVING IN THE COUNTY MAY GO UP, AGAIN, ACCORDING TO WORD FROM THE COURT HOUSE. HERE'S JUDY JOLLY WITH THAT STORY

DAR: County Commissioners today warned taxpayers they may have to bite the bullet to solve the current financial crisis—and biting the bullet in this case may mean a hike in taxes. Following this afternoon's 4-hour meeting at Commissioners Court, County Judge John Jones had this to say:

(Actuality: We have agreed that a tax increase is the county's only way out of the current budget crisis.)

DAR: If the proposed tax increase goes through, it would be the first such increase in 50 years. Judy Jolly, KXXX News, County Court House.

6. Fatalities: Reporters and newscasters sometimes forget that survivors hear fatality stories. Because we *do care* about the feelings of survivors, we treat the names of victims with care. *Never* say "the Smith woman was DOA at Parkland. Instead, "Miss or Mrs. Smith was pronounced dead on arrival at Parkland Hospital." *Mister* Smith died on the operating table an hour later. Minimize use of police jargon in reporting crime stories. "John Smith, white male, 21, was shot in the stomach by an officer as he resisted arrest." Instead, write: Twenty-one year-old John Smith was shot as he resisted arrest. Officer Tom Jenkins said he fired once, striking Smith in the stomach." Don't hesitate to use two, three or four sentences to express the story. *Always* avoid long, complicated sentences.

7. Titles: The names of women will always be preceded by Miss, Mrs., Ms. or any official title such as Councilwoman, Mayor, Congresswoman, etc. The names of men will *never* be preceded by "Mister" (except in cases of fatality); only by such titles as doctor, senator, mayor, major, colonel, etc.

8. Rewrites: Whether it's an overnight done by Mary King or a story from one of the papers, do a genuine rewrite job. *Never, never* use the same syntax; if you can't update the story, at least put a second-day lead on it or otherwise take a fresh approach. But never read the same story twice using the same word and sentence organization. There is time—always—to at least reverse the lead sentence. Here's an example, beginning with a story from the newspaper:

COUNTY VOTES TIGHTER BUDGET

In an anticlimactic finish to several weeks of talk about County taxes, County Commissioners voted with little ado Tuesday to tighten the county budget rather than raise taxes this year.

(Point one: Do not ever, in any re-write, use the phrase, "with little ado;" this is a pet bromide of the newspaper reporter who did the story, and it becomes immediately apparent that you simply lifted the story from the paper.)

County Commissioner Jim Ellis stalled a planned vote Monday to set the 1975 tax rate, by staying away from Monday's meeting in an effort to buy more time on the tax question. But he showed up Tuesday and voted with County Judge John Jones to raise the county's tax rate 3¢—to $1.03 per $100 valuation.

These two were voted down by Commissioners David Pryor, Roy Nicholson and Jim Whitley, who voted to hold the line and retain the present tax rate.

(Point two: "Hold the line" would be another tipoff that you have simply lifted the story from the paper. You *must* watch these bromides; use your own, as you probably must, but don't use someone else's.)

YOUR REWRITE, COLD:

County Commissioners voted three-to-two today to cut expenses rather than raise taxes. Commissioners Pryor, Nicholson and Whitley voted down a 3-cent increase proposed by County Judge John Jones and Commissioner Jim Ellis.

(More details as desired, depending upon time available.)

YOUR REWRITE, WITH ACTUALITY:

County Commissioners decided today to cut expenses rather than raise taxes. Commissioners Pryor, Nicholson and Whitley voted down a 3-cent increase proposed by County Judge John Jones and Commissioner Jim Ellis. Contacted by KXXX News, Commissioner Jim Ellis had this to say about his support of the proposed tax increase:

(Ellis' clip)

Commissioner David Pryor, who opposed the increase, had this to say:

(Pryor clip)

After the vote, Commissioners ordered department heads to make a seven percent cut in the county payroll. This action was taken to provide funds for an increase in pay that was promised county employees last year.

SECOND USE OF COLD REWRITE:

A proposed 3-cent increase in county taxes has been voted down in Commissioners Court. County Judge John Jones and Commissioner Jim Ellis had suggested a tax rate of one-dollar-three cents per one-hundred dollar valuation. Commissioners David Pryor, Roy Nicholson and Jim Whitley united to kill the proposal.

(More details as needed)

SECOND USE OF REWRITE WITH ACTUALITY:

Three against two—that was the vote in Commissioners Court today when a proposed 3-cent county tax increase was voted down. County Judge John Jones and Commissioner Jim Ellis proposed the tax increase as a means of solving the county's economic situation—and Commissioners Pryor, Nicholson and Whitley voted them down. Contacted by KXXX, Commissioner Pryor had this to say:

(Pryor clip)

Judge Jones, who pledged during his campaign for his post that he would try not to raise taxes, put it this way:

(Jones clip)

AD-LIB REWRITE OF ORIGINAL:

Commissioners David Pryor, Roy Nicholson and Jim Whitley today voted down a 3-cent tax increase proposed by County Judge John Jones and Commissioner Jim Ellis. The 3 to 2 vote against means that the county will have to cut expenses to make the budget balance.

9. *Immediate Action:* There has been a tendency away from "deadline" reporting in broadcast journalism. At KXXX, on significant stories, the "deadline" is the minute you get accurate details of the story. This is to say, we *want* to break in on whatever is being programmed with "bulletin" material. Example Opening: We interrupt this program for a KXXX news bulletin.

"A building in Irving has been hit by explosions and fire. First reports indicate there are some injuries. KXXX reporter Mary King is en route to the scene and will have details shortly."

The idea is to present the news in an interesting and exciting manner. The idea is *not* to put an eight column headline on a two-inch story, but rather to present big news in a big way.

Another technique for presenting "bulletin" material is from the mobile news unit. Example:

Contr: Play special news intro.

King: (from unit) This is Mary King in the KXXX mobile news unit. We're en route to the scene of an explosion at a chemical plant in Irving. First reports indicate there have been injuries. Details when they're available.

Contr: Outro cart.

Immediate "bulletin" action is especially desirable on severe weather stories. The minute we receive such information, we should present it in bulletin or "urgent" form, and make *sure* we continue updating our listeners until the watch or warning has been lifted. Our audience includes many persons in the 50+ age range, and weather bulletins are *especially* important to them.

In short, there will be no cavalier treatment of stories that warrant immediate, bulletin action.

10. KXXX news is delivered *straight,* without editorial comment orally or by voice inflection. Commentary, if in good taste, or a "brite" may be used *once* only if it is written into the story. A "brite" is defined as a light, humorous story.

11. *Preemptions:* A *major* news story will *always* take precedence over other programming. A major news story is one that is judged to have a major impact on life, the city, state, nation, world. The most obvious example would be someone killing or attempting to kill the President. Should a story of such magnitude occur, the news department is to preempt *immediately* (including commercial matter) and take the air. THE EDITOR IN CHARGE SHOULD IMMEDIATELY CAUSE THE GENERAL MANAGER TO BE NOTIFIED SHOULD SUCH A STORY BE AIRED.

12. *Story Life Cycle:* No completed story that appears in the morning report should ever appear on the next day's morning report. Our basic rule on the tenure of a story in our news budget is based on appearance of the story in the morning and afternoon newspapers.

When a story is broken in the afternoon paper (even if we had it earlier,) and appears again next day in the morning paper, we will not use it beyond the next day's morning report.

When a story is broken in the AM paper, and it appears again in the evening paper, we will not use it beyond the same day's evening report.

Once a story is completed, it is even more important to follow the guidelines on re-writes. The same story in the same words becomes drudgery for the writer, newscaster, *and the listener*.

On a developing story, new developments, if they are significant, may follow the same cycle as indicated above. However, in a rapidly developing story, a single cycle is indicated. If, for example, the morning paper has Jones charging Smith and we carry it, along with a rebuttal statement from Smith, we would not continue beyond the evening report. If, however, we carry Jones' charges all day, and can't find Smith until, perhaps, 4 p.m. for a retort, then we would run the rebuttal through next day's morning report.

Generally, we will *never* run a story more than 24 hours. We will never pick up a story that we believe hasn't quite died and use it to fill. Instead, we will select a state or regional story for use when there is not enough actual local material to complete the newscast.

13. Anchor persons are *required* to be in news control and prepared to begin at precisely the prescribed time. Program logs will be carefully checked for commercial load, and news material will be timed around that load. PSAs and station promos will not be used to fill commercial availabilities.

14. *Housekeeping:* All personnel have responsibility for keeping their work areas clean, and share in responsibility for keeping the general work area clean. This includes picking up scraps of paper, throwing away used plastic coffee cups and, generally helping keep the place neat and orderly.

15. *Commercial Work:* Each newsperson may be required to record commercial or public service announcements.

The preceding, of course, is only an indication of what a licensee may establish in the way of a Policy Manual. The policy should always reflect the thinking of the licensee and his concept of FCC rules, regulations and guidelines, and the public's needs, tastes and desires. One broadcaster may think it is acceptable to say "The Smith woman was dead on arrival at the hospital," while another may wish to soften the story by saying, "Mrs. Smith was pronounced dead upon arrival at the hospital."

After developing policy and hiring the department head, care must be exercised in the selection of staff. At this point, budget considerations should be reviewed because a maximum staff of top flight professionals is very costly. Let us assume we are putting together an all-news staff for a

50,000 watt AM station in Birmingham, Alabama. The plan is to affiliate with one of the major radio networks and broadcast news 168 hours per week.

Personnel requirements:
1 Managing Editor
6 Anchor Persons
5 Engineers (Operators)
5 Local Reporters
4 Editors
4 Re-write Editors
1 State Capitol Reporter
1 National Capitol Reporter
2 Traffic Reporters (part-time)

Facilities:
NBC Radio Network
UPI Broadcast Wire
UPI Audio Wire
UPI Sports Wire
UPI Business Wire
UPI Regional Newspaper Wire
UPI "A" Wire
Associated Press Broadcast Wire
Reuters News Service
Weather Wire
Two Mobile Units, with 2-way
One Helicopter, with 2-way
Short Wave Receiver-Recorder Setup
Frequency Scanner, Police, Fire

SPACE REQUIREMENTS

The modern all-news operation, tragically, is often housed in make-shift studios and offices that were designed in another age for a different kind of operation. In designing the all-news work area, special consideration should be given to the paper and tape flow, accessibility of edit rooms, desks, telephones and typewriters to news personnel, and to designs and configurations that enable staffers to concentrate on news material.

The plan offered provides desk space for six reporters and three edit rooms where they may break down tapes into actualities and wraparounds. The managing editor's office opens to the main operations area, giving that person immediate access to the staff. Business News and Sports News are given special consideration here, because these two editors do a lot of record-keeping and

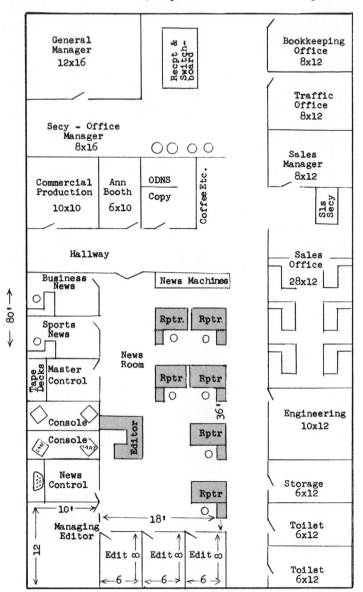

write many complicated, technical-type stories. Their need for more privacy is apparent. It is critically important that all electronic equipment be kept in top repair, as nothing is more frustrating to the broadcast journalist than to have a tape machine break down in the middle of an editing task.

Note that the news room is completely separated from sales and administration, but that it is across the hall from production, operations, and copy. The news room is a world of its own, often housing persons who care or know nothing about the commercial aspects of broadcasting. Newspersons are a breed unto themselves, as are sales and administrative personnel. This should not imply that these groups of specialists cannot coordinate their efforts toward a common goal—because they can—but rather that each group needs its own professional environment to function maximally.

MATCHING PERSONNEL

It is one thing to gather 25 professional broadcasters under one roof to produce a format. It is quite another to gather 25 persons who can *work together as a team*. Careful screening of each employee is essential, to avoid hiring persons who are known troublemakers, loners, and those who lack self-confidence. Even with careful screening, errors will be made in assembling the team. Also, it is essential to observe the moral and legal requisites for ethnic and sex balance on the team. The day of the all-white, all-male staff is gone. Women have proved their ability and their worthiness in broadcast journalism. They no longer are relegated to the role of "news hens" on newspapers or the task of legwork and rewrite with no opportunity for on-the-air broadcasting. Ethnic minorities are similarly entitled and, indeed, broadcasters are legally obligated to give fair treatment. It will not be enough to simply say, "We didn't get qualified applicants and therefore didn't hire females or minorities on our staff." If you do not get such applications, you should make a major search for them.

These are some of the background items the interviewer should look for:

EDITORS: Degree in journalism or broadcasting. Experience on one or more local stations. Some newspaper experience would be helpful. Previous employment should include some staff and/or management work (because Editors must supervise the work of other people.) Voice suitable for air work or "voicers," vacation fill, on-air interviews.

ANCHOR: Same educational background as Editors, but voice quality and ability to interpret news copy are most important factors. Established name would be valuable. Should have the ability to gather, write, edit news. Delivery should convey warmth, authority, sensitivity. This sure-footed image is critical.

REPORTERS: Degree in journalism or broadcasting. Experience as a reporter for other stations, and, hopefully, on a newspaper. Voice quality not important, though an extremely "odd" or high-pitched voice could have a detrimental effect on voicers and actualities. Should have experience in the market, due to the importance of good local news sources. It sometimes takes years to build confidences among newsmakers.

ENGINEERS: These employees may be also referred to as producers or operators. They are an extremely important part of the operation and should have experience operating various kinds of control boards, consoles, and mixers. They must have, or be able to develop rapidly, a sense of flow, as they are responsible for mixing newscasts, commercials, public service announcements, sounders, music backgrounds, and other elements of the format into a smooth, well modulated program. In most cases, these employees are "comers," e.g., persons working their way up through the ranks to become reporters, editors or anchor persons.

Desk
Assistants: These individuals are sometimes called copy persons, gofers, editorial assistants. They indeed may be called upon to run copy from one point to another; to record feeds from reporters, networks, two-way units. They should be able to provide this kind of assistance in several areas.

Re-write
Editors: May or may not have voice capabilities. Must be able to quickly rewrite stories, develop new angles and new facts. Good newspaper background very desirable.

A DAY IN THE NEWSROOM OF AN ALL-NEWS RADIO STATION

The staff is organized into work units that provide some overlap in hours to maintain continuity of work on news material. Remember, any system suggested may be altered in a dozen different ways. In this system, the work schedule is as follows:

The plan calls for 20 full-time employees and 12 part-timers. The part-time persons might get an additional 24 hours work per week as Reporters, Relief Engineers, Relief Anchor Persons, or as Feature Writers. In any event, for an efficient, reliable and believable news operation, a large number of skilled professionals is required. This plan, in fact, calls for fewer personnel than many major market operations such as KNX, Los Angeles; WINS, New York; and WBBM, Chicago. Unions may impose conditions that would make this 32-person staff unworkable. This could be particularly true of producer/

EMPLOYEE	MON	TUES	WED	THURS	FRI	SAT	SUN	TOTAL HOURS	COMMENTS
MG EDITOR	8A-5P ————————→							40	ALWAYS ON CALL
AM ANCHOR	5A-2P ————————→							40	
AM ANCHOR	5A-2P ————————→							40	
AM EDITOR	5A-2P ————————→							40	
AM RE-WRI	5A-2P ————————→							40	
PM ANCHOR	1P-10P ———————→							40	
PM ANCHOR	1P-10P ———————→							40	
PM EDITOR	1P-10P ———————→							40	
OVERNIGHT ANCHOR	9P-6A ————————→							40	
OVERNIGHT ANCHOR	9P-6A ————————→							40	
OVERNIGHT EDITOR	9P-6A ————————→							40	
PRODUCER/OP	5A-2P ————————→							40	
"	2P-11P ———————→							40	
"	11P-8A ———————→							40	
WEEK-END ANCHOR						5A-2P	5A-2P	16	
"						5A-2P	5A-2P	16	
PRODUCER/OP						5A-2P	5A-2P	16	
"						5A-2P	5A-2P	16	
WEEK-END ANCHOR						1P-10P	1P-10P	16	
WEEK-END ANCHOR						1P-10P	1P-10P	16	
PRODUCER/OP						1P-10P	1P-10P	16	
PRODUCER/OP						1P-10P	1P-10P	16	
WEEK-END ANCHOR						9P-6A	9P-6A	16	
WEEK-END ANCHOR						9P-6A	9P-6A	16	
PRODUCER/OP						9P-6A	9P-6A	16	
PRODUCER/OP						9P-6A	9P-6A	16	
RPTR A	9-5 ————————→							40	
RPTR B	9-5 ————————→							40	
AM SPTS	5A-2P ————————→							40	
PM SPTS	2P-11P ———————→							40	
RPTR C			9-5 ——————————→					40	
RPTR D		9-5 ————————————→						40	

CART NO.	TIME	WHO (LOCATION)	DR	A	DAR	DESCRIPTION (SUGGESTED LEADS)	TIME USED
L71	53	PRYOR W/ DALLAS MAYOR WISE			x	THE MAYOR HAS ANNOUNCED THAT HE WILL CONTINUE TO SUPPORT THE UNION TERMINAL PROJECT. PAUL PRYOR HAS MORE	
L72	13	WES WISE, CITY HALL		x		LISTS REASONS FOR SUPPORTING PROGRAM OUTCUE: "ITS SOMETHING DALLAS NEEDS"	
L73	44	PRYOR	X			FEDERAL JUDGE WILLIAM TAYLOR HAS DISMISSED SEVERAL OTHER DEFENDANTS IN THE DALLAS DESEGREGATION CASE. PAUL PRYOR REPORTS	
						DR - Direct Report	
						A - Actuality	
						DAR - Direct Report, with Actuality	

FUTURE FILE

DATE _____10 31_____   FILED BY _____PRYOR_____

TIME _____9:30ᴀᴍ_____   DATE FILED _____9 9 75_____

LOCATION _____DALLAS CITY HALL_____
_____CITY COUNCIL OFFICES_____
_____

DESCRIPTION _____MAYOR EXPECTED TO REVEAL HIS POSITION ON THE UNION TERMINAL____
_____PROJECT BEING INCLUDED IN THE DECEMBER BOND ELECTION_____
_____

CONTACT _____MAYORS SECRETARY CALLED CONFERENCE, MAYOR AND RAY HUNT_____
_____WILL BOTH ATTEND NEWS CONFERENCE_____

PHONE _____748-9711_____

FILE DATES _____9 8 75_____
_____
_____

FOLLOW-UP _____MIGHT GET REACTION FROM OTHER BUSINESS LEADERS, CONCERNING__
_____CITYS ROLES IN PROJECT, DO THEY APPROVE, OR DIS-APPROVE_____

_____CHECK WITH OTHER COUNCIL MEMBERS TO SEE IF THEY_____
_____APPROVE OF JOINT PROJECT_____
_____
_____

engineers, who will spend nine hours in the station with one hour off for a meal or break. If work breaks are required by the union contract, then additional personnel will be required to operate the board during those breaks.

Plan of Action

When the morning Anchor Persons arrive at the station, the overnight team has already prepared most of the material to be aired during the important morning drive period (6–10a.) The material may be in one of the following forms:

Copy, local and wire, edited to be read
Actuality on cartridge, with copy to be read
Direct Report, on cartridge
Direct Report, with actuality, on cartridge

Cartridges are labeled in detail to indicate length, subject, and outcue. Form N-1 will be helpful in maintaining a log of on-going news material. It is absolutely essential that Editors and Anchor Persons communicate accurately to succeeding Editors what has taken place on each story. Union restrictions notwithstanding, anchorpersons can achieve a better flow and better production by inserting and firing their own cartridges. Producer/Engineers handle mixer controls and the firing of commercial, PSA, and promotional cartridges. Paul Pryor, Managing Editor of an all-news operation in Dallas, WRR, assigned each air person a series of cartridge numbers, noting that many broadcast newsrooms label carts with "complete information." The only information shown on Pryor's cartridge was a number (such as L-71) meaning "local" story, Pryor. The anchorperson, using the N-1 log form, referred to the log for details of the story. Often, the "description" column provided enough information for a knowledgeable anchorperson to ad lib an intro and close for the cart. Pryor believes the advantage of his system is that the anchorperson can merely glance at the log sheet and know immediately what taped material is available. He believes this is much more efficient than wading through dozens of different carts. Furthermore, this plan permits the Managing Editor to double-check each reporter's work, in terms of finding and preparing news material. The forms and master tapes are filed daily, giving the newsroom an immediately-available morgue.

Pryor also maintains a "futures" file, using form N-2. In addition, newspaper items relating to the upcoming story are clipped and attached to the form, giving the reporter additional references. Pryor uses the advance file in another interesting manner. "When I see a slow news period developing, I pull the advances and assign reporters to do enterprise pieces for use on our newscasts."

Newsroom files can be critical, at times. Background material on famous local newsmakers can make significant difference when that newsmaker dies or is otherwise involved in a big story. These files may be compiled from station efforts and by clipping stories from magazines and newspapers. Voice clips should also be included in the files, perhaps in a special "tape file" in the station morgue.

The AM Editor and re-write persons, immediately upon arrival at the station, will receive a fill-in on what has broken overnight. They will begin the daily task of updating, following up leads developed overnight, and re-writing overnight material for its frequent use on the morning report. At 6:00 a.m., the anchorperson scheduled to do the first half-hour, will begin. The first period may be scheduled:

6:00-6:05 - NBC Network news

6:05-6:15 - Local, state news. Emphasis on
weather, frequent time checks.
Recap top national news at 13:30.

6:15-6:20 - Sports/ Business/Human Interest Features

6:20-6:25 - World, national pyramid newscast, using
actualities and voicers recorded from
UPI Audio and NBC Network.

6:25-6:30 - Local, state news updates

6:30-6:35 - NBC Network news

And so the daily wheel has begun. The second anchorperson during the 6:00-6:30 period has been assisting in preparing material to be broadcast in the 6:30-7:00 slot. This rotation continues throughout the morning, with Editors and re-writers working steadily, processing the never ceasing flow of materials from the wire services, local reporters, and the network. Anchorpersons are required to take the myriad material and assemble it into an interesting, believable news program. Frequent time checks and weather updates are essential services that should be broadcast conscientiously and continuously. Time, traffic, and weather checks are especially important in the morning drive period, as listeners need this information to help them get to work on time, avoid traffic jams, and dress properly for the current weather.

The AM staff continues producing the half-hour newswheels through the 1:00-1:30 period. At 1:30, the PM staff has had a half-hour to phase into the operation and pick up the pace by producing the 1:30–2:00 p.m. wheel. This procedure continues until the end of the PM shift at 10:00 p.m.

Throughout the broadcast day, Reporters and Editors are checking their own sources and monitoring the competition for new stories or new developments on ongoing stories. The "scoop" attitude prevails in most news departments, but it seems to be more intense in all-news operations. Considerable effort is expended each day in gathering, writing, and producing news features that will be broadcast, perhaps, four or five times in the ensuing 24 hours. Even the all-news operation must be prepared to devote full time and attention to a major news story, and this to the virtual exclusion of all other news. A major disaster or an attempted assassination of a prominent figure will place heavy demands on each staff member. Off-duty personnel may be called in to assist. The *entire* department may become involved and, indeed, should become involved. A station's reputation as a reliable, authentic source of news may well be at stake on stories of such magnitude. This is where radio does its best job. Radio can impose an immediacy not possible on television or in newspapers.

TELEPHONE TALK SHOWS

Broadcasters view telephone talk shows with mixed emotions. Controversy may develop ratings, but it often drives away advertisers and promotes adverse public reaction. A prime case in point was, in the early 70s, when under Fairchild Industries, KLIF in Dallas instituted a "sex talk" show, with Disc Jockey-Program Director Dave Ambrose serving as host. Station ratings had been sagging for several months and, noting the success of Bill Ballance's talk show in Los Angeles, management decided to air a similar program. The program was broadcast live, with Ambrose taking calls from listeners. Crux of the show's format involved opening each day's show with a provocative question, such as, "How do you turn your man on?" The question, and others like it, apparently turned on a great many women, because the next rating book (ARB) showed KLIF improving its audience by some 25,000 women. While the show was obviously "turning people on," more straight-laced listeners were keeping the switchboard at the station busy, and others were writing to the FCC and to advertisers whose messages were heard on or near the two-hour program.

The value of contracts cancelled during the first month of the show amounted to thousands of dollars. Accounts that were sensitive to "public image" were demanding that their spot announcements not be closer than one hour before or after the show. Meanwhile, across the nation other stations were trying to cash in on the apparent success of these shows. The idea was, if they want "sex talk," we'll give them a real dose.

The FCC indicated early in the fracas that it would not interfere with the "chick-chat" shows. The National Association of Broadcasters (NAB) was indicating some official nervousness, because in San Francisco, FCC Commissioner Charlotte T. Reid told the Seventh Annual Radio Program Conference that the "commission is not concerned with individual programs, even if a large number of the audience finds them offensive." She noted that "many people think the FCC is a censorship board," but said she personally wondered, "how such programs fit into the concept of public need."

Congressional hints and continuing harrassment from dissident citizens finally brought the sex talk shows to their knees.

But telephone talk shows, sans the overdose of sex, continued and prospered. KTRH in Houston was broadcasting a steady diet of them, and the ratings were good. WMCA in New York broadcast only talk shows, and some of the best talk show hosts in the nation worked from those microphones. WERE in Cleveland was showing rating successes with talk shows, but the station in 1975 abandoned the "hassle" in favor of NBC Radio's full-time News & Information Service. This was a dramatic new concept in network news that provided affiliates with 50 minutes of news per hour, 164 hours a week.

Telephone talk shows have many advantages in terms of a station "broadcasting in the public interest." A good moderator, who has done his or her homework, can dig into an important story and provide more information in two hours than a regular news program could provide in two weeks. In journalistic terms, the "feedback" is fantastic; public reaction cannot be duplicated in any other kind of show. The problem is that, without controversy, mass audiences won't listen, and station ratings will remain low. *With* controversy, ratings will build, but many advertisers are reluctant to be associated with controversy. Sheer personality can build a talk show audience, but such personalities are rare.

Properly handled, talk shows may be used for in-depth development of the most complicated issues. Normally dull subjects such as tax reform, economics, or psychology can be brought alive by a well-informed moderator, knowledgeable guests, and curious listeners who call in and voice questions and comments. The procedure for a telephone talk show is fairly simple once moderators, operators (engineers), and listeners catch on to the system.

A seven to 30-second delay system is necessary to keep off the air any obscenities or other words not suitable for broadcast. Many listeners, whose names are not known and whose voices are disguised somewhat by the carbon microphone in the telephone, will articulate their hates and biases freely if given half a chance. Moderators may or may not want such expressions edited out of the dialogue, but when station policy prohibits, a delay system is necessary.

Two telephone instruments with "speakers" are needed to produce a talk show with good technical quality. The arrangement may be similar to the following:

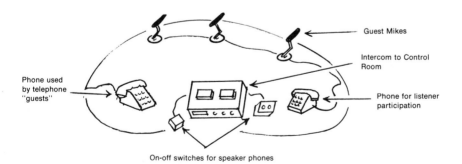

Guest Mikes

Intercom to Control Room

Phone used by telephone "guests"

Phone for listener participation

On-off switches for speaker phones

Under the arrangement, the moderator or "host" speaks directly into a studio microphone connected to a special mixer in the control room. The mixer also controls the three or four guest microphones. Some stations use a volume-control device that is voice-actuated. This simplifies work for the engineer, but more importantly, it opens *only* the microphone or microphones that are actually being used. Accoustics seem to fail in a studio with four or five live microphones open simultaneously.

When the phones are "opened" for listener comment, incoming calls are worked through the phone at the right (the left would be just as good, except that it is good to establish mechanical habits). The moderator who is not familiar with the phone system will concentrate on the mechanics of the show rather than the subject matter. The line on which the calls come in is depressed, followed by the moderator hitting the "on" button of the speaker phone. The conversation is "line fed" to a volume control in the control room for better quality, while the moderator hears the caller through the speaker phone. The conversation proceeds normally, with the audio fed into the "delay" system before being aired. It is a maddening experience to *watch* a talk show through a studio window, and *hear* the dialogue through a radio or a program line-fed speaker. The dialogue heard was spoken 7 to 30 seconds earlier by participants; the words heard do not match the lip movements of participants.

When the conversation is finished, the moderator lightly touches the "off" button of the speaker phone system, and the caller is off the air. The second telephone system is used primarily for "guests" who appear on the show via telephone.

In such instances, the guest could be a nationally known economist who, from an office in New York, might spend an hour or so on a program being broadcast in Houston. The guest simply remains on the telephone, talking with the moderator, and later talking back-and-forth with callers. The guest hears callers' questions and comments from the "caller speaker phone" on the right. This system obviously permits easy discussion of a topic by one caller, three studio guests, and the moderator.

A typical dialogue:

```
HOST:  The inflation-recession the country is exper-
iencing has touched most of us in one way or another.
Gasoline is scarce and expensive; it costs more to build
houses these days, and rates of interest are out of sight.
Pay scales haven't kept pace with the rises in the cost
of living, and those with fixed incomes are in particu-
larly bad shape.  To tell us the "why" of our economic
situation, we've arranged to have as our telephone guest
Dr. So-and-So from San Francisco.
```

Dr. So-and-So is a nationally-known economist who served as economic consultant to the White House during the last administration. He has authored a book on the subject, and we believe he is amply qualified to speak to our listeners today. Dr.-So-and-So, are you on the line?

GUEST: Indeed I am, Bill. And I'm ready to go to work.

HOST: Great. Dr. So-and-So, what has happened to our economy? Why are prices so high? Why are so many people out of work?

(A question and answer session continues for, perhaps, 15 minutes, between the "host" and "the telephone guest." Then:)

HOST: Okay, Dr. So-and-So, all of our phone buttons are lighted, so it's time to find out what's on the mind of listeners here in Atlanta. We'll be back in two minutes.

(At this point, the moderator breaks for commercials, public service announcements, weather, or news headlines.)

HOST: Okay, we're back and this is the Bill Smith Show. And we have Dr. So-and-So, nationally-known economist, on the phone in San Francisco. We've been talking with Dr. So-and-So about the country's economic plight. Now, Dr. So-and-So, if you're prepared, we'll go to the telephones. Let's talk to our first caller.

CALLER: Yes, I wanted to ask Dr. So-and-So if our sale of all that wheat to Russia has had anything to do with the cost of bread.

GUEST: Absolutely. When we sold that wheat to Russia, we created a shortage in this country. Under the laws of supply and demand, etc., the shortage forced prices up. Everybody seems to be making more money except the wheat farmer.

CALLER: I thought so; an article I read in <u>Newsweek</u> blamed that wheat deal for a lot of our problems.

HOST: Yes, and other writers in other publications have said the same thing. Okay...let's go to line #2 for another question or comment. If you wish to talk with Dr. So-and-So, just call us at 234-7765. That number again, 234-7765 (hitting the "on" button). Good morning, you're on the air. Do you have a question for, or a comment to Dr. So-and-So?

CALLER: Dr. So-and-So, I have read your book, and I think you're all wet in your theories. Professor So-and-So at Harvard did a critique of your book -- and it was his opinion, etc...

HOST: Now we've got an argument going, Doctor; how do you feel about Professor So-and-So's criticism?

GUEST: (responds, and the dialogue continues)

The dialogue flows smoothly because the moderator knows the subject and is familiar with the telephone system, while the guest is amiable, and the callers are familiar with the procedures. In other cases, the show does not go smoothly. The following is an example of a poorly produced show, guaranteed to turn listeners away by the thousands:

HOST: Let's go to our telephone lines now, so listeners can chat with our guest. Hello, you're on KXXX.

CALLER: Am I on the air?

HOST: Yes sir! Go ahead with your question or comment.

CALLER: I'm not on the air, either; you're kidding me. I can hear the radio and it isn't me.

HOST: Turn your radio off, sir. We're on a tape-delay system, and you can't listen to the radio and talk at the same time.

CALLER: Well...just a minute and I'll go turn off
my radio.

HOST: Well, while we're waiting for our gentleman
caller to turn off his radio, we'll just kill a few
seconds here with a commercial or two.

CALLER: Okay, I'm back. But I've forgotten what it
was I wanted to ask your guest.

And that's a fairly mild example of how a bad caller can literally destroy
the entertainment value of a talk show. No matter how hard a station tries,
some of these callers will get through. If a "screener" can be employed, the
calls are initially answered in another studio. Callers can be instructed on how
they should participate in the program. Sample of such screening:

SCREENER: Good morning, this is the producer of the
            Bill Smith show.

CALLER: Yes, I want to ask Mr. Smith's guest a
            question.

SCREENER: Fine. Now, is your radio turned off?

CALLER: No, but how will I know I'm on if I
            turn it off?

SCREENER: Turn it off, lady; I'll explain.

CALLER: All right.

SCREENER: Now, when we finish talking, the next voice
            you hear will be that of Mr. Smith. He'll
            say good morning, you're on the air. At
            that moment, you _are_ on the air and should
            make your comment. By the way, keep your
            question or comment very brief; get right
            to the point, because we have five other
            calls holding and we want to give everyone
            a chance to participate. Okay?

Hopefully, with such explanation, the caller will participate in the show,
ask one or two relevant questions, then hang up. The unlucky host will have
callers who ramble, do not know the subject under discussion, or who want to
deliberately disrupt the show. Often, the screener can learn what the caller

wants to say and, if the caller is off-target, suggest that he or she call at a later time when the question would be more relevant. The "mild tempered" host may be unable to cope with certain situations that arise on talk shows. When a host or a guest is insulted or intimidated by a caller, one or both of them may become involved in a mild argument with the caller and try to defend themselves. Some callers may force such a situation by throwing personal insults at the people on the air. A tough-minded host, with supportive station policy, might handle a "hot" situation like the following:

HOST: Good morning, you're on the air.

CALLER: Yes, I've been listening to the garbage you and your guest have been spewing, and I want to say I think you're both disgusting.

HOST: Now just a minute. No one asked you to call and make a comment like that. Go wash your mouth out with soap and try us another time. We'll go to the next line now, because I'm cutting that caller off. (Next caller) Good morning, you're on the air.

CALLER: Yes, I heard you cut that lady off. I think she was right, and you were rude to cut her off (Click!! Cuts her off)

HOST: Good heavens! Ladies and gentlemen -- we're trying to conduct a talk show here on KXXX this morning on the subject of sex therapy. Our guest is the prominent Dr. So-and-So, whose book on the subject has sold over a million copies. Now, if you want to call and make some kind of intelligent remark about Dr. So-and-So and his book, please do, but if you want to call and try to examine our personal morals, just forget it. This is my show, and I intend to handle it the way I want to handle it. Now...let's try another call.

CALLER: Yes, Mr. Smith. I've read Dr. So-and-So's book, and I think it is a valuable work. I

> have two small children, and until I read the
> book I was puzzled about some of their activi-
> ties.
>
> GUEST: Just what activities were you puzzled about?
>
> CALLER: Well, for one thing, my little boy played
> with himself a lot.
>
> GUEST: Certainly. Infantile masturbation is quite
> ordinary, and if you'll read Chapter 2 of my
> book again you'll find some advice on how to
> handle the problem.
>
> HOST: Thank you for calling. (hangs up the phone)
> Now, that's the kind of call we want this
> morning. Doctor...

A steady diet of argumentation would eventually take all value from the program. An occasional outburst by the host may be acceptable, but a steady diet of it would eventually ruin the entire effort. The moderator who can "kid" or cajole callers into conforming with the rules and procedures should be able to maintain an interesting, informative program.

Of course, all talk shows do not deal with "hot" subjects (sex therapy) or controversy (to build or not build an atomic reactor near your city). Many excellent talk programs involve special guests who discuss everything from how to fix appliances in the home to the fun of scuba diving. KTRH in Houston, a top-rated information station, has conducted interviews with sports editors, outdoor editors, sail plane pilots, doll collectors, foot specialists, veterinarians, publishers of underground newspapers, disc jockeys, treasure hunters, hobos, housewives with interesting hobbies, famous chefs—the list is endless; the world is full of interesting people, and a good talk show host will find them and expose them to his listeners.

As a technique for meeting a licensee's commitment to use the facilities to assist in solving community problems, the talk show is matchless. A licensee, through his ascertainment study, for example, might find the following to be his community's top 10 problems:

Crime
Street Lighting
Low-cost Housing
Public Education
Public Transportation
City's Health & Sanitation Facilities
Inflation

Segregation
Public Child Care
Unemployment

The ordinary music station may find the same community problems, and will pledge to address these problems through public service announcements, editorials and perhaps a weekly talk show on Sunday night. But information stations with a heavy schedule of talk shows literally depend upon the existence of such problems for talk show subjects.

The following examples demonstrate how the information station can approach community problems.

> CRIME: Host researches the problem from both local and national viewpoints. This self-education process is absolutely necessary for any host. Then, a variety of guests and circumstances may be indicated. Police spokesmen, ex-convicts, rape victims, and victims of armed robberies and muggings, are contacted for interviews. The rape victim, reluctant to be seen in a studio talking about the crime, may wish to participate via telephone. The host covers all bases: Why is the crime rate in our town so high? How do we compare with other cities our size? What sort of crimes are committed? Are the police equipped to handle them? If not, what would it take to solve this problem?

> UNEMPLOYMENT: Again, the host must educate himself and find experts on the question. How many people are out of work in our town? Who are they? Let's find some of them and have them tell their story on the program. What about the state employment agency? Find a federal official who knows the story. Get an economist to tell us his views on why local and national unemployment is so high.

Public officials have been known to ask for transcripts of programs on such subjects because of the valuable information that can be obtained. The station's objective, again, is not to solve the problem but to aid in finding a solution. Listeners often call in with extremely helpful ideas. Such statements as these, from local citizens, may give public officials a clue as to what the public at large would accept:

"I think people would pay higher taxes, if necessary, to hire another 30 policemen."

"I think some street lights on lower Elm Street would help stop those muggings and beatings in that area."

"I lost my job because my company lost a big government contract." (This call might inspire the host to get the local congressman on the air to explain why the company lost the big government contract.)

In the course of a broadcast day, the information station may deal with all such questions at one level or another. Example of a News/Talk format:

6:00- 9:00 a.m.	Morning Report (All News)
9:00-10:00 a.m.	The Spencer Callison Show (Issues oriented)
10:00-10:30 a.m.	Morton Bounty & his poetry
10:30-11:00 a.m.	Ask Susie (Home Management program)
11:00-12:00 a.m.	Do It Yourself Show (Household chores)
12:00- 1:00 p.m.	Noonday News
1:00- 3:00 p.m.	Nancy Rogers Show (Soft Subjects, not heavy issues)
3:00- 6:00 p.m.	Afternoon Report (All News)
6:00- 7:00 p.m.	Zip Small Show (Sports Talk)
7:00-10:00 p.m.	The Tommy Akins Program (Issues oriented)
10:00-11:00 p.m.	The Don Kraft Show (Astrology)
11:00-12:00 p.m.	Late News (All News)

Obviously, every possible idea and subject may be discussed at length on such a format. Top flight talk show hosts, professional broadcast journalists, and competent engineers each contribute significantly to making the News/Talk format flow smoothly and sparkle with interesting guests on well-researched topics. The "poetry" half-hour would have special appeal to older listeners.

The Nancy Rogers Show would explore everything from women in broadcasting to how to handle a rowdy child. The Spencer Callison program might deal with the morning news, his own and listener commentary on what happened in the world yesterday and last night. Callison might call his a "magazine format"—one that deals with a variety of subjects. Whatever the subject, such programming can be effective if skilled, interested personnel are employed and given the freedom to think and work.

The techniques of producing talk shows and news blocks vary from station to station, but there are certain fundamentals that are necessary if the station is to attract and hold listeners. These fundamentals involve radio's basic services—time, temperature, weather reports. A host may introduce his program in this manner:

"Good morning, I'm Bill Smith, and this is the Bill Smith Show. It's 9:00 a.m. on this Tuesday, the second of April. Our town weather forecast calls for rain today . . . so prepare yourselves. And temperatures will be in the low 40s for most of the day. Okay, today we have Mr. So-and-So in our studios, etc . . ."

The host should avail himself of every opportunity to provide the basic services. "It's 9:13 now, and we'll be back in a minute." (Pause for commercials) "Okay, we're back on the Bill Smith Show at 9:15 and our guest is Mr. So-and-So; we'll open our phone lines in just a second, right now it's 20 past 9, and the weather forecast calls for rain and temperatures in the low 40s; good morning, you're on the air!"

Most talk show programmers set breaks for commercials and other material at regular intervals during the hour. These are helpful to the host in planning the use of guests, prepared taped interviews, etc. A station allowing 18 commercial minutes per hour would be in trouble with 18 interruptions. One solution is to cluster the commercials, perhaps, at 10-minute intervals. It would be permissible, as well, to schedule two or three minute news "update" slots in the hourly plan; and, of course, listeners should be reassured now and then that the show will be interrupted at any time for bulletin news items.

Broadcasters such as John Gambling (WOR) didn't do talk shows as we have come to know them; they excluded what John Henry Faulk in 1975 was calling "open dialogue." Faulk liked the idea of getting strangers (the unknown folks) on the air to voice their feelings about events. Gambling "talked" a lot, and occasionally he did an on-air interview. But it was rare when he actually put an unknown listener on to speak on current events. Gambling also would play music when he ran out of something to say or needed a break. The music wasn't particularly important to the format; people tuned to hear Gambling's light-hearted conversation. The modern talk station doesn't play music, because it "breaks" format and because many stations have special ASCAP/BMI and SESAC licenses that forbid the playing of music. Jingles, background music for commercials, and musical bridges are permissible, but no music programming is permitted.

It is difficult to describe the characteristics of a good talk show host. Certainly, nothing he has been or is now will assure the programmer of success. A topnotch anchorperson who may be adored by the audience may turn them off upon relating and dealing with audiences on a one-to-one basis. The host often is an ombudsman between the citizens and their government, between adversaries in a controversial issue. It may be appropriate for the host to take sides (more often it is not.) But it is always necessary for the listener to identify with the hosts, rather than with those who would attack and malign them. The host must be well-read, well-informed, on a variety of subjects, particularly the one at hand. If the host doesn't know, this should be made plain to the audience; this act of acknowledging ignorance could bring the audience to the side of the station.

8

Religious Formats

"Go therefore and make disciples of all nations"

Matthew 28:16

"Go and proclaim the Kingdom of God."

Luke 9:60

"God has given us powerful tools in radio and television. Let us use them skillfully and faithfully to give light in a dark world."

Ben Armstrong, Editor,
Religious Broadcasting,
February 9, 1977, p. 9.

HISTORY

Religious radio stations started in the 1920s for the purpose of putting church services on the airways. The Lutheran Church-Missouri Synod founded radion station KFUO, December 14, 1924 in Clayton, Missouri, and the Moody Bible Institute began WMBI in Chicago, 1926.[1] KPBC, Pasadena, California, began broadcasting December 25, 1924. Like most other religious stations of that time, KPBC was founded by a minister, Dr. Robert Freeman, to carry the Pasadena Presbyterian Church worship services on Sunday mornings.[2] WMPC, Lapeer, Michigan, was founded by a minister, Reverend Frank S. Hemingway, who believed that radio afforded a great opportunity for reaching thousands of people beyond his own First Methodist Church in Lapeer.[3]

Toward the end of the 1920s the stations began to broadcast instructional programs such as the "Radio School of the Bible," initiated by WMBI. In the

[1]*Religious Broadcasting,* February-March, 1977, p. 30, and September, 1976, p. 13.
[2]*Religious Broadcasting,* February-March, 1977, p. 30.
[3]*Religious Broadcasting,* November, 1976, p. 17.

1930s when radio drama became popular on commercial stations, the religious stations produced radio drama based on biblical stories and themes.

The growth of religious radio stations lessened toward the end of the 1930s, perhaps due to the FCC's attitude toward licensing stations to what were termed "special interest groups," such as labor unions and religious organizations. The Commissioners at that time were concerned about the stations serving all opinions and creeds and not having any one station licensed for any one point of view.[4]

The religious organizations turned from establishing their own radio stations in the late 1930s and early 1940s to forming organizations for securing network time and time on the commercial stations. The Federal Council of Churches, an interdenominational group, was formed to represent many denominations to secure time for religious broadcasts on the networks. The National Religious Broadcasters was formed in 1944, and one of their purposes was to assist churches in getting their share of network time. This was the era of the great preachers on the networks as the sermons of Harry Emerson Fosdick and Walter A. Maier were broadcast over the nation.

In the later 1940s FM broadcasting became a reality, and some church groups turned again toward securing their own radio stations in the FM band. The American people were slow to become FM listeners and entrepreneurship among broadcasters and set manufacturers and merchandisers was slow in getting underway. Because of this lack of marketing enthusiasm, the movement toward FM religious stations stalled out in the early 1950s when religious organizations turned their efforts toward television programming.

In the 1950s many of the church groups set up their own radio programming departments. They sought to devise programs that would not interfere with a commercial station's format, programs that would be airable at times other than Sundays. For example, the news programs produced by the Lutheran Church of America, which were sent to 400 radio stations, featured interviews with national figures and world news. The Baptist Television and Radio Commission produced "Master Control" in 1959. This program featured MOR music and interviews, and was intended to fit into an MOR commercial station's format without any problems.

The cataclysmic events of the early 1960s prompted church groups to try new types of religious programming to reach a public disturbed by the Cuban missile crisis, the assassination of President Kennedy, and the Vietnam war. The Madison Avenue approach with the funny, dead realistic, scary spots of Stan Freeberg were intended to make religion speak to an audience concerned with worldly events. As the Vietnam war escalated and the student protests began, the churches began to try to reach the young people. Religious programs featuring interviews about the war, drugs, and cultural alienation placed in the

[4] Giraud Chester and Garnet R. Garrison, *Television and Radio* (New York: Appelton-Century-Crofts, Inc., 1965), p. 125.

context of Top 40, Rock, and Progressive music were sent to commercial stations to be played at late night when young people were listening. The Methodist Church produced a program called "Night Line." Listeners who were troubled could call in and talk to counselors about their problems. The Baptist Radio and Television Commission created a program with country music stars singing and preaching sermonettes to appeal to young adults.

In the 1960s country music began to win back its fans from rock, and some of the country stars like Johnny Cash, Charlie Rich, and Loretta Lynn began to record what was called "country gospel music." There began to be created a new kind of religious music, with some roots in country songs, traditional hymns, and a bit from the blues and dustbowl laments of the 1930s. The sin and redemption themes of the country music seemed to meld into a natural transition to the new gospel music with its Biblical lyrics and stories of spiritual seeking and salvation. During the latter 1960s and early 1970s this music began to catch on with the young people whom the upheavals of this era were driving into a search for spiritual inspiration and guidance. Country musicians began to form gospel groups. They began to play at churches and public concerts and their records began to sell. This gospel movement seemed to grow in three directions with the more upbeat country sound being called "contemporary Christian music," the traditional country sound being called "southern gospel," and the upbeat rock sound, called "Gospel Rock" or sometimes "Jesus Rock" and "Christian Rock." All of these songs had religious lyrics. As in the case of country and other music types, the play on radio made records popular and the record sales made people want to listen to the radio stations that played gospel music. Because of the emergence of this new religious music and its growing popularity, religious broadcasters saw a way to move back toward station ownership in the 1970s. The number of religious stations grew from 118 stations in 1974 to 415 in 1977.[5] With the growing popularity of the religious music the broadcaster had a ready-made programming format. The bulk of the programming could be recorded music interspersed with educational religious programs and worship services.

The great appeal of this new gospel music made it feasible to have commercial religious stations, because the music drew the listenership and the listenership attracted the sponsors. A kind of full service commercial religious station developed which had commercials, contests, news, weather, and public service spots in addition to religious programs.

With the popularity of FM broadcasting in the 1970s, the number of educational religious stations began to grow. Non-commercial, these stations were supported by churches, schools, educational and religious foundations.

The revitalized interest in religion in the late 1970s, the popularity of religious music, the feasibility of the commercial religious station, and the

[5] *1974 Broadcasting Yearbook,* p. D-4, and *1977 Broadcasting Yearbook,* p. D-79, Washington, D.C.: Broadcasting Publications, Inc.

growth of FM listenership and the educational religious FM station seem to indicate a continued increase in the establishment of religious radio stations in the 1980s.

COMMERCIAL MUSIC STATIONS

The commercial religious station is similar to most commercial stations in that it does have commercials, news, and public service programs, but there the resemblance ends. The programming is mostly religious music, but there is some time given to educational religious programs and worship services. The music may be contemporary Christian, Christian rock, southern gospel, traditional, spiritual, MOR religious, or a mixture of these types. Most stations will emphasize one type such as contemporary or rock, but will play some of the other types also.

The station may be locally owned or part of a group of stations owned by a corporation. Crawford Broadcasting owns nine stations, Universal Stations owns six stations, Mortenson Broadcasting owns six, and Swaggart Broadcasting owns five religious stations. In the case of the group-owned station there may be a vice president who selects the music for all stations. The specific format of the stations, however, may vary from market to market.

Station Organization

The station organization is similar to any commercial station. There is a general manager who is responsible for the whole operation. If the station is part of a group of stations owned by a corporation, the general manager is responsible to the president or vice president of the corporation. The general manager has a special responsibility for sales. Since it is a music station, the general manager may have quite an input to the program director about the music. In the case of the group-owned station, there is a music director who selects the music for all stations. The program director is over copy, traffic, production, music, and announcing. There is a sales manager who shares the responsibility for sales with the general manager. The office manager is in charge of bookkeeping and secretarial work. The production manager handles the production of all commercials, public service spots, public service programs, and locally produced religious programs. In case of group ownership, the production manager of one of the stations in the group will do some production for all stations in the group.

Programming—Commercials

The commercial religious station sells to many religious related clients such as religious bookstores, gospel music concerts, and institutes offering philosophic and religious study programs. One station manager said that fifty percent of his business was "Christian." At the end of one commercial, for car tune-ups at a garage, the jock said that the garage owner was a "Christian." The identification of places of business being "owned and operated by Christians" was in the tag of several commercials. The rest of the commercials are those found on any local commercial station; restaurants, bowling alleys, drug stores, office supplies, printing, and gardening supply greenhouses. There are no beer or wine commercials. Most of the production is fairly simple, the contemporary religious music under an announcer, but some dramatized commercials are produced and sound effects are used to emphasize the straight pitches. For example, in a commercial for a steak house located in a rural area, the announcer's appeal to get out in the "pure country air" was accompanied by coughing and city noises. The commercials for gospel concerts are very similar to those on secular commercial stations for rock concerts: a punch announcer backed by excerpts from the albums of the gospel singers, introduced and closed with very upbeat strings. According to one station manager, great care is taken in production to choose the right theme for a client's commercial "to get people into their store and buy their merchandise." Another consideration is that the music and sound effects are suitable to the station's image. He said there are two main considerations about the programming: (1) to get the religious message out, so that great care is taken that the commercials do not mar or take away from what he termed the "reverence" of the station's sound; (2) to give very good service to the client. As he said, "We are getting the (religious) message out 98% of the day with the music and everything we do at the station, but we want to serve the client well and in a highly professional way."

Music

Station managers program music that is compatible with the market and with the age group. In conservative markets, if they are seeking to appeal to ages 25 through 49, they play contemporary religious music. This music is upbeat, but doesn't get into the rock beat although some of it edges that way. Some of this music sounds like modern country. It is very sad with a yearning feeling. Some of the music has a very melodic, loving, comforting sound. Some has a very fast beat with a joyous sound like a spiritual with almost a rock beat. The music is chosen very carefully. As one station manager said, "This is a very conservative area, and we would lose our audience completely if we played Christian rock. We can play contemporary religious music, but we have to be careful. Some people were shocked when we played it at first, but now they are pleased with it. We couldn't play a higher tempo music because we're right on the edge now." One station manager described contemporary music as follows: "Contemporary music is simply a type that you tap your foot to or snap your fingers. It lifts the morale if you are a little down. It's just a good simple plain down to earth music. It's nothing fancy, but it is appealing because it's not lulling you to sleep.''

In some markets, Christian Rock, sometimes called ''Jesus Rock,'' is very popular. This is basic rock music with religious lyrics. It has a very fast beat, an ecstatic, ethnic sound. The female vocalists go very high, like the old Supremes records. Their voice quality has the sound of old time spirituals at a climactic moment, but with a much faster beat, generally backed by rock guitars and rock piano techniques, some of it a bit like the old barrel-house sound. ''Jesus Rock'' is very popular with teenagers in every market and with young adults in some markets. One station manager reported that young businessmen ages 24 to 34 liked Jesus Rock very much. In conservative markets some stations will program a variety of religious music: (1) tenors and baritone singers backed by piano or full orchestration singing semi-classical numbers with religious lyrics; (2) very upbeat spirituals; (3) traditional hymns rendered in Mantovanni style; and (4) southern gospel numbers that have a distinct country style.

But whatever the rhythm or the tone or the instrumentation or arrangement, all of the lyrics are religious. Some of the themes are ''Let My Light Shine for Jesus,'' ''Slow Down and Know That He is Love,'' ''When I Hear Him Call My Name,'' ''Father I Love You Today,'' ''I Love to be on the Mountaintop Fellowshipping with the Lord,'' and ''Cast Your Cares Upon Him.'' Most of the songs tell about the peace and joy that can be found by believing in God. Some of the songs have plots that are reminiscent of the country songs. ''Old Dan Cotton'' tells of an old man who found his belief in God in the solitude of a woods. It has a mournful country sound but has the nostalgic quality of ''Bojangles'' also. ''Harvest John'' is also in this genre, the story of a religious old man who helped a family to harvest their crops.

Some commercial religious stations program what one station manager called ''sensitive secular music'' which is non-denominational and humanistic. The lyrics communicate everyday homilies about taking care of the family and being thoughtful and considerate with fellow human beings. ''Stop and Smell the Roses'' by Mac Davis is an example of this type of music. One station manager said this secular music is programmed to give variety in lyrics from the denominational lyrics of the bulk of the religious music programmed.

Religious Programs

During the week days the commercial religious station will have five minute inspirational talks from local ministers. Some of these talks are played during evening drive time to lift the spirits of weary workers on their way home. On Sundays the station will ''block out,'' a term used by station managers meaning to sell most of their time in thirty minute blocks to local and national denominational groups and other religious organizations in the form of pretaped worship services and educational religious programs. Syndicated pro-

grams are a part of the program fare of the religious station. These are programs which are pre-recorded and marketed in religious stations all over the
country. They take the form of Bible lessons, worship services, narration of appealing human interest stories with religious themes, and religious music. An
example is "Chaplain Ray" which is sent to 125 radio stations in the U.S. and
Canada. Chaplain Ray is a pastor who ministers to prisoners. He tells stories of
prisoners who have gotten into trouble, have been jailed and then turn to
religion and are rehabilitated. He reads letters from ex-convicts who explain
how religion has helped them rebuild their lives. He records songs sung by
prison inmates and also interviews prison inmates. Chaplain Ray asks for donations to help place the broadcasts on stations where prisoners can hear them. He
also uses the donations to send some 400,000 Bibles and other religious literature to prisons. The program is fifteen minutes long and its theme is the "Pris-
oner Song." Other religious programming is done by the DJs who read scriptural quotations and preach two minute sermonettes.

News

On some commercial religious stations the jock reads the news from the
wire service for five minutes at twenty minutes after the hour. These are state
and national stories followed by the weather. Directly after this comes an audio
service newscast of national and international news for five minutes. The DJ
does a traffic report and a sportscast during drive time. Other religious commercial stations use the wire service audio on the hour and weathercasts on the
thirty and the fifty. Some stations add a religious note to the introduction and
close of the news programs: "K——— presents the news of today and the
promise of tomorrow." "This has been K——— information news, the news
that is now history. Now with the news that never changes, more from the
word of God on K———, Christian Radio." Most of the religious stations that
feature music do not have news departments. The news programming consists
of wire service audio and the jocks reading from the wire service reports.

Public Service

Like any other commercial radio station, religious stations have an obligation to do public service programming. In the Dallas-Fort Worth metroplex
market, KPBC programs a telephone call-in talk show with guest experts on
various issues and non-denominational inspirational talks (five minutes) on
problems of daily living. They also schedule public affairs programs such as
"Black America" and "The Next 200 Years," which deals with issues like the
energy problem. They do the usual PSAs from health foundations like blood
banks and the American Cancer Society. These spots are read live by the DJ,
one spot every hour. In addition KPBC schedules "Dr. Moon's Gardener Calen-

dar," a program about gardening tips with Dr. Robert Moon, Chief Horticulturist, Dallas County Agricultural Extension Service.

KPBC does an interesting spot that resembles an Emergency Broadcast System announcement:

SFX:	Sounder
ANNOUNCER:	For the next 60 seconds this station will conduct a test of the Awake and Awareness Broadcast System. This is only a test.
SFX:	Two shots
SFX:	Sounder with chorus singing.
ANNOUNCER:	Had this been an actual rapture, you who are in Christ would have been with the Lord at the sound of the trumpet and shout. This concludes this test of the Aware and Awareness Broadcast System.

KWJS-FM, also in the Dallas-Fort Worth market, programs spots about traffic safety, college counselling services, church services, and benefit performances. KMGC, also in this market, does the usual spots from national foundations, but in addition produces panel and interview programs that deal with local issues.

Disc Jockeys

Disc jockeys of commercial religious stations have the responsibility of carrying the image of the station. The station managers want them to be cheerful, pleasant, and reverent. In the case of the station that plays contemporary religious music, the jock is expected to adjust his chatter rhythm to that of the music, which is rather upbeat, but not as hot as rock. The disc jockey will weave in some religious content as he moves from record to record. Phrases like "Praise the Lord," "Shalom everyone," "I love Jesus," "Isn't God's love wonderful," "Jesus of Nazareth requests your presence at a dinner in His honor," "That's what happens when Jesus comes into your heart," are woven in around the time and temperature in a quick, deft, cheerful manner. A cart will introduce the jock with a religious note: "It's time to praise the Lord with Alicia Klasky on KWJS."

The jock also recommends scriptural readings for different hours of the day.

Eight fifteen at KPBC 1040 radio in Dallas. Our breakfast this morning, Romans 13:8 through 14. Romans 13:8 through 14 is our lesson in living this morning.

Sometimes the jock will read the scriptures to the listeners.

The jock will preach short sermonettes on familiar themes which are related to everyday living: "Be decent and true in everything you do. Then all can approve your behavior. Don't spend your time in wild parties and getting drunk or in adultery or lust or fighting or jealousy. Ask the Lord Jesus Christ to help you live as you should." Then later on in the shift the jock will repeat one of the phrases from the sermonette, "If you love your neighbor as much as you love yourself you will not want to harm or cheat him." All of this is done in a normal kind of radio speech without any "holy joe" overtones or "prea-cherish" delivery. Of course the jocks work in the usual kind of comment that you hear from most disc jockeys such as, "Getting hot out there." "Where am I?" (sound of pages turning). "Here I am. I didn't turn the page last time." For the most part the disc jockeys on commercial religious stations are very professional and many of them have come out of lay radio. Some of them use religious air names such as "Deacon Bill Smith."

Religious disc jockeys are expected to promote the station and increase their one-to-one relationship with the listeners by being highly visible. They make personal appearances at gospel concerts, religious bookstores, and churches.

Scheduling

At one religious music station the station manager says the morning drive time has a little hotter tempo. He says it is faster then than at any time of the day. He said: "It's the kind of wake-up time, getting them motivated for the day." At mid-morning after drive time this tempo slows and the music gets more mellow for housewives and for background music for office workers. At afternoon drive time the tempo of the music picks up and the disc jockeys get more peppy with the chatter. Then in the late evening some stations begin to play "Jesus Rock" for the young people who make up the bulk of the late evening audience.

Promotion

Some of the promotion at commercial religious stations is handled by the jocks who travel around acting as master of ceremonies for gospel concerts, where the popular gospel music stars are appearing. One disc jockey at KPBC, Dallas, Texas, who calls himself Deacon Evans, was telling the listeners about his appearance at the East Texas Jesus Jamboree, where he was going to be the master of ceremonies:

Hey we just confirmed Sue Ellen Chennault Dodge to be at the East Texas Jesus Jamboree, coming up on next weekend . . . So we got Dogwood, Terry Talbot, Sue Ellen Chennault Dodge, Chris Christian, Mike Johnson,

Keith Green, Crews Family, lotta local groups from as close as Houston and all over Texas. We're going to praise the Lord and he's going to save some souls that weekend. So we want you to be a part of it.[6]

Disc jockeys also appear at churches and religious bookstores. One station has a group of jocks called "King Pins" that become involved in bowling tournaments. In a contest a disc jockey became a prize. If the listener would call in and get on the contest roll call he or she had a chance to win a dinner at an Italian restaurant with the DJ and a popular gospel singing group. As a station manager remarked about the promotion activities of disc jockeys, "In that respect (promotion) we are not different from any other radio station. They (disc jockeys) get requests to be masters of ceremonies for various occasions from people all over town."

Other kinds of promotion are contests and giveaways. Record albums of gospel singing groups are given away. All the listener has to do is call in and ask to be listed in the "East Texas Jesus Jamboree Roll Call." This, of course, is a way of promoting the gospel concert, the station, and gospel music at the same time. One station manager said that the station would give away several thousands of dollars worth of tickets and merchandise in the next three months. Contests are an important part of promotion at religious stations. One station was having a "Scavenger Hunt Quiz." If the listener could answer the question, "Who was the first Apostle to be martyrized?" and then take a pocket comb to a meat market, the winner would get free meat patties. Some stations co-sponsor open air gospel concerts with religious bookstores, where religious posters, plaques, and Bibles are given away every fifteen minutes. Some stations use bumper stickers which are given away at religious bookstores. This promotes the station and the bookstore. Then there is that free trip to the Holy Land for two—a 10-day tour of the Holy Land which stops at Jerusalem, Jericho, Gallilee, Garden of Gethsemane, Mount of Olives, Cairo Museum, and the pyramids of Egypt. The listeners pick up the entry blanks in stores which are clients of the station. One commercial religious station promo'd its giveaway program as follows:

MUSIC:	Contemporary Upbeat Strings
ANNOUNCER: (ECHO EFFECT)	Wonder no longer. One O two and one-half (102.5 MH2) enters a new era. Starting soon. Starting very soon, the sunshine sounds of K will be giving to you prizes and surprises. You'll never know when it happens. You'll have to listen 24 hours a day to one O two and a half. Starting soon. So keep listening to

[6] KPBC transcripts, page 5.

	the sunshine sounds of K_____. Espe-
	cially to you from your friends at one O
	two and a half.
MUSIC:	Contemporary Strings Out.

THE COMMERCIAL BLOCK STATION

There are some commercial religious stations called "block," "blocked," or "blocked out," that act as common carriers simply playing taped programs that are sent to them by various religious denominations, independent groups, and program syndicators. These groups pay the station for playing the programs. The tapes are a mixture of preaching, teaching, and music.

Programming

The programs are similar to a church service with hymns, scripture readings, sermons, and prayers. The minister generally asks for a donation to keep the program on the air. If the program is sponsored by a local group, he will ask the listeners to attend church services. He will describe the prayer meetings, lectures, and sermons for the coming week. The minister promos the program. He tells of the many listeners who have written letters telling how they enjoy the program and that many people visit the church and tell how much the program means to them. He reads letters from listeners telling how they have been helped by "hearing the word" on the program. He reads requests for prayers and he prays.

The other type of program that is frequently in the block schedule is a Bible study program sometimes called a "revival lesson." A minister or an elder gives a lecture around Biblical quotations. Listeners are asked to send in their questions about the lesson. They are offered free copies of the lesson and the church newspaper and are asked to send in a donation.

Another type of program is a religious news program which has news stories about missionary work around the world. Some programs tell of religious lectures which will soon be held in the area. The gist of one lecture is given for about ten minutes and an outline of the other lectures is described. The schedule of seminars in various cities is announced. An example of this program was the description of a prayer school scheduled to be held in several cities over the country.

The sources of the taped religious programs are local denominational groups plus what one station manager called "independents." The independent obtain a charter and give a name to their church. They are independent in that they have no denominational affiliation. The block station is important to this type of religious group since they can use radio to show the kind of church program and worship services they have, and use this opportunity to build the membership if the listener likes the program and visits the local church.

The national religious groups use the block station to let the listener know when one of their traveling church services or revival groups will be coming to the city. They also use the program to promote their television programs. They ask for donations to support their particular mission. The program may consist of excerpts recorded from one of their revival worship services held in various cities. The minister tells the number of conversions in each city and describes incidents of healing.

Audience

The programs of most blocked stations are traditional in nature and the appeal, according to one station manager, is to listeners from age thirty-five up. Some stations do not subscribe to rating agencies and get most of their information about their listeners from the mail received. Because of the many requests on the taped programs for letters, prayer requests, donations, and program evaluations, the mail response may be more revealing than the mail drag of other commercial stations.

Public Service

The block station manager feels a need to serve the station's public service obligation and broadcasts pre-recorded public service programs produced by government agencies and state universities. He or she also schedules spots for service organizations such as American Foundation for the Blind.

News

The block station has news on the half hour and weather on the quarter hour. The newscasts are "rip and read" from one of the wire services and perhaps a commentary written and delivered by the station manager.

Announcers

The announcer function (as opposed to disc jockey) on the block station is chiefly to introduce and tag the various pre-recorded programs giving the name of the religious organization that sponsors the tapes and stating the address where donations may be sent.

Promotion and Sales

Block stations do not have to be very active in promotion or sales efforts. There is quite a flourishing business from the religious denominations and groups who want to program their tapes on the station. The stations do no billboard, print, or television promotion.

One station manager said that his station has the services of two national sales reps in Los Angeles, who handle national accounts. One of the station employees works the local accounts. He said they do very little selling, leaving it to the local religious groups "to come to us." The blocked station does not schedule any commercials. The total revenue is derived from selling time for broadcast of the taped religious programs.

Station Organization

Since the programming function of the station is mostly playing pre-recorded tapes, the block station operates with a small staff. There is a general manager and under him six people who handle the functions of sales, announcing, bookkeeping, continuity, and engineering.

EDUCATIONAL RELIGIOUS STATIONS

The purpose of the educational religious station is to teach. On most stations, lessons are about the Bible and they are taught from the viewpoint of several different Christian denominations. In addition to the Bible, secular literature having religious themes is also used in teaching. Lecture notes, study outlines, and books are sent to listeners upon request without cost. The music played on the station has a teaching function, since all of the lyrics are of a religious nature. The station has a preaching function also. The largest concentration of preaching is on the weekends, although there are sermons and worship services programmed during the week along with the study courses.

Station Organization

Educational religious stations are owned by churches, schools, and educational foundations. All of these organizations are non-profit and there are no commercials scheduled. The stations are supported by contributions from churches and listeners. Syndicated program producers who ask for donations on the air may also contribute, but they are not required to. Churches who block-program may make contributions to the station.

At the helm of the religious station is the president and under this officer is the station director. These two officers acting under the board of trustees of the sponsoring foundation, church, or school set the policies of the station. The station director, with the advice and consent of the president gives the permission for a program to be accepted and the program director with aid from traffic department does the scheduling. A music director, under the program director, assists this officer in the selection of the record play and recorded live music. The announcers are called "operators" at some educational stations and they are responsible for working the boards, doing production, and announcing. They are under both the president and the station manager. Engineering and office manager (secretarial, bookkeeping, and traffic) are under the president.

Station Organization
Educational Religious Station

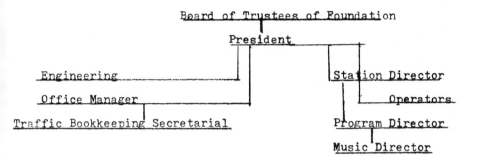

Programming

Educational religious stations do some block programming; that is, they schedule pre-recorded programs from local churches and national syndicators. The local church programs generally start with a hymn, then the minister greets the listeners and reads a psalm. He asks the listeners not to turn the program off, but to stay with him for the next quarter hour. He announces the title of the lesson, for example "City of Prayer." He talks about the importance of poetry and he reads an inspirational poem with organ music in the background. A gospel number is sung which emphasizes the theme of the lesson. The minister lectures and ends by blessing the listeners. A choir sings and the announcer asks for a donation and gives the address. The minister asks the listeners to call the station and say that they are listening. Sometimes the minister will offer a free cassette of his lecture if a donation of $5.00 or over is sent.

An example of a syndicated program scheduled by educational religious stations is "Haven of Rest." It begins with organ music and then the minister, Paul Evans, discusses the soul for two minutes. A hymn "God's Final Call," by a baritone with organ accompaniment follows. The discussion of the soul is continued for two more minutes. Then a quartet sings a hymn, "If I Had Only Jesus." The minister talks of the need to accept forgiveness. He announces a gift, a magazine called *Anchor*. A hymn is played by the organ. The minister tells a human interest story of driving down the freeway and seeing a little dog running down the middle of the freeway. He was terribly concerned for the little dog, but he could not stop because of the rapid traffic behind his car. He knew the little dog was doomed. Then he gave the moral, if you can care that much for a dog, how much can you care about your fellowman? The story was followed by a hymn rendered by a tenor. The minister discusses a parable from the Bible, Jonah 6, in which the Lord shows that Jonah cares more for a garden plant than for the people of Nineveh. Then the minister relates this parable to the story of the little dog on the freeway, saying that we should care more for the souls of men than for little dogs or plants. Then a quartet sings "Sharing the Gospel," and an organ plays "Hour of Prayer." The minister prays. The organ music swells up and out. Then there are sound effects of a boat whistle and the minister asks the listeners to write for the free magazine, *Anchor*. Then he says the program is supported by contributions from listeners.

Another type of syndicated program is the religious drama. An example is "Unshackled," sponsored by the Pacific Garden Mission in Chicago. This is a thirty minute program reminiscent of the radio dramas of the 1930s. It has a cast of professional radio actors whose voices, along with the use of sound effects and an electric organ for transitions, tell the story of how a person's life is changed by being converted to religion. A typical episode told the story of a famous mission preacher who had been a drunkard in his younger years, but after being converted in a mission for drifters, became a leader in the mission field and helped to rehabilitate many people.

Music

The educational station will play several types of religious music, contemporary Christian, southern gospel, MOR, spirituals, traditional, and classic. The contemporary Christian is the same upbeat young adult music played by the commercial religious stations. Southern gospel music is traditional country with religious lyrics and this category also includes quartets rendering "Saints Go Marching In," type music. The MOR music edges toward classical with baritone soloists and ornate orchestrations. Spirituals follow the historic mold, deeply emotional religious music with soaring sopranos and large choirs with quick change in pace and several climaxes. Traditional music consists of the old hymns. Educational stations for the most part do not play Jesus Rock. There are two kinds of classical music played. One kind features piano concertos with familiar hymnal themes. The other classical type features operatic sopranos backed by full orchestration and large choruses performing traditional hymns and inspirational secular music.

News

News at some stations consists of three five minute newscasts at 2:55 p.m., 3:55 p.m., and 4:55 p.m. with headlines every thirty minutes if the religious programming permits. Some of the local religious pre-recorded programs run fifteen minutes and some thirty to forty-five minutes, so that if the program passes over the hour mark the news headlines are omitted. At other stations the news starts with a fifteen minute newscast at 8:00 a.m. This consists of seven minutes of world news and local news, two minutes of church events such as films and seminars, two minutes of headlines, and at 6:00 p.m., fifteen minutes of world, local and sports news. The newscasts are wire service reports read by the announcers. The news of church events is gathered locally, written by the staff, and read by the announcers.

Public Service

According to one station manager the entire schedule consists of public service in that the programs are all teaching, religious, music, and worship services and are not commercially sponsored. However, considering public service in its usual sense, the educational religious station does its share of spots provided by local civic groups, Heart Fund, Lung Association, and traffic safety. The calendar of events type program listing meetings and programs of churches, schools, and civic groups is also produced. The educational religious station is open to public service spots from any civic group.

Announcers

At the educational religious station there are announcers rather than disc jockeys. They do not "chatter" or try to establish a conversation or "one-to-one" relationship with the listeners as do the DJs on the commercial religious stations. Their function is to introduce the programs, give the addresses where donations may be sent, read the news from the wire service agencies, give the time, temperature, and weather, announce station IDs, read promos for camp meetings and religious seminars, and announce give-aways such as free printed copies of Bible lessons. The announcers or "operators" as they are called in one educational religious station, also handle the control board, playing the tapes and the records and doing any recording of local programs.

Scheduling and the Listeners

A typical schedule is set forth below:

7:00 a.m. - 2:00 p.m.   Block programming (church services and Bible lessons)
2:00 p.m. - 6:00 p.m.   Music
6:00 p.m. - 12:00 a.m.   Block Programming (church services and Bible lessons)
12:00 a.m. - 7:00 a.m.   Music

The educational religious station manager will tell you that the station is aiming at everyone, all ages, "The Christian and the non-Christian, too." When asked, "Is there any particular age group that you think is listening at certain times?", one station manager said, "No, that's the reason we rotate our music; middle of the road, contemporary, and southern gospel. It reaches all ages. In the afternoon we put music in drive time. In the morning we have block programming (mostly church services and Bible lessons). We share it, message in the morning and music in the afternoon. We feel that the people who listen to the block programming may not listen to the music programming and vice versa. By segregating the programming off like that we might capture two different audiences.''

THE FUTURE OF RELIGIOUS RADIO

Religious station managers are predicting a large growth in religious radio stations. They say that churches and religious organizations are no longer satisfied with the ''Sunday Ghetto'' programming available to them on the commercial stations, and that they want ''more than just thirty minutes or an hour on Sundays.'' As one station manager said, ''Every day is the Lord's day.''

Station managers believe that there is a growing desire for religious programming on the part of both adults and young people. They say that the complexities of urban living are causing adults to seek solace and inspiration through religious programs. They believe that the young people are also turning to religious radio programs for guidance, for they are perplexed with vocational and social problems. The national media seem to bear out what the station managers are saying about youth turning to religion. A recent network television documentary depicted great numbers of young people turning to religion for spiritual guidance, and the press media tell of young people being attracted to various sects, cults, and spiritual groups.[7]

In addition to this return to religion movement, the young people are attracted to religious radio programming because of their love for the new gospel music; the recordings, the concerts, and the gospel music groups. ''Jesus Rock'' or ''Christian Rock'' is popular with teenagers and young adults, and contemporary music attracts ages 25 through 49. Said one station manager, ''We are just scratching the surface. Christian music is the third highest selling music in the entire market. Without any question it's coming on strong. You take our station in Houston. They have a very strong audience in the Christian rock field.'' He said that young adults at a business luncheon asked him to play more Christian rock music, and that this music was very popular with teenagers and those in their 20s.

Assisting in the growth of religious radio stations is an organization called the National Religious Broadcasters. Established in 1944, the NRB provides a forum where religious broadcasters can exchange ideas and discuss problems. The purposes of the organization are ''to upgrade the quality of religious pro-

---

[7] ''CBS Reports: Born Again,'' July 14, 1977. ''Berkeley: New Brands of Protest,'' *The Dallas Morning News,* July 11, 1977, p. 5A.

gramming and to relate the program producer, the station owner and operator, and others interested in religious broadcasting to the issues and opportunities for carrying the Gospel message on radio and television.'' [8] As in the case of the National Association of Broadcasters, the NRB provides a trade press to promote communication among its members and a code of ethics to encourage quality programming, solid fiscal operation, and sound doctrinal basis for broadcasting.

According to people working in religious broadcasting, there will be a continued growth in the number of religious stations. *Religious Broadcasting* reports that there is one new religious radio station being established each week.[9] Station managers say that we will see more religious stations in the future than we have ever visualized or dreamed. As one station manager put it, ''The problems of the world have made man seek out a higher being, and radio is one of the greatest means of evangelizing the world.''

<pre>
            KMGC   FM   102.5   6/15/77 8:54 A.M.

SOUND: Upbeat Gospel tune "Anywhere I Am." Segues into another

               Gospel tune "Take Me In Your Arms and Carry Me All the

               Way Home." Male vocalist and string band. Has country

               sound. Segues into "If You Would Show Me." Male

               vocalist and Guitar. Modern country sound. Segues into

               "Walking in the Light of the Spirit." Duet singing.

               String accompaniment. Contemporary. Christian music.

ANNOUNCER: You are listening to the new sounds of Sunshine Radio,

               KMGC, Dallas...where the music has been mechanically

               reproduced.

SOUND: Hello, I'm Kenneth Copland. In a moment I'll be back

               with today's message.

MUSIC: Gospel Tune. "I'll Show You the Story." Country sound

               duet with guitar accompaniment.

SOUND: Well Praise the Lord. Here it is Wednesday and time for

               the Believers Voice of Victory Broadcast. Welcomes listen-

               ers to program. Says program goes to Mexico. Develops
</pre>

[8] Virgil Magill, ''The Origins of NRB,'' *Religious Broadcasting,* February, 1977, pp. 36, 65.
[9] *Religious Radio Broadcasting,* February, 1977, p. 65.

theme of once you get into the will of God, life is fun. Says he gets so turned on he would like to finish the broadcast in tongues. He says he is going to sing a song, "His Name is Jesus," and he reads the lyrics of the song. He asks the listeners to sing it along with him and learn the lyrics.

MUSIC: "His name is Jesus." Copland sings slow beat Gospel song with string band accompaniment and quartet.

COPLAND: Says he will play this song several times until listeners learn lyrics. Says song is for worshipping God. Discusses the 4th Chapter of Proverbs: Heart faith is Bible faith. Head faith is human faith. He preaches a sermon. Theme: keep the word of the Bible before your eyes and in your heart. To have a sense-ruled mind is death. Your mind must be ruled by the word of God, which is in the Bible. Ends sermon by saying: "Our time is gone again today." Talks about a book that he is giving away free and postpaid. Tells them to write him and gives address (Ft. Worth). Tells them where to write if they are in Canada. Book is called Trouble Maker. Ending: Until tomorrow at this same time, Kenneth Copland here reminding you that Jesus is the Lord.

MUSIC: Piano under for:

COPLAND: The preceding program is sponsored by the Kenneth Copland Evangelistic Association and its partners in this area.

ANNOUNCER: The following program has been mechanically reproduced.

MUSIC: Male solo with piano. "Jesus Put Your Breakers On." Under for:

ANNOUNCER: This is the faith seminar of the air with Kenneth Hagen, a man whose ministry is attracting many in the principles of Bible faith, the key to receiving word from God. Kenneth

Hagen, Jr. and Dr. Ted Stewart will be with Brother Hagen in

Anaheim, California for a faith, holy spirit, and healing

convention at the Anaheim Convention Center (gives address)

June 19th through the 22nd. Then June 26th through July

2nd we will be in Inglewood, California. This week Dr.

Hagen talks about confession brings possession, and now

with today's Bible lesson, here is Kenneth Hagen.

KENNETH HAGEN: Reads the text, Mark 11:20. Teaches a lesson about the

importance of faith. Uses himself rising from a sick bed

after 16 months as an example. Says Church is sadly lacking

in teaching about the subject of faith. Refers to Acts

2:4, to show the difference between leading and forcing.

Talks about speaking in tongues.

MUSIC: Organ softly under.

KENNETH HAGEN: Confession brings possession. If you would like to have a

free printed copy of this Bible lesson, write to me, Kenneth

Hagen (address in Tulsa, Oklahoma,) and your free printed

copy of this Bible lesson will be sent to you immediately.

Now as we've suggested through this week...better yet, to

those who will send an offering of $5.00 or more we will

send you our Bible Faith study course, and this lesson,

"Confession Brings Possession" is one of the lessons of this

24 lesson Bible Faith study course bound in the beautiful

binder or back. And so if you send an offering of $5.00

or more, then you request that we send you this Faith Study

Course Book. Say, please send me your Bible Faith study

course and include an offering of $5.00 or more and it will be

sent to you immediately. Now we will continue with this

Bible lesson tomorrow, Confession brings Possession,

listen to God's word carefully, friends, put it into

	practice. It will work for you. And now we bid you goodbye.
MUSIC:	Piano with baritone singing "Put Your Faith in God." Under for:
ANNOUNCER:	You have been listening to the <u>Faith</u> <u>Seminar</u> <u>of</u> <u>the</u> <u>Air</u> with Kenneth Hagen. When you write be sure to give the call letters of this station and ask for the lesson Confession Brings Possession. (WITHOUT PAUSE THE SAME ANNOUNCER GOES INTO A CAMP MEETING COMMERCIAL.) The fifth annual camp meeting is July 25th through July 30th at the Tulsa Civic Center. Kenneth Copland and Norvell Hays will be two of the main speakers along with Kenneth Hagen for the most dynamic camp meeting ever, Camp Meeting 1977, July 25th through July 30th. The Faith Seminar of the Air is sponsored by the Kenneth Hagen Evangelistic Association (gives address in Tulsa, Oklahoma).
MUSIC:	PIANO MUSIC OUT.
ANNOUNCER:	KMGC, Dallas.
MUSIC:	SYMPHONIC ORCHESTRA UP AND OUT.
ANNOUNCER:	(STAFF) Good Morning, KMGC Time is 9:29 and here's a brief summary of the news.
NEWS:	ON THE HALF HOUR.
ANNOUNCER:	(STAFF ANNOUNCER READS NEWS)

1. Austin, Special legislative session on school finance.

2. San Antonio. City Council ban on building over the Edwards Aquafier .

3. Fifth Circuit Court of Appeals. TV Newsmen and Filming Executions in Texas.

4. House Ways and Means Committee. Use of Higher Oil Tax Proceeds. U.S. Congress.

5. Spain's First Free Election.

6. Dallas City Council. School Safety Month.

WEATHER: 7. <u>WEATHER</u>

MUSIC: SLOW BEAT GOSPEL NUMBER. FEMALE VOCALIST. BACKED BY

                GUITAR, PIANO AND DRUMS. ALSO MALE VOCALIST. <u>Segues</u>

                into upbeat Gospel number. Male vocalist backed by

                guitar and piano.

MUSIC: OUT.

ANNOUNCER: That's "Losers and Winners" by Daniel Amos. It's

                twenty-one minutes shy of 10 o'clock at KMGC.

MUSIC: Up. Slow beat Gospel Number. "Fly on the Wings of an

                Eagle." Male vocalist and female vocalist backed by

SEGUES: guitar group. <u>Segue</u> into slowbeat mournful Gospel

                number. Male vocalist backed by piano and guitar. Has

SEGUES: country sound. "That's the Way It's Got to Be." <u>Segues</u>

                into upbeat gospel number. "He's Coming Back." Male

                singers and strings.

SOUND: CART. ANNOUNCER WITH ECHO EFFECT BACKED BY UPBEAT

                STRINGS ANNOUNCES GIVEAWAYS "So keep listening to

                the Sunshine Sounds of KMGC."

MUSIC: "This Song for You" Beatle type group.

KVTT FM 91.7   11:20 AM to 12:25 PM   6/16/77

SOUND: Hymn sung by choir. Under for:

SOUND: Minister greets listeners. Quotes Psalm. Asks listeners

                to share faith and friends. Asks listeners not to turn

                program off but to stay with them for the next quarter

                hour. Subject of study this week is "City of Prayer."

                Stresses the importance of prayer. Stresses the impor-

                tance of beauty in poetry and "writing." Thanks listen-

ers for sending in some poetry. Asks listeners to send
in poetry to share the "ministry of poetry in radio land."
Reads poem: "Spring is a Song."

MUSIC: Organ music is under the reading of the poetry.

MUSIC: OUT.

SOUND: Minister speaks of the beauty of spring. Says that we
have seasons in our spiritual life, mountain tops to
deserts. Assures listeners that God has not forsaken
them. Says share with us the ministry of song.

MUSIC: Piano music accompanies soloist. Upbeat gospel song.
Trumpet comes in and takes some licks. Title: "Talk
It Over with the Lord."

SOUND: Minister asks if listeners have tried talking it over
with the Lord. Emphasizes the importance of prayer. Says
that Jesus set a good example. Jesus always found a
place to pray at the close of the day. Someplace to be
alone with the Father.

MUSIC: Organ softly under:

SOUND: Minister tells about how Jesus used prayer. Tells how
prayer brought revelation to the disciples. Emphasizes
the importance of dedication. Uses the example of
a dedicated student. Tells how important it is to
give oneself to Jesus when one is young. Tells about
the faith and confidence of Moses: the Lord helps one to
win the battles. Says that it has been beautiful day
to share these beautiful thoughts. Urges listeners
to have faith in God. Gives Blessing. "If you
will go with God, God will go with you."

MUSIC: CHOIR UP AND UNDER:

ANNOUNCER: Asks for donation to keep this program on the air.
Says to send all donations to Echoes of Faith, Arling-

ton, Texas. Gives P.O. Box. Thanks audience for
listening.

MUSIC: SWELLS UP AND OUT.

ANNOUNCER: GIVES TIME AND WEATHERCAST.

                Gives ID. 11:29 a.m. This is KVTT 91.7 FM in Dallas.

MUSIC: UP. Hymn, "Just Hold His Hand." Women's trio and
                solo baritone, piano. Under for:

DON GEORGE: How do you do friends, this is Don George, and you're
                listening to Gospel Time. I bring you greetings in the
                name of my Savior, Jesus Christ, the Son of God. What
                a joy it is for me to be able to sit down with you
                and just talk to you for awhile about the Lord Jesus
                Christ. Pull up a chair and sit down here with me
                and let's talk about the Lord. God is so good.
                God doesn't want you to be tense or uptight, fear-ridden
                or frustrated. God wants you to be relaxed, at ease, in
                perfect tranquility, in perfect contentment, and in
                harmony with His will. And I believe in the next quarter
                hour as you and me and the Lord Jesus Christ have a good
                talk together, that the Father is just going to pour out
                His Holy Spirit upon you, and regardless of what your need
                is, God is going to minister to your need, I believe that.
                I just believe that God's power is available, and I trust
                Him to do for you whatever you need, to minister unto
                you in whatever area you need help. A good listener
                recently wrote me from the city of Arlington, Texas:
                "Dear Pastor George, I have just listened to your morning
                message, and praise God, you've made my day for me again.
                I'm just home from a serious hospitalization, and with your
                help and instruction, am trusting God for a complete
                recovery. I covet your prayers in my behalf, thank you.

We are relatively new to this area, and I am really excited about being a part of your worship service at our
earliest opportunity. Thanking you in advance for your
current gift offer, I am praying for your ministry to
continue blessing others as it is blessing me. Sincerely."
And I want to pray for you right now, my friend. I want to
trust God right now to minister to you. I just feel a
directive by the Holy Spirit to pray for you personally.
"Father, in the name of Jesus. You see the name of the
individual for whom I pray. It's written on this letter
that I hold in my hand right now. God, I ask you here in
Arlington, Texas to put your hand upon this wonderful
Christian. Minister to this need. Do it now, Father,
in the name of Jesus Christ. Just let your presence,
your warmth, your glory, your personality be experienced.
Oh, Father God, in the life of my friend, and I trust
you for it now. Satan, I find you, I rebuke you, I take
authority over you, in the name of Jesus Christ and I
give God the glory. I give my Father all the praise
for the work that is done. Thank you, God, in the name
of your son, Jesus Christ, Amen." Well praise God, I
believe God heard my prayer. I believe God ministered as
I prayed. Henry and Hazel Slaughter are coming to
Calvary Temple, Irving, Texas one week from this coming
Sunday night. The date, June 26th. The final Sunday
night in the month of June, 6:00 p.m., Calvary Temple of
Irving...June 26th with Henry and Hazel Slaughter. They're
from Nashville, Tennessee.

MUSIC: Organ up.

DON GEORGE: And they come to sing beautiful songs, our glory in the
cross, the Slaughters.

MUSIC: Organ swells into hymn with solo female vocalist backed

            by a quartet.

MUSIC: OUT.

DON GEORGE: There is nothing better to glory in than the wonderous

            cross, of the Lord Jesus Christ, I read to you from the

            Gospel of John, Chapter five, beginning with verse one.

            (He reads from the New Testament.) There are so many

            things that I want to share with you about this beautiful

            narrative that depicts and describes the healing virtues

            and power and compassionate spirit of the Lord Jesus

            Christ. You see there were many, many people at the

            pool of Bethesda in Jerusalem and they were all ill in some

            particular way. Now they believed in the legend of the

            Angel coming down boiling up the water, so that the first

            one to come down would be cured of whatever ailment he had.

            They believed in that, they believed in a magical mystical

            cure of the water, when the mysterious angel would come

            and boil up the water. Well, it was pretty exciting to

            have a try at the waters that supposedly carried healing

            in them. But I know that there was no healing power in

            that water. I also know that a lot of people are sick

            today, and I believe that almost everybody is sick in some

            way, in one way or another, sick. Some people have learned

            the way to exercise the option of divine health, and praise

            God for them, but the vast majority of this world is sick.

            It is a sick, sick world, that we live in. You see sickness

            takes different forms, in the body, in the mind, in the

            spirit, in our relationships, in our attitudes. Especially

            sickness pervades the attitudes of so many people. I

            know some people who need a checkup from the neck up.

            (Chuckles) They need a change in attitude. Their attitude

is sick, the way they look at things is sick, the way
they act is sick, and they need healing. They're a great
deal like so many of the people who were at the pool side
when Jesus came and performed this magnificent miracle.
Well, we're not at the pool side right now, but we are
in the grace and reach and provision of my God. And I
want to pray for you right now. I want to trust God to
set you free. Father, one is listening to my voice who
needs healing in his mind, another needs healing in his
spirit, one needs healing in his attitude, some need
healing in their bodies. Well, Father God, I ask you in
the name of Jesus to release and set free. Those who are
bound, I break the power of Satan, I bind the forces of
the enemy, I claim a victory over you, Satan, in the name
of Jesus Christ and I give my Father God the praise for
healing now in the life of every person listening to my
voice. And I give you praise for it, Father, in the name
of Jesus Christ, Amen. Well, friends, all you need to do
to receive our new book entitled Answers to Entime Questions,
is write to me and request gift offer 127. If you'll get
your letter of request in the mail speedily, I must tell
you there is a limited supply, for the book is free for as
long as it lasts. Answers to Entime Questions. Gift Order
127. It will come without cost and obligation to you.
Write to me, please. My name is Don George. My mailing
address is (gives address in Irving, Texas). This is Don
George. Thank you for listening. Have faith in God.

MUSIC: Hymn up and under for:

DON GEORGE: Henry and Hazel Slaughter, a Christ Exalting ministry
coming to the metroplex. This is Pastor Don George
inviting you to a celebration of praise with Henry and
Hazel. The Slaughters will sing and I will preach the

word, Sunday night, June 26th at 6:00 p.m. Calvary Temple. (Gives Irving Address). For additional information phone (gives phone number).

MUSIC: Hymn quartet up. CUT TO piano music backing another quartet singing a different hymn "Jesus the Lamb of the Soul."

ANNOUNCER: From Dallas, Texas we bring the international radio broadcast sponsored by World Missionary Evangelism, Dr. John Douglas, Senior, Founder. The World Missionary Evangelism is supporting more than 30,000 children in homes and schools in many countries around the world. Thousands of national ministers are supported so that they can tell the story of Jesus in many lands. And now Dr. Douglas and daughter Evonne are here to share with you the thrilling story of caring for the homeless children, the destitute lepers, and winning the lost to Jesus.

DR. DOUGLAS: Offers free book, God Wrote Only One Bible. Says only a few left. Says to ask for Gift Packet 45. Gives mailing address.

KWJS FM 94.9   3:55 to 5:07 PM   6/4/77

SOUND: PSA Traffic Safety.

ANNOUNCER: "I Found It All In Jesus" Jack Price on KWJS.

MUSIC: Tenor backed by organ. Does some talking of the lyrics. Backed by choir. (This is turn of the century light classical type tenor number. "Ah Sweet Mystery of Life" type.)

COMMERCIAL: Upbeat strings. Punch Announcer. For Battle of Songs Concert. Features several Gospel groups and inserts of their albums used in this commercial. Groups: Inspirations, Florida Boys, Dixie Echoes, The Hintons.

ANNOUNCER: All the way from California to the Dallas-Ft. Worth

Metroplex, Nancy Harmon and the Victory Voices, "I

Thank you Lord." (Fast pace, lots of pep.)

MUSIC: Very upbeat spiritual type. "I Thank You Lord."

MUSIC: Very mellow strings. Mantovanni type. Under for:

ANNOUNCER: All that thrills my soul is Jesus. The Otis Skillern's

orchestra takes us right up to news time. I'm Alicia

Clasky. See you back in about seven minutes.

BREAK:
MUSIC: Mantovanni type strings. Harp breaks.

ANNOUNCER: (CHANGES FROM WOMAN ANNOUNCER TO MALE ANNOUNCER FOR

THIS STATION BREAK) This is KWJS 95 FM, Arlington.

We now join the United Press International Audio Net-

work News.

MUSIC: STRINGS UNDER.

ANNOUNCER: KWJS presents the news of today and the promise of

tomorrow. Now KWJS Information News.

MUSIC: Segues into sounder.

SOUND: HIGH FREQUENCY DOT DASH.

SOUND: UPI Audio News

1. Rosaline Carter in Peru

2. President Carter's Tax Reform Package

3. Agriculture Secretary on Tour to Japan

4. Off Shore Oil Leasing. Secretary of the Interior.

5. Dutch Hostage Story.

6. Chicago Bomb Blast

7. Organized Crime and the Interstate Commerce
    Commission

8. New Soviet Constitution

9. Israeli Troop on Alert

SOUND: SOUNDER UNDER:

UPI ANNOUNCER: From the world desk of United Press International this

is Tom Wendell.

ANNOUNCER: From the United Press International Audio News Network

	this has been KWJS Information News. The news that is now history. Now with the news that never changes, more from the word of God on KWJS, Christian Radio, serving the Dallas-Fort Worth Metroplex, twenty-four hours a day.
SOUND:	Sounder.
MUSIC:	Very upbeat contemporary music under:
ANNOUNCER:	It's time to praise the Lord with Alicia Galasky on KWJS.
MUSIC:	Upbeat contemporary music segues into very slow beat modern country sound with male duet backed by guitars. A contemporary Christian number, "Praise the Lord."
SOUND:	PSA for convention of the Pentacostal Church of God. Announcer only.
COMMERCIAL:	Commercial for concert of Gospel music groups called "Battle of Songs." Punch announcer plus inserts of album cuts.
A.C. (DJ is Alice Galasky)	"The Precious Love of Jesus," Jimmy Swaggart on family gospel radio, four ten, ninety six degrees. (the record is under as the DJ starts to speak.)
MUSIC:	"The Precious Love of Jesus". Southern gospel type with country sound.
MUSIC:	Guitars under for:
AC:	The Spears, "I Never Shall Forget The Day."
MUSIC:	"I Never Shall Forget the Day," Southern gospel type. Male vocalist lead plus women trio.
AC:	"The Spears" on KWJS, four fifteen, ninety seven degrees outside.
MUSIC:	Record begins.
AC:	Gettin' hot out there.
MUSIC:	Record up.

AC: Roger McGaff and "Shattered Dreams."

MUSIC: "Shattered Dreams." Slow beat southern gospel, male

                   vocalist and guitar backed by quartet.

AC: Four nineteen, partly cloudy sky, at least that's what

                   the weather service says. I haven't been out for awhile

                   so I'm not sure, ninety seven degrees outside, thirty-

                   seven degrees celsius, and winds out of the south

                   southwest at nine miles per hour. We're expecting fair

                   and hot temperatures through Monday. Our revised fore-

                   cast through Sunday and now it's going to be hot until

                   Monday, high today 100 degrees, low tonight in the low

                   seventies and winds light to southern five to ten miles

                   per hour.

AC: She reads PSA about college counselling for high school

                   students from TCU.

MUSIC: Intro to record.

AC: There's something in the air besides all that hot wind.

                   There really is. The Downings.

MUSIC: "There's Something in the Air." Downings. Contemporary

                   Christian. Women in duet. Upbeat.

MUSIC: "Happy Road is Taking Me Home." Southern Gospel. Male

                   vocalist. Guitars.

SOUND: PSA Temple Bethel Church Anniversary Service.

                   Announcer only.

SOUND: Station ID. Male announcer with strings under. Upbeat.

AC: "The Happy Goodmans featuring Johnny Cook, "Looking for

                   a City."

MUSIC: "Looking for a City." Southern gospel. Guitar and

                   fiddles. Segues into:

MUSIC: "I Want to be More Like Jesus Everyday." Upbeat

                   spiritual.

AC: The Blackwood Brothers featuring James Blackwood from
                    their live concert in Nashville. There's a lot of
                    people there.

COMMERCIAL: Kings Village Dinner Theatre. Announcer and upbeat
                    piano.

COMMERCIAL: Car dealer. Announcer plus upbeat contemporary music.
(Note:
Christian   Says they are Christian owned and operated. Tag on
owned and
operated.)   times they are open by female announcer.

AC: The Florida Boys. "Here They Come".
                    Four-thirty-five, ninety-seven degrees.

MUSIC: The Florida Boys, "Here They Come." Spiritual.

MUSIC: Record intro.

AC: A song written by Bill Gaither, sung by Richard
                    Roberts, "It is Finished."

MUSIC: "It is Finished." Baritone plus full orchestra.

AC: Richard Roberts on KWJS. This is Alicia Calasky and
                    I certainly have enjoyed being with you this afternoon.
                    Thanks for all the calls and I'm sorry we just didn't
                    have time to play all of your requests, but Vicki
                    Jamieson and Dwight Thompson are coming up in just
                    a minute.

COMMERCIAL: Benefit concert for the Fowlers Christian Music School.
                    Gospel Music. Donations of $2.50 will be asked at the
                    door.

COMMERCIAL: Word of Faith Singles Class at Ramada Inn.
                    Announcer backed by choir.

MUSIC: "Hallelujah." Contemporary. Slow beat. Female
                    vocalist backed by guitars. Vicki Jamieson.

AC: Vicki Jamieson, freely, freely, Jesus gives so let's
                    give to others.

MUSIC: Intro to record.

AC: Dwight Thompson, "Rise and be Healed."

MUSIC: "Rise and be Healed." Slow beat Gospel. Baritone

               solo backed by woman's choir and piano.

AC: Dwight Tompson on KWJS, four-fifty-one, I am Alicia

               Calasky, sitting in with you this afternoon.

               Partly cloudy skies outside and ninety-seven degrees

               thirty-six degrees centigrade, winds out of the south

               southwest at nine miles per hour. Fair and hot through

               Monday, high today near 100. Low tonight in the low

               seventies. Winds light and southerly five to ten

               miles per hour. And here's a hint for those of you

               who may be sitting out in the sun. Sun worshippers

               can minimize their risk of skin cancer and still enjoy

               the great outdoors. Call the information services for

               simple preventative measures. Sponsored by Andy Anderson

               Hospital.

MUSIC: Intro to record.

AC: David Sapp, "His Banner Over Me is Love." Praise the

               Lord with him.

MUSIC: "His Banner Over Me is Love." Contemporary Christian.

AC: I certainly hope that you have enjoyed this after-

               noon, I certainly have. God Bless you and have a

               great week.

D. J.: Deacon Don Evans   1   6/14/77   Tuesday

                                                       7:55 a.m. to 8:55 a.m

KPBC   1040   Contemporary Christian Music

Commercial: COMMERCIAL. GUITAR SHOP. Announcer with Guitar music

               under him. Frets and Strings.

MUSIC: Woman trio singing jingle, "Lead the Good Life"under

               for:

D. E.	This is Deacon Don Evans. Join me at the Good Life Bookstore, Saturday June 18th from 1:30 to 3:30 for a giant
JOCKS FROM 0	jamboree give away and open air concert by the Bread of Life. You'll have a chance to win Bibles, posters, **plaques** , and gifts, and they'll be giving away something great every fifteen minutes, and we'll be broadcasting live from the Good Life. That's the Good Life Bookstore in Hurst. Take the Brown Trail Exit off **Airport** Freeway to the Bellaire Shopping Center and the Good Life.
SOUND:	Jingle I. D. (women's trio).
MUSIC:	"Say, I'm a believer, now." Dallas Home and Frame
SOUND:	Sunbreak 77 Contest. Announcer plus strings under. Sunbreak 77 Contest continues all summer long. Be listening for details. You'll get your share of the fun.
MUSIC:	STRINGS UP
D. E.:	Shalom everyone. A minute before eight.
MUSIC:	"I'll Have The **Strength** To Carry On."
COMMERCIAL:	OX INN STEAK HOUSE. CART. ANNOUNCER PLUS SOUND EFFECTS OF COUGHING AT BEGINNING TO SHOW NEED TO GET OUT OF TOWN IN THE PURE COUNTRY AIR WHERE THE INN IS LOCATED. STRING MUSIC UNDER. FEATURES COUNTRY COOKING.
SOUND:	SOUNDER. INTRO'S **DR. MOON'S** GARDENER CALENDAR. DR. Robert Moon, Chief Horticulturist. The Dallas County Agricultural Extension Service. This is a public service giving gardening advice to the listeners. 30 seconds.
COMMERCIAL:	Commercial. Foreign Flare Greenhouse. Announcer with strings under.
D. E.:	That's what I said. One ninety-nine (he's repeating the price quoted on the commercial) That's your cue, fellows.
SOUND:	Jungle I. D.
MUSIC:	UNDER FOR

D. E.   It's six after eight at KPBC with Deacon Evans and "Har-
                   vest John".

D. E.:   "Harvest John," Reverend Walt Mills, on KPBC, ten after
                   eight. Good Morning everyone, how are you today?

COMMERCIAL: Commercial. East Texas Jamboree. Gospel Music Concert.
                   Artists voice invitation to attend, followed by announcer
Promotion   with contemporary gospel music under. Bumper stickers
                   may be picked up at Christian Book and Music Store in Ft.
                   Worth, or any Peter and Paul Store. Also get more infor-
                   mation about the Jamboree at these stores. Add your name
                   to the Jamboree Roll Call today by calling Metro Line
                   429-7870. CONTEST. This will give you a chance to win
                   dinner for two at the Italian Village with the D. J. and
                   Dogwood (a gospel music group) in person. Also can win
                   gospel msuic albums to be given away on the air.

COMMERCIAL: Thompson Transmission. Jock reading with contemporary
                   Gospel Music under.

SOUND: Jingle I. D.

MUSIC: "Rain". Take Three.

D. E.:   (Over ending of record.) Take Three and "Rain".

D. E.:   (I. D.) 8:15 at KPBC 1040 radio in Dallas. Our breakfast
                   this morning, Romans 13:8 through 14. Romans 13:8 through
                   14, our gravy is Hebrews 13 verse 18. I just look at ...
                   (SOUNDS OF PAGES TURNING) Where am I? Here we are. I
                   didn't turn the page last time. O.K., Romans 13, verse 8,
                   let's look at it together: "Pay all your debts except the
                   debt of love for others. Never finish paying that, for if
                   you love them you are obeying all of God's laws, fulfilling
                   all his requirements. If you love your neighbor as much
                   as you love yourself, you will not want to harm or cheat
                   him, kill him or steal from him, and you won't sin with his

wife, or want what is his or do anything else the ten com-
mandments say is wrong. All ten are wrapped up in this
one, to love your neighbor as you love yourself. Love does
no wrong to anyone. That's why it fully satisfies all of
God's requirements. It's the only law you need. Another
reason for right living is this. You know how late it is.
Time is running out. Wake up for the coming of the Lord is
nearer now than when we first believed. The night is far
gone. The day of his return will soon be here. So quit
the evil darkness and put on the armor of right living.
As we who live in the daylight should. Be decent and true
in everything you do. Then all can approve your behavior.
Don't spend your time in wild parties and getting drunk
or in adultery or lust or fighting or jealousy. Ask the
Lord Jesus Christ to help you live as you should. And
don't make plans to enjoy evil.

MUSIC:	Contemporary Gospel under.
D. E.:	Romans 13:8 through 14. Lesson in Living this morning, **folks**. Karen Lassity, "Bird in a Golden Sky."
MUSIC:	"Bird in A Golden Sky."
SOUND:	Sounder introduces news.
D. E.:	Good Morning, it's 8:20 and "News Headlines"

    1. Tom Clark Story. (National and state item).

    2. Governor Briscoe and Carter's **Energy** Program.(State item)

    3. Odessa, Texas Newspaper Editor resigns. (State item)

    4. Eugene McCarthy (National and State item)

    5. Weather

Michael O'Neal is next with world news.

COMMERCIAL:	Thompson Printing and Office Supply. Announcer with fast strings under.

SOUND: Michael O'Neal with UPI World News. This is an audio ser-

                  vice newscast.

                  1. President Carter - Flag Day, Budget.

                  2. USSR charges USA newsman with spying.

                  3. European Security Council and Human Rights.

                  4. Organization of American States and Human Rights.

COMMERCIAL: Deeper Life Bookstore. Jingle plus straight pitch.

                  Music, Contemporary Gospel under. Pushing a particular

                  book title.

SOUND: UPI WORLD NEWS CONTINUES

                  5. President Carter's public works proposal.

                  6. Senate reporter. Actions in Senate on Social Security.

                  Actuality, Senator Long. Pamela Taylor, reporter.

                  7. Prison Escape.

                  8. President Carter - Amnesty.

                  9. Murder in Oklahoma, three girls.

                  10. Mine Workers.

                  11. Gubernatorial Election in Virginia.

SOUND: Jingle I. D. Christian Radio for Today. KPBC a leader.

MUSIC: "I Want To Be Ready" segues into "Glad I Came By Here"

                  Dogwood.

D. E.:   That's Dogwood, "Glad I Came By Here", on KPBC for Tuesday

                  morning, the 14th of June, it's eight thirty-two with Dean

                  Evans, and there are some congratulations in order, we are

                  congratulating Dawn Weikel of Bedford, she just won a Tom

                  Autry album, that's a good album too. She won it by put-

                  ting her name in the East Texas Jesus Jamboree Roll Call,

                  Folks, I advise you to do that. Dawn, D-A-W-N, Weikel

                  of Bedford, congratulations. And speaking of the East

                  Texas Jamboree, Bob Gary just called me from over there,

                  after seven o'clock this morning and said, hey we just

                  confirmed Sue Ellen Chennault Dodge to be at the East

Texas Jesus Jamboree, coming up on next weekend, weekend
after this one coming. 24th through the 26th. It will
be in Lufkin. So we got Dogwood, Terry Talbot, Sue Ellen
Chennault Dodge', Chris Christian, Mike Johnson, Keith
Green, Crews Family lotta local groups from close as
Houston and all over Texas. We're going to praise the
Lord and he's going to save some souls that weekend. So
we want you to be a part of it. It's 8:33 at KPBC.

MUSIC: Up

D. E.:   Something else we want you to be a part of too. KPBC is
giving away a ten day tour of the Holy Land for two which
stops at Jerusalem, **Jericho**, and Gallilee, Garden of
Gethsemane, Mount of Olives, Cairo Museum, and Pyramids
in Egypt, **trip** of a life time and its yours free if you
are a winner in KPBC's Summer Sun Break 77 Contest. We'll
award the trip, June 30th. But our Summer Sun Break 77
Contest continues all summer long, so stop in and enter
today at Stretch and Sew, (Gives addresses for all), Thompson Printing and Office Supply. That's in Dallas.

COMMERCIAL: Weary Lee presents another hour of our Jesus Festivals
Featuring Reba Gardner and Dallas Home with his group:

SOUND: Excerpt from Dallas Home Album

COMMERCIAL: The meeting begins at 7:30 Friday, June 17th, at the
Bronco Bowl **Coliseum**, 2600 St. Worth Avenue, and the
admission is free, doors open at 6:30 and the **concert**,
will be video-taped for a future TV special. (Gospel
Music is under)

SOUND: Jingle I. D.

MUSIC: "He Has Risen, Hallelujah"

COMMERCIAL: Chiropractic Life Centers. Straight Pitch plus testi-
monial.

COMMERCIAL: Mustard Seed Restaurant. Dramatized.

SOUND: This is a test.

SOUND: Sounder under.

SOUND: For the next sixty seconds this station will conduct a

                test of the Awake and Awareness Broadcast System.   This

                is only a test.

SFX: Two shots

SOUND: Jingle

SOUND: Sounder with Music, chorus singing.

ANNOUNCER: Had this been an actual rapture, you who are in Christ

                would have been with the Lord at the sound of the trumpet

                and shout.   This concludes this test of the Awake and

                Awareness Broadcast System.

MUSIC: "Come On Down Lord Jesus"

9

The Classical Format

Concert Music; Fine Music; Serious Music

Music is no longer confined within the four walls of concert halls and opera houses. Radiotelephony has freed the captive bird from its prison, and it is now at liberty to soar and to sing for all who may care to hear.

C. E. Massens, 1922[1]

The purpose of classical music radio stations is to provide great music in a style which is pleasing to the listener. The commercial classical music radio stations seek to do this while realizing a profit on the sale of time to advertisers. Classical music stations program the "recognized music" of all eras—from the renaissance through the baroque, classical, romantic and modern periods—by the "important" classical composers. Their "bread and butter" is the music of composers from the time of Bach to the romantics of the late nineteenth and early twentieth centuries. The "gray area" in which the stations differ includes the "new" music of this century and music of the "electronic era."

More than two-thirds of the member stations of the Classical Music Broadcasters Association are non-commercial. Managers of classical music stations

---

[1] "How the Opera Is Broadcasted," *Radio Broadcast,* August, 1922, in Lichty, Lawrence and Malachi Topping, *American Broadcasting,* New York: Hastings House, 1975, p. 285.

distinguish their stations from "semi-classical" stations which they prefer to group with "good music" and "beautiful music" formats. There are commercial classical music stations in most major markets with 27 stations in the top 25 markets.[2] There are now less than 40 commercially-operated classical music stations in the nation.[3]

The paradox of the classical music stations is apparent in the "format change" controversy. Classical music stations may only reach a small audience but when they have attempted to abandon serious music for more popular formats they have been faced with highly organized protests from irate listeners. Citizens groups—sometimes with the support of the courts—have successfully blocked some changes and thwarted the attempts of some owners to sell their stations to others who sought to change the format. The prospects are dim that other stations will adopt classical music formats or that potential owners will invest in classical stations because of the fear that they will be bound to serious music formats.

Classical music stations in some cities have been quite successful with programming that includes short selections, several commercials, glib announcers and station promotions that are not very different from other formats. Other classical stations get by with longer selections interrupted for very few commercials and a minimum of talk between records. Some stations program talk programs, show tunes, folk music, and light classics in addition to serious music while others play only concert music.

UNADULTERATED CLASSICAL

With the exception of a 15-minute book review program once a week, WRR-FM, Dallas, programs classical recordings, taped concerts, tapes, and live opera performances eighteen hours a day.

WRR-FM is licensed to the City of Dallas and operates as a commercial station. Tapes of the Chicago Symphony, the Boston Symphony, and the New York Philharmonic in concert are aired two evenings a week and on Sunday afternoons. Concerts from North Texas State and Southern Methodist University are also regularly scheduled. Performances from the Metropolitan Opera are broadcast live on Saturday afternoons.

Most of the programming on WRR-FM is from recent recordings. The station may have as many as 30 different recordings of a particular work to choose from. The music is selected more than a month in advance and listed in the station's program guide. WRR-FM plays slightly more chamber music and some other types more frequently than other classical stations but it generally plays

---

[2] Federal Communications Commission, "Development of Policy re: Changes In the Entertainment Formats of Broadcast Stations," *Memorandum, Order and Opinion,* July 30, 1976. Washington, D.C.: The Commission.

[3] McGavren-Guild Ranks Radio's Most Popular Program Formats," *Broadcasting,* May 2, 1977.

the "bread and butter" music. Station Manager Edward Hill lacks the personnel to enable the station to program other types of music: "If you aren't adequately staffed it is wiser not to get into certain areas," he says. Listeners are more likely to complain about a work being played too often than to ask that a work be repeated. Hill explains that the listeners buy the recordings they like and are more interested in hearing new or different recordings.

"We try to give an adequate representation of all classical music," Hill says. Most stations conscientiously avoid alienating segments of their audience, but Hill has a different point-of-view: "We couldn't play a wide range of classical music without running-off listeners, because no one likes all of that kind of music, they just don't."

Some listeners don't like vocal recordings and others don't like modern music so Hill believes it is best to schedule these at specific times. "People get up in arms when you insert a type of music at a time they feel is inappropriate, but if on a specific time of day we have a program designed to play that type of music we don't run into opposition." Opera is usually scheduled at prescribed times—in blocks on Wednesday and Sunday nights and on the Saturday afternoons for the Met. broadcasts. The alternative would be to play only a few types of music designed to hold a larger share of the audience for longer periods of time. Eddie Hill rejects this idea. "Since we don't attempt ever to program for a majority, we can't see why we should do only the majority out of the minority we have."

The audience for WRR-FM, like other classical music stations, must be judged on its "quality." The manager describes his station's audience as "mature, older, affluent," but he is quick to add that there are many listeners who are students and musicians who wouldn't fit this category and there are "possibly a bit more men than women." It is generally considered that between 5–7½% of the population of any area is the potential market for classical music stations.

Listeners to WRR-FM also listen to public radio station KERA-FM and the morning news on KRLD (AM). Hill explains that "people who listen to classical music are a natural for news and other types of radio where you are required to listen." The station's listener surveys indicate that much of its listening is from 7 to 10 p.m. so Hill considers television to be his greatest competition. "We have an alert audience. They just aren't going to sit glued by the television set to watch whatever program comes on."

Some ratings data support Hill's contention that most of the listening to WRR-FM is done at night but they also indicate that morning and afternoon drive-times are peak listening times for the classical station. Eddie Hill programs the 6 to 9 a.m. and 4 to 7 p.m. periods separately. The announcer on duty during those hours selects the music—usually "short selections" of under 12 minutes. The music played during these time periods may be repeated quite often, unlike other recordings on the station which are usually not repeated within a month.

There are eight full and part-time announcers at WRR-FM who perform administrative duties at the station in addition to working their air-shifts from 6 to 9 a.m., 9 a.m. to 3 p.m., 3 to 7 p.m. or 7 to midnight. During the five and six hour shifts longer selections are aired. The announcers select records, program the station for the up-coming listener's guide, catalog records, or perform traffic chores.

The announcers have little freedom. The station manager believes 30 seconds is enough time to indicate when a piece of music was written or some interesting feature about it. He sees little need to educate the audience. "They could read about Dvorak's Symphony in a book. The people tune us in to hear the music, but we do give them tidbits of information about it." Some programs have their own copy but most of the music introductions are ad-lib. Hill expresses little interest in individual staff members' musical preferences but he admits that if he could afford a larger staff he would air "succinctly-stated, well-researched background pieces."

WRR-FM selects announcers for their interest in music, and broad background. Most have a bachelor's degree. Many of the announcers have been with the station for more than four years. This is consistent with the stability evident at other classical music stations such as WQXR, New York where many announcers have been employed for more than 15 years.

According to Eddie Hill most owners of classical music stations *want* first to be in the classical music business and second to make money. The commercially-oriented stations seek to make a profit, but the owners are content not to make as much money as they can.

About 60% of the station's revenue is from local business. Four commercial minutes are programmed within most hours and up to 10 minutes during drive times. Commercials are clustered with two or three per stop. If all of the available minutes were sold the station would be doing quite well, notes Hill.

"High ticket items," like airline tickets and expensive cars are sold on the station along with classical records, antiques, books and other merchandise with appeal to a limited market. "Our listeners listen to us if they want classical music," says Hill. "We get good advertising results with the right client because we deliver an audience that is going to be responsive."

The classical musical station is usually not offered commercials for products that might be considered "distasteful" but it does receive spots for nationally advertised products which are produced in a style not suited to the format. Eddie Hill admits that he cannot turn away the business so he is left with three choices: to find a different commercial for the product; air it and let people adjust to it; or program it in such a way that it is separated from the music. There are few objections if the spot is aired during adjacencies or in newscasts or after other announcements. On the other hand, if an inappropriate spot is run at the end of a symphony where a listener is likely to be "involved with the emotional experience of the music" ill-will is created for the product and the station.

On-air promotion is used to boost listenership for special programs and to

Mozart: Piano Con. No. 21 in C maj., K. 467 (Lupu, Segal, Eng. Cham.) 27:43
3:00 Bruckner: Sym. No. 4 in E♭ maj., "Romantic" (Barenboim, Chi.) 1:03:39
4:10 Until 7:00 pm, a variety of musical selections & news. Today, celebrating the birthdays of Leo Delibes & Widor.
7:00 THE CONCERT HALL
Tippett: Little Music for String Orch. (Marriner, St. Martin) 10:56
Stravinsky: Firebird (complete ballet) (Boulez, NY Phil.) 44:18
8:00 NEW RELEASES
*Francaix: Aubade for 12 Celli (Ber. Phil. Cello Ens.) 14:47
*Sibelius: Lemminkainan Suite, Op. 22 (Kamu, Helsinki Radio Sym.) 345:19
9:10 *Brahms: Violin Con. in D, Op. 77 (Kremer, Karajan, Ber. Phil.) 41:35
10:00 MUSIC FOR PIANO
*Beethoven: Piano Sonata No. 21 in C maj., Op. 53, "Waldstein" (Brendel) 24:50
10:30 THE BAROQUE MASTERS
*Vivaldi: Concerti, Op. 7 Nos. 10-12 (I Musici) 26:51
11:00 MONDAY SYMPHONY
Mahler: Sym. No. 10 in F♯ min. (Performing Version by Derycke Cooke) (Ormandy, Phila.) 1:09:34

TUESDAY, FEBRUARY 22

6:00 THE EARLY PROGRAM
Until 9:00 am, a variety of musical selections, news & weather reports
9:00 THE MORNING PROGRAM
Wagner: Tannhauser Overture & Venusberg Music (Walter, Col.) 24:52
Haydn: Sym. No. 76 in E♭ maj. (Dorati, Philh. Hung.) 24:45
10 00 CPE Bach: Flute & Harpsichord Sonatas, Nos. 1-3 (Rampal, Veyron-Lacroix) 20:21
10 25 Handel: Con. Grossi, Op. 6 No. 7 in B♭ maj.; No. 8 in C min. (Marriner, St. Martin) 28:10
11 00 Mozart: Sym. No. 38 in D maj., K. 504, "Prague" (Klemperer, Philh.) 25:45
Rachmaninoff: Piano Con. No. 1 in F♯ min., Op. 1 (Pennario, Previn, Roy. Phil.) 27:02
12:00 News
12:05 THE AFTERNOON PROGRAM
Until 12:30 pm, a variety of musical selections
12:30 Walton: Variations on a Theme by Hindemith (Szell, Cleve.) 22:42
1:00 Vaughan Williams: English Folk Song Suite (Gould, Orch.) 10:19
Prokofieff: Sym. No. 5, Op. 100 (Martinon, Paris Consv.) 40:14
2:00 Orch. Selections by Coates, Elgar, German, Fletcher, Quiter & Wood (Weldon, Pro Arte) 23:05
Paganini: Violin Con. No. 2 in B min., Op. 7 (Rudolf, Ricci, Cin.) 26:07
3:00 Music for Piano by Chopin, Debussy, Ravel & J. Strauss (Pennario) 25:28
3:30 Vorisek: Sym. in D maj. (Prague Cham.) 24:45
4:00 Until 7:00 pm, a variety of musical selections & news.
7:00 THE CONCERT HALL
Copland: Music for a Great City (Copland, Lon. Sym.) 24:46
Schumann: Sym. No. 4 in D maj., Op. 120 (Karajan, Ber. Phil.) 30:11
8:00 THE CHICAGO SYMPHONY ORCHESTRA PROGRAM
Ravel: Le Tombeau de Couperin
Berg: Violin Con. (Samuel Magad, violin)
Ravel: La Valse
Tchaikovsky: Sym. No. 6 in B min., Op. 74, "Pathetique" (Sir Georg Solti, Chicago Sym. Orch.)
0:00 THE CHAMBER MUSIC HOUR
*Schubert: String Qr. No. 1, K. 18 (Melos Qr.) 17:18
*Glinka: Trio Pathegique (Hacker, Lange, Burnett) 17:03
*Brahms: Trio in E♭, Op. 40 (Grumiaux, Sebok, Orval) 28:16
1:10 TUESDAY SYMPHONY
Respighi: Pines of Rome (Kertesz, Lon. Sym.) 21:00
Rodrigo: Concierto de Aranjuez (Williams, Ormandy, Phila.) 20:58

WEDNESDAY, FEBRUARY 23

6:00 THE EARLY PROGRAM
Until 9:00 am, a variety of musical selections, news & weather reports
9:00 THE MORNING PROGRAM
Weber: Clarinet Con. No. 2 in E♭ maj., Op. 74 (Goodman, Martinon, Chi.) 22:23
Vivaldi: La Cetra, Op. 9 Nos. 11 & 12 (I Musici) 24:06
10:00 Tchaikovsky: Capriccio Italien, Op. 45 (Szell, Cleve.) 14:45
Beethoven: Sym. No. 7 in A maj., Op. 92 (Jochum, Concertgebouw) 37:16
11:00 Bach: Well-Tempered Clavier, Book II Nos. 13-17 (Martins) 21:13
11:30 Debussy: Nocturnes (Nuages, Fetes, Sirenes) (Giulini, Philh.) 26:27
12:00 News
12:05 THE AFTERNOON PROGRAM
Until 12:30 pm, a variety of musical selections
12:30 Poulenc: Model Animals Suite (Pretre, Paris Consv.) 21:35
1:00 German Dances by Mozart & Schubert (Brott, No. Sinf.) 26:33
Saint Saens: Carnival of the Animals (Whittemore, Lowe, Dervaux, Philh.) 22:13
2:00 Ravel: Rapsodie espagnole (Stokowski, Lon. Sym.) 14:30
Brahms: Sym. No. 2 in D maj., Op. 73 (Leinsdorf, Bos.) 39:11
3:00 Music of Palestrina (Willcocks, King's College Choir) 22:04
3:30 Stravinsky: Le Baiser de la Fee: Divertimento (Reiner, Chi.) 23:52
4:00 Until 7:00 pm, a variety of musical selections & news. Today, celebrating the birthday of Handel.
7:00 THE CONCERT HALL
Mozart: Sym. No. 29 in A maj., K. 201 (Davis, Sinf. of London) 23:31
Rozsa: Violin Con. (Heifetz, Hendl, Dallas Sym.) 26:25
8:00 NEW RELEASES
*Music of Pachelbel & Corelli (Auriacombe, Toulouse Cham. Orch.) 20:45

9:00 THE OPERA HOUR
Puccini: Tosca (Highlights) (Pretre, Soloists, Paris Consv. Orch.) 57:00
10:00 SPECTRUM
Spisak: Symphonie Concertante No. 2 (1956) (Wislocki, Warsaw Phil.)
Tahourdin: Sym. No. 2 (1963) (Post, So. Australian Sym.)
11:00 WEDNESDAY SYMPHONY
Scriabin: Sym. No. 1 in E maj., Op. 26 (Svetlanov, USSR) 49:46

****

* An Asterisk indicates a new recording, or a recording which we have scheduled for the first time.

251

increase the number of subscribers to the station's monthly program guide. The guide had been distributed free but increased costs forced the station to charge $7.50 per year for a subscription. Circulation dropped from 18,000 to 4,000 copies a month although it is believed that proper promotion could raise that figure as much as 50%. The low circulation had hindered sales of ad space in the guide. A section of WRR-FM's 30-page, typescript program guide is reproduced below.

OTHER STATIONS

Some stations differ in the type of classical music they emphasize and the way in which they program it. We might call it variations on a theme. KFAC (AM) Los Angeles will air "Switched On Bach"—played on a synthesizer—while its own FM is more "typical" and favors lengthier, romantic orchestral works.

The program director of New York's WQXR says he offers a "fine arts service" and the station is programmed "the way Bernstein programs a Philharmonic concert." He refers to some other stations as "classical music jukeboxes." A station may have a "Music for Dining" program which plays lighter works, and—like KFAC—may offer lengthier cuts at night.

Non-classical music—jazz and show tunes—is played on some stations. For several years the most popular programs on WFMT (FM) Chicago have been its radio drama and folk music comedy programs. KFAC-AM and FM simulcast a midday talk program and WCRB, (FM) Waltham, Mass. provides eight hours a week of black-oriented programming. The classical format has proven flexible enough to allow for the lively (almost pop) sound of WGMS (AM and FM) Bethesda, Maryland—which featues many promotions and short musical selections during drive-times.

WFMT (FM), Chicago airs a maximum of four minutes of commercials an hour—and the spots are read live—while LA's KFAC (AM) will program up to 12 minutes' worth.[4]

HISTORY

Developments in the broadcasting of classical music correspond to developments in the technology of recorded music and broadcasting. Classical music was transmitted via radio waves even before there was "broadcasting." In 1903 the British Victor Talking Machine Company marketed recordings by noted opera singers, in 1904 Victor began its "Red Seal" series, and in 1905 Edison's phonograph company featured stars of the Metropolitan Opera on its

---

[4] "Classical Formats: A Distinct Breed," *Broadcasting,* September 27, 1976, pp. 68–69.

"Diamond Disks." A year later Reginald A. Fessenden was awarded "the first patent issued for voice transmission by electronic waves."

In 1910 Enrico Caruso and Emmy Destinn sang from the Metropolitan Opera House into Lee de Forest's microphones. Listeners to the "radiophone" in New York state, New Jersey and on board ships at sea heard them. The early transmissions were largely of an experimental or amateur nature and were usually meant to relay information, not to entertain. But by 1916 David Sarnoff, an employee of the Marconi Wireless Telegraph Company of America predicted there would soon be a "Radio Music Box" in every home. And there might have been had World War I not channeled developments in the "radiophone" toward the war effort.

Dr. Frank Conrad, an engineer for Westinghouse, became bored while speaking into the microphone of his post-war experimental radio station in Pittsburgh. So he placed his microphone in front of the speaker of his phonograph. In the summer of 1920 a department store advertised that broadcasts of two orchestra numbers and a soprano solo had been received and invited the public to the showroom to hear their radios. Conrad's experimental station became KDKA, the station credited with ushering in the era of broadcasting when it broadcast the results of the Harding-Cox elections.

By 1922 there were 569 radio stations serving 700,000 radio sets. New Yorkers heard the first broadcast by the New York Philharmonic Orchestra and the first remote pick-up of an opera—"Aida," from Kingsbridge Armory.

By the middle of the decade record companies were featuring their artists on the radio. A New Year's Eve concert featuring tenor John McCormack and soprano Lucrezia Bori was broadcast on WEAF, New York and 13 other stations in 1925. One critic called these broadcasts "the most significant development in radio programs since broadcasting was started." The newly created NBC and CBS radio networks featured opera programs along with drama, sports, politics, news, and popular music. In 1928 "concert music" comprised more than 40% of network radio evening programming.

In 1931 WJZ, New York flagship station of the "Blue Network," rebroadcast an international transmission of the Vienna Philharmonic. WJZ joined with WEAF of the "Red Network" to broadcast "Hansel and Gretel," the first radio presentation from the Metropolitan Opera House. Radio was bringing fine music to every corner of the nation and it stimulated sales and improvements in the quality of records.

In 1937 NBC formed its Symphony Orchestra with Arturo Toscanini as conductor. Two technological breakthroughs were about to change the complexion of broadcasting: Major Edwin H. Armstrong was given the go-ahead by the FCC in 1939 to develop FM radio and a television "network" was demonstrated in upstate New York with signals originating from WNBT in New York City. Stars of the Metropolitan Opera appeared in a televised version of "Pagliacci," a first, in 1940.

There were more than 50 million radio sets in 1942, and 400,000 of them could receive FM broadcasts. Forty-five of the nation's 800 stations broadcast FM signals. During World War II adoption of television and FM was curtailed but developments continued. Allies in Europe were impressed by developments of the "magnetophone," a German magnetic tape recorder. Subsequent improvements would make live programs unnecessary. In 1944 *The New York Times* purchased WQXR (and WQXQ) for $1 million.

In 1945 RCA introduced vinyl plastic records. By the end of World War II there were more than 500 applications for FM stations. The number of television stations was increasing, the price of television sets dropped rapidly, and color television experiments were proceeding in 1947 when 93% of all U.S. homes had radios—nearly 40 million sets. A year later there were 1,621 AM and 374 FM stations on the air.

An estimated 370,000 viewers saw a 1948 telecast of Maestro Toscanini conducting the NBC Symphony in a performance of Beethoven's "Ninth Symphony." Two years later the maestro toured 20 U.S. cities. ABC networked the first full-length telecast from the stage of the Met—Verdi's "Otello," in 1948. There were more than 2,000 AM stations and more than 700 FM stations and 72 television stations on the air in 1949 when former NBC President M. H. Aylesworth declared "radio is doomed." FCC Chairman Wayne Coy echoed his sentiments.

Aylesworth was predicting the demise of *network* radio and Coy predicted that half the U.S. homes would have television within five years. However, the FCC soon imposed a "freeze" on television channels, set costs were still relatively high, and there were few television networks and no daytime television.

Columbia Records developed a 33⅓ rpm microgroove 12-inch record which could play up to 50 minutes of material. Columbia remastered its classical music catalogue and reissued it in its new "LP" package while successfully warding off a challenge from RCA, who was promoting its new 7-inch, 45 rpm disk. The era of high fidelity—"hi-fi" to its millions of devotees—was launched.

By 1955 concert music accounted for only 5% of network radio's evening programming but all network music programming was down to less than 25% (from 62% in 1928).[5] Music had become the substance of local radio. Specialization meant the listener could choose from several stations offering different types (and even the same type) of music. Receivers were purchased because classical music sounded great via the quality FM signal and there were fewer commercials than on the more competitive AM band. The introduction of stereophonic transmission by FM "multiplexing" sparked a demand for new recordings in stereo.[6] Record companies recorded the classics in stereo and re-

[5] Lichty, Lawrence W. and C. H. Sterling in Lichty and Malachi Topping's *American Broadcasting,* New York, Hastings House, 1975. Table 25, p. 429. See also Orrin E. Dunlap, Jr. *Radio and Television* Almanac, New York, Harper and Brothers, 1951 for chronology to 1950.

[6] See Barnouw, Erik, *The Image Empire,* New York, Oxford University Press, 1970 for history from 1953.

leased more than 3,000 budget classical albums featuring lesser known artists and re-issues of their earlier monophonic recordings. Tape networks provided local stations with recent concerts by major orchestras from all over the world which were recorded on the finest multi-track recorders with the latest noise-suppression devices. Music lovers became accustomed to hearing their favorite works in the car, at the beach, and at work as well as at home.

FORMAT CHANGE

The radio listener can choose from a wide variety of programming and often has a choice of station offering one kind of music. What happens if there is only one classical music station in a community and that station plans to change to another type of music? In the '70s listeners formed groups and pressured to block such changes. These groups place "citizens' rights" above broadcasters' rights and the Courts have held that they have a right to be heard before a proposed change is approved. The format change issue raises fundamental questions about the rights of broadcasters and listeners and the role the Federal Communications Commission should play in regulating program content.

In 1970 the FCC rejected the complaints of citizens' groups who protested a change from classical music to middle-of-the-road by WGKA-AM and FAM, Atlanta. The U.S. Court of Appeals overturned the Commission and ordered a hearing on grounds that the wishes of listeners must be considered. Six months later the Court, citing WGKA, reversed the Commission when WONO, the only full-time classical station in Syracuse, New York sought to change its format. It required the Commission to exercise closer scrutiny of proposed changes in programming when the buyers of WEFM (FM) Chicago sought to replace a classical music format with pop and rock music in 1974.

An impasse was avoided in suburban Washington, D.C. in 1972 when the FCC waived its AM-FM non-duplication rules to allow WGMS to continue programming classical music on both AM and FM. Listener groups, aided by the Stern Community Law Firm, had filed formal petitions with the FCC to deny the change. Congressmen, politicians, their wives and 10,000 signers of a petition sought to tie renewal of the station's license to retention of its classical format. New Yorkers "dug up" 10,000 signatures and protested the change of classical station WNCN to progressive rock by that station's new owners until the station was sold in 1975 to a corporation which agreed to maintain the classical format. The buyer of WRVR (FM) in New York agreed to keep its jazz format after the seller reimbursed a citizens' committee for $10,000 in legal fees. Other cases involved an Ohio station, WXEZ (FM) which sought to change from progressive rock to M-O-R and Denver station KBTR (AM) which wanted to go country from its all-news format in 1972.

In 1975 the Federal Communications Commission initiated an inquiry to determine the role it should play in respect to changes in the entertainment formats of broadcast stations. The FCC studied the diversity of formats in the 25 largest markets and in July of 1976 it announced a policy of "non-interference." The Commission lacked the constitutional and legal authority to interfere with program changes, it concluded, and it didn't know how to determine what a format is, or if one had been changed. The Commission's study found diversity within formats as well as among different formats but Commissioner Benjamin Hooks felt mechanisms should be found to ensure that minority needs are not abandoned in format changes.[7]

The arguments favoring government intervention in programming matters emphasize the rights of listeners to pick and choose from formats rather than the rights of broadcasters to make a profit. They cite the Red Lion decision which placed viewers and listeners above broadcasters in a fairness case. The groups seek programming for "significant minorities"—e.g. classical music listeners. Public participation in programming changes is sought so that all cultural groups are represented to the greatest degree possible.

Those who argue against government interference in format changes—especially broadcasters—feel that competition ensures diversity in programming and they believe the First Amendment precludes the FCC from interfering with program content. The FCC itself generally believes that broadcasters need flexibility and discretion. The Commission has indicated it doesn't want broadcasters to come to it seeking prior approval for changing a format and it will act only when an adverse affect on the public interest is demonstrated.

The Citizens' Communications Center, a public interest law firm, has vowed to take the format change issue to the Supreme Court to win support for the concept of the supremacy of listeners' rights. *Broadcasting* magazine reports, "a hearing order at transfers is probably fatal to the sale."[8] The city of Dallas decided to retain its classical station WRR-FM when it offered its all-news AM for sale.

The issue is clouded because broadcasters may side with protesters to avoid competition with other stations which switch to their station's format. In the future hearings may automatically be held if complaints about a proposed format change arise. Until the issue is clearly settled a broadcaster wishing to change a format—especially if it is the only service of its type in the community—would be wise to check with an attorney.

TRENDS

Increasing wealth, better education, and more leisure time have created a "culture boom" in the U.S. Attendance at concerts has grown to 25 million a

[7] Federal Communications Commission, "Changes In the Entertainment Formats of Broadcast Stations," *Memorandum, Opinion and Order,* July 28, 1976. Washington, D.C.

[8] "Court Asked For Basic Rule: Who Chooses the Format?" *Broadcasting,* August 7, 1972, pp. 18, 21.

year, cultural events in many cities outdraw sports, and this year more than 10 million will see an opera performed.[9] However, commercial classical music radio stations have not felt the impact of this boom.

The classical music format, with lengthy selections and few commercial interruptions, works against the increasing demand for air and advertising time on FM. The classical programmer must play shorter selections or run more commercials in a stop. Non-commercial "public" radio stations which program classical music compete for the attention of listeners in many cities.

Most industry predictions indicate that quadraphonic recordings and the quadraphonic transmission now being tested will not have a great impact on classical music stations.

The format change controversy may have discouraged potential owners from acquiring classical music stations but it reveals a fierce listener loyalty and dependence on classical stations. These stations face the challenge of holding on to these audiences while attracting new listeners. Young people exposed to classical forms by rock musicians may develop a taste for classical music and some stations have been successful in luring new listeners with less serious musical forms. WQXR New York reports that it has become "more serious." Eddie Hill, manager of classical WRR-FM, Dallas speaks for many classical stations when he says: "Our basic goal is to do what we do now, but to do it better."

Transcript   January 20, 1977

WRR-FM   8:00 - 9:00 p.m.

ANNOUNCER: Our concluding selection on tonight's "Concert Hour" has

                been "Music for Strings, Percussion and Celeste." This

                was a Columbia recording with Pierre Boulez conducting

                the BBC Symphony Orchestra.

CM: Van Winkle Motors (Mercedes-Benz cars).

SOUND: (Promo-cart.) Live opera broadcast. Mozart's opera, "Magic

                Flute," on Saturday night.

ANNOUNCER: (live tag) 12:30 this Saturday afternoon.

SOUND: Musical interlude (approximately 1 and half minutes)

CM: The Ivy House (tableware)

ANNOUNCER: It's exactly 8:00. This is the world of music, WRR-FM,

                Dallas. Welcome to "New Releases." Tonight our two hour

[9] "The Culture Boom," *US News and World Report,* Vol. 38, No. 6, August 8, 1977, pp. 50–53.

program will consist of three works; first of all, a rather

long one - "Piano Concerto Number One in D Minor," by

Johannes Brahms. That will be during our first hour of

new releases between eight and nine. Between nine and ten

we'll begin the hour with the "Suite #1 in G Major for Solo

Cello," by Johann Sebastian Bach and then "Symphony #1 in

A Major" by Felix Mendelssohn. That's our music tonight

on "New Releases" and we begin the program right after

this word.

CM: Great American Cover-Up (quilt tops, dresses, clothing).

ANNOUNCER: Our first work tonight on our "New Releases" program will

               come from a new disc by Seraphim. "Piano Concerto No. 1 in

               B Minor for Piano (opus 15)"by Johannes Brahms. Pianist

               will be Claudio Arrau. Carlo Maria Giulini conducts the

               Philharmonic Orchestra.

MUSIC: Brahms: "Concerto No. 1 in B Minor."

ANNOUNCER: During the first hour of our "New Releases" tonight we have

               been listening to "Piano Concerto No. 1 in D Minor, opus 15"

               by Johannes Brahms. The pianist on this new recording by

               Seraphim was Claudio Arrau, Carlo Maria Giulini conducted

               the Philharmonic Orchestra.

CM: Ciro's Restaurant.

SOUND: (Promo.) Symphony Orchestra Programs on Saturday Night.

CM: The Market (furniture, antiques).

MUSIC: Trumpet Fanfare.

10

Educational Facilities

Some people still consider public radio a forum for culture and political magpies—where everyone speaks in deepest tweed, solving the problems of the world in a spate of throat-clearing, academic swamp gas.

L. A. Times Critic James Brown, 1977[1]

All educational radio stations are not public radio stations but public radio stations are educational radio stations. There are about 750 noncommercial, educational stations licensed by the Federal Communications Commission to educational institutions and community groups. More than three quarters of these stations are operated by colleges and universities, one fifth are licensed to local boards of education and schools, and others are operated by churches, religious organizations, libraries and state and local municipalities.

Most educational radio stations operate on one of 20 channels located between 88.1 and 91.9 Mhz on the FM band. These stations may have up to 100,000 watts of radiated power but nearly half of them are "class-D" 10-watt stations which radiate only a few miles beyond the campus of a high school or college. About two dozen educational stations broadcast on the AM band where some have been operating since the 1920s. Some stations, like those in Wisconsin and Minnesota, are members of a state educational network.

Educational stations are licensed to "nonprofit educational organizations . . . for the advancement of an educational program." In many cases the sta-

[1] Brown, James. "No Snobs Now On National Public Radio", *The Indianapolis Star*, March 20, 1977.

tion is student operated and exists primarily as a laboratory for training in broadcast practices. These "electronic sandboxes" often program an imitation commercial format or combine several formats. They will, for example, play Top-40 hits during school hours, getting "heavier" in the evening with progressive rock and jazz. KALX-FM at the University of California at Berkeley combines progressive music with ethnic programs. Live or taped school sports events are an important part of most school stations and these programs may be fed to a regional network. Educational stations may have simple rip'n'read newscasts or provide an in-depth service supervised by the school's journalism department with access to a national voice network. Other educational stations air locally produced or nationally syndicated religious programs.

More than 200 noncommercial stations have "qualified" for assistance from the Corporation for Public Broadcasting (CPB) and membership in National Public Radio (NPR). Qualified stations have met criteria set by CPB by: being on the air for 18 hours a day every day of the year; having full time paid staff of five; an effective radiated power of 3,000 watts; studios adequately equipped for local program origination and production; and "programming intended for a general audience." Programming which is "designed to further the principles of a particular religious philosophy" or "programming "designed primarily for in-school or professional in-service audiences" does *not* meet CPB qualification criteria. A daily broadcast schedule of "programming of good quality which serves demonstrated community needs of an educational, informational and cultural nature" *is* considered appropriate for Corporation support.[2]

CPB qualified stations are eligible for community service grants of more than $15,000 per year which can be used for personnel, programming or promotion but not for equipment. Eligible stations may receive station development grants of up to $25,000 the first year and $15,600 for a second year. Some public radio stations receive program production unit grants up to $200,000 for which they are required to develop and produce special programs of one type—public affairs, drama, education, or agriculture—for distribution by National Public Radio.

Public radio stations are located in 47 states and the District of Columbia and Puerto Rico. Together they serve about two-thirds of the country. Public radio stations may program everything except a full schedule of religious and instructional programs. Many of them have one of three types of formats: a schedule almost totally of one thing, such as classical music; a block format with large blocks of classical or other music and blocks of public affairs and talk; and a variety schedule built on a program-by-program basis. A CPB study of ratings diaries for seven NPR member stations revealed that "listeners to public radio—like listeners to commercial radio—tend to listen to stations

    [2] Corporation for Public Broadcasting, *Policy for Public Radio Assistance and Qualifying Stations,* Washington, D.C., May, 1973; and National Public Radio, *Fact Sheet,* Washington, D.C., June, 1977.

rather than to *programs."* It was found that listeners would tune to specific programs but would tune out right after them. Listeners would stay tuned to those stations which offered "a consistent service either all day long or through major parts of the day five or seven days a week." [3]

Many public radio stations program special interest programs—live or recorded jazz, black or other ethnic affairs, big band music, nostalgia radio programs, folk music, or language programs—on a weekly or block basis. NPR members receive up to 32 hours of network programs a week with 26 hours of information and other cultural and live special events coverage, and eight hours a week of music programs on stereo tapes. NPR programs include: the award-winning "All Things Considered," a 90-minute daily news magazine; "Voices In the Wind," a weekly hour of the arts hosted by Oscar Brand; "Folk Festival U.S.A.," concert and jazz programs; comedy programs from the British Broadcasting Corporation (BBC); "Options," documentaries for four days a week; "Options in Education," Congressional hearings; and live coverage of talks from the National Press Club. NPR initiated and distributed a popular series of new radio dramas in a project called "Earplay" produced by WHA, Madison, Wisconsin. NPR programming makes up about one-fifth of the programming of its member stations. NPR member stations may submit programs to the network for which they are compensated.

Public radio stations receive 15% ($15.4 million) of the CPB total annual expenditure of $103 million. CPB qualified stations must have an annual operating budget of $75,000 though many public radio stations have a budget of $100,000 or more. In May of 1977 National Public Radio merged with the Association of Public Radio Stations (APRS). APRS represents the interests of public radio stations before Congress and the FCC. It has put the following issues before the FCC: support for the all-channel radio bill which will require that all radios costing $15.00 or more be equipped to receive FM signals; standards for licensees under which educational radio licenses would be granted; interference with tv channel 6 and 90% coverage of the U.S. [4]

Noncommercial stations air programs provided free by religious groups and other nonprofit agencies, Government agencies, and foreign and international broadcasters. They also acquire programs from syndicators and tape libraries and exchange and purchase programs from other stations.

The purpose of public broadcasting is, by its own definition, to provide an alternative to commercial broadcasting. There is a group of noncommercial radio stations which call themselves "alternative," "community" or "community access" stations. Thirty-two of these stations are on the air, three are in the construction permit stage, and another 37 are in the application process. Community alternative stations are characterized by the predominance of ethnic

---

[3] National Public Radio. "Report on ARB Diary Entries of Seven NPR Member Stations," n.d., Mimeo.

[4] Simkins, Tania. "Public Radio: Coming Out of Hiding," *Educational Broadcasting,* May/June 1974, pp. 15–20.

music and minority group talk programs and programs for special interests and have a disproportionate number of volunteers to paid staff on the air. To the uninitiated these stations often sound "weird," "amateurish," and "radical."

Alternative/community stations program "music that other stations wouldn't touch" and open their microphones to those groups and individuals—of the left and the right—who are denied access to the airwaves. These stations vary from 100,000 watt stereo KCHU-FM in Dallas with a volunteer staff of 125 (with most of them on the air) to KBDY-FM at 20 watts in a St. Louis neighborhood. WGTB-FM in Washington, D.C. will play western swing music of Texas while KCHU in Dallas airs 1950 rhythm 'n' blues music from the ghettoes of Washington, D.C.[5]

The National Federation of Community Broadcasters (NFCB), headquartered in Washington, D.C., enables community stations to exchange ideas about fund raising, coordinates efforts to promote the interests of the stations, and aids potential community stations. NFCB maintains a tape exchange and lobbies for the interests of its members.[6]

Some communities are served by several non-commercial stations, each different from the other and each offering a service not available from commercial broadcasting. Community-licensed public radio station WETA/FM in Washington, D.C. provides a schedule of classical and jazz music, old radio programs, NPR programs and local public affairs and syndicated programs. WETA-FM features concerts recorded locally and live coverage of public affairs. Washington's American University provides NPR programs and ethnic, music and talk programs. It has featured marathons of radio nostalgia and has carried NPR features—like a weekend-long blues festival not carried on other area stations. WGTS-FM in suburban Takoma Park is another public station. It is licensed to Columbia Union College and provides a mix of NPR programs and classical music and as well as locally produced public affairs programming. It is distinguished by the high percentage of religious programming it broadcasts. WGTB-FM of Georgetown University proudly announces that it gets no support from government agencies and foundations. Its "alternative" style includes large amounts of progressive rock music and feminist programs as well as music for specific audiences and locally recorded programs featuring new artists recorded in clubs. Washington also has a listener-supported station of the Pacifica Foundation.

HISTORY

Broadcasting in the United States began as noncommercial radio. One of the first regularly scheduled stations, WHA, Madison, Wisconsin, which began

---

[5] The philosophy of community/alternative stations is discussed by its prime mover, Lorenzo Milam in his *Sex and Broadcasting: A Handbook for Starting a Community Radio Station*. Saratoga, California, Dildo Press, 1975.

[6] National Federation of Community Broadcasters. *The Constitutional Convention Report.* Madison, Wisconsin, 1975 (mimeo).

as 9XM in 1919 is still on the air. In 1922 a wavelength on the AM band near 830 Khz was authorized for "lectures and sermons" and other special types of transmission. In 1923 more than one out of ten stations were licensed to educational institutions. Non-profit institutions and educational organizations operated 171 of the 571 stations which were on the air in 1925.

Between 1922 and 1925 a series of four National Radio Conferences recommended changes in frequencies and power, and sought time limitations to meet the needs of educators. The National Association of Broadcasters (NAEB) with headquarters at the University of Illinois was established in 1925.

In 1929 representatives of education, broadcasting, and related fields appointed by the Secretary of the Interior met as the Advisory Committee on Education by Radio to study the use of radio in education and the development of educational radio. Some of its recommendations influenced Congress and the legislation created the Federal Communications Commission in 1934. Groups wanted fixed percentages of time to be set aside for non-profit educational, religious, and cultural institutions within the provisions of the Communications Act. The Wagner-Hatfield Amendment to the Act would have required that 25% of all radio broadcasting be allocated to educational groups. The Amendment received the votes of 23 Senators. Congress, recognizing the need for "the rightful place of broadcasting in education," directed a study which a year later reported: "there is no need for change in the existing law." It was believed that there was sufficient access to existing facilities and stations had an obligation to cooperate with educators. A Federal Radio Education Committee in 1936 recommended that "ultra high frequencies" be reserved for noncommercial use by organized education agencies.

By 1937 only 38 of the 202 stations which had been operated by educational institutions between 1921 and 1936 remained on the air. During the depression years these stations were unable to compete with the growing number of commercial stations for frequencies, increases in power and the demand for channels. In 1938 the FCC set aside some AM channels between 42 and 43 Mhz for educational stations. In 1941 it allocated five (out of an available 40) available FM channels 42-43 Mhz for noncommercial FM use and in 1945 it reserved 20 FM channels between 89 and 92 Mhz for education.

The post-WW II years saw the number of FM radio stations increase from nine in 1945 to 123 by 1955. Some of this growth was due to the establishment of low-power 10-watt FM stations which the FCC had authorized in 1948. The Commission eased technical requirements for the operation of these stations.

In spite of the interest in television during the '50s the number of educational radio stations grew steadily—to 162 by the end of 1959. Aided by a fund from the Kellogg Foundation, the NAEB started a tape network which supplied stations with up to 600 hours of programs a year. In 1964 the NAEB tape network and the Educational Radio Stations division of the NAEB were merged to form the National Educational Radio division (NER) of the NAEB. It had 600 members who paid membership fees based on the size of their station and the amount of programming they used. A round-robin interconnect in several

Northeastern states heightened interest in "live" national educational radio network.

NER achieved success with its coverage of an international peace conference, "Pacem In Terris" and in 1965 70 stations were interconnected for a live international feed results of the German National elections. A permanent interconnect was sought.

A 1966 FCC inquiry found strong support for continuation of the lowpower 10-watt stations and a need for an allocation table for them was indicated. Herman Land Associates reported results of an in-depth survey of educational radio stations. This study revealed a wide range of functions which the stations served and a direct relationship between the size of stations and their quality. The Land study found a need for educational radio stations to serve special groups—"forgotten audiences"; a lack of facilities and research; and uneven coverage of the country. It recommended permanent financing and the establishment of a national and international interconnect.[7]

The Land report was taken into account with passage of the Public Broadcasting Act of 1967. The NER division of the NAEB had lobbied for the inclusion of radio and the provision of funds for radio facilities in the Act. The term "public" had come from recommendations of the Carnegie Commission on Educational Television. The 1967 Act established the non-profit Corporation for Public Broadcasting (CPB) and charged it with making "noncommercial, educational radio services available to all citizens of the United States." It called for programming of diversity and excellence . . . responsive to the interests of the people. Under the provisions of the Act educational radio stations became eligible for grants for facilities from the US Office of Education.

A 1969 study of public radio stations revealed that most operated on a budget of $10,000 per year and had little permanent staff. CPB established a private non-profit corporation, National Public Radio (NPR) "to produce, acquire, and distribute programming for the nation's public radio stations." In 1970, its first year, it was given $1 million by CPB. In 1971 NPR inaugurated national transmissions with the Senate Foreign Relations Committee's hearings on Vietnam and pioneered its daily news magazine, "All Things Considered." CPB established the policy that not all stations would be eligible for its funds and minimum criteria for qualification were established.

The National Educational Radio (NER) network became part of NPR in 1971 as its "scheduled tapes" division. In 1972 CPB proposed changes in the FCC's rules which would restrict the authorization of class-D (low-power) stations. In 1973 the Association of Public Radio Stations (APRS) was incorporated to represent the interests of "qualified" stations. In 1973 NAEB became an association of professionals in all areas of educational broadcasting. That year the CPB joined with the National Association of FM Broadcasters to support the all-channel radio bill.

---

[7] Land, Herman W. Associates. *The Hidden Medium: A Status Report on Educational Radio in the United States,* Washington, D.C. The National Association of Educational Broadcasters, 1967.

In 1977 APRS and NPR merged to form a "new NPR" and 14,000 listeners in the US and France telephoned whistles to NPR stations as part of an experiment in the composition of new music. Two-thirds of all noncommerical educational radio stations have gone on the air within the last ten years.[8]

PUBLIC RADIO

KERA(FM) in Dallas is licensed to the Public Communication Foundation for North Texas, a community organization which also operates KERA-TV a public television station. KERA(FM) reaches more than 42,000 listeners a week, about 2% of the potential adult population of the area. In 1977 KERA changed its format to one which is more than 65 per cent classical music, 15% public affairs, 15% jazz and the remainder folk music, foreign language, and talk. Station Manager Bruce McKenzie describes it as "excellent music, fine arts, and public affairs."

KERA devotes each Saturday's programming to a "block buster" which features 12 hours of a particular kind of music, comedy, fine arts or works of one artist. Blockbusters have been devoted to big band jazz, blues music, folk ballads, British comedy shows, nostalgia radio programs, Texas artists, '60s rock music, and compositions by Bach.

Week-days programming begins with "The Morning Program" (news, weather, sports and interviews) until 9:30 and music until noon. Classical music is aired between noon and five o'clock with NPR's "All Things Considered" from five to six-thirty followed by another NPR public affairs program, like "Options." Evenings are devoted to classical music from syndicated tapes, foreign broadcast organizations, or recordings. A jazz program is heard from 11:30 to 1:00 a.m. each weekday.

On Sundays classical music and opera broadcasts are aired as are a weekend edition of "All Things Considered," radio dramas, a German language program and discussions of new recordings. Big band jazz, folk music, and minority talk programs are also scheduled. Less than one-fifth of KERA's programming originates with NPR.

The classical music is selected by a music director who holds several degrees in music. Music on the jazz, folk, and other music programs is selected by the hosts of those programs. KERA's manager McKenzie says, "if you're going to be a music station then you ought to be really interested in music, not just play it." The music played on KERA is often of earlier or later periods than the music played on the area's commercial classical music station WRR-FM. McKenzie would like to see his station exploring new areas, becoming "more academic . . . bringing people new experiences." He would like to do more live and live-on-tape concerts, and air master classes and performance

[8] Federal Communications Commission, *Educational Radio,* Washington, D.C., The Commission, 1972 (mimeo), and National Public Radio, *A Growing Force,* Washington, D.C., July, 1977.

competitions. KERA aims to "present works that wouldn't otherwise be heard in ways that others would not present them" for example, playing the "Beggar's Opera" in its entirety.

KERA had a "TV-type" format until March of 1977. It had its morning public affairs program until 9:30 a.m. and followed it with the Jean Shepherd, Heywood Hale Broun, or Carlton Fredericks talk programs and other "canned" (taped) shows. McKenzie felt a change was necessary because the stations' membership was stagnant and the station was having difficulty achieving an image and significant impact on the community. Projections made by the station's management indicated that it would have to "harangue" people into joining by spending more time and effort soliciting subscriptions if the station was to pay for itself. A study by a local university found that KERA was working harder at increasing its membership than other public radio stations. The study suggested people would be motivated to join the station and new listeners would be attracted to the station by increased promotion and changes in programming. Many members joined the station because of its variety in programming but were unaware of some of the programs featured on the station.

According to station manager McKenzie, KERA was left with three options: talk and public affairs, jazz, or classical music. The talk/public affairs approach was considered too costly and jazz too risky. The station had shown it could program classical music effectively and it had been successful on other public radio stations. By eliminating the "canned" programs and some of the "see saws" in the schedule people would stay tuned in, value the station, like it and therefore support it. The classical music would be used to build an audience from large programming blocks, by exposing new and larger audiences to programs like "All Things Considered."

McKenzie believes a station like KERA will attract those people who listen to the kind of programming the station is interested in airing. He says public radio doesn't speak in terms of a target audience but he knows that KERA's audience is higher than average in income and education and upwardly mobile. KERA gets limited ratings information but these are often months behind because CPB, who pays for them, analyze them before the station gets to see them.

"Public broadcasters have an obligation to find the right compromise between doing all of one thing and something else that's important to do, that the station can do, and that isn't being done by other stations," says McKenzie. The public radio station is forbidden to make announcements which promote a product or service. The station was permitted to delete commercials from its taped talk shows and sometimes it changes them to underwriter's credits. There are few special technical requirements for the public station though McKenzie feels that at times his station has been lax in not rejecting a program for technical reasons.

KERA airs locally produced on-air promotions from carts at natural breaks in its programs, usually on the half hour. It receives promotions from NPR feeds on a daily basis and tags them locally. Public service announcements are read live. KERA would like to devote only two or three weeks a year to fundraising but it now spends more than that. During membership weeks the station has featured week-long marathons of folk music, jazz, old radio shows or other special programs. KERA's monthly schedule is included in *Prime Time,* a slick magazine mailed to members of the television or radio station, pages of which follow.

There are five announcers on the KERA staff. Some work shifts from six a.m. to noon, or noon to five p.m., and others engineer during the taped evening classical music programs and host the jazz program until 1 a.m. Host announcers work five days a week but one afternoon announcer works on the Sunday classical program.

KERA differs from other public radio stations in that it puts public affairs programming in morning drive-time. Its blockbusters are designed "to do something completely different, and do it for 12 hours." McKenzie says the public station differs from the alternative/community access radio station KCHU because of their differing goals: "We're trying to be a full-blown, professional communication service. We've had some people think this station exists for *their* benefit, but it really does exist for the community's benefit. KCHU is there for people to come in and indulge themselves . . . fine, but I'm not going to put them on the air."

According to KERA station manager Bruce McKenzie the question the public radio station must continually ask is, "why would someone pay $15 for something they can hear somewhere else?" The station needs to concentrate at what it is really good at, he says. To KERA that means public affairs, classical music and jazz. This format, McKenzie believes, "fulfills the mission and the role that public radio ought to be . . . I don't know if there's anything else that it could be . . ."

ALTERNATIVE RADIO

In late August of 1975 North Texas listeners, tuning to the educational radio portion of their FM dials, heard an unusual combination of rare Texas blues records, interviews with radio "personalities" who lived right next door to them, a live broadcast from the Charlie Parker festival at a Dallas night spot and much clowning around. A new station, KCHU, was on the air with 100,000 watts at 90.9 FM. During the weekend listeners could have heard music from India blended with readings from esoteric magazines, blues and jazz from very old or very new recordings and the '50s rock 'n' roll antics of Screamin' Jay Hawkins', "I Put a Spell on You," followed by a rare classical recording by Enrico Caruso. Later in the week they may have tuned to a feminist talk program, a program for the gay community of North Texas, a 12-tone music program, poetry, a noon-hour interview with a Flamenco guitarist,

October on 90 FM

SUNDAYS

7:00am SUNDAY'S STORIES Stories and music for children.

8:00 SUNDAY THEME AND VARIATIONS

12noon FIRST HEARING A guest joins regular panelists Martin Bookspan and Edward Downes to evaluate new recordings.

12:45 THE VOCAL SCENE With George Jellinek
10/2 Hamlet and Ophelia
10/9 Brevity, the Soul of Wit
10/16 De Luca and Schlusnus: Two of a Kind
10/23 The Vocal Dvorak
10/30 *La Forza del Destino:* An Opera of Duets

1:30 VOICES OF THE MASTERS Host Barry Brenesal
10/2 *The Long and the Short of It.* A closeup on the long careers of such singers as Olivero, Gigli and Marcoux; and on the tragically short careers of Supervia, Schmidt, Scotti, and others.

The 1977 San Francisco Opera International Season. A ten week series of taped live recordings.
10/9 Cilea, *Adriana Lecouvreur.* With Giacomo Aragall, Giuseppe Taddei and Elena Obraztsova.
10/16 Mozart, *Idomeneo.* With Eric Tappy, Maria Ewing and Carol Neblett.
10/23 Janacek, *Katya Kabanova.* With Elizabeth Soederstroem.
10/30 Wagner, *Das Rheingold.*

5:00 DE KOVEN The world's sauciest classical disc jockey plays anything that is "Barococo" in spirit.

6:00 ALL THINGS CONSIDERED The weekend edition of this award-winning news magazine.

7:00 EVENING AT SYMPHONY Featuring the Boston Symphony Orchestra. Simulcast with Channel 13.
10/2 Seiji Ozawa, conductor; Joseph Silverstein, violin. Bartok, *Music for Strings, Percussion and Celesta.* Vieuxtemps, *Violin Concerto, No.5.*
10/9 Seiji Ozawa, conductor; Andre-Michel Schub, piano. Wagner, *Overture to 'Tannhauser'.* Beethoven, *Piano Concerto, No. 5.*
10/16 Seiji Ozawa, conductor. Wilson, *Voices.* Rimsky-Korsakov, *Scheherazade.*
10/23 Klaus Tennstedt, conductor; Phyllis Bryn-Julson, soprano. Mahler, *Symphony No. 4.*
10/30 Seiji Ozawa, conductor. Beethoven, *Overture to 'Prometheus'.* Brahms, *Symphony No. 1.*

FRANZ JOSEPH HAYDN

8:00 KUNTERBUNT AM ABEND (German)

9:00 OL' JIM LOWE AND THE BIG BAND SHOW

MONDAYS

6:00am THE MORNING PROGRAM Host Glenn Mitchell; news and in-depth reporting by Bob Ray Sanders and the KERA public affairs division (7—7:45); Norm Hitzges with sports.
THE MONDAY SPECIAL
10/3 Mozart, *Ascanio in Alba.* Mozart was fifteen when he wrote what one critic called "a musico-dramatic jewel, structurally perfect from first to last."
10/10 *T.S. Eliot.* Featuring Eliot reading his poetry, including *The Love Song of J. Alfred Prufrock* and *Ash Wednesday.*
10/17 Purcell, *King Arthur.* The stellar combination of Henry Purcell's music and John Dryden's drama was all the rage in the late 17th century.
10/24 Haydn, *L'infedelta delusa.* Writes one Haydn scholar: "L'infedelta delusa is perhaps the finest opera Haydn ever wrote; the care he lavished on the music is evident on every page of the score."
10/31 An appropriately spooky and mysterious Monday Special for Halloween is in the works. (Boo.)

11:00 TEXAS WEATHER With Caitriona Bolster and Catherine Wilson
10/3 Berlioz, *"King Lear" Overture.* Nielsen, *Symphony No. 2 ("The Four Temperaments").* Brahms, *Ballades, Op. 10.* Torelli, *Concerti Grossi, Op. 8.* Delibes, *Suite from 'Coppelia'.*
10/10 Prokofiev, *Lt. Kije Suite.* Fritz Wunderlich sings songs by Beethoven. Ginastera, *String Quartet No. 2.* R. Strauss, *Concerto for Horn in E Flat, No. 1, Op. 11.* Chopin, *Etudes, Op. 25.*

10/17 Ravel, *Le Tombeau de Couperin.* Mendelssohn, *Symphony No. 1 in C Minor.* Khachaturian, *Violin Concerto.* Mozart, *Piano Trio in B Flat Major.* Britten, *Five Flower Songs.*
10/24 Schumann, *Three Romances, Op. 94.* Dvorak, *Concerto for cello in B Minor, Op. 104.* Ives, *Holidays Symphony.* Arne, *Sonatas for harpsichord.* Florent Schmitt, *La Tragedie de Salome.*
10/31 Villa Lobos, *Quartet for flute, oboe, clarinet and bassoon.* Tchaikowsky, *Symphony No. 6 in B Minor, Op. 74 ("Pathetique").* Cimarosa, *Symphonie Concertante in G for two flutes.* Vaughan Williams, *Fantasia on a Theme by Thomas Tallis.* Debussy, *Sonata for violin and piano.*

5:00pm ALL THINGS CONSIDERED NPR's Peabody and DuPont Columbia Award-winning news magazine.

6:30 IN BLACK AMERICA Interviews with celebrities and newsmakers.

7:00 BBC SCIENCE MAGAZINE

7:30 CONCERT STAGE Leonard Marcus, Editor-in-Chief of *Hi-Fi/Musical America,* and renowned singer Phyllis Curtin welcome a guest each week for an hour of informal conversation and music.
10/3 Raymond Leppard
10/10 Waverly Consort
10/17 Illana Vered
10/24 Gerard Schwarz
10/31 Gary Karr

9:00 IN RECITAL
10/3 Michael Hume, tenor; William Fred Scott, piano; Peter Hume, guitar. Handel, *Silent Worship.* Faure, *La Bonne Chanson.* Seiber-Bream, *Four French Folksongs.* Poulenc, *Three Songs.* Warlock, *Five Songs.*
10/10 Paul Tobias, cello; Elizabeth Moschetti, piano. Valentini, *Sonata in E.* Beethoven, *Sonata in C, Op. 102, No. 1.* Debussy, *Sonata No. 1 in D Minor.* Ginastera, *Pampeana No. 2.*
10/17 Edmund Battersby, piano. Beethoven, *Andante Favori.* Albeniz, *Iberia (excerpts).* Debussy, *Two Etudes.* Rachmaninoff, *Moment Musical in B Minor, Op. 16, No. 3.* Kreisler-Rachmaninoff, *Liebesfreud.*
10/24 Roberta Long, soprano; Russell Woollen, piano. Copland, *Four Songs.* Lees, *Songs of the Night.* Woollen, *Two Songs.* Barber, *Hermit Songs.*
10/31 Donna Turner Smith, piano. Bach, *Toccata in D Major.* Schumann, *Novelette in F Sharp Minor.* Hindemith, *Sonata No. 3.* Chopin, *Andante Spianato* and *Grande Polonaise.*

10:00 MUSICA ANTIQUA Music from the Middle Ages and the Renaissance.

11:00 EASY DOES IT The best of quiet jazz. Host Dave Thomas.

TUESDAYS

6:00am THE MORNING PROGRAM
10/4 Brahms, *Clarinet Sonata in F Minor, Op. 120, No. 1.* Seixas, *Harpsichord works.*
10/11 Schedrin-Bizet, *Carmen Ballet Suite.* Boccherini, *Sextet in D Major, Op. 24, No. 3.*
10/18 Schumann, *Variations sur le nom "Abegg," Op 1; Studies after Caprices of Paganini, Op. 3; Impromptus on a theme of Clara Wieck, Op. 5.* Distler, *Totentanz.*
10/25 Debussy, *String Quartet in G Minor, Op. 10.* Basque composers of the 18th century.

11:00 TEXAS WEATHER
10/4 Schubert, *Symphony No. 7 in C Major.* Poulenc, *Le Bestiaire.* Stamitz, *Trio Sonata in G Major, Op. 14, No. 5.* Castelnuovo-Tedesco, *Quintet for guitar and string quartet.*
10/11 Rossini, *Overture to 'La Gazza Ladra'.* Lennox Berkeley, *Symphony No. 3.* Chopin, *Songs.* Gottschalk, *A Night in the Tropics.* Rachmaninoff, *Piano Concerto No. 3 in D Minor, Op. 30.*
10/18 Telemann, *Trio in D for two flutes and continuo.* Haydn, *Symphony No. 11 in E Flat.* Bartok, *The Miraculous Mandarin.* Brahms, *Piano Trio in C Major, Op. 87, No. 2.* Roque Cordero, *Concerto for violin and orchestra.*
10/25 Mozart, *Symphony No. 25 in G Minor, K. 183.* Schoenberg, *Violin Concerto, Op. 36.* De Falla, *Nights in the Gardens of Spain.* Schubert, *Sonata in A Minor, D. 821 ("Arpeggione").* Xenakis, *Medea (extract).*

5:00pm ALL THINGS CONSIDERED

6:30 OPTIONS IN EDUCATION The only regularly scheduled news program covering policies and people in the field of education.

7:00 GREAT PERFORMANCES Live From Lincoln Center: Massenet, *Manon.* Beverly Sills stars in the New York City Opera production conducted by Julius Rudel. Simulcast with Channel 13.

7:30 EVENING CONCERT HALL
10/4 Rimsky-Korsakov, *Russian Easter Overture.* Brahms, *Concerto in A Minor, Op. 102 for violin and cello.*
10/11 Benjamin, *Overture to an Italian Comedy.* Chopin, *Grand Fantasy on Polish Airs.* Songs of Stephen Foster.
10/25 Bizet, *Jeux d'Enfants.* Vaughan Williams, *A London Symphony.*

9:00 INTERNATIONAL CONCERT HALL Classics from around the world.
10/4 The Detroit Symphony Orchestra; Paul Freeman, conductor;

Natalie Hinderas, piano; Linda Anderson Baer, soprano; The Billy Taylor Jazz Ensemble. Chevalier de Saint-Georges, *Sinfonie in D Major, Op. 11, No. 2.* George Walker, *Concerto for Piano and Orchestra.* Adolphus C. Hailstork, *Celebration!* Hale Smith, *Ritual and Incantations.* David Baker, *"Le Chat qui Peche,"* for orchestra, soprano and jazz quartet.
10/11 National Symphony Orchestra; Antal Dorati, conductor; William Conrad, narrator. Miklos Rozsa, *Tripartita.* Gunther Schuller, *Concerto No. 2 for Orchestra.* Ulysses Kay, *"The Western Paradise."* Beethoven, *Symphony No. 8 in F Major, Op. 93.*
10/25 Czech Chamber Soloists. Handel, *Concerto Grosso in F, Op. 6, No. 2.* Telemann, *Suite in A for flute, recorder and cembalo.* Corelli, *Concerto Grosso in C, Op. 6, No. 3.* Vivaldi, *Concerto for Two Violins.* Mozart, *Divertimento in F, K. 138.*

11:00 EASY DOES IT

WEDNESDAYS

6:00am THE MORNING PROGRAM
10/5 Brahms, Piano Concerto in B Flat Major, Op. 83.
10/12 Mozart, *Piano Concerto No. 26 in D, "Coronation," K. 537.*

10/19 Benda, *Concerto in E Minor for Flute, Strings and Basso Continuo.* Saint-Saens, *Septet for Trumpet, Piano and Strings, Op. 65.*

10/26 Ives, *Piano Sonata No. 1.* Every Wednesday Father Ralph March joins Glenn Mitchell at 10am for a discussion of a particular work, a style, a composer or a form.

11:00 TEXAS WEATHER
10/5 Saint-Saens, *Symphony No. 3 in C Minor, Op. 78 ("Organ").* Kabalevsky, *Piano Pieces for Children.* Bernstein, *Symphonic Dances from 'West Side Story'.* Pleyel, *Wind Sextet in E Flat Major.*
10/12 Coleridge-Taylor, *Danse Negre.* Bach, *Orchestral Suite No. 2 in B Minor.* Suk, *String Quartet in B Flat Major, Op. 11.* Shostakovich, *Symphony No. 5, Op. 47.* Brahms, *Violin Concerto in D, Op. 77.*
10/19 Robert Ward, *Prairie Overture.* Beethoven, *Symphony No. 3 in E Flat, Op. 55.* Reger, *Serenade in G, Op. 141a.* Luciano Pavarotti sings arias by Verdi and Donizetti. Vivaldi, *Sonatas for lute and harpsichord.*
10/26 Sibelius, *Incidental Music to 'The Tempest'.* Franck, *Symphony in D Minor.* C.P.E. Bach, *Quartet for piano, flute, violin and cello.* Copland, *Music for a Great City.*

5:00pm ALL THINGS CONSIDERED

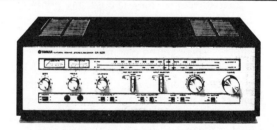

music of the Caribbean, news from the Reuters wire service and tapes of speeches by political activists of the '60s. Programs wouldn't necessarily appear at the right times, some announcers had difficulty pronouncing the titles of the works they were introducing, microphones wouldn't always be opened in time to allow a speaker to be heard, and much laughter was heard.

Two years later things hadn't changed very much. There would be a Chicano program in Spanish, one devoted to Jewish music, more '60s rock and less '30s and '40s big band music, but over all things would sound about the same.

KCHU went on the air after more than four years of hard work and some luck for a couple of young Dallasites who had been bitten by the alternative radio bug while attending colleges in other cities. The station took advantage of the experience, guidance and financial backing of Lorenzo Milam. Milam and his friend, Jeremy Lansman, helped establish more than a dozen alternative or community radio stations which earned them the label "Johnny Appleseeds of home-grown radio" from *Broadcasting* magazine.[9]

Milam became manger of KCHU in early 1977. He explains that the station is a reaction to commercial radio: "We borrow some tools from commercial radio but we have to provide a type of broadcasting that's not available anywhere else. People will support us if we're filling needs that aren't being met by other stations." Therefore KCHU plays music which is not played on any other station in the area. Volunteer announcers—Milam calls them mini-program directors—may choose any combination of selections from the station's "collection." The record library is composed of original folk music and blues, foreign music from every country, and classical and spoken-word recordings. There are no commercial jazz, popular music, rock, or easy-listening records to tempt the newcomer. Some KCHU on-air people may bring records from their personal collection if the works are rare or unusual and the announcer can discuss them intelligently. The predominance of ethnic music from South America, Africa, China, and Scandinavia gives the station its unique sound. Milam describes it as "music that other stations wouldn't touch, even the non-commercial stations—it's just too weird."

Based on his experiences at several community stations Milam has concluded that a mix of 60% music and 40% talk is ideal for such stations. "Just Before Dawn," a program by and for the gay community of Dallas and Fort Worth is considered to be the best of many minority-interest talk programs on KCHU. The hour-long program is carefully produced and well-placed with musical bridges between the talk segments which feature news, interviews, phone-ins, plays, poetry and other things of interest to gays. Milam notes that until recently the gay community was, like other minority groups, ignored by the media and so it was one of the first groups to be offered air time on the sta-

    [9] "Milam and Lansman: Johnny Appleseeds of Home-Grown Radio," *Broadcasting*, September 3, 1973, p. 24.

tion. "Just Before Dawn" is aired live Wednesday evenings and repeated from a tape on Thursday afternoons. Some program segments are recorded during five or six hours of pre-production prior to air-time.

Another long-running program on KCHU is produced by a tenants' alliance which uses its time to inform renters of their rights and how to deal with landlords. When militant feminists were given 12 hours of air time to discuss rape they read the names of convicted rapists. Some listeners complained that they were not given a fair hearing when they called in to comment on statements made during the controversial program. Milam explains that "people deeply committed to a philosophy tend to ignore, or be resentful of, more common philosophies." He encourages minority groups to use their air-time to bring about unity within their organizations and to inform the general public about how they have been victimized. He says controversial interviews bring "PR types out of their shells" and increase listener interest.

News on KCHU has varied from in-depth documentaries on local issues to lackluster reports from a newswire or newspaper clippings to well-produced, brief taped features which are aired by announcers at will. The news is "alternative" in that local news of minority affairs or alternative lifestyles is favored over international and national stories covered by other stations. Re-broadcasts of international stories from foreign shortwave radio stations have been proposed.

KCHU's daily operations are to be supervised by six professional staff: a station manager, business manager, chief engineer, program director, news and public affairs director, and a director of promotion and membership. It is assumed that staff members will work for a subsistence salary matched by donations from station benefactors. In fact both salaries and matching grants are usually non-existent though a few employees have been subsidized under short-term training grants from national and community agencies. Among some people at the station there exists the belief that a paid staff might become complacent and less innovative. "New blood" is brought in to operate the station which brings in new ideas but often results in programming which is irregular at best, unlistenable at its worst.

There is always a cadre of young men and women who love radio and those with a specific cause to promote which provide the station with as many as 125 volunteers who become involved in its operation each week. Some volunteers have air shifts of from one to five hours during which they play music they have selected from the collection, engineer talk programs, and roll tapes as required. Anyone will be put on the air if he or she plays or discusses things not heard on other area stations, uses time "wisely and excitingly," and doesn't expect to get any money. Announcers who talk down to people, or in stentorian voices, or who sound too commercial with a "Hi, I'm . . . ," approach, play top hit tunes and "cliché records" are removed from the air. A "commercial sound" is o.k. when that means a style which excludes the "ahs, uhs, and uhms" often heard on the station. Volunteer announcers who put together interesting programs which appeal to a wide audience are given "prime time" slots in early evenings and on weekends. The station educates its volunteer staff as well as its audience by encouraging them to listen to "role models"—those people on the station who speak casually and make smooth transitions between speech and records.

KCHU aims to reach "anybody with brains, those who are dissatisfied with existing media and need an alternative voice." Milam says he can "feel it in the air" when people are listening. Listeners come from the upper class, students and intellectuals. The station attempts to reach listeners in the minority communities by dealing with problems that concern them which aren't discussed on other media. A station like KCHU "can't be all things to all people," says Milam, "but it can be an *alternative* to all things."

Each on-air person is expected to solicit a number of station memberships for $15.00 or more. Members, or subscribers, have voting rights at station meetings, and receive a monthly program guide, participate in station functions and get discounts from local merchants. Announcers may use their own style to encourage memberships but when the station is confronted with a financial crisis the announcer will interrupt a program for a mini-marathon during which he refuses to play any music until a specific amount of money is pledged. Milam says pleas for funds "shouldn't be the be-all and end-all of these stations. Programming should come first, then education of the on-the-air people, then education of the audience." If the station fulfills a need in the community—even if it's a need the station created itself—the people will support it. The station's program guide, a 20-page newsprint amalgamation of letters, poetry, essays, cartoons and station notices is distributed free at area shops and schools. A program listing from a guide follows.

Stations which have many amateurs must have equipment which is simple to operate and sturdy. KCHU has offered training classes in radio engineering and production techniques.

Alternative stations should "supplement" rather than compete with other stations, according to Lorenzo Milam, who says KCHU differs from public radio station KERA because of KERA's membership in National Public Radio and because KERA receives grants from national sources which limit local involvement. He adds that KERA fills a definite need in the area, is competently managed and is very listenable. KCHU differs from other alternative community stations because it is more powerful than most. Its management is "more enlightened" and the station is deeply involved in minority communities. Some of the other community stations, he says, are "elitist" but "KCHU talks *with* rather than *at* its listeners."

Manager Milam would like to see KCHU's programming become less "amorphous" by "punctuating music programming with talk and talk with music." For example, "International Hotline" (a daily program of ethnic music) could devote each day of the week to music of a different region. Book, movie and concert reviews would be blended with music, news, commentaries and tightly-produced half-hour specialty programs.

Alternative stations are "organic beings" which will not be very much different ten years from now, says Milam. There will still be a gay radio program in one form or another and they'll still be playing Indian music." He predicts such stations will survive because they have created a need for themselves in the community and KCHU will "grow old gracefully."

Two years after it went to the air KCHU signed off, the building which housed its studios and offices was offered for sale, and there was a mad scramble for the frequency by educational institutions and interest groups. It was not surprising that the station was in financial trouble but an imminent takeover by a community group had been thwarted when an individual not connected to the station agreed to assume responsibility for the station's debts. Bills of more than $70,000 were overdue on a $212,000 loan which was used to purchase equipment and put the station on the air. It costs $230 a day to run KCHU for one day—without salaries. If the station were to lease office and tower space its debts would still accumulate at more than $5,000 per month. An interim steering committee set out to find a permanent station manager and funding from national sources.

KCHU represents the "ideal" alternative community station to Lorenzo Milam, whose philosophy is quite clear: "Radio is the salvation of the world, the panacea. A station will use the elements of a community to talk back to itself. We're a feedback mechanism and a machine must have a feedback mechanism to control itself . . ."

OTHER STATIONS

The five listener-supported non-commercial stations of the Pacifica Foundation combine the independence of the alternative/community stations with the professional qualities of the public stations. Pacifica stations are located in Berkeley (KPFA), Los Angeles (KPFK), New York (WBAI), Houston (KPFT), and Washington, D.C. (WPFW). Pacifica stations have qualified for grants from the Corporation for Public Broadcasting but do not air programs from National Public Radio.

The Pacifica Foundation, organized in 1946, uses radio to "explore the causes of strife between individuals and nations which plague mankind with war." It programs for "young people, peace people and women" and opens its microphones to "cultural, political, and religious facets of society." Radio is elevated to a high art on Pacifica stations and much time and effort is spent preparing the documentary, panel discussion, interview, lecture, humor, readings and musical performance programs heard on them. Local news and public affairs programs are offered along with such diverse topics as the architecture

SUNDAY

12:00-12:30
UNCLE CHUBSUCKER SHOW- This show has yet to receive critical acclaim for its comic content. Could it be that everyone is afraid to criticize an ex-highschool English teacher?

12:30-3:00
KALEIDOSCOPIC- A mixture of Jazz and contemporary sounds for you by Johnnye

SUNDAY

6:00-9:00
GOSPEL SHIP- Robert Brown plays gospel music new and old, soft and loud, and sometimes live.

9:00-12:00
THE JEWISH MUSIC HALL- With Barry Somerstein you can hear something to make you feel nostalgic, bring an appreciative smile to your face, make you turn and sneer knowingly and to send you into the week. He does his best to bring you all the varieties of the Jewish experience through radio.

12:00-2:00
THE FORT MUDGE MOAN- Albert has been hopping to Kchu with his amalgam of bluegrass, novelty songs, country swing some of the goldarnest things you ever heard for a long time now.

2:00-4:30
THE BLUES- James and James may sometimes be mistaken as a newly rediscovered jug band duo but in reality they are playing records of rural and urban blues and stringband music and have someone play it for you live when they can find it.

4:30-6:00
JAZZ STREET- When Dale McFarland was told that his show could move from that late night shift to Sunday afternoon he said, 'That's better'n switching your paper bag in for a plunger for a trumpet mute.' Dale's program features Jazz musicians in the DFW area. He plays tapes, raps, sneaks into every Jazz club he can and runs down everywhere that Jazz can be heard. You should call him if you have an addition to his club listings and concert calendar.

6:00-7:00
REVERIE- Reverie means 'lost in thought' Lisa Fenton and Tom Sime explore diverse themes with literature and music.

7:00-8:00
LOOKING AND FEELING GOOD- You look your best by taking care of yourself and feeling good, that's what Madeline Anderson is saying with this program.

8:00-9:00
BLACK WOMENS' UNITED FRONT- Carol Parks brings information through music and interviews and poetry and news.

9:00-10:00
HUNGRY EARS- Robert Wisdom has been ravaging the halls of popular music since the fifties and has begun to find patterns in the music whether it is blues, r & b, rock or sweet pop it is fair game for his hungry ears.

10:00-12:00
SUNDAY AFTER DARK- A couple of hours of uninterrupted listening pleasure for jazz lovers with Johnnye Hughes.

12:00-6:00 am
NIGHT MOVES- Night Moves is a talk show that will feature subjects ranging from bed-wetting to the price of wool in Turkey. Don Smith likens his show to a news magazine with the added touch of up-beat sounds. Tune in— Listeners are invited to call in, 742-6262 or 263-0585.

MONDAY

6:00-9:00
MORNING MUSIC- Provided by Khalil Ayoub; mostly baroque and, of course, early music.

9:00-12:00
FLEXUS- Terry Lance seems to be saying that if he has to bear an hour and a half of international folk music then you can bear the same of his poem play. Also some of the records of contemporary humorists played.

12:00-1:00
OVER THE GARDEN FENCE- David White brings gardening and food news mixed liberally with music by the acoustic guitar crowd.

1:00-4:00
THE RETURN OF- Crab Nebula was what Alan Stovall called his last program. He has yet to see what the day will bring. Tune in if you like the unusual in jazz and classical and sound. The return of the ?!

4:00-5:00
NEWS- Done by those who care.

5:00-6:00
DE COLORES- ?Cual es la function de la Iglesia en la comunidad? ?Donde esta el sentimiento revolucionario de la Iglesia Cristiana? ?Es la Iglesia un instrumento del establecimiento para tenernos de rodillas? Escuche al Deacono Juan Gonsalez platicar de estos y otros temas con miembros de la comunidad. Juan Gonzalez and his wife and Father Frances discuss the role of the church in the community.

6:00-7:00
LA MUJER- Yolanda Gutierrez dice este es una programa para las mujeres. A program about, for and by women of the Chicano community.

7:00-8:00
CONTRIBUTIONS: PAST AND PRESENT- Cultural, artistic and social contributions have been made by Blacks to American life and the world. This program explores these with music and talk.

8:00-9:30
VOICE OF FREEDOM- Ernie McMillian, spokesperson for the People United For Justice For Prisoners discusses events and topics important to those whose freedom is threatened within and outside of the prison system.

9:30-10:00
DALLAS ARCADE- I've been told that as soon as the public is ready for the comedy and humor of the Gruben Brothers they will leave us and forget all about their humble beginnings here at Kchu. Both Roger and Bill tell me to rest assured.

10:00-12:00
JAZZ ETC.- Jazz has come to Kchu with a vengence.

12:00-3:00
BAROQUERY- Khalil Ayoub is making a big move bringing his cantatas, sonatas, suites and fugues with him into the night.

TUESDAY

6:00-9:00
THE MORNING AFTER- Richard of 'Sinners' fame has returned with more music than talk.

9:00-12:00
INTERNATIONAL HOTLINE- Geoffrey is equally uncertain of his new role as the subscription lady as he is to the exact location of Estonia. "I believe they play polkas there' sez he. You call to request the country that we hear from- 742-6262.

12:00-1:00
THE VOICE OF THE IRANIAN PEOPLE- A program presented by the Iranian Students Association (World Confederation) that elaborates the conditions of life in Iran mixed with progressive music from around the world. The program is in two parts, one in English the other in Persian.

new program to be announced.

4:00-5:00 NEWS

5:00-6:30
HERE'S SUMPIN- Benny Arredondo has blown his trumpet with the best of them. Who are them? The giants of jazz, and now Benny is playing them on the radio and making pertinent comments. Hey, one more thing that's extra special, Benny has a picture of him jiving with Sarah Vaughn and Charles Parker and an old friend, Don in some club in Kansas City in '49. If you become a member of KCHU on Benny's program then you can have one.

6:30-7:30
FREEDOM'S JOURNAL- Dr. Emerson Emory holds one thing higher than the truth and that is the real truth, not what some people might represent as the truth. Dr. Emory always keeps a smile and good bedside manner when he is going for the jugular.

7:30-8:30
ETHIOPIA- This month we will see the emergence of a new program featuring news and cultural items from the Ethiopian Student Union.

8:30-10:00
FOLK SEIGE- Pete Hansell has been playing traditional American and English folk music for a long while and he may not always play your favorite. If not give him a call and tell him what your favorite is and it may become the new favorite.

10:00-12:00
JAZZ ETC.- Don finds a wide variety of musical sounds that go under the name of Jazz.

12:00-3:00
THE NEW ROCK SHOW- There are so many cliches about how rock is here to stay that I won't repeat very many of them. The real question is where is rock going and why and what has really happened (not the Kirschner Report either).

July 19- DAVE EDMONDS. If you remember one of the few decent songs on the (ack) AM radio in the early '70's 'I Hear You Knocking' or the wild guitarist and writer of the music for the movie 'Stardust' you have only a vague idea of who Dave Edmonds is.

July 26- NEW WAVE This is not a dance. The dance is the Pogo if you believe what you read in Slash magazine. Since the British rock bands that bust out of England in the sixties was called the British Invasion now they call themselves New Wave.

August 2- BEZERKLEY CHARTBUSTERS A label ,Bezerkley, that seemed to be more of a legend than a record company, has recorded Earthquake, Gregg Kihn, the Rubinoos and a couple of others but Johnathan Richman and the Modern Lovers appear to be destined-

August 9 The local band that the club owners love to hate has gotten an inside track with this kid Mike and he says he is going to play them over and over until the city council abdicates or they get a contract. I think it will just end up with a contract being taken out on them. Oh Yea! they are called the NERVEBREAKERS.

WEDNESDAY

6:00-8:00
THE MORNING AFTER THE MORNING AFTER- Richard says he will keep it up as long as he can. Mostly music.

8:00-9:30
DALLAS AT DAYBREAK- This woman swears that her name is Camile and that she is looking for the frozen chickens. Music with drama notes, reviews and a few scenes.

9:30-11:30
MANANA- Ms. Norma Garcia plays music of South, central and Norte Americano and the Caribbean and provides interesting bits of information about the people and cultures that these musics come from

11:30-12:30
EL LATINO- Alphonso le toca la music

274

mejor y les da noticias nueves y estorias nuestra vida Chicano. Alphonso mixes music with comments and news for the Chicano community.

12:30- ?
DALLAS CITY COUNCIL MEETING- Sometimes we think that the council tries to hide the most important issues in the most boring proceedings. Tune in and hear the wheels of city government grinding along.

? TIL 6:00
Owing to the variance in the length of the city council meetings the NEWS will be played by Katie along with mostly jazz between ? and 6pm.

6:00-7:00
IRAN: A COUNTRY WITHOUT JUSTICE- Bejan and Barry host a program in which they demonstrate the oppression of the Iranian people by the dictator with the longest run in any country in this century-The Shah of Iran.

7:00-8:30
JUST BEFORE DAWN- News, commentary and entertainment from the Gay community.

8:30-9:00
TRALFAGAR PRODUCTIONS- Kchu seems to attract a lot of funny people and sometimes they make it on the air and you get to see exactly how funny they are.

9:00-10:00
TRISH THE DISH- Big band, cool jazz, music from tinpan alley and more .

10:00-12:00
JAZZ ETC.

12:00-3:00
KATZ KOFFEE HOUSE- Kat Sherman thinks that too few of us have any real idea of what a folk coffee house is like and she will bring it to us via radio. Just sit back.

THURSDAY

6:00-9:00
AMANECER- Musica international en espanol para todos los gustos. Music sung in Spanish from all around the world for all people played by Perfecto.

9:00-12:00
INTERNATIONAL HOTLINE- here to allow you to hear something new, folk music from countries all over the world. If you have a request for a country call 742-6262 or 263-0585.

12:00-1:30
JUST BEFORE DAWN- A repeat of Wednesday nights program.

1:30-4:00
JAZZ AFTERNOON- Kchu has an incredible amount of jazz on the air these days. Are you listening?

4:00-5:00 NEWS

5:00-7:00
LA VOZ DEL CHICANO- Todos los jueves de la tarde escuche musica de protesta y las voces de los activistas de Dallas y del estado. Las lineas telefonicas siempre estan abiertas para platicar con gente de la comunidad. Alejandro plays Spanish language protest music along with news.

7:00-8:00
COMMUNITY REVIEW- Jean Freeling's interests lie in politics and government. Every day something happens that affects us all, Blacks and lower income people of all races, She works to stay informed and to inform you. The telephone lines are always open and she brings guests in that you may want to question. For instance-
July 14 Ms. Freeling will be discussing different aspects of Dallas County law enforcement with Sheriff Carl Thomas.
August 4 Ms. Freeling will place District Attorney Henry Wade on the firing line with questions about our criminal justice system, white collar crime, Grand Jury selections, jury selections, Black employees in the D. A.'s office, the up coming bond election and anything else that you'd like to ask him. Extra time will be available if Mr. Wade proves to be in demand.

?:00-10:00
'OT O' MUSIC- Dave Liggions, Finny Mo and Benny Arredondo work together to bring you music by the senior citizens band and local talent.

10:00-12:00
FINGER POPPIN' TIME- Jim Yanaway lets out a hoot and a hollar with 50's rock and r & b. In the past he has featured Buddy Holly and Gatemouth Brown, tune in for more.

12:00-3:00
JAZZ REFLECTIONS- Jazz, jazz and more jazzz.

FRIDAY

3:00-6:00
COUNTRY CARAVAN- Did you ever hear a country station in the wee hours years and years ago? With this program you would swear you can hear the tumbleweeds scratching at the window and the dust, the dust rattling and scratching.

6:00-9:00
THE MORNING PROGRAM- Mike Rush must play it right to make all the excitement that he does at such an hour. You can be sure of hearing some pleasant jazz. What else.

9:00-12:00
INTERNATIONAL HOTLINE- Jerry Brown does the honors this morning and he ranges mostly in the African countries and blends in early soul, Memphis sound and international news.

12:00-2:00
UPPITTY WIMMIN- Kay does interviews, news commentaries and whatever else she can to present the changes for women in society.

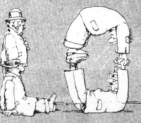

2:00-4:00
RAIN'S PROGRAM- So called since it is replacing Kevin's program with music and an occasional reading of poetry or prose by women. One recommendation is for the traditional American music that she plays.

4:00-5:00
NEWS- Fridays news includes a news program prepared by the National AFL-CIO.

5:00-6:00
EVENING FOGG- Art Fogg discusses alternative lifestyles.

6:00-7:00
STAR WORLD- A sci-fi radio melodrama performed right here in the Kchu studios.

7:00-8:00
XANADU- Joe has found that many poets will not come onto his show to read their work, despite his efforts. He also does programs with readings of major contemporary poets from Lorca to Corso to Tzara to you.

8:00-9:00
GRASS ROOTS- Issues of the inner city, focusing on housing and neighborhoods from the vantage point of East Dallas.

9:00-10:00
THIS IS SCOTLAND: THE CRAZY CAJUN On alternate weeks you hear Campbell Read on Scottish music and culture and Leo Perron with Cajun music.

10:00-12:00
JAZZ MESSAGES AND MOODS- Art Thornton with jazz to end a long week and jazz to make you think.

12:00-1:00
ANOTHER ROADSIDE ATTRACTION- Jim Thompson supervises this zany use of radio.

1:00-3:00
LOVE IS THE DRUG- There are rumors that they have returned to the air.

SATURDAY

6:00-9:00
REFUGIO- El Mexicano, el Chicano, es estranjero en territorio que en un tiempo fue suyo. No tenemos fuerza politica o economica. El amor a nuestra cultura esta siendo arrancado de nuestros corazones. Sin esto ultimo, nunca podremos iniciar una verdadera lucha de liberacion. Nuestros lideres han puesto su lealdad en los partidos politicos establecidos. En su lucha por progresar dentro de estos, se han olvidado de las necesidades de Pueblo Oprimido Mexicano. Somos Mexicanos, y se now debe respetar, no solo por nuestras contribuciones a la humanidad.

9:00-12:00
LA VOZ DEL BARRIO- Este programa es bilingue. Benito les toca musica de su Barrio y habla de los problemas de nuestra comunidad. Escuchen todo los Sabados de las 9am a 12pm. Mi raza is primero y se necesita estar informarda de lo que pasa con nuestra raza. Las lineas estan abiertas para platicar con la gente. Los numeros son 742-6262, Dallas y 263-0585, metro y Fort Worth. This program is in Spanish and English and is for the local community.

12:00-2:00
BOB TRAMMELL- didn't give his program a name yet but I can tell you something of what to expect. He is one of the few people to play really!!!!!! modern or as they used to say, avante garde jazz also reads poetry, plays any other music that he can fit in, interviews artists and passing through Dallas and does one of the worst new member talks on the station.

2:00-4:00
JAZZ FOR A SATURDAY AFTERNOON- Brought to you by Lisa and Katie. Play it girls.

4:00-6:00
MUSIC DRAMA-   Dee Mitchell
July 16 THE MOTHER OF US ALL The music is by Virgil Thompson and words by Gertrude Stein.
July 23 ELEPHANT STEPS The play or scenes if you will are by Richard Foreman and music by Michael Silverstain.
July 30 RAFT OF THE FRIGATE MEDUSA The event most resembles a cantata but definitely has an intensly dramatic presentation. Hans Werner Henze
August 6 ☆ ☆ VAUDEVILLE ☆ ☆ AND ☆ ☆ BURLESQUE ☆ ☆ What else can be said?

6:00-8:00
VOICE OF WOMEN- Music that emphasizes women along with appropriate comments.

8:00-9:00
ALL THAT JAZZ- Paul tries to pull it off with jazz and poetry and sometimes he does.

9:00-10:00
EL DISCONTENTO ES LA MADRE DEL PROGRESO- Music and Talk Plus En Julio 29, 30 se llevara a acabo el maraton para ayudar a los campesinos de tejas que marchan hasta Washington, D.C. On July 29, 30 a food raising marathon will be held for the Texas Farm Workers march to Washington D.C

10:00-12:00
JAZZ MESSAGES AND MOODS- Art Thornton.

275

of Frank Lloyd Wright, an historical analysis of Shakespeare, political debate among the far left and right, and "Erotic Art and Women."

Programming on the Pacifica stations varies between cities so that progressive country music receives play on the Houston station while New York features many ethnic, talk, media criticism, and political programs. The stations receive program materials from an archive of 12,000 taped programs and Pacifica's Washington news bureau. Programs are made available to schools and libraries via Pacifica Tape Library and Pacifica programs are used on over 100 educational radio stations. Pacifica stations have small staffs which work for moderate salaries and many volunteers assist in the administration of the stations, fund raising activities and program production.

In 1964 the FCC renewed the licenses of three Pacifica stations and approved a fourth after investigating alleged Communist affiliation by Pacifica staff members and the airing of several controversial programs. At issue was a broadcast of Edward Albee's play "The Zoo Story," a poetry reading by Lawrence Ferlinghetti, a discussion with eight homosexuals and other broadcasts. The Commission's decision stands as a landmark in radio's fight for freedom of speech. The Commission:

We recognize that as shown by the complaints here such provocative programming as here involved may offend some listeners. But this does not mean that those offended have the right, through the Commission's licensing power, to rule such programming off the airwaves. Were this the case, only the wholly inoffensive, the bland, could gain access to the radio microphone or TV cameras.[10]

Another example of a combination of public and community radio is WAFR-FM which serves the black community around Durham, North Carolina with jazz, rhythm 'n' blues, gospel music and community-oriented public affairs. Funding for WAFR-FM has ranged from cocktail sips to beer blasts and week-long marathons to facilities grants from HEW and programming funds from the CPB and religious organizations. People of the community write and produce the programs to involve the station's audience—an estimated 60% of which is black—in a "mass meeting of the airwaves." WAFR has been an NPR affiliate.[11]

Other educational radio stations have established satellite studios for the origination of programming from urban neighborhoods and rural areas within the station's coverage area.

[10] Federal Communications Commission. "Memorandum, Opinion and Order. In re Applications of Pacifica Foundation." Washington, D.C., January 22, 1964.

[11] Erwin, Carolyn K., "A Black Voice In Durham," *Ebony*, Vol. 28, No. 8, June 1973, pp. 114–22.

ISSUES

Although Washington, D.C. is served by five non-commercial educational services about one-third of the U.S.—including 30 major population centers— is not reached by a public radio facility. There are no NPR stations in Nevada, Idaho, Wyoming, Vermont, New Hampshire and Connecticut, and some Southern states have only one station. Coverage is concentrated in the northeast and midwest. Public radio broadcasters hope to cover 90% of the country and to provide multiple services in areas to offer the public a wide range of programming choices.

Federal matching grants for the construction of educational facilities and the improvement of existing stations will increase the availability and variety of services offered to the public but raise important questions of who is to receive the allocations. Some argue that religious institutions serve narrow interests, that educational institutions are concerned mainly with training, and that government-subsidized public stations represent the establishment to the detriment of smaller local stations. To some degree they are all right.

Noncommercial broadcasters and citizens groups were divided on the "ascertainment" issue which requires educational stations, like commercial stations, to survey their community's needs. Low power and instructional stations were given exemptions, and ascertainment requirements for all non-commercial radio stations are less stringent than those of their commercial radio counterparts and public television stations.

Public radio stations lobby for increases in federal appropriations to the Corporation for Public Broadcasting and fight for a larger share of the total for radio, citing British and Canadian broadcast systems which allocate a third of their resources for radio. CPB qualified stations would like the Corporation to provide more information on their audiences and successful fund-raising techniques, develop corporate underwriters for radio and provide more funds for promotion. Those stations which do not receive CPB grants are frustrated by the lack of flexibility in the standards for qualification.

There is a schism among educational radio stations between the public and community/alternative stations. Public broadcasters admit that their plans for expanded coverage necessitate the reallocation of existing low-power stations and they have come out against the granting of licenses to new low power stations. Their differences are summed up in this strong response to the CPB proposal to reallocate the low-power class-D stations:

The CPB proposal represents the classic conflict between the well-funded, expensive, heavily bureaucratized, heavily narcotized institutions—and the rowdy, slightly seedy, mostly poverty-stricken non-institutional community stations and of course—given past history, the giant college and school departments of "communications" will win out—both in money and influence.[12]

THE FUTURE OF EDUCATIONAL FACILITIES

The future of educational radio stations will be affected by proposed changes in the federal financing of public television and radio broadcasting, the development of multiple stations and extended coverage of the nation, changes in the formats of stations, and the use of satellites and cable systems in the transmission of radio signals.

The Carter administration has proposed amendments to the Communications Act which would substantially increase the funding and availability for grants to educational radio and television stations for facilities and new programming. The bill, which would go into effect on October 1, 1978, will make grants;" a) to extend delivery of public radio services to as many citizens as possible . . . b) significantly increase public television and radio services for minorities and c) strengthen the capability of existing public television and radio stations to provide educational or cultural services. The Corporation for Public Broadcasting will present a five-year plan for the development of public broadcasting and a National Programming Fund would be established. The bill assures that "each eligible licensee and permitee of a public radio station receives a basic grant." It proposes matching funds for public broadcasting of up to $200 million per year by 1981 to be distributed from a Public Broadcasting Fund.[13]

The National agencies in public radio have proposed a goal of reaching 20% of the American population a week by fiscal year 1980. At present 6% of adults in areas where there are public radio stations say they listened "last week." To reach 20% of the population multiple services and multiple distribution systems will be needed—at least three main channels on broadcast or cable systems and three or more specialized services in metropolitan areas and two or more in some others. Each channel of "main services" would appeal to a different audience: a news/talk information service for 10% of the population; a good music/fine arts service which would reach 5% of the population, and a specialized service for groups which represent less than 5% of the population.

Educational radio stations will be helped by the all-channel radio bill which will require that all radios costing over $15.00 be capable of receiving FM as well as AM signals.

[12] *Alternative Radio Exchange,* #13, 14, July 12, 1972.
[13] "Public Broadcasting Financing Act of 1978," Special Supplement to *ETV Newsletter,* Ridgfield Connecticut: C. S. Tepfer Publishing Co., Inc., October, 1977.

With the increases in national coverage of the country by the establishment of educational facilities and increases in potential audiences will come changes in programming. A survey of the planned format changes of half of the public radio stations indicated that many believe their audiences are underestimated by Arbitron rating services. Stations responded that in their programming they: "a) try to serve several different audiences that are unserved or poorly served by commercial radio; b) have a primary target audience whose tastes and needs we try to reflect while giving information and other material it might not otherwise seek out; and c) try to have something that will interest almost everyone in the community." Seven stations indicated they plan to move from a) above toward c) and b).

Stations which responded to the survey indicated they were reaching an average 8% of their potential audience but they hoped to reach more than 20% by 1980. Stations listed their priorities as: drama, news, documentaries, events coverage and classical music. Most stations plan to present 17 types of programs. Classical music, news summaries, jazz, and an omnibus package will be presented on most stations with some providing rock/progressive music, soul music, show tunes, and MOR/pop music. The study concluded that "NPR stations are not planning to go very far down the commercial road of specialization." The average number of hours to be presented of each type of programming, it found, "is remarkably low." Most public radio stations plan to offer more than four types of music each week.[14]

NPR will increase the type of specialized services it offers its member stations. It has introduced a package of specialized programming features, or "modules," which allow for flexibility by the local station, and it works harder at personnel and station development.

The NPR board has approved the development of a four-channel radio satellite system with 15 uplink sites around the country with a potential of 189 participating stations. This development, to be completed by 1980, will enable the national interconnect to provide live coverage of news events and stereo concerts, and will allow for the distribution of several programs simultaneously to provide greater flexibility and choice by member stations, origination of national programming from anywhere in the nation, regional networks, and multilingual transmissions.

The development of cable radio or the carriage of radio on cable TV systems will increase the distances covered by educational radio signals. Cable systems have two-way capability which will allow the listener to respond to a program. Cable systems interconnected by satellites will provide public radio stations with an infinite variety of programs and will enable smaller stations to originate programs which could be fed to state, regional, or national networks.

---

[14] "Results of Survey of NPR Member Stations on Audiences and Formats in FY 1980," Washington, D.C. National Public Radio, 1973 (mimeo).

Transcript

| KERA-FM | 8:30 - 9:30 p.m. | March 16, 1977 |

SOUND: Applause.

ANNOUNCER: For the past hour we have been listening to a live perfor-

              mance from the BBC Concert Hall (pause). This series of

              programs is recorded by the British Broadcasting Corporation

              for the enjoyment of listeners around the world. (pause)

              The BBC Concert Hall comes to listeners in the United States

              from Parkway America's fine arts broadcasting service.

PROMO: (on cart) Jazz music under for . . .

ANNOUNCER: 90FM jazz tonight at 11:30. I'm Dave Thomas your host for

              "Easy Does It," tonight at 11:30. Join me for a late night

              tour de force of cool and bebop jazz, some unusual jazz

              imports from England, France and Holland, and at midnight

              we'll take a tour of some of the activities in the Dallas

              and Fort Worth clubs. Tonight at 11:30 - 90FM on "Easy

              Does It . . ."

MUSIC: Up.

FIRST
ANNOUNCER: (on tape) During the next hour the University of Alberta's

              string quartet will be heard live, "In Recital." (pause)

              (applause under for) Each week the world's greatest concert

              artists are heard "In Recital." (pause) In live performances

              recorded by the BBC (pause).

SOUND: (crowd concert noise)

SECOND
ANNOUNCER: (on tape, veddy British) From the 28th Cheltenham Festival

              the BBC presents a recital given in the Pittfield Pump Room

              by the University of Alberta string quartet.

              Thomas Ralstan . . . and Lawrence Fisher, violinist (he in-

              troduces the performers) . . . (pause). They will play two

              works . . .

MUSIC:	String quartet
SOUND:	Applause
SECOND ANNOUNCER:	The other work in the recital is . . . (he gives background and introduces the string quartet)
MUSIC:	String quartet.
ANNOUNCER:	(over applause) You've heard a performance by the BBC . . .
FIRST ANNOUNCER:	Each week world famous artists are heard "In Recital" (pause). In a live performance recorded by the BBC (pause). Next week we shall hear Yehudi Menuhin, Maurice Jandra and Benjamin Britten, "In Recital" (pause) "In Recital" originated with the BBC and came to listeners in the United States from Parkway, America's fine arts broadcasting service.
PROMO:	(on cart) "All Things Considered" (NPR) special five part report on old people and terror.
TAG:	Crimes Against the Elderly, a special feature on All Things Considered. This week at five p.m.
FIRST ANNOUNCER:	Classical showcase, a program in stereo featuring well known German and international chamber music ensembles.
ANNOUNCER:	In 1974 on the initiative of UNESCO, the international musical world celebrated the Czechoslovakian music year. Among the composers featured were Smetana and Janacek and also Antonin Dvorak. In 1974 was the 70th anniversary of his death (pause). Dvorak's music reflected the awakening national consciousness of the Slavonic peoples in the last century. The sources of his inspiration were the folk songs and infectious dance tunes of his homeland, as a result his compositions have the character of popular Czech national music, (pause). In the following work too, the echoes of Slavonic folk music can be so clearly heard. It's his "Waltz In A-Major, Opus 54 For Solo Piano." Here

it's played in a recording made by Heinz Cheurter, long-

time director of the Music Academy in Cologne.

MUSIC: Piano solo.

Transcript

KCHU-FM   9:40 - 10:40 p.m.   January 16, 1977

Tricia Ramsey

MUSIC: "Porgy"

MUSIC: Oliver Cobbs

MUSIC: Louis Armstrong

MUSIC: "Panama Limited Blues"

TRISH: And you are listening to Bertha "Chippie" Hill and that was

                the "Panama Limited Blues" and before that you were listen-

                ing to Louis Armstrong and before that you were listening

                to Oliver Cobbs and before that you were listening to "Porgy,"

                and before that you were listening to me tell you that I

                would like you to become a member tonight. And once again

                the number to join the station is 742-6262 or you can make

                out a check for ten dollars, fifteen dollars or twenty dol-

                lars and send it to 2516 Maple Avenue (pause) or if you want

                to call and get a program guide tonight we're open for that.

                You can have a listing of all of our programs. We'll send

                that to you free of charge so that if you don't know any-

                thing about the station you can read our literature and

                read all the propaganda about us. So why don't you go on

                and do that tonight (pause). Once again I will be taking

                requests, the number is 742-6262 or that famous number for

                Fort Worth is 263-0585 (pause). And we're gonna go on now

                to music of the twenties and this is Helen Kane with the

                orchestra directed by Leonard Joy and this is called "I

                Wanna Be Loved By You," Scooby-doo!

MUSIC:	"I Wanna Be Loved By You," Helen Kane.
MUSIC:	"I Kiss Your Hand, Madam," Leo Reisman.
MUSIC:	"C-O-N-S-T-A-N-T-I-N-O-P-L-E," Kentucky Serenaders.
TRISH:	And that was Johnny Hamps' Kentucky Serend . . . (laugh), hold it, stop, wait a minute, one more time, Johnny Hamps' Kentucky Serenaders, my dentures slipped, there . . . that was "Constantinople" and before that "I Kiss Your Hand, Madam" with Leo Reisman and his orchestra, the vocal with Van Weeks, and before that "I Wanna Be Loved By You," with Helen Kane, the orchestra directed by Leonard Joy, (pause) I hope you enjoyed tonight's show, I want to thank all of you who called and made their pledges tonight and we're gonna end with some Clifford Brown . . . stay tuned for about eight minutes of news and then Crabbe Nebulae and this is KCHU Dallas and I guess we'll see you again next Wednesday at this time, eight to ten.
MUSIC:	Clifford Brown (jazz).
ANNOUNCER:	Shaw Whitney now has the news.
SW:	(Reads report about racism in Ontario, Canada.)
SOUND:	(Tape) "In the Public Interest," Edward P. Morgan, (about urban planning) provided by the Fund for Peace, Washington, D.C. (short commentary program).
SW:	Story about forty-seven million dollar suit filed by Black Panthers in Chicago. Now we have a couple of public service announcements: 1. Michael Harrington to speak at a local meeting (on public policy). 2. Shakespeare Festival of Dallas needs workers. 3. Radio journalism -- join KCHU, news team -- "Especially if you disagree with the political leanings of this newsman."
ALAN:	Thank you Shaw Whitney. This is KCHU, Dallas and you're

now tuned to Crabbe Nebulae. (pause) Going to start off
the show tonight with Sun Ra. (pause) Just like to remind
you that albums for tonight's show have been donated by
Peaches Records and Tapes.

MUSIC: Sun Ra (progressive jazz).
                Woody Herman, "Apple Honey" (big band jazz).

ALAN: And that was Woody Herman who was naming off all the musicians
                there. That was from a new album called "Woody Herman and
                the New Thundering Herd," it's a double album on RCA that
                features, as you could tell, quite a few musicians which
                Woody Herman got back together. This is the 40th anniversary
                Carnegie Hall Concert that was recorded last year and the
                piece, "Apple Honey." Before that we started off with Sun
                Ra and his orchestra from "Bad and Beautiful" and the piece
                was ANK, which is the Egyptian symbol for life eternal.
                (pause) This is Crabbe Nebulae, the multi-hued show (pause).
                I'm going to be playing mostly new releases tonight. We're
                gonna start off with a new album by Barry Miles, it's called
                "Sky Train" and this is sort of follow the trend of the new
                fast jazz using lots of electronics, etc. etc. etc . . . and
                after that we're gonna hear from the new Return to Forever
                album with Chick Corea and Stanley Clarke and later on we're
                going to be hearing from the new Jeff Beck, and I've got one
                other new one here if I can think of it. Anyway, it's com-
                ing up. This is Crabbe Nebulae, I'm your host, Alan and this
                is Barry Miles.

MUSIC: Barry Miles (big band electronic jazz).

MUSIC: "The Musician" (jazz and vocal).

MUSIC: Chick Corea and Return to Forever (jazz-rock).

11

Adult Block (Variety)

In the "golden" days of radio, stations were programmed much as television is today. Programs were laid out in "blocks," and many of those early techniques are currently in use in markets of all sizes. The scheme attempts to provide something for listeners in every demographic category. It may include several categories of music, newscasts, talk shows, sports talk shows, play-by-play accounts of baseball, football, soccer, hockey, and basketball. Theoretically, block programming in major, highly-competitive markets is not profitable. In small markets, however, it is not only profitable, but necessary, if the station is to provide the community with adequate broadcast service. Block programming differs from "formula" programming in many ways. There is no effort to develop an aural "image," as there is in formula formats. The quality of talent, written materials, and music may be equal, but the execution and schedule configurations exhibit huge variations. The thinking of leading broadcasters is that without a different and highly definitive "sound," ratings cannot be achieved, and without ratings principal advertisers will avoid the station. Stations such as WCCO in Minneapolis and WSB in Atlanta are two representative exceptions. These operations are successful and their programming has withstood barrage after barrage of rock-and-roll competition. Both have stuck to the format for many years and while the music and personalities have changed to keep up with the times, the service concept of the stations has not. Power of the station opting for an adult block format is a major consideration because such stations must depend upon distant audiences for listenership. It is not uncommon for a 5,000-watt rock and roll station to achieve number one position in a metropolitan area and lose out to strong, adult stations in the ADI and TSA areas. Strong, dense signals are essential to consistent, repetitive listening. The circumstances under which a licensee would establish an adult block commercial format require very delicate interpretation.

Two interesting examples of relatively new adult block formats may be found at KRLD in Dallas and WOAI in San Antonio. These are both 50,000-watt facilities, and both are in highly competitive markets. Each includes in its program schedule a conglomeration of adult music, news and sports. WOAI patterned its plan after KRLD, so it is perhaps more appropriate to examine the original concept.

KRLD was the first Dallas station to implement a news "block," that is, it was the first station to program more than 15 minutes of news continuously. The block ran from 5:30 a.m. until 9:00 a.m. and sounded, during that period, very much like an all-news concept. At 9:00 a.m., the station programmed "adult music," a variety of highly-orchestrated pieces that have come to be called "lush" music. This continued until noon when a 30-minute news segment was programmed. Music followed until 4:00 p.m. when a two-hour news block was again aired. A sports talk (open line) show followed, and at 7:00 p.m. the audience was treated to five hours of country and western music. The station returned to lush music until 5:30 a.m. when it began repeating the cycle.

Principal considerations in KRLD ultimately instituting the format was the formidable competition being offered by a host of other stations. KLIF and KNUS were in head-to-head battle for the teen and 18–34 audiences. WBAP and KBOX were only two of the country and western formats being offered, and both stations had a big head start in the field. So-called "good music" had been adopted by several full-power FM stations, and the MOR rock formats were being programmed at KFJZ and KVIL. All of these were well-established in the Dallas-Fort Worth market, and it would have taken years and virtually unlimited exploitation dollars for the station to make a showing.

Faltering attempts were made at programming rock music, but it became apparent to management that this *was not* the best direction. KRLD was one of the oldest facilities in the market and was affiliated with the CBS Radio Network. In the dimming years of the '30s and '40s, KRLD was an entertainment and information mainstay for radio listeners. Because of its enormous reach (50,000 watts at 1080 khz) the station had programmed to farmers, ranchers, and city dwellers alike. It carried the soap operas and nighttime dramas of CBS and generally was a prosperous and respected operation.

No format is ever permanent in every detail. Programmers and management continually strive to upgrade, update, and otherwise improve the palatability of the station sound. This was certainly the case with KRLD. When surveys indicated geriatric demographics, management decided to change the lush music to a younger variety. Some rock was included in the play list. After WRR began programming News & Talk, KRLD instituted a talk show in the 7:00 p.m.–10:00 p.m. period. Later, noting WBAP's huge cumulative audiences with country music, KRLD began programming C&W in the evening hours. It was believed that the station could grab a sizable share of WBAP's listeners when WBAP was broadcasting nighttime play-by-play accounts of Texas Ranger Baseball. While these changes are by no means minor adjustments to a format, they are representative of the constant manipulation required to keep a format current and workable.

The adult block format produces a cume audience change that is difficult to read and consequently may result in time buyer misinterpretation of figures. Normally, a ''skew'' graph will indicate to the experienced observer the specific audience the station is trying to reach.

Again using KRLD as an example, an October-November Arbitron audience estimates in the 6-county Dallas Trading Area, showed KRLD with a total audience of 417,600 persons, 6:00 a.m. to 12 midnight, Monday through Sunday. Of this audience, 29.4% were over 50 years of age, and 51.7% were males, while 48.4% of the station's audience was in the important 25–49 age groups. More than *half* of the station's total audience was garnered over the weekend, and 125,300 of those were found between 10:00 a.m. and 3:00 p.m. Sunday. Why? Because KRLD carried the Dallas Cowboy professional football games on Sunday afternoon, resulting in the relatively extremely high weekend and Sunday figures. A progressive rock station featuring, perhaps, three hours of ''Sly & the Family Stone'' in a special Saturday afternoon concert might produce the same results. There's nothing intrinsically wrong with this kind of specialty programming, but unless time buyers are alert they are likely to misread the tone of the station if they attempt to make a buy based on total audience and total week. Formula stations may safely be purchased in this manner, but adult block stations may not. Another indicator is average quarter hour figures. For the total week, KRLD's *average* quarter-hour audience was 25,300. For the 10:00 a.m.–3:00 p.m. period on Sunday, it was 45,100!

KRLD's total average quarter-hour adult audiences by daypart, Monday through Friday:

$$6–10 - 54,000$$
$$10– \; 3 \; - 21,100$$
$$3– \; 7 - 22,000$$
$$7–12 - \; 6,900$$

It is immediately apparent that the station's main strength is in the morning drive-hours (6–10.) This is true with almost all AM stations, but the drop from 54,000 average quarter hour in the morning drive to 21,100 in mid-day represents a more dramatic decline than one finds on other AM stations. The

audience loss amounts to 60.9%. Let's compare with KLIF, a Top 40 operation, and KBOX, a C&W station:

	KLIF	*KBOX*
6–10	26,600	19,600
10– 3	13,200	12,400
3– 7	15,500	12,800
7–12	6,200	3,700

KLIF lost 50.4% of its *adult* audience after the morning drive period
ended, while KBOX dropped only 37.0% of its listeners. By contrast, KOAX,
an adult "lush" music operation, actually gained audience in the 10–3 period
compared to that of the 6–10 period. The station had an average quarter-hour
audience estimated at 9,200 in morning-drive, compared to 9,400 in the mid-
day period. The afternoon-drive period showed 7,400 persons listening, with
5,600 listening at night. The reason for this differential in audience levels is
principally because the station is FM. The AM stations show a huge automobile
audience, while FM does not, due to the relatively small percentage of autos
with FM radios.

KRLD's drop would also be a clue to the "block nature" of the format.
Listeners tuned to the station in the morning for the news, which included high
quality reports from the CBS Radio Network and the ABC Information Network, as well as local news. Those persons tuning for news *tuned out* when the
station began programming music at 9 a.m.

Another factor is the *availability* of audience. Teens, for example, are not
available to listen to radio during school hours. Thus, a surge of teen listening
in the 3–7 period and the 7–12 period is normal for rock stations. And while
FM listening overall is increasing dramatically, FM listening in cars progresses
slowly. The automobile audience simply is not available to FM stations because
the sets aren't there. Because FMs *are* available in homes, offices, and stores,
during non-drive hours, it is logical that most adult FM listening will be during
those hours.

Listeners to FM stations programming rock music take on a picture similar
to that of the AM rockers, except that the decline in audience from morning to
mid-day is not so pronounced. Remember, the rock stations attract *youth* audiences; KOAX-type lush music stations attract older listeners. KNUS showed an
average quarter-hour audience of 15,500 in morning-drive, 9,000 in mid-day,
11,500 in afternoon-drive (availability of teens), and 6,000 in the 7–12 period.
The drop between morning drive and mid-day was 42%, compared to 50.5 for
KLIF, 60.9 for KRLD, and a *2.2%* gain for KOAX.

The news blocks programmed on an adult block format may be exactly the
same as those programmed on an all-news or a news/talk format. The music
may be the same as that programmed on a solid music station. The essential
difference is that a "block" formatted station will pick and choose among elements of all formula formats for its program ideas. A sports talk program

would approximate in quality that of an all talk station, such as WMCA in New York.

A musical hour on a block station may appear:

0:00 – 0:05 — Network News
0:05 – 0:30 — Easy Listening Sounds of KXXX
0:30 – 0:35 — Local News
0:35 – 0:60 — Easy Listening Sounds of KXXX

Commercials, public service announcements, and promotional announcements may be clustered, perhaps on the 0:10, 0:20, 0:40, and 0:50, giving the listener long periods of uninterrupted music. Another programmer may decide to break between each piece of music for announcements, including time checks and weather updates.

12

Total Service:

The Only Station in Town

Single-station markets are recipients of a radio service not usually found in multi-station markets. These are usually daytime-only facilities and may be equated with the country weekly newspaper. Frequently, such stations provide more *genuine* service than their big city counterparts. In a metro area served by 30 stations, it is difficult for licensees to really believe that people depend upon them for hour-by-hour service. But in a town of 3,000 in the heart of a farm area, the licensee knows, by day-to-day contact with the audience, that the area depends upon the station for many vital services.

Major market stations simply cannot be "all things to all people," but in the small, one-station market, the station *must* be just that. A day of programming should sound the way a magazine reads. There should be music and information that *specifically* suits the needs, tastes, and desires of the people living within the service area. The country newspaper prints local news principally, as it has neither the resources or challenge to dig up national and international news. "Locals" are stressed, and often the printing press is an ancient flatbed. Any photographs run are from engravings that have been secured from a distant larger city. Local small-town radio is much the same. Frequently, the station is *owned and operated* by a local citizen who has lived in the area for many years. Such operations do not lend themselves to absentee ownership, except perhaps in cases where the local manager is also a substantial partner in the owning company or corporation.

Following is a typical Monday-through-Saturday broadcast schedule for a daytime-only station (500 watts at 1410 kcs) in a small southern farm community. Assume the township has 2,500 persons and that the county has an additional 18,000 persons, most of them farmers, mercantile employees, and housewives.

Hour	Program Title	Description
6:00–6:02	Sign On	Sign On. National anthem, followed by station ID, ownership identification, station motto.
6:02–6:15	News	Local, state news from wire. Long-range weather forecast. Current weather. Closing stock markets.
6:15–7:00	Morning Melodies	C&W music, personality DJ, interspersed with commercials, PSAs, local names. Time checks.
7:00–7:05	News	Local news. State news headlines. Weather.
7:05–7:15	Gospel Time	Ten minutes of gospel music.
7:15–7:30	Morning Melodies	C&W music
7:30–7:35	County Agent	County Agent talks to farmers about crop conditions.
7:35–8:00	News	Local news, state news headlines, weather.
8:05–9:00	Morning Melodies	C&W music
9:00–11:00	Mildred's Show	Local female plays MOR music, gives recipes, talks with listeners on phone about local happenings. Everything is localized, keyed to female audience.
11:00–11:05	News	Local, state.
11:05–12:00	Mildred's Show	Continues as above.
12:00–12:15	News	Considered a major newscast, probably

		done by owner or manager. Contains weather, current and forecast, stock market reports, perhaps an interview with local businessman on local economy.
12:15-12:30	Noonday Sermon	This quarter-hour is rotated among all churches in area, with local ministers giving light sermons with non-denominational approach. Perhaps include local church news, coming events at minister's church this Sunday.
12:30-1:00	Gospel Time	Half-hour of old time gospel, interspersed with ad-lib PSAs.
1:00-1:05	News	Local, state.
1:05-2:00	Bill Jones Program	Personality program with variety of musical favorites. Announcer indicates knowledge of community by ad-libbing local news items, mentioning as many names as possible.
2:00-3:00	Good Music Hour	Non-personality program on which big band, semi-classical music is played. Might be handled by wife of owner or manager.
3:00-5:30	Teen-Time	Local student plays current hits in manner of Top-40 station. Ad-libs school events calendar.
5:30-Sign Off	Quittin'Time	Jones comes back to play C&W music with gossip and news.

You think this is hokey? That it won't work? That it will drive listeners to tune distant stations? Wrong. KRIH, a daytimer in Rayville, Louisiana, had a similar daily schedule and held the attention of around 90% of residents surveyed. The *only* competition was a weekly newspaper; ownership was local, and everything was keyed to local needs, tastes and desires. Possible staffing of a small station:

Position	Duties
Owner	Manager, runs board and morning show until 9 o'clock. Sells time, writes copy, handles some production balance of day.
Office Manager	Handles bookkeeping and billing. Makes up daily log. Answers phone. Types orders.
Announcer	Female, handles "Mildred's" program. May be part-time lady from Home Extension Service or person who has "retired" from full-time broadcast work in larger market. Should be socially prominent. Some selling.
Announcer	Does "Bill Jones Show," sells, writes copy, does some maintenance.
Announcer	Part-time student does afternoon teen show, such other duties as station budget will allow. Runs board Sunday morning.

Under such a plan, all personnel work a six-day week, with engineering handled by a contract engineer from a nearby city. This is legal with non-directional, low-power local stations. Persons running the board must have a third class license. Sunday afternoon may be handled by another student part-timer.

It is the manager's task to formulate the programming, set policy and lay down objectives. Every aspect of the schedule must relate faithfully to the community. It is better to have *local* people working in the offices, studios, and in sales. A station that is totally dedicated to serving just that community—and living within the means provided by that community—will be a success. Quality, as compared to programming in a highly competitive market, may be minimized, so long as everything relates and is done in good taste. A "blue" story told on the air in a small market may cause a local uproar, while it might go unnoticed in a major market.

Ward L. Quaal and James A. Brown, in their book, *Broadcast Management,* pointed out the station's duty toward its community. The statements are particularly applicable to stations that enjoy a local monopoly.

The station should be known as a champion for civic improvement and for the promotion of public safety, racial and religious understanding. Always regularly expose any community "evils" which come to its attention. Mere notices, brief announcements, colorless paragraphs sandwiched in the day's schedule are not enough! Whenever the station reaches the stage where it is a true mirror for the community, then the person who has guided it to that accomplishment can take pride in this achievement. The station will enjoy acceptance and approval.

Most small market operations are not highly profitable, but they may provide a decent living for the owner and staff, and they may be operated economically. Equipping such a station is relatively inexpensive because sophisticated equipment simply is not needed—nice to have, perhaps, but not essential. In fact, many daytime-only stations do not have production rooms, per se; the control room is used to produce materials after the station has signed off for the day. Two turntables, a couple of cartridge playbacks, and one record playback will handle the job. Such operations may have an overhead of no more than $3,000 a month, while revenues of $4,000 to $5,000 per month are not uncommon.

It is particularly important in these small markets for ownership to participate in community affairs. Editorials are appropriate, even though the owner never thought of himself as a writer or commentator. Citizens look to broadcasters for leadership. While weekly newspapers normally take positions on important public issues, radio stations are wont to sit back and let others do the arguing. Responsible licensees who feel compassion for their communities are more and more getting into the fight. Any person capable of obtaining a license to operate a station is certainly capable of commenting on the affairs of the service area.

While the format outlined in this chapter relates to a small southern market, its principles may be applied in any small market where the station has a monopoly. Minorities must be considered, whether they are Chicano, European or Black. Programming *must* be addressed to these groups, not only because they are entitled to it, but also because the FCC *expects* stations to pay attention to the needs, tastes, and desires of all citizens in a community. If it is a farming area, then programming should emphasize farming. If it is an industrial area, programming should mirror that environment. Daytime-only stations may go back on the air at night during such emergencies as freeze warnings, civil strife, or destructive storms. Any time the community faces any sort of general danger, the station should take to the air and give warnings, information, and advice. This situation is covered in FCC Rules & Regulations.

GLOSSARY

AP — Associated Press. A news wire service.

ASCAP — American Society of Composers, Authors and Publishers. A music licensing service.

actuality — News report from the scene, or voice of newsmaker from any location.

adult-block variety — Format which provides a range of program types in lengthy segments. Often m-o-r music, news and sports.

album oriented rock (AOR) — Replaced "progressive rock" as name of format that features laid-back announcers and popular album cuts.

alternative station — A "buzz" word used by many stations to indicate format differences. Most commonly used by non-commercial stations.

anchor — The person or persons who tie various elements of a newscast together. Usually the strongest member of a news team. Walter Cronkite, for example, *anchors* the CBS evening news.

Arbitron — A major broadcast rating service which uses diaries mailed to listeners' homes.

ascertainment — FCC requirement that stations survey community leaders and the public to identify problems and needs of their community.

automation (automated) — Technical equipment designed to reproduce audio material in pre-designated sequence.

average quarter hour — Different numbers of persons listen to a station in each hour of a given day part (6–10, 10–3, etc.). Ten may be found to listen between 6–7 a.m., while 40 may listen 7–8 a.m., 30, 8–9 a.m., and 20, 9–10 a.m. The total number of persons is 100, and the number of quarter-hours is 16. The average quarter hour audience then is 6.

bg — Background, usually a music "bed."

BMI — Broadcast Music, Inc. An industry-supported music licensing service.

back announce — Announcing the titles and artists of records after they have been played, usually after a set of two or more records.

back-to-back — Program units that are adjacent to each other. Music, "back to back"; news and sports, "back to back", etc.

bed — Instrumental portion of singing jingle and/or background music in a commercial or i.d.

block programming — A format in which programming appealing to entirely different audiences is "blocked out" on the schedule.

blocked or blocked station — Receives revenue from broadcasting syndicated programs or programs from churches or other religious organizations.

"blue" — Off-color joke. Jocks often referred to as "blue" personality.

break — Usually means "station break" in which station call letters and location are announced. Also used to indicate interruption in any sequence of program elements.

broadcast day — The time period in which a station conducts normal operations (sunrise-sunset, 6 a-12 m, continuous, etc.)

broadcaster — May be anyone engaged in any station job; usually, a licensee, manager, or other experienced radio or TV executive, program manager, personality.

butted — Music editing jargon, meaning to abut one sound against another.

carousels — Juke-box-like component of an automated programming system which moves cartridges into position for broadcast.

charts — Published list of hit records, often organized by category, e.g., country, pop, or soul.

class-d station — Low power (10 watt) FM station licensed to an educational institution.

clear channel station — Operates over a far-reaching area free from interference from other stations.

clock — Sometimes called a "wheel." Indicates, in the fashion of a clock, the sequence of program events within a given hour.

clustering — Airing several commercials in succession to allow for longer uninterrupted segments of music.

commercial load — The amount of commercial matter calculated into any format. Load may vary from 8 minutes to 21 minutes per hour, depending upon format.

community station (community access) — Type of educational station which provides large amounts of air time for programs presented by community groups and non-professionals.

compressor (compression) — Technical device that compresses dynamic range of sound and increases audio density.

contemporary music format — Any of several types of popular or hit music station.

contemporary religious music — Contemporary music with religious lyrics.

counter-programming — Programming specifically designed to offset the appeal of a competing station, or attract a different segment of the audience.

cross-over — 1. Music which is played on two or more formats, e.g. country-pop, soul-rock, rock-pop. 2. Record which appears on two types of hit record chart.

cume — Survey term used to designate unduplicated audience.

dbs — Term used to describe loudness of audio output.

daypart — Term used to describe various parts of the broadcast day. Radio dayparts are 6–10 a.m. (morning drive), 10–3 (midday), 3–7 (afternoon drive), 7–12m (evening) and 12–6a (overnight). A station "dayparts" when it makes changes in music. Dayparting for teens would require heavy teen-oriented music in afternoon drive and evening.

daytimer — Radio station authorized for daytime only operations. Usually, local sunrise to sunset, although some facilities have "pre-sunrise" authority, depending upon frequency and geographic location.

demographics — Demo (people) graphic (picture). A picture of people, described by rating services in terms of audience age, sex and numbers.

drive-time — Classified as morning or afternoon, refers to heavy traffic times of the day when drivers are coming to and from work.

echo effect — Used in commercials and radio drama to sound like an echo and create mood and environment.

educational station — Station licensed to an educational institution or community group. Usually a non-commercial FM station operating on one of 20 frequencies reserved for that purpose.

facility — Used as alternate to "station," "radio station," "plant," etc. Usually means the entire operation, including transmitters, studios, towers.

fairness doctrine — A policy of the Federal Communications Commission under which stations are required to present both sides of controversial issues of local importance.

filter mike — Eliminates frequencies. Used in commercials and radio dramas to sound like police radios and telephones.

format — Any "plan" of action for programming a station. Asking a person about a format is similar to asking his name.

formula — The ingredients of a format. The formula for producing an AOR format is a company secret.

frequency — Various industry meanings, including a station's position on the dial, how often the average person hears a given commercial schedule, how often a spot announcement is aired.

fulltimer — Station with authority to operate 24 hours daily.

golden oldies and gold nuggets — Old records that are still popular.

good music — Format which features lush orchestrated arrangements of popular songs. Also known as beautiful music format.

hz (Hertz) — Replaces "cycles" as term to describe station frequency. Name derived from Heinrich Hertz, discoverer of the cyclical characteristics of radio waves.

hype — A slang term taken from "hypodermic", meaning to stimulate or promote. Stations attempt to "hype" audiences during rating periods. Also, heavy promotion of a specific record.

i.d. — Station identification. The broadcasting of the station's call letters and location.

ips — Inches per second. Used to designate the speed at which audio tape travels on a recorder.

Jesus rock — Sometimes called "Christian rock", is rock music with religious lyrics.

jingle package — A series or collection of musical commercials used by a station to establish an audio logo. Range in length from two seconds to sixty seconds.

licensee — The entity to which the FCC issues a license. May be an individual, partnership, corporation, association, or any other legal entity.

limiter — Electronic device used to prevent overmodulation, which is illegal. Also called a "peak limiter." Overmodulation creates distortion of signal.

listener sponsored station — Non-commercial station financed largely by contributions and subscriptions from listeners.

live — All broadcasts are live or recorded. Programs recorded locally may be logged as "live." Indicates, in vast majority of cases, whether material is pre-recorded for later broadcast or whether broadcast at time of occurrence.

mor (middle-of-the-road) — Any of a number of formats which fall between hard rock and beautiful music.

mastering — Product of final editing and a copy of a program or piece of music from which all other copies will be dubbed or made.

metro share — Station's relative position expressed in "shares" of an audience within a standard metropolitan statistical area (SMSA).

mil — One thousandth of an inch. Used to designate the thickness of recording tape.

mobile reporter — A news person who broadcasts live over two-way transmitter-receiver gear that is mounted in an automobile, van, truck, etc.

monitor — Recorded or written report on a station's performance.

music director — Individual responsible for selecting, cataloging, and scheduling musical selections on a station.

NAB (National Association of Broadcasters) standard — An "NAB cart" or "reel" is one that will fit equipment at most stations. A term describing a system of standardization.

news wheel — Same as clock, except that a news wheel indicates positioning of commercials, psas, national, local, regional news. The sequence in which each component will be broadcast.

non-commercial station — Station which, under terms of its license, cannot accept advertising.

non-entertainment — Usually such program items as news, talk shows, religious programs.

operations manager — Title used instead of program director to mean person in charge of everything that goes on the air.

pd (program director) — Individual responsible for selecting and scheduling on-air personnel and material heard on a station.

psa (public service announcement) — An announcement for which no charge is asked or received and which promotes a non-profit or charitable event or cause. When station charges for such announcements they must be logged "commercial".

payola — Illegal payment to a station employee in exchange for air play of a record.

personality (air personality) — Disc jockeys in general, or format which features recognized disc jockeys.

pressure — Applied to delivery of announcer, or station's general sound. High-pressure jock is one who puts pressure behind voice to develop intense or fast-paced delivery. Low-pressure delivery would indicate quiet, laid-back delivery.

produced i.d. — Recorded station identification prepared by a station or jingle firm.

program verb/noun — The station will "program" good music (v), and the format will include a news program (n).

progressive country — An upbeat country sound which shows contemporary and rock influence.

progressive rock — Rock music that varies dramatically from the norm. May feature new lyrics, musical styles, unknown artists, though not necessarily. Term has fallen into disuse in recent years, being replaced by album oriented rock (AOR).

promo — Promotional announcement. Any announcement that "promotes" an upcoming event or program. Normally used in association with a station-sponsored event.

psychographics — Used to describe audience characteristics beyond age, sex, numbers.

public station — Station which meets criteria established by the Corporation for Public Broadcasting to receive federal funds. Often used to denote all educational facilities.

Pulse, The — A nationally-known audience survey organization that uses the personal interview method of gathering data.

rating — Research term, meaning a percentage of the "universe" or of total population within a survey area.

reach — (Also known as cume, circulation) — Number of different persons who listen to a station in a given period. *Net* reach is the number of different persons estimated reached by a specific schedule of announcements.

reverb unit — Audio time-delay that creates echo effect. Is in limited use today, but was thought originally to enhance technical sound of station.

rhythm 'n blues (R&B) — Term used to describe Black-oriented music or music that appeals mainly to Black people. Also called soul music.

"rigged" contest — A contest in which the station takes covert action to either establish a win date or otherwise mislead listeners into believing anyone has a chance to win at any time during the period of the contest.

rotation — System of ensuring that a variety of musical selections are played within a given period of time.

SESAC — Society of European Singers, Artists and Composers. A music licensing service.

SFX — Used to mean "sound effects" in scripts.

SMSA — Standard Metropolitan Statistical Area. Areas designated by the Census Bureau of the Federal Government to indicate trade or retail areas. The City of Dallas is the hub of a six-county SMSA.

schmaltz — Sentimental or florid music. Lush, soft, syrupy.

Sec. 315 — Part of the Communications Act of 1934. Deals with handling of political advertising.

segue (pronounced seg-way) — Unbroken phasing of one piece of program material, usually music, into another.

service area — The area into which a station broadcasts an interference-free signal, or, in some instances, the area in which the station is "licensed" to operate. KABL, for example, is licensed to Oakland, California, but San Francisco is in the station's "service area."

side men — Professional musicians who accompany singing stars.

"soaps" — Describes old-time radio dramas and present-day TV dramas, usually broadcast during mid-day and sponsored by soap companies, such as Procter & Gamble.

soul format — Black-oriented programming featuring a particular type of music.

sounder — Bars of music used to provide audio identification. NBC's famous "chimes" are most notable example.

southern gospel music — Country music with religious lyrics.

stop set — In certain formats, the period when music stops and commercials, public service announcements, and promotional announcements are inserted.

support — Music editing jargon, meaning to increase amplitude of sound.

sweep — The period in which an audience survey is taken. Arbitron conducts 3–4 week "sweeps" during April–May and during October–November periods.

syndication — Distribution of a program on a station-by-station (rather than network) basis.

tape network — Programs are recorded on tapes and mailed to the stations for broadcast.

throwaway — Used to describe something useless, or low in value. Sunday night, at some stations, is a "throwaway."

tight — 1. Music playlist which allows for minimal entry of new records. 2. Format which allows for little variation in its music or talk. 3. Rapid transitions between program elements.

top 40 — Format which features hit music from charts (lists) of best-selling records.

total survey area (TSA) — The total area in which audiences are studied or measured. Contrasts with the Area of Dominate Influence (ADI), and Metro Survey Area. Terms are most common to Arbitron surveys.

turnover — Research term used to indicate length of time a person listens to a given station. All-news stations with relatively low average quarter-hour audiences and high cumes are said to have high turnover. Schmaltzy music stations have reverse situation and are known as low turnover stations.

"20-20 news" — Scheduling of brief news reports at 20 after and 20 minutes before an hour.

UHF/VHF — In television, ultra-high frequency and very-high frequency. "V" stations operate on channels 1 through 13, while "U" stations operate on channels 14 through 83.

UPI — United Press International. A news wire service.

unstructured — Free-form, without format or formula. Early acid rock stations were said to be unstructured.

voicer — Newsroom term. Indicates story recorded (voiced) by someone other than the anchor person.

wall-to-wall — Phrase meaning solid music. May be applied to any format where long sweeps of music are aired.

wheel — See "clock".

wire re-creation — Refers, usually, to a play-by-play broadcast of a sports event in which the announcer is *not* at the scene of action and "re-creates" the play using cryptic reports of play action.

BIBLIOGRAPHY

"A Century of Recorded Sound," Special Issue of *Billboard,* May 21, 1977.

Arbitron Radio, *Research Guidelines for Programming Decision Makers,* Arbitron, New York, 1977.

Barnouw, Erik, *A Tower in Babel,* Oxford University Press, New York, 1966.

———, *The Golden Web,* Oxford University Press, New York, 1968.

———, *The Image Empire,* Oxford University Press, New York, 1970.

Barrett, Marvin, ed. *The Politics of Broadcasting,* Thomas Y. Crowell Company, New York, 1973.

Buxton, Frank and Owen, Bill. *The Big Broadcast,* The Viking Press, New York, 1972.

Chester, Giraud, Garrison, Garnet, and Willis, Edgar. *Television and Radio* (4th ed.), Appleton-Century-Crofts, New York, 1971.

Clift, Charles III and Greer, Archie. *Broadcast Programming:* The Current Perspective, University Press of America, Washington, D.C., 1977.

Coleman, Howard W. *Case Studies in Broadcast Management* (2nd Edition, Revised and Enlarged). Hastings House, New York, 1978.

Dary, David. *Radio News Handbook,* Tab Books, Blue Ridge Summit, Pa., 1970.

Diamant, Lincoln. *The Broadcast Communications Dictionary* (Revised and Enlarged Edition). Hastings House, New York, 1978.

Dunning, John. *Tune In Yesterday: The Ultimate Encyclopedia of Old-Time Radio (1925–1976),* Prentice-Hall, Englewood Cliffs, New Jersey, 1976.

Editors of Broadcast Management/Engineering, *Interpreting FCC Broadcast Rules and Regulations,* (in 3 volumes), TAB Books, Blue Ridge Summit, Pa., 1968, 1972.

Gifferd, F. *Tape, A Radio News Handbook.* Hastings House, New York, 1977.

"Growth Market in Black Radio," *Broadcasting,* January 24, 1972, pp. 16–21.

Hall, Claude and Barbara. *This Business of Radio Programming,* Billboard Publications, New York, 1977.

Head, Sydney W. *Broadcasting In America,* (3rd edition), Houghton-Mifflin, Boston, 1976.

Hilliard, Robert L. *Radio Broadcasting* (2nd Edition). Hastings House, New York, 1976.

Hirsch, Paul. *The Structure of the Popular Music Industry,* Institute for Social Research, University of Michigan, Ann Arbor, 1973.

Hoffer, Jay. *Organization and Operation of Broadcast Stations,* TAB Books, Blue Ridge Summit, Pa., 1968.

Kahn, Frank J., editor. *Documents of American Broadcasting,* Appleton-Century Crofts, New York, 1972.

Krasnow, Erwin G. and Longley, Lawrence D. *The Politics of Broadcast Regulation.* St. Martin's Press, New York, 1973.

Lawton, Sherman P. *The Modern Broadcaster,* Harper & Row, New York, 1961.

———. "The Poetica of 'Top 40'," *Journal of Broadcasting,* Vol. 9, No. 2, pp. 123–128, Spring, 1965.

Lazarsfeld, Paul and Kendall, Patricia, *Radio Listening in America,* Prentice-Hall, New York, 1948.

Lichty, Lawrence and Topping, Malachi. *American Broadcasting,* Hastings House, New York, 1975.

"McGavren-Guild Ranks Radio's Most Popular Program Formats," *Broadcasting,* May 2, 1977.

Mendelsohn, Harold. "Listening to Radio," in Lewis, Dexter and White, David, *People, Society and Mass Communications,* Free Press, New York, 1964.

Milam, Lorenzo, *Sex and Broadcasting:* A   Handbook For Starting A Community Radio Station, Dildo Press, Saratoga, California, 1975.

Moomey, Robert and Skolnick, Roger. "Typologies of Radio Station Target Audiences," *Journal of Broadcasting,* Volume XIV, Number 4, Fall, 1970.

National Association of Broadcasters, *A Broadcast Research Primer,* 1971.

———. *Radio Financial Report* (annual), N.A.B. Washington, D.C.

———. *Standard Definitions of Broadcast Research Terms,* The NAB, Washington, D.C., 1970.

Oringel, Robert S. *Audio Control Handbook* (4th Edition). Hastings House, New York, 1972.

Passman, Arnold. *The Deejays,* The Macmillan Company, New York, 1971.

Quaal, Ward L. and Brown, James. *Broadcast Management* (2nd edition) Hastings House, New York, 1976.

Reinsch, J. Leonard, and Ellis, E. I., *Radio Station Management,* Harper & Row, New York, 1960.

Routt, Edd. *The Business of Radio Broadcasting,* TAB Books, Blue Ridge Summit, Pa., 1972.

———. *Dimensions of Broadcast Editorializing,* TAB Books, Blue Ridge Summit, Pa., 1974.

Ruffner, Marguerite, "Women's Attitudes Toward Progressive Rock," *Journal of Broadcasting,* Vol. 17, No. 1, pp. 85–94, Winter 1972–73.

Scott, Walter. *Personality Parade,* Grosset & Dunlap, New York, (n.d.)

————. *Million Seller Records,* 1970 edition. Phono-Graph Publications, Woodland Hills, California.

Simon, George T. *The Big Bands,* The Macmillan Company, New York. (3rd edition, 1974).

Summers, Robert and Summers, Harrison, *Broadcasting and the Public,* Wadsworth, Belmont, California, 1966.

Surlin, Stuart, "Black-Oriented Radio: Programming to a Perceived Audience," *Journal of Broadcasting,* Vol. 16, No. 3, pp. 289–298, Summer, 1972.

Taylor, Sherril W. *Radio Programming In Action:* Realities and Opportunities, Hastings House, New York, 1967.

"The Many Worlds of Radio, 1976," *Broadcasting,* September 27, 1976, pp. 33–76.

Wimer, Arthur and Brix, Dale, *Workbook for Radio and TV News Editing and Writing,* Wm. C. Brown, Dubuque, Iowa, (2nd edition), 1969.

INDEX

Educational facilities, 259-84; future of, 278-79; history of, 262-65; transcript illustrating, 280-84

Educational religious station, 220-24; announcers on, 223; audience for, 223-24; music on, 222, 224; news programs on, 222-23; organization of, 220-21; programming for, 221-22; public service programs on, 223; scheduling for, 223-24

Effective radiated power (ERP), 44-45

Eisenhower, Dwight D., 18

Ellington, Duke, 14, 15

Erwin, Carolyn K., 276*n*.

Ethnic music, 11

Etting, Ruth, 14

Evans, Deacon, 216, 240-45 *passim*

Evans, Paul, 221

Ezra, Uncle, 100

Fairchild Industries, 34, 196

Fairness Doctrine, 178

Faith, Percy, 151, 158

Faulk, John Henry, 206

Federal Communications Commission (FCC), 8, 20, 24, 26, 27, 30, 32, 33, 38, 39, 41, 61, 65, 66, 158, 186, 196, 209, 248*n*., 253, 254, 255, 256 and *n*., 259, 261, 263, 264, 265*n*., 276 and *n*., 294; and Fairness Doctrine, 178; Rules and Regulations of, 294; three-year-rule of, 42

Federal Council of Churches, 209

Federal Trade Commission (FTC), 32, 33

Feminine Mystique, The (Friedan), 20

Ferlinghetti, Lawrence, 276

Fessenden, Reginald A., 253

Financial and technical limitations, 41-43

First Amendment, 256

Fisher, Eddie, 19

Fitzgerald, Ella, 15

Fleetwood Mac, 87

Flow and mix, 148 and *n*., 151

FM radio, 8, 9 and *n*., 26, 33, 34, 35, 44, 45, 111, 128, 129, 133, 139*ff*., 147, 209, 210, 211, 253, 254, 257, 259, 263, 267, 286, 288

Fogelberg, Dan, 87

Form and style, in news broadcasts, 181-86

Format(s): adult block (variety), 61, 285-89; all-news, *see* Information formats; all-talk, 170, 289; black ethnic, *see* Black ethnic formats; classical, *see* Classical format; contemporary music, *see* Contemporary music formats; country music, *see* Country music formats; educational, *see* Educational facilities; good music, *see* Good music formats; information, *see* Information formats; religious, see Religious formats; specialization in, 40-41; top 40, *see* Top 40 format; variety, 40

45-RPM records, 91

Fosdick, Harry Emerson, 209

Four Tops, 137

Frampton, Peter, 86, 87

Francis, Connie, 19

Franklin, Benjamin, 4

Fredericks, Carlton, 266

Freeberg, Stan, 209

Freed, Alan, 19, 138

Freeman, Robert, 208

Friedan, Betty, 20

Gambling, John, 3, 22, 206

Garrison, Garnet R., 209*n*.

Gavin Report, The, 92

Gay community, and KCHU (Dallas), 270

Gaye, Marvin, 137

General manager, of station with information format, 177, 178

George, Don, 231, 232, 233, 234

Gershwin, George, 14

Glass Menagerie (Williams), 17

Godfrey, Arthur, 6

Gold/Oldies, 12, 13

Good music, 13, 24, 41, 61, 286; defined, 12, 145

Good music formats, 145-64; automation equipment for, 150, 152, 158-64; consultation and advice for, 153; and detail, attention to, 154-58; history of, 145-48; monitoring techniques for, 153-54; and Schulke Music Library, 149-52; technical requirements for, 152-53

Goodman, Benny, 15, 17, 19, 151

Gordy, Berry, Jr., 137

Gospel music, 12, 126, 133, 137, 210, 211, 213, 217, 222, 224

Grable, Betty, 17

Grand Ole Opry, 99, 100, 107, 111